TUAIRIM, INTELLECTUAL DEBATE AND POLICY FORMULATION: RETHINKING IRELAND, 1954–75

Manchester University Press

Tuairim, intellectual debate and policy formulation

Rethinking Ireland, 1954–75

Tomás Finn

Manchester University Press
Manchester and New York
distributed in the United States exclusively by Palgrave Macmillan

Copyright © Tomás Finn 2012

The right of Tomás Finn to be identified as the author of this work has been asserted by him in accordance with the Copyright, Designs and Patents Act 1988.

Published by Manchester University Press
Oxford Road, Manchester M13 9NR, UK
and Room 400, 175 Fifth Avenue, New York, NY 10010, USA
www.manchesteruniversitypress.co.uk

Distributed in the United States exclusively by
Palgrave Macmillan, 175 Fifth Avenue,
New York, NY 10010, USA

Distributed in Canada exclusively by
UBC Press, University of British Columbia, 2029 West Mall,
Vancouver, BC, Canada V6T 1Z2

British Library Cataloguing-in-Publication Data is available

Library of Congress Cataloging-in-Publication Data is available

ISBN 978 0 7190 9543 6 *paperback*

First published by Manchester University Press in hardback 2012

This paperback edition first published 2014

The publisher has no responsibility for the persistence or accuracy of URLs for any external or third-party internet websites referred to in this book, and does not guarantee that any content on such websites is, or will remain, accurate or appropriate.

Printed by Lightning Source

*In memory of my parents,
Tom and Maura,
and brother, Liam*

Contents

List of figures	ix
Acknowledgements	xi
List of abbreviations	xiii
Note on terms used in Irish	xiv
Introduction	1
1 Tuairim and the intellectual climate in Ireland	14
2 Representation and reform: Tuairim, the government and the Oireachtas	59
3 North and south: Tuairim and a divided island	102
4 Discourse and discord: Tuairim's challenge to the conservative consensus on education and childcare	150
5 Sense and censorship: Tuairim and cultural conservatism	210
Conclusion	225
Select bibliography	232
Index	245

Figures

1. The Tuairim member Jim Doolan became one of the first Irish people to work in the World Bank in 1962. Courtesy of the *Irish Times* and the National Library of Ireland. *page* 17

2. Conor Cruise O'Brien published an article on Katanga (now in the Democratic Republic of the Congo) in the London branch's *An Occasional Bulletin* in 1962. Courtesy of the *Irish Times* and the National Library of Ireland. 32

3. David Thornley, Brother Gerard of the Taizé Ecumenical Community in France and Rev. P. J. Brophy of St Patrick's College (left to right) at a Tuairim meeting on 'Christian unity' in 1965. Courtesy of the *Irish Times* and the National Library of Ireland. 37

4. Seán Lemass, Taoiseach, 1959–66, inspecting a pennon in government Buildings in 1966. Courtesy of the *Irish Times*. 44

5. A group of people in attendance at a Tuairim weekend at which Lemass spoke in 1957. Courtesy of the *Irish Independent* and the National Library of Ireland. 45

6. Speaking at a debate on PR in 1959 were (left to right) Donal Barrington, Erskine Childers, the chairperson, Rev. Gabriel Bowe, Seán MacBride and Declan Costello. Courtesy of the *Irish Independent* and the National Library of Ireland. 75

7. Val Finnegan, Margaret Hurley and Garret FitzGerald (left to right) spoke at a Tuairim meeting in Cork in 1972. Courtesy of the *Irish Examiner* and the National Library of Ireland. 129

8 The Ministers Brian Lenihan, Charles Haughey, Erskine Childers and Patrick Hillery (left to right) outside government buildings in 1965. Courtesy of the *Irish Times*. 167

9 Gemma Fallon seemed to enjoy a cheese, wine and art evening organised by the Limerick branch at King John's Castle. Courtesy of the *Irish Independent* and the National Library of Ireland. 214

Acknowledgements

This book has evolved from a doctoral dissertation in the Department of History at the National University of Ireland (NUI), Galway. Thanks, therefore, must go to those who helped me to see the dissertation to fruition. I am deeply grateful to Dr Mary Harris of the Department of History at NUI, Galway, for her invaluable advice and assistance. She has been a very helpful mentor and a supportive colleague. Professor Steven Ellis, head of the Department of History, NUI, Galway, and Professor Gearóid Ó Tuathaigh have also provided guidance and encouragement over the course of this project. Professor Ó Tuathaigh and Professor Dermot Keogh acted as examiners for the thesis and offered various suggestions to improve this work.

Access to a wide range of sources has been critical to this project. Thanks to the staff of the following libraries and archives for their assistance and co-operation: the James Hardiman Library, NUI, Galway, in particular the staff of the Special Collections Reading Room, the National Library of Ireland, the National Archives of Ireland, Dublin Diocesan Archives, University College Dublin (UCD) Archives Department, University College Cork's Special Collections and the Archive of the Irish in Britain at the London Metropolitan University. I am also grateful to the Departments of Education and Health as well as the History Department at Trinity College Dublin.

My thanks are especially due to the staff of Manchester University Press for their hard work in preparing the manuscript for publication. I am also grateful to their anonymous readers for their helpful comments. The Faculty of Arts, NUI, Galway, and Dún Laoghaoire Rathdown Co. Council have provided financial support in relation to this project while Professor Lionel Pilkington and the School of Humanities and Professor Ellis and the History Department have assisted with the costs of the illustrations for this book.

I wish to thank my friends and colleagues in Galway and elsewhere for their companionship and support. Dr Ger Power, Kieran Hoare, Dr Chris

Maginn, Dr Orla Power, Martina Krocová, Conor Hand, David O'Connell, Michael Anglim, Dr Adrian Patterson, James O'Donnell, Professor Jim Doolan and Michael O'Hanrahan have read different versions of this work, shared their wisdom and been generous with their insights. I would especially like to thank Héloïse Vincent for her suggestions, support and encouragement. I am also grateful to Dr Jonathon Hore, Brian Wallace, David McBride, Paul Roche, Darragh Doyle, Tom O'Leary, Tessa van Keekan, Dr Jackie Uí Chionna, Dr Kevin Forkan, Dr John Cunningham and many others for their advice and friendship.

NUI Galway's history seminar series and many other conferences and seminars have provided valuable opportunities to present earlier version of this work. Together with University College, Dublin and, in particular, Professor Tom Garvin and Dr Maurice Manning, who introduced me to historical scholarship into modern Ireland, these have helped to shape me as an historian.

Tuairim's members and others have shared their valuable insights with the author concerning the development of the society and its contribution towards a changing Ireland. Many people including Donal Barrington, Maurice Manning, Barry Desmond, Michael O'Hanrahan, Miriam Hederman O'Brien, William Peacocke, Ann Boland, Margaret Hurley, Val Finnegan, Cian O'Carroll, Brian O'Connor, Ann Barry, Muiris MacCarthaigh and Geordie Rudd have supplied me with important documents relating to Tuairim. I would like to thank each of them and everyone who has given so generously of their time, through interviews, correspondence and by responding to queries.

Finally, thanks to my family – Pádraig, Máire, Fergal and Austin, and in particular, my parents, Tom and Maura, and my brother Liam, who are sadly missed. I am deeply grateful to all of them, especially my parents, for their unfailing love, support and encouragement. This book is dedicated to them.

Abbreviations

AD	Archives Department
AEDE	European Association of Teachers (Association Européenne des Enseignants)
DDA	Dublin Diocesan Archives
DEA	Department of External Affairs
DFA	Department of Foreign Affairs
DJ	Department of Justice
DT	Department of Taoiseach
EEC	European Economic Community
IRA	Irish Republican Army
IRSP	Irish Republican Socialist Party
L & H	Literary and Historical Society
MP	Member of Parliament
NAI	National Archives of Ireland
NFA	National Farmers' Association
NILP	Northern Ireland Labour Party
NLI	National Library of Ireland
NUI	National University of Ireland
PR	proportional representation
PR-stv	proportional representation by single transferable vote
RTÉ	Radio Telefís Éireann
SDLP	Social Democratic and Labour Party
TD	Teachta Dála
UCC	University College Cork
UCD	University College Dublin
UCG	University College Galway
UNESCO	United Nations Educational and Scientific and Cultural Organisation
UUP	Ulster Unionist Party
VTA	Vocational Teacher's Association

Note on terms used in Irish

'Tuairim' means 'opinion'. Teachtaí Dála, or TDs (Teachta Dála is the singular form), are the members of Dáil Éireann, the lower house of the Oireachtas (the Irish parliament). Seanad Éireann is the Senate, the upper house. The Taoisigh or Taoiseach, in its singular form, is the Prime Minister of the country while the Tánaiste is the Deputy Prime Minister. The Ceann Comhairle, the speaker of the house, oversees the debates in Dáil Éireann while his deputy is the Leas-Cheann Comhairle.

Introduction

This book examines Tuairim ('opinion' in Irish), an intellectual movement which was active in Ireland from 1954 to 1975. Tuairim's significance lay in the ideas put forward in the pamphlets it published as well as at the meetings it organised; these addressed several burning issues at the time, including Northern Ireland, electoral reform, education and censorship. This study examines Tuairim's ideas and assesses their influence on the transformation that took place during the 1950s and 1960s. The society is important in that it was influential in relation to a number of issues but also because its members went on to play important roles in a variety of areas of Irish life from the 1960s. Prominent individuals active in Tuairim included Donal Barrington, a future Supreme Court justice, Garret FitzGerald, a future Taoiseach, David Thornley, subsequently a lecturer in Trinity College Dublin and later a Labour Party TD, and Miriam Hederman O'Brien, a future Chancellor of the University of Limerick and chairperson of the Commission on Taxation and the Commission on the Funding of the Health Services. These and other Tuairim members helped transform Ireland beginning in the 1950s, a decade which has traditionally been characterised as one of uniform mediocrity and episcopal hegemony in intellectual and social life. While the Irish state could be said to have been dominated by a conservative political elite and a powerful Catholic Church during its early decades, this situation changed in the 1950s and 1960s. On the one hand, during much of the 1920s, 1930s and 1940s, the national question permeated political thought and informed public policy. Political events, such as the 1921 Anglo-Irish Treaty and its dismantling, the politically motivated economic war and the 1937 constitution, had dominated the agenda. On the other hand, the fact that Tuairim existed and was able to operate is one indication that the 1950s and 1960s were different. These decades witnessed a transformation in the state's approach to policy formulation, much of which was the result of new ideas. The consequence was that Ireland evolved into a country which in many ways scarcely resembled that which had existed in the earlier decades.

The transition that took place in the 1950s and 1960s included a new economic thinking, which facilitated a rejection of protectionism and the adoption by the state of a central role in the planning of the economy and the education system. There was also an early intimation that irredentist nationalism would be replaced by a policy of conciliation in relation to unionism and a move towards a more open attitude generally. This was reflected in the reforms of censorship and the education system as well as the establishment of a national television station in 1961. Notwithstanding the economic difficulties and the powerful position in which the Catholic Church remained during the 1950s, that decade had witnessed the first major challenges to the authority of the Catholic hierarchy. Moreover, the new economic thinking of the 1950s facilitated unprecedented economic prosperity and social and cultural change in the 1960s.

As previously noted, the transformation in the state's approach to policy formulation was the result of new ideas. Tuairim and its influence on key policy decisions, as well as the intellectual climate that informed them, are the subject of this book. It is important that ideas, intellectuals and their influence in persuading governmental institutions to adopt new policies are placed at the centre of an understanding of how Ireland evolved during the 1950s and 1960s. The transition in the Irish economy, society, politics and culture was the consequence of original ideas and new policy decisions. While the body politic, through its democratic mandate, was responsible for the change of direction, the degree to which non-political forums for debate influenced public policy has not been the subject of detailed historical analysis. Dramatic adjustments to economic, educational and censorship systems as well as the emergence of a new approach to unionism could not have occurred without a climate of opinion that at least acquiesced in these developments. Though the task of ensuring support for their policies lay with the political elite that was implementing them, the political establishment was in the 1950s also reacting to the crisis in which the state found itself as well as to outside stimuli and pressures to adopt alternative strategies. One important forum that challenged the existing order and advocated a new approach was Tuairim, a society which explored many issues crucial to the transformation of Ireland during this period.

The extent to which Tuairim facilitated the formulation of and discussion on new policies is the central question addressed by this book. Specifically, the monograph investigates how new ideas were disseminated in Ireland. Tuairim's meetings and pamphlets touched on a wide variety of areas. These include the European Economic Community (EEC) and the United Nations, fisheries, social security and healthcare.[1] This book focuses in particular on Northern Ireland, the economy, politics, education, childcare and censorship, reflecting the areas in which Tuairim had most impact as well as the issues that generated much debate in the country, in Tuairim and among its participants. The book also addresses subjects of continuing relevance for contemporary Ireland, including a consideration of Tuairim's anticipation of more recent approaches to peace on the island and its investigation into the issue of institutional care of children.

Tuairim's members challenged traditional attitudes and orthodoxy in a number of different areas. Initially a reaction to the economically depressed and intellectually stultified 1950s, the society demonstrated an ability to question conservative constraints. Though Ireland experienced a period of relative economic prosperity and significant social change during the 1960s, there remained many problems in Irish society that needed to be examined. Tuairim claimed that its independence of the Catholic Church and of political parties gave it the freedom to examine controversial issues and, if necessary, put forward unpopular solutions.

More broadly, an analysis of Tuairim raises questions about Ireland as well as the character, nature and place of the intellectual within society. The organisation's commitment to the articulation of new ideas and the need for members to be able to defend their position at lively meetings and thereafter, perhaps in writing, point to the need for a new understanding of the role of ideas and intellectuals in Irish life. Though a number of historians including Diarmaid Ferriter and Dermot Keogh have in recent years repudiated the stereotypical image of the 1950s and 1960s as the worst and best of decades and contributed to a more nuanced interpretation of this period,[2] the role of intellectuals in Ireland has not been studied in detail. Increasingly, scholars such as Gary Murphy and Tom Garvin have, however, recognised as crucial the variety of experiences during the 1950s, and particularly the economic and political changes that took place during that decade. While John Bradley and Tom Garvin argued that the economic crisis which saw the emigration of an average of 40,000 people each year from Ireland during the 1950s was vital in forcing a new approach from the government,[3] Murphy contends that Ireland also assumed a greater role on the international stage during that decade.[4] Keogh and Ferriter have respectively concluded that alongside conservative attitudes, a 'vibrant counter-culture' and a 'questioning culture' existed during the 1950s.[5]

This book maintains that Tuairim had a central place in this new culture of enquiry. While the society was concerned with the present and future narrative of Ireland, it existed during a period which became known as historical revisionism, when the traditional view of Irish history began to be revised. Tuairim helped to give rise to a spirit of enquiry which questioned orthodoxy but at the same time was impartial to the history of Ireland. The society marked a break from tradition and the historical narrative which demanded that one be partial in relation to events such as the Irish civil war of 1922–23. The 'revisionist debate',[6] which became the controversy upon which Irish history revolved, was mainly centred on earlier periods and formed some of the intellectual backdrop to Tuairim.

The pages that follow are concerned with intellectual and broadly cultural developments in the context of assessments of the 1950s and the process by which the transition towards a more 'open' society occurred in the 1960s. Emblematic of the generational, social and cultural changes that took place during these decades, Tuairim explained international developments, notably the Second Vatican Council (1962–65), and facilitated improved relations between Catholics and Protestants as well as reforms in education and censorship that would not have been possible in earlier decades. All was not change for the better, however. This study examines the continued resistance of elements of the political establishment as well as the Catholic Church to the ideas put forward by Tuairim. It thus supports the arguments of Keogh and Ferriter, who have pointed to the persistent existence of poverty and the exclusion of segments of Irish society alongside new opportunities in the 1960s. The book also reinforces the case for not treating the Catholic Church as a monolith: it contained liberal as well as conservative elements during this period.

The lack of literature on intellectuals in Ireland extends to most fields. There are, for example, few Irish memoirs, autobiographies and 'letters' by leading figures in the political or intellectual life of modern Ireland; distinguished contributions are fewer still.[7] Ireland's political culture, which political scientists have claimed includes anti-intellectualism and a pressure to conform,[8] combined with significant deficiencies in strategic thinking, and the quality of ideas has been a factor in informing a dismissive attitude towards intellectuals in the country. The extent to which Irish life contains anti-intellectualism has, however, yet to be fully considered. The original suggestion echoes similar assertions in relation to other countries such as the USA.[9] Recently, such views have generally given way to a tendency among scholars to examine the context in which intellectuals exist.[10] In an Irish setting, the country's 'intellectual infrastructure' has been criticised by the historian Joe Lee.[11] It was to this, the market for ideas, that Tuairim contributed.

In contrast to France, for example, where ideas and the question of the role of intellectuals have been the subject of academic thought and general polemic since the Dreyfus Affair, Ireland and Britain have been characterised as notable for the absence of such individuals.[12] Stefan Collini in *Absent minds* has argued that intellectuals themselves, to reinforce the concept of British exceptionalism, often deliberately denied the existence of such individuals in that country. Bryan Fanning, who has examined the debates in periodicals such as *The Bell, Studies, Administration, Christus Rex* and *The Crane Bag*, arrives at similar conclusions in the Irish case. This study concurs with the views of Fanning. Tuairim's unwillingness to use the term 'intellectuals' reflects the sense that, similarly to Britain, it was associated with impracticality, unproductivity and aloofness and had other negative connotations.[13] In that context, it could undermine Tuairim's ability to attract active individuals and to influence public policy.

More generally, scholarship since the 1990s suggests that ambivalent attitudes exist or have existed towards intellectuals not only in Ireland but in many other countries including Britain and the USA; this is even the case in France, which has been viewed as exceptional in the status that it granted to its intellectuals, at least in the period immediately after World War II. Definitions of intellectuals, their place in society and their role as agents of social, political, economic and cultural change are contested. There are divergent views as to the extent to which intellectuals constitute a coherent elite rather than a number of individuals, can be or need to be truly independent, and retain that detachment while being active politically. It is, however, generally accepted that intellectuals shape, or seek to shape, public opinion. In this context, a study that examines intellectuals' impact on public opinion and public policy in Ireland is all the more necessary. Authors who have considered their place in Irish society have at least so far shown that such individuals existed and that they engaged in various debates in relation to the ideas and policies that were pursued in the country.[14] Such studies have taken a comparative approach, have examined intellectuals from a nationalist and class viewpoint, and have tended to define the term broadly. The extent to which they influenced the public agenda has, however, not received detailed consideration. Fanning's study *The quest for modern Ireland* is, for example, a valuable contribution to the intellectual history of Ireland, but fails to explore fully the impact of the ideas within the periodicals he examines. Most particularly the journals on which Fanning has based his study are largely dealt with in isolation; he does not consider their role in the dissemination of ideas, their influence upon governments or the electorate as reflected in government files, parliamentary debates and other publications such as newspapers.

Most significantly, however, Tuairim's role in the intellectual life of the country has only briefly been discussed. Fanning does not elaborate beyond a short reference to Tuairim,[15] although he does discuss the contributions of the society's members to the debates in the periodicals. Moreover, among the general histories of twentieth-century Ireland, only Joe Lee and Diarmaid Ferriter attempt commentary on intellectual history (or the history of ideas and their impact): neither provides much discussion of Tuairim as an agenda or as a conduit to critique Irish society. Roy Foster's *Luck and the Irish: a brief history of change, 1970–2000* examines the transformation that has taken place in Ireland since 1970;[16] that is, however, the period after Tuairim existed. Tom Garvin has produced the most complete account of Tuairim's activities, while Diarmaid Ferriter acknowledges the breadth of topics that the society addressed and quotes from Garret FitzGerald's claim that its role in the modernisation of Ireland deserves study.[17] Louise Fuller and Garvin respectively refer to Tuairim's critique of censorship and the education system.[18] Specialist histories of the educational system contain the majority of references to Tuairim: John Walsh has pointed to the importance of the role played by the society in provoking debate, while Seán O'Connor, the former Secretary of the Department of Education, noted that Tuairim criticised existing educational policy.[19] None of these authors has, however, provided more of an insight than Eileen Randles, who though viewing Tuairim as having made an important contribution to debate on the education system, condemns the negative nature of the London branch's views.[20]

It is the London branch's pamphlet in relation to industrial schools, which has, in recent years, proved to be the most controversial that Tuairim produced. Garvin has claimed in *Preventing the future* that it was significant that it was the branch outside Ireland that was most critical in its views. Mavis Arnold and Heather Laskey and Mary Raftery and Eoin O'Sullivan have, however, criticised Tuairim's pamphlet for not including an account of the abuse children suffered in industrial schools.[21] On the other hand, Diarmuid Whelan, who published the personal story of a former industrial school pupil, sought a more complete explanation for the absence of such testimony.[22] Most significant is the assertion as to the importance of Tuairim in the 2009 *Report of the Commission to Inquire into Child Abuse* (henceforth known as the Ryan report after its chairperson, Mr Justice Seán Ryan).[23] These authors, have, however, not sought to explain fully why there were differences between the London branch's views and those of the other branches. This study explains why the London branch seemed to have a more radical perspective than Tuairim in Ireland.

The book also sheds new light on Tuairim in Ireland and its relations with the political and religious establishments. Tuairim's pamphlet in relation to University College Dublin (UCD) was considered in Donal McCartney's study of that college. He illustrates that though Tuairim failed to influence government policy, the society made a considerable impact on the debate surrounding the college's future.[24] Tuairim's articulation of views that seemed to threaten the hegemony exercised by those in influential positions of power is underlined by John Cooney's claim that the Archbishop of Dublin, John Charles McQuaid, infiltrated the society's activities with a 'priest-spy'.[25] It is clear from these accounts that despite the Catholic Church's opposition to independent thinking, Tuairim was part of a wider debate regarding the future direction of the country, to which at least some politicians contributed. Mary Daly, for example, shows that the society added to the momentum for reform in relation to local rates as well as a farm apprenticeship scheme, while a book of essays on David Thornley, a member of Tuairim and a politician, is important in illustrating the range of issues fundamental to Ireland's future discussed by the organisation.[26] The relationship between Tuairim and politicians was crucial to the society influencing government policy. It thus seems curious that Niamh Puirséil has insisted that Tuairim 'shunned party politics'.[27] While the society was independent of political parties, and its orientation was certainly more liberal than that of the establishment, Tuairim encouraged its members to join the parties. Furthermore, individual politicians both co-operated with and criticised Tuairim. This relationship was thus a complex one, and it is central to a full appraisal of the society and of the politics of this era.

This work is based primarily on empirical research. The range of primary source material includes personal communications, unpublished documents and personal papers as well as papers and manuscripts in public archives. The attitude of the Irish government towards Tuairim was the most critical determinant of its success or otherwise in influencing public policy. Accordingly, an important feature of this monograph is a thorough examination of government files at the National Archives of Ireland. Many of the society's pamphlets and newspaper reports relating to these publications and its meetings are found therein; a full study of government views as revealed within these files indicates the kind of influence Tuairim exerted during these decades. (This book assesses the ideas that Tuairim put forward with a view to ascertaining both the extent to which they were novel and impacted on the body politic.) Critically, government files reveal the attitude of senior civil servants to the society. Records of parliamentary debates are also vital in illustrating the impact that Tuairim had on those in positions of power and how prevalent the ideas expressed by the society were among Oireachtas members. Archbishop John Charles McQuaid's papers in the Dublin Diocesan Archives and collections pertaining to individuals, including Ernest Blythe's papers in the UCD Archives Department, are instructive with regard to the political and religious establishments' attitude to Tuairim. The *Irish Independent*, a mainstream southern Catholic newspaper, and the *Irish Press*, which was associated with Fianna Fáil and was traditionally irredentist in its mentality, as well as the formerly unionist *Irish Times*, which during the 1960s represented a relatively liberal readership, are the most important daily newspapers to take into account in considering the type and amount of publicity that the society received. These, along with periodicals such as *Studies*, *Christus Rex* and *Hibernia*, disclosed much about the intellectual climate and the formation of public opinion at this time. Tuairim members contributed to these publications while the society's pamphlets and meetings were sometimes the subject of articles therein. Regional newspapers, particularly the *Cork Examiner*, also a daily, and others which were associated with a particular viewpoint, such as the Connolly Association's *Irish Democrat*, contained information about the different branches of the society and public attitudes of certain organisations to Tuairim.

Additional archival research has been conducted in relation to the London branch at the Archive of the Irish in Britain at the London Metropolitan University, while the Department of Health in Dublin and the Department of Education in Athlone and Owen Sheehy Skeffington's papers at the National Library of Ireland have provided essential information in regard to the industrial schools question. The minutes of Tuairim's Dublin branch for the years 1964–70 were consulted in the History Department at Trinity College Dublin.

In addition to written materials, we have oral interviews with many leading figures in Tuairim. Interviews of and correspondence with seventy-one individuals, the majority of whom were Tuairim members, have been crucial in acquiring a more complete understanding of this period. These sources have illustrated individuals' motivations, experiences and idealism. Although there are exceptions, details could be partially or wholly inaccurate and dangers of exaggeration and problems of hindsight were ever present. Donal Barrington has been particularly helpful regarding his own role and Tuairim's interaction with the political establishment during the late 1950s. Enda McDonagh, Frank D'Arcy, Miriam Hederman O'Brien, Jim Doolan and many others have also provided valuable insights into how and why they became involved as well as the context in which Tuairim operated. Certain former members retained personnel papers relating to Tuairim and have kindly made them available. These contain detailed material about the society in the late 1950s and early 1960s and more general information with regard to the late 1960s and early 1970s. Joy Rudd's papers include correspondence from the early 1960s between the London branch and Tuairim in Ireland as well as letters between the branch and other individuals and organisations. Michael O'Hanrahan has made his folder of press cuttings regarding the London branch from the early 1960s available, while Margaret Hurley's and Val Finnegan's papers include information relating to the Cork branch during the early 1970s. Barry Desmond and Maurice Manning have papers that include some of the minutes and correspondence of Tuairim's parliamentary study group from the early 1970s. While there obviously are years for which there is more information than for others, interviews and archive sources, combined with abundant newspaper coverage, make this study of Tuairim possible, thus contributing to a more complete understanding both of the period in which it operated, and of the role in Ireland of public intellectuals which this movement exemplified.

The extent to which Tuairim's viewpoint prompted debate on Ireland's future and influenced those in positions of power illuminates the nature of intellectual ferment and policy formulation in the country and among its diaspora. Tuairim's vision of a more active citizenship encouraged certain politicians, civil servants and other individuals in the consideration that they were giving to new directions for government policy. The society also provoked, however, much criticism from conservative elements, thus pointing to possible limits to its influence.

Tuairim's impact, as well as the limits to its influence, is the focus of this book. The evolution of church–state relations and the part played by intellectuals in Irish civil society as well as among the Irish diaspora in the changes taking place in the Irish economy and society are recurring themes. The book examines the particular contributions of Tuairim's most significant branches, notably those in Dublin and London. The London branch and the different milieu of which it was part of are examined. The extent to which this gave the society in London a unique perspective is considered. The book argues that Tuairim played a crucial role in the debates that shaped modern Ireland and contends that the connection between intellectual debate and policy formulation is central to an understanding of the deepening complexities of this period.

This book consists of five chapters. The first chapter considers the society's membership, its methods, the range of matters it examined, the nature of its views, the reaction the society provoked and the wider debates to which it contributed. It also examines the intellectual climate in the wider Western world during the post-war period and the factors that made the society unusual in both a national and an international context. The reasons why the society was established and the factors involved in its demise are assessed. By analysing the attitudes of prominent figures towards Tuairim, light is shed on the environment in which the society operated and how it sought to influence those in positions of power. Chapter 2 examines Tuairim's contributions to debates on both administrative reform and the quality of ideas informing public policy. This chapter considers the society's attempts to change political culture, to influence the nature of the electoral system and to convince the political establishment of the need for Oireachtas reform. Tuairim's challenges to traditional nationalist attitudes, and its attempts to promote reconciliation between the two states – Northern Ireland and Ireland – and between the two communities within Northern Ireland are assessed in Chapter 3. It examines how radical Tuairim's views were in relation to Northern Ireland and the means by which they were disseminated. This chapter argues that the society prefigured some of the thinking behind the peace process (and ultimately the Good Friday or Belfast Agreement) which emerged some decades later. Chapter 4 evaluates Tuairim's important contribution to the debate on the education system and its views on industrial schools as well as its attempts to retain UCD in Dublin city centre and to foster good relations between that college and Trinity College Dublin. Tuairim's challenge to the earlier commitment of the political and religious establishments to a Catholic university in the suburbs (UCD was originally established in the nineteenth century as Ireland's Catholic university) is compared with the society's influence on the government in relation to primary and post-primary education as well as childcare and the increased willingness of the government as the 1960s progressed to consider reforms in areas where the Catholic Church held a vested interest. Pamphlets by both the Dublin and London branches are examined in this chapter, which assesses the reasons why Tuairim in London seemed more radical than in Ireland. Chapter 5 is concerned with censorship. This chapter examines Tuairim's support for authors who had books banned and the interaction between a representative of the liberal wing of the Catholic Church and Tuairim in its quest for reform of the system of censorship in operation in Ireland. The contrast between the attitude of one priest and that of other members of the Catholic Church is considered in this chapter.

The central theme of this book is Tuairim's role in the transformation of Ireland in the 1950s and 1960s. This study considers the extent to which the society informed the debates that shaped Ireland's future direction. Consisting of members of the first generation born since independence, Tuairim was an example of active citizenship and represented a key cohort of intellectuals in twentieth-century Ireland. An evaluation of Tuairim's contribution to rethinking the country illuminates the nature of debate and the role of ideas and intellectuals in the creation of modern Ireland.

Notes

1 For an evaluation of Tuairim's debates in relation to those areas see Tomás Finn, 'The influence of *Tuairim* on intellectual debate and policy formulation in Ireland, 1954–1975' (Ph.D. thesis, NUI, Galway, 2009).
2 Diarmaid Ferriter, *The transformation of Ireland, 1900–2000* (London: Profile Books, 2004); Dermot Keogh, *Twentieth-century Ireland: nation and state* (Dublin: Gill and Macmillan, 1994). For more traditional accounts of this period see John A. Murphy, '"Put them out!" Parties and elections, 1948–1969', in J. J. Lee (ed.), *Ireland, 1945–70* (Dublin: Gill and Macmillan, 1979), p. 3; Fergal Tobin, *The best of decades: Ireland in the nineteen sixties* (Dublin: Gill and Macmillan, 1984).
3 John Bradley, 'Changing the rules: why the failures of the 1950s forced a

transition in economic policy-making', in Dermot Keogh, Finbarr O'Shea and Carmel Quinlan (eds), *The lost decade: Ireland in the 1950's* (Cork: Mercier Press, 2004), pp. 105–17; Tom Garvin, *Preventing the future: why was Ireland so poor for so long?* (Dublin: Gill and Macmillan, 2004); Tom Garvin, *News from a new republic: Ireland in the 1950s* (Dublin: Gill and Macmillan, 2010); Gary Murphy, *In search of the Promised Land: the politics of post-war Ireland* (Cork: Mercier Press, 2009).

4 Gary Murphy, '"A wider perspective": Ireland's view of Western Europe in the 1950s', in Michael Kennedy and Joseph Morrison Skelly (eds), *Irish foreign policy, 1919–66: from independence to internationalism* (Dublin: Four Courts Press, 2000), pp. 247–64. See also Miriam Hederman, *The road to Europe: Irish attitudes, 1948–61* (Dublin: Institute of Public Administration, 1983); Dermot Keogh, *Ireland and Europe, 1919–1989* (Cork: Hibernian University Press, 1990); D. J. Maher, *The tortuous path: the course of Ireland's entry into the EEC, 1948–73* (Dublin: Institute of Public Administration, 1986). For the economic crisis see Mary E. Daly, *Social and economic history of Ireland since 1800* (Dublin: Educational Company, 1981); Mary E. Daly, *The slow failure: population decline and independent Ireland, 1920–1973* (Madison: University of Wisconsin Press, 2006).

5 Ferriter, *Transformation*, p. 23; Keogh, *Twentieth-century Ireland*, p. 223.

6 Ciaran Brady (ed.), *Interpreting Irish history: the debate on historical revisionism, 1938–1994* (Dublin: Irish Academic Press, 1994).

7 Not the only exception, Garret FitzGerald's *All in a Life* is the most obvious one. See Garret FitzGerald, *All in a life: an autobiography* (Dublin: Gill and Macmillan, 1992).

8 Basil Chubb, *The government and politics of Ireland* (Harlow: Pearson, 1992), pp. 19–20. See also John Coakley, 'Society and political culture', in John Coakley and Michael Gallagher (eds), *Politics in the Republic of Ireland* (London: Routledge, 2003), p. 36.

9 Ron Everyman, 'Intellectuals in historical and comparative context', in Liam O'Dowd (ed.), *On Intellectuals and intellectual life in Ireland: international, comparative and historical contexts* (Belfast: Institute of Irish Studies, 1996), pp. 31–49.

10 Charles Kurzman and Lynn Owens, 'The sociology of intellectuals', *Annual Review of Sociology*, 28 (2002), 63–90.

11 J. J. Lee, *Ireland, 1912–1985: politics and society* (Cambridge: Cambridge University Press, 1993), p. 605.

12 Stefan Collini, *Absent minds: intellectuals in Britain* (Oxford: Oxford University Press, 2007); David Drake, *Intellectuals and politics in post-war France* (Basingstoke: Palgrave, 2002); Jill Forbes and Michael Kelly (eds), *French cultural studies: an introduction* (Oxford: Oxford University Press, 1995); Bryan Fanning, *The quest for modern Ireland: the battle for ideas, 1912–1986* (Dublin: Irish Academic Press, 2008); Jeremy Jennings and Anthony Kemp-Welch (eds), *Intellectuals in politics: from the Dreyfus affair to Salman Rushdie* (London: Routledge, 1997); John Flower, 'Intellectuals', in Michael Kelly (ed.), *French culture and society: the essentials* (London: Arnold, 2001), pp. 138–9.

13 Collini, *Absent minds*, pp. 32–4, 39. See also Edna McDonagh, 'The Christian and Catholic intellectual', in Yseult Thornley (ed.), *Unquiet spirit: essays in memory of David Thornley* (Dublin: Liberties Press, 2008), p. 97.
14 Fanning, *The quest*; Maurice Goldring, *Pleasant the scholar's life: Irish intellectuals and the construction of the nation state* (London: Serif, 1993); O'Dowd (ed.), *Intellectuals*; Liam O'Dowd, 'Intellectuals and political culture: a unionist–nationalist comparison', in Eamonn Hughes (ed.), *Culture and politics in Northern Ireland, 1960–1990* (Milton Keynes: Open University Press, 1991), pp. 151–73. See also Thomas Duddy, *A history of Irish thought* (London: Routledge, 2002).
15 Fanning, *The quest*, p. 214.
16 R. F. Foster, *Luck and the Irish: a brief history of change, 1970–2000* (London: Penguin Books, 2008). See also Ferriter, *Transformation*; Lee, *Ireland*.
17 Ferriter, *Transformation*, p. 526; Garret FitzGerald, *Reflections on the Irish state* (Dublin: Irish Academic Press, 2003), p. 194; Garvin, *Republic*, pp. 33, 152, 186, 194–6, 202–5, 210.
18 Louise Fuller, *Irish Catholicism since 1950: the undoing of a culture* (Dublin: Gill and Macmillan, 2002), pp. 62, 136; Garvin, *Future*, p. 150; Garvin, *Republic*, pp. 194–6.
19 John Walsh, *The politics of expansion: the transformation of educational policy in the Republic of Ireland, 1957–72* (Manchester: Manchester University Press, 2009), pp. 78–79; Seán O'Connor, *A troubled sky: reflections on the Irish educational scene, 1957–1968* (Dublin: St Patrick's College, 1986), pp. 23, 64, 100, 109. See also Donald Harman Akenson, *A mirror to Kathleen's face: education in independent Ireland, 1922–1960* (Montreal: McGill-Queen's University Press, 1975), pp. 73–5; John Coolahan, *Irish education: its history and structure* (Dublin: Institute of Public Administration, 1981), p. 132; John Coolahan, 'Educational policy for national schools, 1960–1965', in D. G. Mulcahy and Denis O'Sullivan (eds), *Irish educational policy: process and substance* (Dublin: Institute of Public Administration, 1989), pp. 47, 66; Séamas Ó Buachalla, 'Investment in education: context, content and impact', *Administration*, 44:3 (1996), 12.
20 Eileen Randles, *Post-primary education in Ireland, 1957–1970* (Dublin: Veritas Publications, 1975), pp. 66–7, 75–7.
21 Mavis Arnold and Heather Laskey, *Poor Clares* (Belfast: Appletree Press, 1985); Mary Raftery and Eoin O'Sullivan, *Suffer the little children: the inside story of Ireland's industrial schools* (Dublin: New Island, 1999). See also Dáire Keogh, 'Letterfrack: Peter Tyrrell and the Ryan Report', in Tony Flannery (ed.), *Responding to the Ryan Report* (Dublin: Columba Press, 2009), pp. 56–81.
22 Diarmuid Whelan, *Founded on fear: Letterfrack industrial school, war and exile* (Dublin: Irish Academic Press, 2006); Diarmuid Whelan, 'Document study: Peter Tyrell's account of Letterfrack, war and exile', Sheehy Skeffington papers, National Library of Ireland (NLI); *Saothar*, 31 (2006), 111–18.
23 *Report of the Commission to Inquire into Child Abuse* (2009), www.childabusecommission.com/rpt, accessed on 22 December 2010.
24 Donal McCartney, *UCD: a national Idea: the history of University College Dublin* (Dublin: Gill and Macmillan, 1999).

25 John Cooney, *John Charles McQuaid: ruler of Catholic Ireland* (Dublin: O'Brien Press, 1999), p. 398.
26 Mary E. Daly, *The first department: a history of the Department of Agriculture* (Dublin: Institute of Public Administration, 2002), pp. 417, 598 n. 106; Mary E. Daly, *The buffer state: the historical roots of the Department of the Environment* (Dublin: Institute of Public Administration, 1997), p. 505; Miriam Hederman, 'The Tuairim phenomenon – a forum for challenge in 1950s Ireland', in Thornley (ed.), *Unquiet spirit*, pp. 66–76.
27 Niamh Puirséil, *The Irish Labour Party, 1922–73* (Dublin: University College Dublin Press, 2007), p. 194. See also Niamh Puirséil, 'Political and party competition in post-war Ireland', in Brian Girvin and Gary Murphy (eds), *The Lemass era: politics and society in the Ireland of Seán Lemass* (Dublin: University College Dublin Press, 2005), p. 20. In this discussion of politics and party competition, Puirséil identified the absence of ideas among the political parties as the reason for Tuairim's establishment.

1

Tuairim and the intellectual climate in Ireland

The intellectual climate in Ireland during the 1950s was not conducive to the development of new ideas. Nevertheless, the serious problems which marked that decade meant that traditional policies were increasingly questioned. As emigration soared, the political establishment became convinced from the late 1950s of the need for a more open economy and began to recognise the benefits of investment in education. Faced with the failure of existing anti-partitionist policies, it also sought to improve relations with unionists in Northern Ireland. The pages that follow consider how Tuairim was able to contribute to the debates that informed these policy shifts. Firstly, Tuairim members saw, during the 1950s, the need for new policies and to challenge what they perceived as the dominance of a powerful Catholic Church and conservative political elite. This factor explains the urgency with which the society sought reform of political, economic and social policy in Ireland. Tuairim's independence of the Catholic Church, unusual in an Irish context in the 1950s, and of political parties was critical to ensuring that the society was in a position to influence intellectual debate and policy formulation in Ireland. The perception that the political and religious establishments had of Tuairim and the way in which this changed during the 1950s and 1960s highlight not only the difficulties the organisation faced but also the high regard in which it was held. Tuairim's attempts to subject problems to intellectual analysis and to influence elites and public opinion in general ensured that many people in positions of power were aware of the society. This was particularly evident in the London branch, which provides an interesting example of attitudes within Tuairim and the expectations that certain civil servants had of the society. Tuairim's development from a Dublin-centred organisation to a nationwide society with diaspora elements was, however, not sustained. This chapter examines this growth as well as the factors that gave rise to Tuairim's birth and the reasons for its demise. The international context will shed further light on Tuairim and Ireland, with comparisons being made with organisations in other Western countries. Before all this, Tuairim's formation, objectives, membership and methods are considered with a view to indicating the extent to which these were novel.

Tuairim's establishment, objectives and membership

Tuairim's purpose was to move debate from issues surrounding the civil war, the event around which Irish politics and society continued to turn, to the more immediate problems facing Ireland. The impetus for the society came from the shared frustrations of its founding members, Donal Barrington, a barrister, and Patrick Kilroy, a solicitor and businessman, with the stagnation and conservatism evident throughout the country.[1] Barrington and Kilroy determined that an independent movement was necessary to examine the political, economic, social and cultural problems of contemporary Ireland. The need for independence from political and religious establishments in order to influence public policy reflected a wider tension, perceived by intellectuals in other countries, between the necessity for detachment from the state and the desire to effect change.[2] Tuairim was established in the hope that Ireland could have a new beginning. Barrington and Kilroy created the society as a forum for young people to put forward new ideas and develop a fresh approach. The name Tuairim ('opinion') indicated a questioning attitude, while also reflecting the interest many of its members had in the Irish language. The society's logo showed two faces, that of a woman superimposed on that of a man, representing the society looking to the future, the sense of 'pioneering for a new world'.[3] The most formal statement of its intentions was found in a document that Barrington and Kilroy prepared for the society's first meeting in February 1954. This document, Tuairim's constitution, stressed that Tuairim was not a political party and had no connection with any existing political party. Each member was to be between the ages of twenty-one and forty and had to accept the document, including its reference to the principles enshrined in Articles 40 to 45 of the Irish Constitution. Potential for controversy arose with Article 44, which recognised the 'special position' of the Catholic Church. This reference to the Irish Constitution was a reaction to a campaign by Maria Duce, a right-wing Catholic society, which, as discussed below, sought a referendum to amend the Irish Constitution and replace 'special position' with 'one true Church'. Barrington and Kilroy hoped that Tuairim would contain neither right-wing Catholics nor communists; that it would be seen as a respectable organisation which consisted of what its founding members perceived to be responsible, altruistic and independent-minded citizens. Barrington's view, that Article 44 in the Irish Constitution represented a reasonable compromise, was reflected in Tuairim's document.[4]

A questioning attitude was the most significant requirement for Tuairim membership. According to its constitution, the society was to examine the social, economic, political and cultural problems of modern Ireland. Couched in a formal language, the document set as the society's principal objective the provision of a platform for the younger generation to put forward and discuss new ideas that it hoped would prove influential. Each member was to develop expertise in a particular subject, deliver a paper analysing a problem in that area and suggest a solution at one of the society's monthly meetings, held from September through to the following May. These papers occasionally formed the basis for pamphlets that the society published. The age range for members proved to be one of the most controversial features of the constitution. While the upper limit was overlooked from time to time, most members felt that retaining the rule, at least for officers, was important to ensure the continued vitality and youthful appearance of the society. Furthermore, it reflected their determination to move the debate from issues surrounding the civil war towards the more immediate problems confronting Ireland. It was hoped that those not already in positions of power and influence, would after the age of forty, having formed their ideas in Tuairim, be equipped to impact on the body politic.

Originally a society of fifteen graduates from various parts of Ireland but based in Dublin, Tuairim expanded initially mainly through word of mouth but also through press coverage. The society established twelve branches in addition to its Dublin branch and at its peak in the early 1960s had as many as 1,000 members.[5] Prominent members included Frank Winder, a future professor in biochemistry at Trinity, Dr Miriam Hederman O'Brien and Ronan Keane, a future Chief Justice. Frank D'Arcy, who later became a lecturer in the Department of Adult and Continuing Education at Magee College, Derry, James Scott, a professor of dentistry at Queen's University Belfast, and the businessmen Ronan Brocklesby and Richard Dennis were also involved. In these years, however, these individuals were all young civic-minded Irish citizens. They shared Barrington's and Kilroy's determination to examine the problems of modern Ireland in a non-partisan manner. It was hoped that Tuairim's independence of political parties would allow members of all parties and those in none to come together to address Ireland's political, economic and social difficulties. While Tuairim's orientation was more radical than existing policies, the society took an active interest in politics and encouraged its members to join a party. Barry Desmond and David Thornley of Labour, Garret FitzGerald of Fine Gael, Michael Woods of Fianna Fáil and the socialist Jim Kemmy, for example, were all in their youth members of the society. Thornley later formed part of the Labour Party's 'intellectual' TD grouping alongside individuals such as Justin Keating and Conor Cruise O'Brien. The later involvement of Tuairim's members in politics indicated that they were acquainted with individuals in the parties and were part of the same social circles. This was also the case with Donal Barrington, who unsuccessfully ran for Fianna Fáil in the Seanad election in 1961 and married Eileen O'Donovan, a member of the Boland political dynasty, while Jim Doolan (see Figure 1), a future professor of the Management Department at University College Galway (UCG), is brother-in-law to George Colley.[6] Tuairim's independence of political parties also enabled civil servants such as Maurice Doyle and Diarmuid Ó Cearbhaill, both in the Department of Finance, to join the society, thus facilitating further access to members of the government.

Early Tuairim members such as Donal Barrington, Frank Winder and Ronan Keane left the society in the early 1960s. The most prominent reason for this was the society's age limit of forty, but they also became busier in their careers and many married and started their own families. Around that time, individuals such as David Thornley and John Whyte, respectively of the Political Science Departments at Trinity and UCD, became active members. They and others such as Franklin O'Sullivan, a solicitor who had been involved since the 1950s, assumed the officer positions. As chairmen of the Dublin branch, Barrington, Winder, Thornley and O'Sullivan were crucial to deciding which issues Tuairim examined. Thornley's involvement was particularly important: his oratorical ability attracted many individuals from his college, thus varying the profile of Tuairim's members.[7] Heretofore Tuairim's Dublin branch had been dominated by graduates from UCD. Thornley and other Tuairim members went on to play significant roles in the high society and intelligentsia of Ireland, many of them becoming involved in the structures of power and pursuing careers in areas such as academia and law. At this point it should be noted that though Tuairim's members derived from an educated elite, a number, including Barrington and Kilroy, would have found it impossible to go to college without scholarships. There was also a range of clerical and lay

Mr. James Doolan, of 70 Trimleston park, Booterstown, Co. Dublin, who, as announced in our later editions yesterday, has left for Washington to take up a new post as financial analyst with the World Bank.

1 The Tuairim member Jim Doolan became one of the first Irish people to work in the World Bank in 1962.

people, such as Rev. Enda McDonagh, the Professor of Moral Theology at Maynooth College, Rev. Gabriel Bowe and Sr. Margaret MacCurtain of UCD, Protestant members such as Arthur Carter and Harold Clarke and the first Jewish Lord Mayor of Cork, Gerald Goldberg.

The members of Tuairim did not describe themselves as intellectuals or their organisation as an intellectual society. As previously noted, an unwillingness to use the term would have been understandable given that it was not in favour in Ireland. Its utilisation in relation to individual Tuairim, members such as Garret FitzGerald, Donal Barrington, David Thornley and others is, nevertheless, appropriate. That is also the case in regard to Tuairim, since the society discussed a range of ideas and gained a reputation for a balanced and incisive approach. That its members or those who referred to Tuairim do not seem to have countenanced the term underlines its lack of use in the country.

Tuairim's objective to create an environment conducive to discussion was reflected in the background of its members and their intellectual formation. A cursory glance at their reading habits prior to the society's establishment and during its early years suggests a keen interest in international developments. Well educated, they followed among other matters the fate of the Labour Party and the welfare state in post-war Britain as well as the emergence of the Common Market in continental Europe. An early and sustained enthusiasm for the European project, following the establishment of the European and Steel Community in 1951, was to be found in particular in Miriam Hederman O'Brien, Donal Barrington and Brian O'Connor, a solicitor. Hederman O'Brien also demonstrated a familiarity with more radical political and religious alternatives. She briefly flirted with communism while studying music in Rome before returning to undertake degrees in law and in French at UCD and attending to what became her long-standing involvement in the Irish Council of the European Movement. Though Hederman O'Brien may have been more eclectic in her interests than most, she and her future husband, Bill O'Brien, a solicitor and Tuairim member, independently read books by Carew Hunt on communism, and she, Paddy Kilroy and others learnt more about Marxism after they graduated.[8] This pointed to a wide range of interests among at least some Tuairim members. Though the society was certainly not a radical left-wing organisation, and nor were Hederman O'Brien or others communists, her thirst for knowledge was an illustration of the society's active interest in ideas. This was also reflected in the reading of other members such as Frank D'Arcy and Enda McDonagh. Including as it did the English Catholic periodical *The Tablet* and writings by intellectuals in France such as Gabriel Marcel and Jacques Maritain,[9] it points to an engagement with deeper philosophical questions and a familiarity with the more radical thinking emerging within the Catholic Church in continental Europe. Though few could have foreseen the changes brought about by Vatican II, members believed that those alternative interpretations of Catholic teaching were more reasonable than the hard-line views represented by Archbishop John Charles McQuaid of Dublin.

Not only were individuals expected to challenge the perceived wisdom in society on a particular issue, but implicit in the nature of Tuairim was the need to study and acquire further knowledge. Information, members have stressed, was readily available if one was willing to seek it. Nor do they seem to have been inhibited by their background. In interviews, Hederman O'Brien dismissed any sense that her house was 'priest-ridden', while Barrington claimed that politically Tuairim viewed itself in the constitutional republican tradition in that one's religion should be separate from one's politics.[10]

Following its establishment in 1954, Tuairim as a society focused on pragmatic matters. These were years of consolidation for the organisation. This was partly due to concerns that the establishment of branches outside the capital would take up too much time and energy but also to a need to ensure the vitality of the Dublin branch. That the society did become active outside the capital owed much to the prodigious energy of Lean Scully. Scully, subsequently a successful businesswoman, travelled the country establishing contacts that helped to form new branches: in Cork in 1958; in Limerick, Athlone (referred to as the Midlands branch), Clonmel, Waterford and Sligo in 1959; in London, Belfast, Galway and Tralee in 1960; and in Nenagh and Birmingham (a short-lived branch) in 1962.[11] The establishment of so many branches, particularly in 1959 and 1960, placed the society for a brief period under considerable financial strain. Keeping in regular contact with each branch remained a constant difficulty for the society throughout its existence. Geography was the main factor that inhibited a closer relationship between branches.

Tuairim's increasing organisational sophistication prompted it to adopt a revised constitution in 1966. This document reiterated the society's commitment to democracy as well as its role in putting forward new ideas. Its main innovations were in its definitions of a branch and in Tuairim's governing structure. It thus reflected the reality of a more numerous and complex body. More significant was what the document retained, albeit in a revised format. Pressure in 1965 from two Cork members, Gerald Goldberg and Jim Barry, both working in the legal profession, to abolish the age limit of forty was resisted. A relaxed version which allowed older people to be associate members was, however, adopted. This meant that these individuals over forty years of age could be involved but were ineligible to be elected chairperson of their branch or to the Council of the society. This did not satisfy Barry and Goldberg, who upon reaching forty in 1967 established a rival to Tuairim's Cork branch, a debating society called the Speakers' Club.[12]

The revised document omitted, however, the reference to Articles 40–5 of the Irish Constitution. This omission does not appear to have caused any controversy and probably reflected the perception that it had fulfilled its function, in that Maria Duce's campaign to amend Article 44 had failed. Had Archbishop McQuaid been aware that Tuairim's original document had been a reaction to Maria Duce's campaign he might not have been as content as he subsequently appeared. Years later, in 1965, writing to the Apostolic Nuncio, Joseph M. Sensi, McQuaid claimed that it was 'a significant fact' that membership was conditional upon an acceptance of the 'special position' of the Catholic Church.[13] McQuaid, however, viewed Catholicism as the 'one true Church' and thus disagreed with Donal Barrington's view as expressed in an article published by the Catholic Truth Society. Barrington wrote that because the Irish Constitution was meant to apply to the whole island of Ireland, the existing article represented the best solution and a referendum to change it would be unwise.[14] A referendum on this matter was finally held in 1972; that removed, however, the reference to the 'special position' of the Catholic Church. With *Economic development* in 1958, the introduction of free post-primary education and reforms to the system of censorship in 1967, this was a concrete example of the new thinking emerging during this period and landmarks in the modernisation of Ireland.

During the 1950s, it was perhaps surprising how little dissension there was among Tuairim's members regarding the reference in the society's document to Articles 40–5 of the Irish Constitution. The fact that members of all religions accepted the earlier version is an indication of the climate of the time and the fact that Catholicism was the religion of the majority of people in Tuairim. The hope, as expressed by Frank D'Arcy, Enda McDonagh and James Scott, that this would be a thinking Catholicism, respectful and understanding of other religions, differentiated the society from many people, especially McQuaid and other members of the Catholic hierarchy, who in attempting to maintain the dominant position of the church in Irish life resisted the independent reasoning that Tuairim promoted.[15]

Tuairim's objectives as outlined in its constitution, despite some initial concern, did not give any genuine cause for anxiety to the political establishments. The society's first meeting, in Jury's Hotel, Dublin, on 26 February 1954, attended by more than 100 people, prompted the Minister for Justice, Gerald Boland, to request the Garda Special Branch to 'report on the bona-fides…of "Tuairim"'.[16] The gardaí responded that 'there does not appear to be anything significant in its aims and it is unlikely to make any progress'.[17] This seems to have allayed any fears that Tuairim might have had subversive aims. While surveillance would, the gardaí said, continue, no further reports were sent to the minister. There was, indeed, no reason for concern on the part of the authorities since Tuairim was partly a response to anti-democratic sentiment that lingered on from the 1940s.[18] Tuairim hoped Ireland would move away from what it perceived as the sterility of political debate and that the country would renew its democratic process. This was reflected in newspapers that responded enthusiastically to Tuairim's establishment. The author of 'Irishman's diary' in the *Irish Times*, for example, claimed that it was one of the 'most sensible manifestos' that he had read, while the *Evening Herald* stated that it was a 'welcome sign of the increasingly adult outlook which our citizens are adopting towards problems of national importance' and that it possessed a 'tremendous potential influence for good in the affairs of the country'.[19] Thus established, this precedent of a supportive attitude and generous coverage in national newspapers was generally followed.

The intellectual climate in Ireland

Tuairim believed during the 1950s that that there was a lack of ideas and discussion, and during the 1960s that there was a continued need to examine problems. This view was partly due to the rhetoric of the period prior to Tuairim's establishment, which stressed that the role of the state should be limited in relation to economic and social matters, particularly following the failure of the Mother and Child scheme in 1951. In addition to demands to make the country a truly Catholic state, the international context of the Cold War increased the difficulty of finding solutions to national problems. This was because of the existing tendency to portray the individuals who put forward new ideas as communist and therefore hostile to Catholicism. The pervasive influence of the Catholic Church throughout Irish life made dissent from orthodoxy difficult. This period, however, witnessed pressure for new policies, resulting from changes that included the Irish population's increasing rejection of rural Ireland and a demand for a higher standard of living, as illustrated by emigration to Britain. The establishment in 1940 of the periodical *The Bell* by Seán O'Faoláin and its subsequent criticism of the system of state censorship in operation points to the emergence of a questioning of what values should be central to the country and the beginning of a wider intellectual and cultural debate of which Tuairim was part.

With emigration peaking at 60,000 in 1957,[20] the sense of crisis deepened in the mid- to late 1950s. The need for new policies was increasingly recognised in articles in periodicals such as the intellectual Jesuit journal

Studies, founded in UCD in 1912, and the civil service journal *Administration* but also *Christus Rex*, a publication established by priests in a society of the same name in Maynooth in 1947. Among all these journals, the transition of *Christus Rex*, which had been focused on the dangers of excessive state interference, was perhaps the most dramatic in that it began to adopt a more critical attitude to social issues in the late 1950s.

The evolution of arguments within these periodicals reflected wider debates within the country. Like *Christus Rex*, *Studies* had during the 1940s and early 1950s opposed increased state activity while *Administration*, established by the Association of Higher Civil Servants in 1953, focused on the need for administrative and economic reforms almost to the exclusion of social issues. From later in the 1950s, *Studies* and *Administration* favoured the abandonment of protectionism and membership of the EEC, while the former also criticised the lack of understanding in relation to Unionism. Bryan Fanning, in his study *The quest for modern Ireland*, indicates that Tuairim members such as Donal Barrington, Garret FitzGerald and David Thornley made significant contributions on questions such as the economy, sociology and Northern Ireland both during and following their involvement in the society. These journals became a forum for people to publish papers that previously had been read at Tuairim's meetings. Before they were published by the society, both Barrington's and Thornley's papers, for example, appeared in *Studies*, while Thornley also had an article published in *Christus Rex*.[21]

Although politicians responded with reforms (further discussed in Chapter 2 below), the 1950s were more notable for the sense of despondency caused by the economic situation. The electoral volatility which resulted in four changes of government from 1948 to 1957 suggested a lack of leadership. This was the context in which Tuairim emerged and existed. It would, nevertheless, be an exaggeration to refer to the 1950s as moribund. Periodicals were just one of the signs of vitality during this decade. And from the late 1950s the political establishment adopted certain proposals advocated within these journals in relation to the economy, Northern Ireland and education. These policies resulted in a period of unprecedented economic success and facilitated significant social change.

A further indication of the variety of experiences during the 1950s was the number of organisations which were striving for the realisation of their ideal of Irish society, thus underlining the extent to which Tuairim was unusual for this period. Many of the voluntary organisations, such as Muintir na Tíre, the Christus Rex Society, the Knights of St Columbanus and the Catholic Truth Society of Ireland, were during these decades part of an extended social-Catholic network, each promoting the application of Christian social principles as outlined in papal encyclicals. The latter two were proactive in defending the Catholic view and upholding the status quo, while a similar claim could be made of Christus Rex in its early years. These three organisations focused on influencing the attitudes of the elite of Irish society. On the other hand, Muintir na Tíre wished to have these principles applied to rural Ireland first and from there to all of Ireland. Its desire to develop agriculture, which was seen as the driving force behind the economy, and maintain people on the land was shared by many organisations including Macra na Feirme, the National Farmers' Association (NFA), the Irish Agricultural Organisation Society, the Irish Creamery Milk Suppliers' Association and the Irish Countrywomen's Association.

The concern with making rural areas attractive to live in was closely linked to attempting to protect a traditional way of life. This objective was shared by religious organisations. The Catholic rural life was also bound up with the idea that Gaelic should be the vernacular, a view close to Eamon de Valera's heart. An Comhchaidreamh, Conradh na Gaeilge and Gael Linn were among those societies that promoted the Irish language. A fear was prevalent throughout the country that industrial development and the movement from rural to urban areas underway in Ireland would, as had already occurred in Europe, introduce secular and materialist, not to say English, ideas damaging to family life. It was, indeed, the assumption behind much government policy at least until the late 1950s. Successive Irish governments hoped to ensure the viability of rural areas and facilitate the growth of the spirit of self-reliance evident in these groups. In this regard, the government hoped that Foras Éireann, 'a permanent conference of voluntary organisations' directed towards strengthening the sense of community, would be more successful in co-ordinating the activities of these bodies.[22]

Tuairim's methods of widening its circle of influence

The methods Tuairim used in seeking to create an informed public opinion and influence government policy were wide and varied. They included monthly meetings, study weekends, research groups, publication of pamphlets, and articles in newspapers and periodicals, establishment of new branches, an extern lecturer scheme and involvement in other organisations. Meetings were the first and the main activity in which the society was engaged. They fulfilled a number of functions including attracting new members, introducing particular subjects and discovering whether they required further investigation. Study weekends and research groups allowed these issues to be studied in detail. With the Dublin branch holding one in 1954 and three in 1957, study weekends became increasingly important to the society. Research groups would often be established as a result of a weekend, or else a weekend would be organised to give a group or members an opportunity to present a paper. These groups were increasingly used from the late 1950s to study controversial matters, with pamphlets occasionally resulting from their deliberations. Tuairim published sixteen pamphlets between 1958 and 1970. These challenged many of the assumptions underlying government policies and endeavoured to define progressive politics into the future. Pamphlets had various origins: some were reactions to particular government proposals; others resulted from Tuairim's initiative. Generally, interest in a particular matter would lead a member or group of members to agree to study this in detail and present a paper, which, following feedback, could form the basis of a pamphlet. Each article intended for publication had to reach a certain standard. The executive of the society, which was democratically elected by its members, would decide whether an article was to be published. Pamphlets would generally carry a note emphasising that the views therein were the views of the author(s). These indeed often caused controversy among Tuairim's members.

The costs involved in running the society could be considerable. Generally, the expense of publishing a pamphlet was paid by whoever commissioned it, while others within or outside Tuairim made contributions to this and the costs involved in establishing branches, organising meetings and weekends. The most expensive item proved to be the pamphlet against UCD's proposed move to Belfield (1960), which, owing to the cost of printing, was at first available only in stencilled form. Those who financially supported the publication were probably members of UCD staff and graduates of that college. The cost seemed prohibitive because of the size of the pamphlet (seventy-four pages) and seems to have worsened the society's financial position. This could have been a factor in its failure to publish Peter Connolly's article 'Censorship' (1959). The main reason for the absence of a pamphlet on censorship was, however, that cultural issues were not central to the society. While the system of censorship that existed represented everything that Tuairim stood against, and writers were involved in the society, individuals like Ulick O'Connor did not form its main driving force. Nor was reform of censorship Tuairim's *raison d'être*. The society was more concerned with pressing economic, political, educational and social problems. Certainly, censorship did not command as much attention as the future location of UCD. As for finances, though the initial outlay of money on a pamphlet could place a branch under strain, it is also the case that generally the society did not make a loss on its publications. Each branch, despite this, could be vulnerable, as it depended on the voluntary efforts of its members for its financial well-being as well as a reasonable level of activity and standard of debate.

It was Tuairim's intention, at least initially, to send each pamphlet to every member of the Oireachtas.[23] While this seems to have occurred only with a minority of pamphlets, it raises the question of the extent of the society's ambition. In a letter to the Apostolic Nuncio, Joseph M. Sensi, in 1965, Archbishop John Charles McQuaid claimed that Tuairim, as a 'group of intelligent University graduates', had influenced the government. He went on to suggest that the society would continue to do so through 'through membership of...instruments of policy-control'.[24] As has been previously noted, Tuairim's members were involved in other organisations and contributed to the same debates as periodicals such as *Studies* and *Christus Rex*. Furthermore, the society hoped that its events and publications would receive the maximum amount of publicity and at times actively sought the same. Moreover, politicians and even civil servants spoke at Tuairim's meetings. However, contrary to what was implied by McQuaid, the society's members were generally not appointed to state bodies or commissions. The individuals who were involved in Tuairim would have been considered either too young or too radical for such positions. Nor did Tuairim members actively network with those in positions of power. Civil servants generally did not become involved in the society or attend its meetings.[25] They believed that Tuairim's meetings could be controversial and were, in any event, anxious to retain their traditional anonymity. While Tuairim's members were often in the same social circles as civil servants and politicians, they usually did not actively seek to persuade civil servants or politicians of the need to implement a particular policy. Rather Tuairim seems to have been most concerned with ensuring that the general climate was conducive to the articulation of new ideas. The society was not in itself committed to any particular viewpoint, but acted as a forum for individuals to put forward ideas. While it was hoped that these would lead to a more open debate and a change in policy, it was generally left to the author(s) of certain papers and pamphlets to decide whether a matter should be actively pursued.

The confidence that members demonstrated when articulating their views and that of the society when confronting the country's problems was striking, especially considering that many had only recently graduated. As the first generation born since independence, they seem to have been imbued with idealism and a determination to ensure that Ireland would be a success. Their sense of patriotism most likely emanated from the generation of their parents, those born in the pre-independence era. The success of many of Tuairim's members both at university and subsequently in their careers was also crucial. Part of the elite of society, they displayed an active altruism which was reflected in Tuairim's relatively novel methods. Certainly in a twentieth-century context, the pamphlet was rare, although it had a distinguished history in earlier centuries. Research groups and weekends were more common if still unusual. Generally, meeting different individuals, the interchange of ideas and the questioning of existing norms were what appealed to people and made Tuairim events interesting, and, at times, exhilarating. In contrast then to the dismal perception many people in contemporary Ireland have of the 1950s, at least some of the society's members view it as an exciting period. There was a genuine sense of anticipation at the social engagement that would take place at these events.

It was hoped that the society would in time consist of individuals who were experts in a wide range of subjects. On 1 January 1959 Tuairim's Honorary General Secretary, Miriam Hederman O'Brien, claimed in a letter to the *Irish Independent* that the fulfilment of this objective had given rise to the extern lecture scheme. Announcing its inauguration, she stated that under its terms the society would send members to organisations in any part of Ireland to speak on one of a list of forty-two subjects ranging from Thomas Davis and the Seanad to the Irish language and free trade. Individuals named included Hederman O'Brien, Donal Barrington, Frank Winder, Garret FitzGerald, the future Taoiseach, John Kevin Clear, the Secretary of the National Fish Industrial Development Association, and Riobard MacGabhrainn, the manager and co-founder of Gael Linn, and the writer Ulick O'Connor. Academics such as Colm Ó hEocha, future President of UCG, David O'Mahony, appointed head of the Economics Department in University College Cork (UCC) in 1964, and Gerard Quinn, a lecturer in economics at UCD, were also on this list. For the first six months, the scheme was a 'qualified success', with twenty-seven lectures given by eleven individuals.[26] Thereafter, Foras Éireann took over its organisation, although it remained under Tuairim's name, with one member, Richard Dennis, appointed to the committee as its administrator.

Tuairim was keenly aware of the need for greater co-operation between different organisations in Irish society. To this end, it facilitated contacts between various groups. Tuairim was also anxious that the society's members should become involved in other organisations. In this way, it hoped to influence attitudes, encourage the drive towards economic progress and contribute to social harmony. One contribution that it made to Irish civil society was to organise conferences designed to solve some of the problems of rural Ireland. These were attended by a number of prominent individuals and organisations from throughout the country. Tuairim's success in organising such weekends, as well as the confidence others had in the society's ability to ensure that they ran smoothly, was particularly well reflected in its involvement with local and national developmental bodies. One conference in February 1961, attended by 200 delegates from sixty-seven development associations and companies, with the support of the Taoiseach, Seán Lemass,[27] ultimately led in 1963 to the establishment of a national body to co-ordinate the activities of these local bodies. Another example of Tuairim's attempts to provide solutions to rural problems was a study weekend in Dublin in December 1957. Described as 'one of the most representative gatherings of agriculture ever assembled',[28] it was convened to discuss the recently announced Farm Apprenticeship scheme, which had been jointly proposed by the NFA and Macra na Feirme, and facilitated the involvement of these organisations in the formulation of government policy. This was an indication that rural as well as urban bodies valued Tuairim's role, a point underlined by the society's meetings at which the Irish section of the European Association of Teachers (Association Européenne des Enseignants, or AEDE) and the West Cork Economic Development Association were established.[29]

During these decades Tuairim gained a reputation among various organisations and at least some politicians and other influential individuals for an altruistic interest in the welfare of the country. Its contribution to resolving pressing social and economic problems, together with its provision of a forum for discussion, indicated that the society could serve a vital purpose that few other organisations seemed capable of or were willing to fulfil. Tuairim did not represent any particular section of Irish society, unlike many of those groups heretofore discussed or others such as political parties or trade unions. Furthermore, as previously noted, Tuairim claimed that it was not committed to a particular policy. This was not entirely true, for a liberal tendency was implied in Tuairim's very existence. The society would have shared a conviction of the need for new policies with at least some influential individuals. This enabled it to examine political, economic or social problems either in combination with such individuals or organisations or by itself. Combined with the fact that the society was not constrained by the necessity to appeal to sectional interests and had a vision of a more tolerant Ireland, this caused it to succeed in developing a place of its own in Irish society.

Tuairim hoped that it would widen its circle of influence by its members becoming involved in other organisations. Frank Winder, for example, was on the standing committee of local development organisations, while Miriam Hederman O'Brien and Eilish MacCurtain were successive secretaries of the Irish Council of the European Movement. Hederman O'Brien and Frank D'Arcy were involved in the Irish Association of Catholic University Students, which was affiliated with the liberal international Catholic movement Pax Romana. Donal Barrington and Frank Gibney were in the Anti-Emigration Society, Richard Dennis was in Foras Éireann, Brian O'Connor was in the Irish United Nations Association, Mary Power was the Publicity Officer of the Community Consultative Council, and Mona

Stanton was in the Irish Council of Women.[30] This was an indication of the variety of interests. Many were at least as active in these societies as in Tuairim: Hederman O'Brien's involvement in the Irish Council of the European Movement was one such example. Nevertheless, Tuairim believed that, by co-operating with other bodies, its views would reach and influence a wider audience. To this end, it occasionally held joint meetings with these societies, at which where one of its members or an invited guest would speak. Alternatively, a Tuairim member might present a paper to one of these organisations. Much of this activity was a further indication that during these decades there were options for those concerned about the future of Ireland or with an interest in events outside the country.

As Tuairim grew and established branches, and as Irish society changed, its members responded to the need for a more sophisticated organisation. Initially the structure was, of course, very simple, with one branch in Dublin run by a chairperson, secretary and treasurer and committee. A social secretary, a press secretary, an art secretary and a pamphlets officer were subsequently added to the Dublin branch. Following the establishment of the Cork branch in April 1958, there was a need for a governing structure. This was vested in the Council, whose executive included the President of Tuairim, the vice-president, general secretary and treasurer. The Council, which was the sole interpreter of the constitution and ultimately responsible for the direction of Tuairim, also included the previous president and members elected by the branches as well as up to three extra co-opted members. It was to be democratically elected; each branch was entitled to be represented by its chairperson or her or his nominee and by one person for each fifty members up to 200 and one for each 100 above that. There were also provisions therein defining a branch and mechanisms to remove individuals from office if they failed to attend meetings of the Council or acted contrary to Tuairim's interests. Generally, all officer positions were changed after one year or at the most two with the possible exception of the society's representatives to other organisations, who could remain in these positions for longer periods of time, owing to the diverse interests of Tuairim's members and the difficulties of becoming familiar with the methods of different bodies.

Tuairim's demise

Tuairim's constitution stated that each branch would be responsible for its own finances and was thus effectively independent. The fortunes of the different branches varied in response to the development of a more liberal society in the 1960s. A precondition for a successful branch was, obviously, a number of well-educated young people. Dublin, Cork and Limerick, which boasted larger younger populations than other cities, were at an advantage in this regard and accordingly had the longest-lasting branches. As well as their core members, these cities acquired more new members, particularly those interested in being elected officers or becoming active in research groups. In addition, these branches attracted audiences to attend their meetings, and a local or national press that would cover their activities. Membership in Dublin had by 1963 grown to 250 and seems to have remained above 200 for much of that decade, while those in Cork and Limerick varied between 60 and 100 people.[31] On the other hand, the branches in the other towns and cities found it difficult to sustain a high level of activity over an extended period of time. A figure of 35 members for Clonmel in 1965 seems representative for the smaller branches. The lack of a sufficient number of young people interested in the society and particularly of an influx of new members to renew the organisation after its initial consolidation was the greatest difficulty that Tuairim faced.

It is difficult to overstate the importance of diverse activities to the success of a branch. In addition to regular meetings, study weekends and the publication of pamphlets, the Dublin branch had the most variety, with an art-lending scheme, dances and, generally, an active social side. These social events were important not only in raising funds but also in attracting new members. The art-lending scheme, for instance, was a significant achievement, with more than £1,000 having been spent by 1971 on paintings since the scheme began in 1962. Following its successful involvement in adult education, the Cork branch also introduced an art-lending scheme in 1972. That branch was responding to the need to create new roles for itself. Dealing with what was described as the 'crippling' costs of advertising, travelling and accommodation expenses for speakers and meetings were problems faced by each branch.[32] Suffering from significant debts and a relatively inactive general membership in 1970, the Cork branch briefly prospered by diversifying its activities, namely into the art-lending scheme, literary evenings and adult education. The literary evenings developed into a series of short-term courses, some of which were run in conjunction with the Cork Vocational Educational Committee, on topics as diverse as literature and psychology, Irish political development and the EEC. Its success encouraged the society to invite around twenty organisations, including the Cork City and Cork County Vocational and Educational Committee, Cork Community Council, the Education and Adult Education Department at UCC, to a meeting about co-ordinating and developing adult education in Cork. Though addressing a need in this area, the branch was building on the programmes of adult education already in place. The Cork Council of Adult Education was established and Margaret Hurley, the branch's first female chairperson, was appointed public relations officer. This council provided information to and promoted co-ordination between voluntary and statutory bodies involved in adult education. The council highlighted, however, a weakness of Tuairim: the Cork branch had a limited number of active members and could not meet the increased demand for adult education.

The economic, social, cultural, educational and generational changes of the 1960s meant that there were more alternatives to Tuairim during this decade than during the 1950s. Developments in the media, for example, included an increased number of publications, the evolution of national newspapers, with more investigative journalism and less political affiliation, and the establishment of Radio Telefís Éireann (RTÉ) in 1961. RTÉ, in particular, adversely affected Tuairim's ability to draw well-known individuals to speak at its meetings. While it also facilitated increased questioning of social and political orthodoxies, members maintained that the current affairs programmes being broadcast diminished attendance at Tuairim's meetings.[33] Politicians made more regular appearances as guests on television from the late 1960s. This made it more difficult for Tuairim to attract new members and sustain their interest. However, the society had also contributed to its own demise: its reliance on volunteers prevented it from responding effectively to television and the opportunities it presented.

In the 1960s, there were more options for people intent on contributing to the betterment of Ireland. These included increasingly active student societies in universities and a more open political establishment. The Cork branch, for example, was by the end of the decade competing with meetings in the university and the Speakers' Club. In a similar vein, the *Irish Press* claimed that it was 'a tribute [to the] success' of the London branch that the literary and debating societies of the Irish Club and the National University of Ireland Club were 'devising such attractive and serious programmes'.[34] Meanwhile, in 1967 the Dublin branch noted that the society had been established partly because it perceived the political parties to be inaccessible: a situation which it felt had changed.[35] While Tuairim encouraged members to join a political party, its formation had, indeed, been a reaction to the closed nature of the body politic. Responding to the changes of the 1960s, politicians seemed to be more open to fresh ideas and welcoming to young graduates, a development that was reflected in the increasing attention that they paid to their university branches and the new policies that were adopted.

The establishment of a range of policy-formulation bodies from the 1950s was a further factor in Tuairim's demise. Organisations such as the Economic and Social Research Institute, An Foras Forbartha, An Foras Talúntais, the Institute of Public Administration and the National Industrial and Economic Council were alternative forums for the formulation of policy in an increasingly crowded market for ideas. The establishment especially in the 1970s of societies, many with specific aims rather than the more general objective that was Tuairim's, also brought further competition. As previously noted, Tuairim's reliance on voluntary efforts meant that it found it impossible to respond to the demand for increased professionalism in the provision of services such as adult education in Cork. The greater numbers in higher education, especially from the late 1960s, led to increased specialisation and seem to have created the sense that Tuairim was no longer necessary. In this way, Tuairim's demise reflected a difficulty that intellectuals were perceived to be experiencing in many countries. The assumption that during this period intellectuals, with their more universal perspective, became alienated by the increase in educational opportunities and disciplinary specialisms has been criticised by Stefan Collini, who in *Absent minds* pointed to similar concerns in the nineteenth century. During the 1970s, Tuairim, nevertheless, did not meet the need among the public for the articulation of specific viewpoints. Irish membership of the EEC in 1973 may also have decreased, among the population generally, the necessity it perceived for debate in relation to Ireland's future and hence individuals' desire to become actively involved in Tuairim. These factors resulted in a reduced membership. For example, a mere eighteen people attended Cork's annual general meeting in 1972. The reality was that the logic of Tuairim's age limit and the nature of the society had led to its demise.

The relative economic prosperity of the 1960s was a particularly significant factor in the decision in 1967 to disband the London branch. With a high turnover rate of 50 per cent, many of its most active members, including Michael O'Hanrahan, an accountant, and Joy Rudd, a teacher, returned home. This meant that the branch's attempts to attract young people succeeded only in ensuring a static membership of around eighty, with a figure of twenty-five more representative of the number of active members. The shortage of dynamic individuals and financial problems, which had plagued the branch throughout its existence, resulted in the ninth and final edition of its publication *An Occasional Bulletin* being issued in 1964. An 'organ of informed Irish opinion in Britain',[36] it had been valuable as an outlet for members to publish articles and as a source of publicity for the branch. This meant that its loss was considerable. See Figure 2 for a photograph of Conor Cruise O'Brien, who in 1962 wrote an article for *An Occasional Bulletin*. The London branch's *An Occasional Bulletin* had been a significant innovation within Tuairim. The suggestion, which the branch resisted, that it should be adopted as the society's official publication underlines the high regard in which it was held. Around 2,000 copies of each edition were printed and circulated among a wide readership in London and Ireland.

Tuairim's London branch argued that it was confronted by particular

2 Conor Cruise O'Brien published an article on Katanga (now in the Democratic Republic of the Congo) in the London branch's *An Occasional Bulletin* in 1962.

problems, including the need to establish its autonomy with other organisations, difficulties with an ambivalent local press and a dispersed Irish community. While the latter might have been true regarding graduates, heavy concentrations of working-class Irish existed in parts of London. This fact, combined with the venues, such as hotels and the National University of Ireland Club, which the branch decided on for its meetings once its independence was established, suggests that the society intended to focus on the middle class.[37] The change in its choice of venues from November 1961 was prompted by the need for a more permanent location and the shortage of active individuals, but also by a genuine concern for the welfare of migrants. In contrast to the branch's decision to remain aloof from the Connolly Association, which was perceived as communist, from 1962 members served on the Irish Welfare Fund Committee and the Council of the Irish Centre, and as its contribution to the 1916 commemoration the branch showed Gael Linn's film on the Irish revolution, *Mise Éire*.[38]

As a group of liberal intellectuals, the London branch did not share a world view with the working-class majority of the Irish in the city. John Jackson, a lecturer in social science at Sheffield University, pointed out this very difficulty at the society's first meeting in London in May 1960: he identified a class divide as the principal factor in preventing leaders from uniting the community. This was the background to a debate as to whether members of the Irish community should organise themselves, one to which Tuairim contributed. Roy Johnston, a scientist, claimed that they should follow the lead of the Irish Party during Parnell's time and 'wield the Irish vote in the Irish interest'.[39] Another Tuairim member, Miriam Daly, subsequently a lecturer in history at Queen's University Belfast, argued, however, that such a policy would 'postpone the integration of individual Irish men in Britain, and tend to embitter Anglo-Irish relations'.[40] As one centrally involved in the society, Daly more accurately reflected Tuairim's viewpoint than did Johnston, who was also active in the Connolly Association. Daly believed that the only rational solution was for the Irish state to assume responsibility for its citizens, a view that reflected Tuairim's interest in Ireland rather than Britain. The branch from the outset was much more interested in examining problems in Ireland than in its host country. It produced two pamphlets, one on the Irish education system and the other examining industrial schools. This was contrary to the situation in the Belfast branch, the other one outside the southern state, whose members became involved in the local politics of Northern Ireland. The crucial difference was that the members of the London branch were not from that city and unlike many members of the working-class majority in London, were able to return to Ireland. In the longer term, the branch hoped that migrants would be able to find work at home or, if they remained, integrate into the society in which they lived and thus help break down barriers between the two nations. While Tuairim provided a forum for the Irish in London to express their views and succeeded in having a range of issues debated, its influence upon attitudes among the diaspora and in the host country was limited. In this regard, the branch decided to retain respectability among the political and religious establishments in Ireland and remain aloof from controversial left-wing and Republican organisations in London. Tuairim's independence, combined with the wide range of opinions contained within the society, would in any case have made it difficult for the branch to provide the leadership that was required. Whereas other issues were more significant in the downfall of Tuairim in Ireland, this independence contained the seeds of demise for the London branch. The supply of graduates was declining, and therefore the branch's decision not to attempt to interest the working class in the society in London caused it to close in 1967.

Other factors impeding Tuairim's development were specific to certain branches. According to the future government minister and former Tuairim member Michael D. Higgins, discord over its future direction was a factor in the disbandment of the Galway branch in 1965. The establishment of a third-level educational institution in Limerick in 1972 adversely affected the branch in that city. In view of the divisions in Northern Ireland, it was decided that no branch should be established in Belfast unless it had equal numbers of Catholic and Protestant members. Contrary to Tuairim's non-sectarian nature, this was, however, a practical recognition of the political-religious divide in that state. The branch, though, made little progress as its members concentrated their energies on National Unity, an organisation explored below in Chapter 3. Similarly, the Waterford branch failed to capture the public imagination. Kerry and Sligo were arguably in a worse position, with the former seemingly largely dependent on the Cork branch while many people in the latter focused on the W. B. Yeats Society, which had been established in 1958.[41]

The Dublin branch's active social side created its own difficulties. Some members seemed more interested in dances and the art-lending scheme than in Tuairim's primary purpose of examining social, political, economic and cultural problems. A sub-committee established to examine the question of recruitment had reported that certain individuals, which it did not identify, had cynically implied that these social activities had led to an increasing number of female members and an imbalance between the sexes. This suggestion ignored, however, the number of very intelligent women who were involved in Tuairim and the issues relevant to their gender that the society considered.[42] Tuairim's sub-committee nevertheless found in its 1965 report that members became less active as the society grew increasingly respectable from the late 1950s. It had become more and more difficult to replace Tuairim's founding members, who were leaving the organisation, with similar people who would share their commitment to studying issues and presenting their findings. The loss to the society of dynamic individuals such as Barrington, Winder and Scully was considerable, if not fatal.

During the 1960s, it was generally people from outside the society rather than members who spoke at the organisation's meetings. A consequence of this was the decreasing number of pamphlets published by the society from the middle of that decade, which in turn led to less publicity. While meetings continued to serve an important purpose in putting forward new ideas, the Dublin branch's 1965 report argued that people who wished to improve the country no longer automatically joined Tuairim. The society's image had changed: Tuairim was no longer identified with challenging orthodoxy or as a provocative organisation in terms of debating issues. There was a need for more members to read papers, for speakers to be controversial, for further discussion at meetings and for general changes in the image of the society if young graduates were to continue to join. This led the Dublin branch to undertake a recruitment campaign. Tuairim used press releases, advertised meetings and pamphlets, informed specific people of their events and even organised an essay-writing scheme for people aged under twenty-five. Appeals for more young people to become involved, however, had only limited impact. Had the society sought new members earlier, particularly from the late 1950s, it might have had more success. The attempt to recruit new members was made from a position of weakness, and financial difficulties increased such difficulties. The absence in 1970, for the first time since 1967, of a single theme linking the branch's meetings underlined the sense that Tuairim in Dublin was facing a crisis.[43] The commitment in time and effort that each committee gave to organising its branch's events was difficult to sustain, particularly without the influx of new members. This finally led to the Dublin branch's decision to dissolve itself in 1973, with the Limerick and Cork branches following in 1974 and 1975.

Hibernia

The role of Tuairim's members in the evolution of *Hibernia* from a Catholic magazine to an independent and influential periodical was significant. Originally dedicated to the 'cause of the social apostolate' and striving for the application of Christian social principles, the review had articulated the interests of its members in matters relating to the Catholic Church's welfare since its establishment in 1937.[44] As *Hibernia* increased its circulation from the mid-1950s, the workload of its owner and editor, Basil Clancy, became heavier, which in turn underlined the need for further investment. This presented Patrick Kilroy and another Tuairim member, the businessman Con Smith, with the opportunity in 1959 to attempt to develop *Hibernia* as an intellectual journal. Frank D'Arcy, also a member of the society, became its editor. While these individuals acted independently of Tuairim, this venture followed from the failure of the society's plan to publish its own liberal newspaper. That proposal floundered in the face of an increasingly crowded marketplace and competing demands, not least from Archbishop John Charles McQuaid. McQuaid later recalled that he had offered £6,000 to Tuairim members to establish a Catholic review.[45] That he should offer this amount to the society underlines the high regard in which Tuairim was held as well as his commitment to establishing an intellectual Catholic publication. It also suggests that as the society in the late 1950s was becoming increasingly active in the public sphere, Tuairim's intentions were not yet completely understood by some, including McQuaid.

At the announcement that *Hibernia* would become a weekly, the periodical on 25 September 1959 stressed that the individuals who now controlled it were independent of other organisations. An informed journal, it gave increased attention to political, social and economic matters. Many of the contributors had, however, begun to do so prior to the change of ownership, including Tuairim members such as Donal Barrington, James Scott and Michael McKeown, who were among those who used it as a forum to present their views to a wider audience. Yet the venture failed financially, and *Hibernia* and was sold back to Clancy in 1961 before John Mulcahy became its final proprietor in 1968. This initial period, nevertheless, seemed to have left a lasting impact upon the evolution of *Hibernia*. During the 1960s it continued to consider a wide variety of issues and became an influential review. Moreover, the change of emphasis elicited praise from a future Conservative Party MP, Norman St John-Stevas, who claimed that Tuairim had 'inspired a newspaper "Hibernia" and published some excellent and impartial reports on controversial questions'.[46] On the other hand, the Connolly Association's *Irish Democrat* criticised the '*Hibernia*-Tuairim line of thought' because it advocated a more conciliatory nationalist policy towards unionism.⁴⁷ That newspaper was incorrect insofar as the organisations, despite sharing the objective of informing a more liberal society, steadfastly remained independent in their identity and point of view.

The Catholic Church

There was a fundamental change from the poor relations between the Catholic and Protestant churches in Ireland, from the late 1950s to the ecumenical rapprochement that followed Vatican II. The Vatican Council itself resulted in far-reaching changes to the Catholic Church, including the introduction of the vernacular and greater participation by the laity in the sacraments. Tuairim's interest in these developments was reflected in meetings at which the society attempted to explain the changes to a lay audience. Barrington, meanwhile, forcefully put forward his view on the Catholic boycott of Protestants at Fethard-on-Sea, a small village in Co. Wexford, which began on 12 May 1957. An illustration, albeit an extreme one, of the generally limited understanding between members of the two religions during the 1950s, the boycott was prompted by the belief that the Protestant community had assisted Sheila Cloney and her two children in leaving their home rather than have the children educated at the local Catholic school. Speaking to the Social Study Congress in June, Barrington criticised the boycott as an 'unjust and terrible thing'.⁴⁸ According to Barrington, Bishop Michael Browne of Galway threatened to excommunicate him following his criticism of the boycott. There was thus a significant contrast between the opinion of some Catholics, who were dismayed by the boycott, and that of at least one member of the Catholic hierarchy, who defended it. Shortly afterwards, the Taoiseach, Eamon de Valera, stated that it was 'ill-conceived, ill-considered and futile'.⁴⁹ The mother and children eventually returned home as the boycott came to an end towards the close of 1957. In the present discussion, its significance lay in the difference between Bishop Browne's attitude and that of Barrington and Tuairim, who hoped that members of the two religions could openly discuss such difficulties.

Such views resulted in Archbishop McQuaid's becoming increasingly suspicious of Tuairim. This study focuses on McQuaid partly because he was such a dominant figure but also because it was in his Dublin diocese that Tuairim had its most active branch. One of the most intransigent figures in relation to ecumenical matters, McQuaid demonstrated his commitment to the segregation of Catholics and Protestants in his warning to one priest, Fr. Edward McElroy, of the need to ensure that a Tuairim meeting was not a 'combined Catholic-Protestant affair'.⁵⁰ McQuaid was also concerned about the influence that he believed Tuairim was exerting on the government.

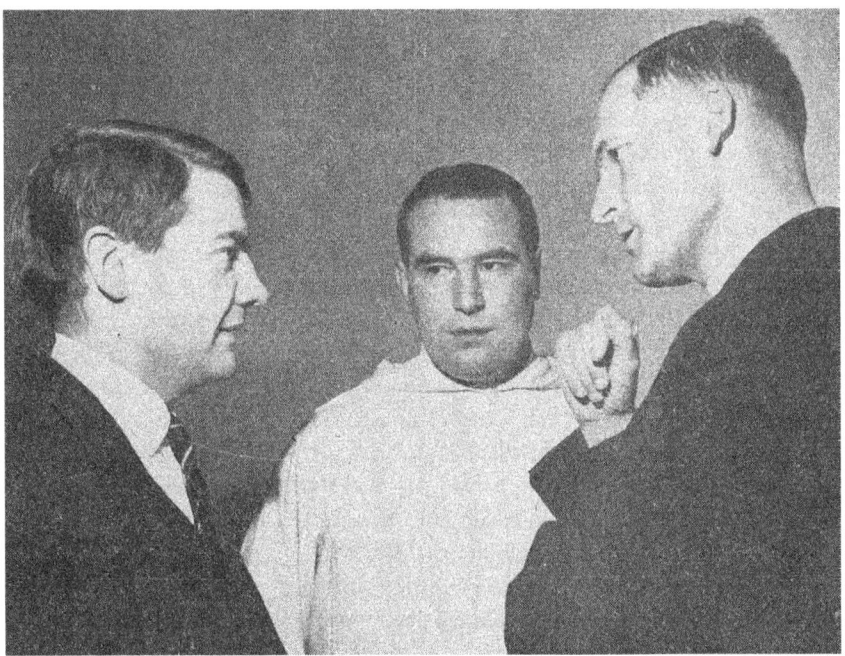

3 David Thornley, Brother Gerard of the Taizé Ecumenical Community in France and Rev. P. J. Brophy of St Patrick's College (left to right) at a Tuairim meeting on 'Christian unity' in 1965.

This might have led him to arrange for Fr. Bertram Crowe, a lecturer in ethics and politics at UCD, to send him information regarding the society. Crowe sent McQuaid some reports over a short period in early 1965 and asked the archbishop if he was 'considering infiltration'.[51] Though to suggest, as John Cooney does in his biography of McQuaid, that Crowe was a 'priest-spy' sensationalises his role,[52] Crowe's actions point to McQuaid's increased concern regarding Tuairim and the archbishop's wish to be better informed of the society's plans. Its timing seems to have been motivated by a demand by the Apostolic Nuncio, Joseph M. Sensi, for information about Tuairim upon reading a newspaper report of the meeting at which Brother Gerard of the Taizé monastic community in France had spoken (see Figure 3). This ecumenical community's work for Christian unity was reflective of the new theological thinking that was emerging in Ireland and particularly continental Europe at this time, which aimed at fundamental reform of the Catholic Church and improved relations with Protestants, as was evident in Pope John XXIII's call in 1959 for unity between Christians. McQuaid feared, however, that increased contact with Protestants would damage the Catholic faith.

Tuairim supported many of the new ideas that were apparent within and outside the Catholic Church. In 1963, for instance, Maynooth's Fr. Enda McDonagh wrote an article for the London branch's *An Occasional Bulletin*, which appeared alongside another by Rev. Canon C. M. Gray-Stack, the Rector of Kenmare and Precentor of St Mary's Cathedral, Limerick. Both were liberal thinkers who favoured the changes introduced by Vatican II and promoted ecumenical attitudes in their respective churches in the interests of harmony among Christians. McDonagh's progressive views were illustrated further at a 1964 meeting of the Dublin Laurentian Society, a society established in Trinity in 1953 to work for facilities for Catholic students, of which Tuairim's John Boland was a founding member. McDonagh argued that as a 'contribution towards ecumenism [and in] their own spiritual interests', Irish Catholics should read the Bible.[53] In 1959 he had claimed that the 'faithful' had a genuine part to play in the development of church teaching and called for 'dialogue of partnership' between the church and an 'interested and well-informed laity'.[54] This was, of course, in the pre-conciliar era, when the church was in a position of authority and maintained a distance from the people, who were generally passive during religious services. While ecumenical activity remained minimal at the level of the Catholic hierarchy, there had, however, since the late 1950s, been echoes in Ireland of the continental European thinking that led to Vatican II. The new generation which emerged in both church and society included Tuairim members such as McDonagh, who argued that the church as a whole needed to adapt to rather than be shielded from secular influences. The interaction between Catholic and Protestant laity and clergy which Tuairim facilitated at its meetings was a significant innovation during this period. It underlines the range of views within the church during this period.

Towards the end of his episcopate in 1971, McQuaid remained aloof from these developments. The archbishop's hostility towards ecumenical trends meant that it was unsurprising that he was unavailable when Tuairim invited him to speak alongside the Chief Rabbi, Isaac Cohen, and an unnamed Protestant representative.[55] This meeting reflected Tuairim's hope that an intelligent and active citizenship would fully contribute to the future development of the country. McQuaid, on the other hand, attempted to exert a degree of control over the members of his diocese. He was of an era when paternalistic values were to the fore. Ill equipped and unwilling because of his background and education to respond to ecumenical developments, he had at least been partly overtaken by the changes in Irish society during the 1960s.

Tuairim, through its meetings and writings, highlighted the absence of a strong intellectual tradition among the Catholic laity. The society criticised not only the lack of new thinking on religion in Irish society but also what it described as the 'puritanical' nature of Catholicism in Ireland.[56] In his pamphlet *Ireland: the end of an era?*, David Thornley argued that the lack of a particular academic study of the Catholic Church's social and political influence was absurd. John Whyte, who spoke at a Tuairim weekend in 1964, addressed that anomaly in his seminal study *Church and state in modern Ireland*. His move from UCD to Queen's University Belfast was undoubtedly a significant loss to both UCD and Tuairim. Whyte, a distinguished academic, wrote the Tuairim pamphlet *Dáil deputies* before leaving Dublin in 1966.[57] As vice-chair of the Dublin branch in 1964–65, Whyte had worked closely with Thornley, then chairperson of the Dublin branch. The interaction between Whyte in UCD and Thornley in Trinity reflected the society's attempts to develop in public a synthesis of its religious and political beliefs. In Thornley's case, this was complicated by his commitment to finding a resolution to the conflicts between his Christianity, his socialism and his Republicanism. His subsequent concern with a lack of interest in politics in Ireland and the difficulties intellectuals encountered in becoming active in political life seemed, with hindsight, sadly prescient.[58] The potential he showed in his writings and fascination with the EEC contrasted with a brief and largely unsuccessful political career, which contributed to his poor health. He died in 1978 at the young age of forty-three.

Attitudes towards Tuairim

Influential figures had different views of Tuairim, from hostility to praise for its active interest in the country. The coverage given in the press indicates that it held Tuairim in high regard. This was especially true of the relatively liberal *Irish Times*, which took a major interest in the fortunes of the society. Provincial newspapers understandably tended to focus on the local branch, if one existed, while news of Tuairim also appeared in other publications. At the time of its foundation, the London branch, in particular, received considerable coverage in national newspapers, which reflected the society's idealistic examination of a wide range of issues but also what was seen as the considerable potential of Tuairim in London. There was a belief within the media and the civil service that the society would make a significant impact on Ireland and among the diaspora. Their view was that Tuairim was different from Republican and socialist groups such as Sinn Féin and the Connolly Association, which, according to the *Irish Times*, wasted their time and energy on irrelevant matters. In the words of Valentin Iremonger, poet and diplomat in the Irish Embassy in London, Tuairim was an 'eminently respectable organisation'.[59] This followed an earlier comment in 1959 by another poet, Máire Mhac an tSaoi, then also a civil servant in the Department of External Affairs, who claimed that Tuairim, along with the Irish-language organisation Gael Linn, was one of the 'most dynamic movements' among the country's young people.[60] She suggested that the fact that the society used an Irish word as its name was indicative of an increased familiarity with the language. This was correct insofar as many of Tuairim's members were comfortable with Irish but it went too far. As discussed in Chapter 4, the language remained an emotive topic throughout this period.

In 1962, officials in the Department of External Affairs expressed disappointment that the hopes they had had for Tuairim in London did not appear to have been realised. The society was 'stimulating the opinion of younger Irish people,'[61] and, it was argued on a handwritten note appended to a report by Tadhg Feehan of the London embassy, included some very intelligent individuals. It was claimed that the society was different from other Irish organisations in the city in that its appeal was more intellectual than social. Tuairim in London had not, however, according to this view, developed in either an intellectual or a social direction. It was possibly the first secretary, Frank Coffey, who claimed that the branch was not a 'vigorous' society and accordingly had 'not lived up to expectations'.[62] Coffey believed that it had not done enough to generate interest among Irish people and ensure a sufficient number of active members. While it looked forward to the results of its research on issues such as education, it seemed to the Department of External Affairs that the branch had not fulfilled its potential. This was partly due to the lack of social activities. Nevertheless, members of the London embassy maintained good relations with the society, with many including the ambassador attending its activities. What was really significant, however, was that senior civil servants were familiar with Tuairim and were interested in its future development.

Tuairim's relationship with politicians

Tuairim's relationship with politicians varied from occasional non-co-operation and even confrontation to a shared concern for the future of the country. Conflict due to Tuairim's steadfastly maintaining its independence of political parties was countered by the society's encouraging its members to take an interest in politics and to join of one of the parties. There were, however, those who objected to Tuairim and its attempts to influence public opinion in a more tolerant direction or who viewed it as an alternative attraction, even a threat, to the political establishment. The division in attitudes to the society was partly reflective of that between different generations of politicians, which were, in turn, highlighted by the views of Fine Gael's John A. Costello and his son Declan. John A. Costello, the Taoiseach of two inter-party governments, had already come across Tuairim after it had contacted him and many other influential figures in an attempt to raise awareness and funds for the Hungarian people in the aftermath of the 1956 revolution.[63] Though Costello's government did not accept Tuairim's proposal, this does not suggest that he was hostile towards the society. At his party's Ard Fheis in February 1958, defending Fine Gael against the *Irish Times*'s suggestion that it should merge with Fianna Fáil, Costello claimed, however, that independent societies damaged the country. He argued that 'study groups...may do a real disservice to Irish democracy if they seek to imply that there is some virtue in aloof neutrality or if they condemn the political function'.[64] Costello's view was that societies such as Tuairim prevented talented young people from entering public life. Similarly, a recent recruit to the Dáil, Richie Ryan, the party's future Minister for Finance, supported Costello's view in a letter published in the *Irish Times* on 8 February that also seemed to refer to Tuairim. These serious charges suggest that hostility towards Tuairim went as far as the highest echelons within the political establishment during the late 1950s.

Costello's and Ryan's view of Tuairim as damaging to democratic politics provoked a strong response from Tuairim. Frank Winder, the chairperson of the Dublin branch, in a letter to the *Irish Times*, stressed the importance of study groups in the 'formulation of political philosophies and programmes and the formation...of public opinion'.[65] He referred both to the Fabian Society in Britain and to the establishment of study groups by Irish political parties in support of his case. Fine Gael's Research and Information Centre, ironically established by, among others, Costello's son Declan, was one of the few examples of such study groups among the political parties.[66] The centre, though, was confronted by lethargy and opposition from within Fine Gael and ultimately had little success in modernising the party's policy. Meanwhile, in his letter, Winder argued that because Tuairim was independent of politics, it could put forward any policy, however unpopular, which it thought would be in the interests of the country. Furthermore, he wrote that Tuairim also had the advantage that it provided a platform for many people from a wide range of professions and with contrary political preferences to discuss their views.

Winder's view was in direct contradiction to Costello and Ryan. If the trend towards 'political "neutrality"' was as serious as Costello implied,[67] it could indeed be a danger to democracy, which depends on political parties. Costello and Winder also differed as to who was responsible for the apathy to democracy that was prevalent in Irish society. For Costello, Tuairim hindered the natural development of democracy, whereas Winder blamed the political parties. Many individuals within Tuairim, other correspondents to the *Irish Times* and the newspaper's editor held similar views to Winder's, maintaining that the parties lacked new ideas, were too alike and were dominated by expediency and intellectual dishonesty. Winder argued that individuals' involvement in groups such as Tuairim highlighted the ineffectualness of political parties. Contrary to the parties, Tuairim could only offer the hope that its ideas would influence public policy or public opinion. Costello also ignored the fact that though Tuairim was independent, it encouraged its members to join the parties. If he was as much concerned about the dangers that societies such as Tuairim inflicted upon democracy as his statement suggested, it seemed strange that, during his tenure as leader of the opposition, Fine Gael paid so little attention to the recruitment of new members. Costello perceived a problem with politics but did not actively seek a solution. While his part-time leadership was a factor in preventing such initiatives, his wish that young people become active members of political parties was probably genuine. Furthermore, the indifference that Costello demonstrated to the development of youth party organisations was shared by many politicians of his generation. The reality was that though there had, under his leadership, been improvements to Fine Gael's image, the party remained remote from many young people.

As previously noted, this, in many ways, represented a clash of generations. Donal Barrington suggested as much when he wrote in *Hibernia* in August 1958 that the 'central problem of Irish politics in the next ten years will be the transfer of power from one generation to another which differs fundamentally in its approach to life and to politics'. The society itself could have become directly involved in politics when this transfer in fact took place. Barrington's view was that a group such as Tuairim, as one of the few outlets for the younger generation, should consider forming its own party only when the solutions it put forward were ignored by politicians. Though he recognised that some steps were being taken, he warned the parties of the need to address the 'poverty of ideas' if the 'survival of democracy' in Ireland was not to come into question. This concern about Ireland's future was a major reason why Tuairim retained a belief that it had an important role to play; similarly to Winder, Barrington argued that it was crucial to formulate 'a new set of social and economic ideas such as can form the basis for the programmes for political parties in the years ahead'. Generally, rather than directly criticising politicians, the society chose to try to persuade them to implement these new policies. The wide variety of views within the organisation would, in any case, have made entering politics difficult, and it was never seriously considered. It is, nevertheless, the case that more of Tuairim's members could have run for election individually. In this Tuairim reflected a problem that seems to have been encountered by intellectuals elsewhere: the apparent need to remain independent as against becoming directly engaged in politics. It was also the case that the sense of crisis, if not the underlying problems, receded with the relative economic prosperity of the 1960s. As for Costello's charge as to the damage that Tuairim inflicted upon politics, his target was misplaced, for even though the society retained its independence, it was committed to democracy. The reality was that, rather than discouraging individuals to become involved in politics, it actually promoted an interest in politics through its discussion of such matters. It certainly did not prevent individuals such as Fine Gael's Garret FitzGerald, Labour's Barry Desmond and Fianna Fáil's Michael Woods from entering politics.

The explanation for Costello's distrust seems to have been that Tuairim provided an alternative attraction to the political parties for many individuals. Costello was interested in ideas or at least those of his son Declan, his son-in-law Alexis FitzGerald and his former advisor as Taoiseach, Patrick Lynch; his view seems then not to point to the existence of anti-intellectualism in Irish life. More accurately, it reflected the adversarial nature of politics, Costello's occasional belligerence and the need he perceived to defend the political system against criticism thereof. Tuairim was challenging the culture that informed politics and society, and therefore Costello's reaction to it was that of a conservative political elite which resisted the questioning culture that it represented. Though he would have preferred it to be active in a political party, it seems unfair to suggest that Costello viewed this as a means to 'control' such individuals better. He was, nevertheless, uncomfortable with Tuairim and its independent thinking. Meanwhile, Declan Costello contributed to some of Tuairim's meetings and was a judge on the essay-writing competition which it was hoped would help recruit new members to the society.[68] He was open to the society, encouraged citizens to engage actively in the organisation and shared its hope that the new ideas found in Europe would influence Irish politics.

The emergence of an inquisitive culture during the 1950s undermined the existence of conformism and authoritarianism as values in Irish life. This, combined with Tuairim's increasing respectability from the late 1950s, removed the sense that the organisation was a threat to democracy. Ryan, for example, later praised Tuairim in the Dáil in 1966 following the publication of its pamphlet on TDs and was willing to speak to the Limerick and Cork branches in 1964 and 1974. At the first of these, he nevertheless defended politics, choosing instead to criticise the Irish people, rather than Tuairim, for their political indifference.[69] While Ryan was steadfast in his defence of politicians, his change of attitude towards Tuairim reflected the increasingly open nature of political parties. Winder, despite his negative view of the parties in 1958, had predicted that the political situation would improve and maintained that independent societies would be vital to this change. The developments that took place were partly due to

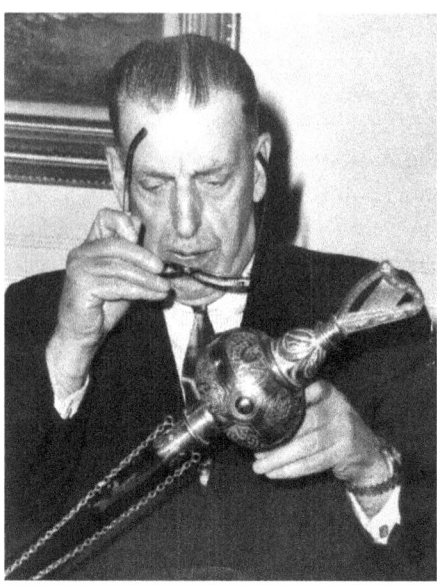

4 Seán Lemass, Taoiseach, 1959–66, inspecting a pennon in government buildings in 1966.

the new generation that entered politics. This, in turn, helps to explain the political parties' increased openness to the society. In a wide-ranging examination of the social and cultural changes taking place in Ireland, David Thornley however, had, in his pamphlet *Ireland:– the end of an era?*, published in 1965, argued that the political parties had not adapted to the changes in contemporary Ireland and needed to encourage young people to join them. Parts of the political establishment continued to resist new ideas.

On the other hand, Seán Lemass, Fianna Fáil Taoiseach from 1959 to 1966, was one of those who welcomed Tuairim or at least some of its ideas (see Figure 4). In 1959, in his first Dáil speech on the budget for the Department of Taoiseach, Lemass commented that Tuairim was one of the organisations facilitating a greater understanding of the country's problems and was part of a 'new spirit' in the country, a spirit which was to be greatly encouraged.[70] The contrast with John A. Costello's comments could hardly have been greater. Lemass, who had previously spoken at a Tuairim meeting in 1957, claimed that it was not important whether the government agreed with the society's views. This comment must be seen in the context of Tuairim's having published pamphlets on Northern Ireland and economics, each of which put forward a basis for a new government policy. Lemass had views similar to some of those presented in these pamphlets, welcoming what he perceived to be good or progressive ideas. Accordingly, he may have seen the society as an ally, albeit an unreliable one, in his attempts to change his party's policies and to introduce economic and social reforms. As Chapter 2 below illustrates, however, Lemass was more likely than Costello to resist the direct input of intellectuals as well as others into policy. This reflected the wish of many politicians to retain control of the policy agenda. Lemass's Dáil speech, nevertheless, claimed that organisations such as Tuairim were important as they represented the desire of younger people for a greater influence on policy and hoped that they would continue to be successful.

5 A group of people in attendance at a Tuairim weekend at which Lemass spoke in 1957.

Similarly, ministers such as Erskine Childers, George Colley, Brian Lenihan and Donogh O'Malley engaged with the society and welcomed the consideration it was giving to new ideas and policies (see Figure 5 for a photograph of a group of people at a Tuairim weekend at which Lemass spoke in 1957).

Under Lemass's leadership the government was aware of and seemed sensitive to comments made at Tuairim's meetings. One example of this was a speech criticising the Cork branch by the outspoken Minister for Health, Seán MacEntee, at the party's 1963 Ard Fheis. MacEntee claimed that he no longer believed Tuairim to be independent because it had provided his predecessor, Fine Gael's T. F. O'Higgins, with a platform from which to attack the government during a by-election in the city. Tuairim responded by stressing its impartiality and noting that the meeting had been held before the need for a by-election arose. The society also stated that Charles Haughey, Brian Lenihan and Brendan Corish had all spoken to the Cork branch in 1963. This statement led MacEntee to apologise for questioning the society's motives. MacEntee's suspicion, indeed, seems to have been unusual in that the minister held Tuairim in high regard, and, following its publication of the pamphlet *University College Dublin and the future*, he praised the society. The episode seems to have been mainly the result of MacEntee's penchant for argument and the differences he had during the early 1960s with O'Higgins over the future direction of the country's health policy.[71] For the present discussion, it suffices to note Tuairim's access to these and other influential figures.

Since Fianna Fáil was in government during most of the period of Tuairim's existence, good relations between the two were crucial for the society to influence public policy. Given that Tuairim was criticising existing policies, it, could, however, have seemed at least to some ministers that the society was implicitly criticising the government. It was in this context that members of the opposition were more likely than the government to refer to Tuairim in Oireachtas debates. It is possible that this resulted in some members of the governing party viewing the organisation as being anti-Fianna Fáil. As

Fianna Fáil saw itself as the 'natural' party of government, it may not have welcomed these alternative views from outside the Oireachtas. An arrogance which resulted from continuing electoral success was perhaps most evident in younger ministers such as Charles Haughey. This was probably a factor in the pointed criticism Tuairim aimed at Fianna Fáil during the late 1960s. At its meeting in May 1968 the society was particularly critical of Fianna Fáil's conduct while at another meeting in June 1969 it appealed to all the political parties to refrain from personal abuse during the ongoing general election campaign. Such views undermined the neutrality that Tuairim had hitherto steadfastly maintained between the political parties. Reasons for Tuairim's view of Fianna Fáil were probably the nature of the party, its links with business, its apparent disinterest in democratic reform and its attempts to link the Labour party with communism. It also reflected the increasing prominence of the idealistic Franklin O'Sullivan, who was then the chairperson of the Dublin branch.[72]

Tuairim was at times unimpressed with all the political parties. The parties in turn, it seemed, would participate in the society's events only when they perceived it to be in their interests to do so. Tuairim's criticism of the quality of debate in the political system represented a continuation of the active interest that the society had in how democracy operated. Its success in attracting politicians to speak to its meetings had indicated a concern with ensuring that is was accountable to the people. Members suggested that the public audience at the society's meetings was crucial to politicians' presence, while some politicians welcomed the opportunity that Tuairim provided to examine the country's problems and to interact with its members. A further factor was the increased profile they might have gained, for Tuairim was clearly considered newsworthy by the national and local press. Some members believed that these meetings were valuable in that they filled a vacuum: they claimed that the Oireachtas and media were not holding politicians to account. Television was, moreover, an unsuitable medium in this regard. Such criticism of television's effect on the quality of public debate was reflected in the comment by the French intellectual Pierre Bourdieu that it 'turns intellectuals' discursive advantage – sustained attention and nuanced analysis – into a disadvantage'.[73]

International and Irish comparisons with Tuairim

Many people in Ireland during the 1950s realised that they needed to take an active interest in integrationist developments in Europe, particularly the creation of the EEC. The turmoil of World War II had resulted in a need for new ideas and institutions to replace discredited regimes throughout Western Europe. It has been argued that this, combined with the birth of the welfare state and increased educational provision, seemed to give rise to 'new intellectual elites' as well as greater opportunities for their employment to solve society's problems.[74] Though Ireland was not an exception to these trends, these developments took longer there because the challenge to Ireland's political establishment seemed less immediate. Neutrality had saved the country from the hardships suffered by other countries during the war, and the birth of a new political party, Clann na Poblachta, which had briefly challenged the existing parties, did not result in a re-orientation of the party system. This meant the continuation in power of the individuals who had established the state. The closed nature of their political parties left the generation that emerged during the 1950s with the dilemma of how to respond to the economic and social challenges of the post-war period. Tuairim was one response, and in its wish to contribute to the creation of an active civil society in Ireland it was part of a larger trend in the Western world. Fears that communist governments would come to power throughout Europe, for example, encouraged American trade unions as well as their government to attempt to influence labour movements in Europe. This was part of a greater debate on the Cold War during the 1940s and 1950s to which intellectuals in American society contributed.[75]

Tuairim was part of a wider discussion in a number of countries regarding their future nature. Models for Tuairim, understandably, came from closer to home. Given the society's rejection of the use of violence for political purposes, it was ironic that a crucial link in Ireland's violent nationalist tradition, the Young Irelanders of the 1840s, was one inspiration for Tuairim.[76] The Young Irelanders had organised a failed rebellion in 1848. Tuairim, would, however, have been attracted to the Young Irelanders' idealism and their hopes for a united nation, one in which both Protestants and Catholics would play a full part. The Young Irelanders' most prominent figure, Thomas Davis, had argued for the need to find common ground between the different religions in Ireland and feared the replacement of a Protestant ascendancy with one that was Catholic. A reaction against Daniel O'Connell's politics, which identified the nation as Catholic, the Young Irelanders also differed from O'Connell in that he was opposed to the use of violence.

Closer to the ideological mark was the Fabian Society, the oldest think tank in Britain. The Fabian Society aimed to influence attitudes by holding regular meetings, at which papers discussed political and social problems, and through the involvement of its members in other organisations. It was, however, socialist in orientation, while Tuairim did not hold a particular view but facilitated its members and others in putting forward a range of opinions. In this regard, the London branch pointed out that, unlike Tuairim, the Fabian Society and the Bow Group were both affiliated to political parties. Tuairim's independence, it hoped, would allow it to 'exercise a greater freedom of approach to national problems' as well as to attract people who were both members of and not involved in a party.[77] Its neutrality can be explained by the absence in Ireland, unlike Britain and Europe, of a strong liberal or left-wing party to which the society might have been associated. Affiliation to political parties was a feature of think tanks not only in Britain but also in continental Europe.[78]

A more accurate comparison could be drawn between Tuairim and Cité Libre (or 'Open Society') in Canada. A periodical established in 1950 and co-edited by the future prime minister Pierre Trudeau, Cité Libre became a 'focal point' for those opposed to the regime of Maurice Duplessis.[79] The role of the *Citélibrestes*, as they became known, in questioning orthodoxy prior to the 'Quiet Revolution' in Quebec in 1960 had certain echoes in Tuairim's attempts to influence the political establishment in Ireland in a more liberal direction. The tactics of the two societies and the circumstances in which they found themselves were, however, very different. Tuairim attempted to influence politicians while *Citélibrestes* created 'a political movement' to challenge the Prime Minister, Duplessis, directly.[80]

Ireland is in an unusual position regarding its relative lack of think tanks. Those that have existed have tended towards having a specific policy. The 1913 Club, for instance, was a left-wing society in the late 1950s, established by David Thornley, while 'Themis' was affiliated to the Labour Party in the late 1990s. Other think tanks such as the Committee on Industrial Organisation, the Economic and Social Research Institute, An Foras Forbartha, An Foras Talúntais, the Institute of Public Administration, the National Industrial and Economic Council, the Institute of European Affairs and the Edmund Burke Institute have been linked to the government or have focused on certain issues. Following its establishment in 1953 the Irish Management Institute had been concerned with business, while more recently the Centre for Public Inquiry has sought to promote higher standards in Irish public life and business life, and Tasc is dedicated to combating inequality, but none of these organisations seems to have had a general membership like that of Tuairim.[81] The important role attached to think tanks in the development of political thinking in many countries has underlined the case for more to be created in Ireland. This increases the importance of a consideration of Tuairim's influence in overcoming resistance to new ideas.

Conclusion

Tuairim's independence of the Catholic Church set it apart from other organisations in Ireland. Its non-affiliation to political parties also made it unusual internationally. The society's objectives, membership and methods were particularly distinctive in an Irish context during the 1950s. Its promotion of new ideas and ability to tackle controversial matters in an impartial manner were noted and encouraged in the press and by politicians such as Seán Lemass. Other individuals and organisations welcomed the platform Tuairim provided for examining problems in Irish society. In this way, Tuairim facilitated consideration, both by itself and in co-operation with others, of a wide diversity of political, social, economic and cultural issues. Public criticism of the society from politicians such as John A. Costello and private concern from Archbishop McQuaid indicate that resistance to independent thinking went to the highest echelons of the political and religious establishments. The corollary of this was that there was an increasing awareness of the need for new policies. During the 1950s Tuairim was part of an emerging culture that questioned existing thinking, and it facilitated the creation of a new policy agenda. It was thus somewhat ironic that the changes that occurred during the 1960s made Tuairim redundant by the early 1970s. From an early stage, it was, nevertheless, clear that many powerful individuals had high expectations of Tuairim. This led to renewed hopes from McQuaid that a Catholic review would finally be established. In a similar vein, senior civil servants and influential opinion-makers hoped for a more sensible approach among the Irish in London. Tuairim's priority was, however, to create an intellectual climate which would facilitate reforms in Ireland. It was this, its vision of a country that would encourage heterodoxy, that provoked a reaction from some in positions of power. As Tuairim's challenge to orthodox attitudes became more pronounced during the late 1950s, any earlier misunderstanding that McQuaid, for instance, had as to the society's nature was replaced by a more clearly articulated view. What follows assesses Tuairim's examination of a range of issues and the reaction these provoked and considers their import.

Notes

1 Interviews with Donal Barrington, Dublin, 19 May 2005, and Patrick Kilroy, Dublin, 26 May 2005; *Irish Times*, 26 January 1964. See *Irish Times*, 28 February 2009, for Kilroy's obituary.
2 Jennings and Kemp-Welch (eds), *Intellectuals*, p. 17; Collini, *Absent minds*, pp. 63, 232, 240.
3 Interview with Barrington, 19 May 2005. An early member of Tuairim, Gary Trimble, an artist, produced the logo.
4 Donal Barrington papers, 'Tuairim constitution', 1954; Donal Barrington, *The church, the state and the constitution* (Dublin: Catholic Truth Society of Ireland, 1959); interview with Barrington, 19 May 2005. See also interview with Bríd Foy, Dublin, 25 August 2005. Foy, an educational psychologist in Dublin,

claimed that she had to accept the article if she wished to be a member. For the Irish Constitution see Brian Girvin, 'The republicanisation of Irish society, 1932–48', in J. R. Hill (ed.), *A new history of Ireland*, vol. vii: *Ireland, 1921–84* (Oxford: Oxford University Press, 2003), pp. 140–1; John Whyte, *Church and state in modern Ireland, 1923–1979* (Dublin: Gill and Macmillan, 1980), pp. 52–6.

5 NAI, DJ, S.4/54, 'Tuairim (Voice of Young Ireland) Party', *Evening Mail*, 24 February 1954; *Irish Independent*, 26 January 1964; interview with Barrington, 19 May 2005.

6 For example, interviews with Barrington, 19 May 2005, and Jim Doolan, Galway, 10 December 2003. See *Irish Times*, 15, 16 February 1962. See also Joy Rudd papers, Barrington to John Boland, 24 October 1961. It is important to note that none of Tuairim's members who stood for election did so as a member of the society. Barrington insisted that it would be wrong for him to seek any imprimatur from the society, as that would obviously weaken Tuairim's independence. He said that if elected, he would attempt to express in the Seanad the ideas he had formed through Tuairim. See NAI, DT, 98/6/501, Tuairim general, handwritten note, 7 January 1964, for Lemass's expression of regret that he was unable to speak to the society; this was in response to an invitation from Tuairim's Diarmuid Ó Cearbhaill, then a civil servant.

7 Correspondence with W. E. Vaughan, 12 March 2004; interview with Enda McDonagh, Maynooth, 24 June 2005.

8 Interview with Miriam Hederman O'Brien, 12 August 2009. Miriam Hederman O'Brien, Donal Barrington and Brian O'Connor were members of the Irish Council of the European Movement. A priest in adult education, on an informal basis and for a short period, taught Hederman O'Brien and Kilroy about Marxism. See R. N. Carew Hunt, *Marxism: past and present* (London: Geoffrey Bles, 1954); R. N. Carew Hunt, *The theory and practice of communism: an introduction* (London: Geoffrey Bles, 1951).

9 Interview with Frank D'Arcy, Derry, 1 June 2010; Enda McDonagh, 'The Christian and Catholic intellectual', pp. 97–113.

10 Interviews with Hederman O'Brien, 12 August 2009, and Barrington, 2 September 2009.

11 For example, *Irish Independent*, 28 November 1960; *Irish Times*, 2 July 1962; Rudd papers, Lean Scully to Boland, 21 October, 24 November, 17 December 1959, 25 January 1960.

12 Rudd papers, 'Revised constitution', 19 February 1966. The lower age limit was also reduced from twenty-one to eighteen. See *Irish Times*, 3 July 1961. Associate membership seems to have been introduced in 1961. See also interviews with Margaret Hurley, Limerick, 3 December 2005, and Michael Collins Powell, Cork, 28 July 2005; Rudd papers, 'Tuairim National Council meeting', Kilcoran Hotel, Cahir, Co. Tipperary, 19 February 1966; 'Minutes of committee meetings of Tuairim's Dublin branch', 15 March, 20 April 1965. I would like to thank Tuairim's secretary, Carmel Kelly, for placing the minutes of the Dublin branch from 1964 to 1970 with the History

Department of Trinity College Dublin, and Professor Eunan O'Halpin and Dr Niamh Puirséil for allowing me access to these records.
13 DDA, McQuaid papers, Tuairim file, Archbishop McQuaid to Apostolic Nuncio, 23 January 1965.
14 Barrington, *The church*. On the other hand, see Rev. Thomas Marsh, DD, 'A booklet on church and state', *Christus Rex*, 14 (July 1960), 180–3 for praise for Barrington's article.
15 See Frank D'Arcy, 'A movement on the fence', *Catholic Truth Quarterly*, 11:1 (1959), 27–31; Enda McDonagh, 'The Christian life, xi: tolerance', *The Furrow*, 12:1 (1961), 49–55; James Scott, 'A letter from Ireland', *The Furrow*, 9:4 (1958), 300–1; *Hibernia*, December 1962.
16 NAI, DJ, S.4/54, 'Confidential note from Mr. Berry to commissioner, Garda Síochána', 25 February 1954.
17 NAI, DJ, S.4/54, 'Confidential note from P. Carroll to secretary, Department of Justice', 5 April 1954.
18 Interviews with D'Arcy, 21 May 2005, and Enda McDonagh, Maynooth, 24 June 2005. See R. M. Douglas, *Architects of the resurrection: Ailtirí na hAiséirghe and the fascist 'new order' in Ireland* (Manchester: Manchester University Press, 2009).
19 *Evening Herald*, 14 October 1954; *Irish Times*, 25 February 1954. See also *Evening Mail*, 24 February 1954; *Irish Independent*, 27 February 1954.
20 *Irish Times*, 31 January 1959.
21 Donal Barrington, 'Uniting Ireland', *Studies*, 46:184 (Winter 1957), 379–402; Donal Barrington, *Uniting Ireland* (Dublin: Tuairim, 1958), pp. 1–24; David Thornley, 'Ireland: the end of an era?', *Studies*, 53:209 (Spring 1964), 1–17; David Thornley, *Ireland: the end of an era?* (Dublin: Tuairim, 1965); David Thornley, 'The development of the Irish labour movement', *Christus Rex*, 18 (January 1964), 7–21. Thornley delivered the paper on the labour movement at a Tuairim weekend in 1963.
22 NAI, DT, S17138A/61, Community development in Ireland: federation of local development associations, 'Report on community development by the Economic Development branch of the Department of Finance', August 1961, p. 17. See also *Irish Times*, 4 December 1959. For Muintir na Tíre and the Christus Rex society and Christian social principles, see Stephen Rynne, *Father John Hayes: founder of Muintir na Tíre people of the land* (Dublin: Clonmore and Reynolds, 1960) and Seán L'Estrange, 'The Catholic clergy as counter-revolutionary vanguard: the Christus Rex society, 1941–71', paper read at conference, 'Intellectuals and ideology in twentieth-century Ireland', St Patrick's College, Drumcondra, Dublin, 9 April 2005.
23 Michael O'Hanrahan papers, H. H. MacErlean, 'On *Tuairim*'. This document was probably written in 1960. MacErlean claimed that 'it is a standard practice of Tuairim to send a copy of each pamphlet to every TD and Senator at Stormont'.
24 DDA, McQuaid papers, Tuairim file, McQuaid to Apostolic Nuncio, 23 January 1965.
25 See NAI, DFA, 366/1/32, The foundation in London of Tuairim,

correspondence between Valentin Iremonger to T. J. Horan, Assistant Secretary, Department of External Affairs, 30 December 1959, 13 January, 6 February 1960. The file also contains the first four Tuairim pamphlets.
26 Miriam Hederman O'Brien papers, 'Report of Tuairim Council', 1958–59. See also NAI, DT, S16603A, Tuairim general, *Irish Independent*, 1 January 1959; *Irish Times*, 29 December 1958.
27 *Irish Times*, 1 April 1963; NAI, DT, S17138A/61, *Irish Press*, 27 February 1961, Tadhg Ó Cearbhaill, Assistant Secretary to the Department of Taoiseach, to Dr J. P. Beddy, chairman, Industrial Development Authority, 28 February 1961.
28 *Irish Independent*, 14 December 1957. See also NAI, DT, S16105A, 'Adjustment of conacre: provision of farms for young farmers'; Daly, *First department*, pp. 416–21; Finn, 'The influence of *Tuairim*', pp. 148–51.
29 Dublin branch of Tuairim in co-operation with Irish section of the AEDE, *Educating towards a united Europe* (Dublin: Tuairim, 1962); *Irish Times*, 25 June 1962; *Hibernia*, June 1959.
30 For example, Hederman, *Europe*, p. 97; *Irish Times*, 1 November 1969; Minutes of committee meetings of Tuairim's Dublin branch, 15 May 1967, 21 May 1968; O'Hanrahan papers, Tuairim, 'Chairman's report for 1956–57'.
31 *Irish Times*, 18 July 1963, 10 June 1967; Rudd papers, 'Tuairim central council meeting', 25 April 1965.
32 Margaret Hurley papers, Hurley, 'Minutes of AGM', 12 May 1973, 'Tuairim AGM', 8 May 1973; interview with Hurley, 3 December 2005. See also *Irish Independent*, 1 February 1973; Val Finnegan papers, Hurley to Cork branch, 6 August 1971, 'Tuairim – Cork, leaflet', 1973–74, newspaper articles, Hurley to Neville Keery, 4 December 1973; Hurley papers, Hurley, 'Minutes of AGM', 12 May 1972. See Denis O'Sullivan (ed.), *Social commitment and adult education: essays in honour of Alfred O'Rahilly an Irish adult educator* (Cork: Cork University Press, 1989) for adult education in Cork. For more on the Dublin branch's art-lending scheme see *Irish Times*, 21 July 1962, and the *Irish Independent*, 20 February 1971.
33 Interviews with Anne Reidy, Paddy Glynn and Cian O'Carroll, Limerick, 3 December 2005; *Irish Independent*, 11 June 1966. See John Horgan, *Broadcasting and public life: RTE news and current affairs, 1926–1997* (Dublin: Four Courts Press, 2004), pp. 38, 50–2, 148. See also interview with D'Arcy, 21 May 2005; *Irish Times*, 8 February 1958, 19 November 1964, 15, 16 February, 4 March 1965; *Irish Press*, 18, 19 February 1965; Rudd papers, 'Central Council', 25 April 1965, 'Tuairim – London, Emigration: the problems of a return', 6 March 1964; www.rte.ie/culture/people/hedermanobrienmiriam.html accessed on 14 July 2003. In 1964 and 1965, the Cork branch, however, had two symposia televised. Miriam Hederman O'Brien, Frank D'Arcy and David Thornley also appeared in the different media of radio and television, as did two members of the London branch as part of a television panel which discussed emigration in 1964. Furthermore, the Fine Gael TD Richie Ryan, without identifying the society, implied that an unnamed member of Tuairim had appeared on Radio Éireann's programme 'Question box'.

34 *Irish Press*, 26 May 1967; William Peacocke papers, 'Report of Cork branch'.
35 *Irish Times*, 10 June 1967.
36 Rudd papers, 'Tuairim – London, report by chairman, Boland, AGM', 30 March 1962. See NLI, Leslie Daiken papers, MS33500, Boland to Leslie Daiken, 26 February 1961. Initially a means of providing information on Tuairim's activities, from 1961, the bulletin consisted of eight to twelve pages and contained articles covering a wide range of issues. See also NAI, DFA, 2002/19/70, The foundation in London of Tuairim, Tadhg Feehan, 'Report of second annual general meeting', 2 May 1962; Rudd papers, 'Tuairim – London, report by chairman, Tony Fahy, AGM', 26 March 1965, 'Tuairim – London, AGM of council of Tuairim', 8, 9 July 1961, Fergus Pyle to Boland, 17 May 1961, Boland to Scully, 21 November 1959. See Hurley papers, 'Minutes of AGM', 12 May 1972; and *Irish Times*, 7 June 1973, for information on the Cork and Dublin branches.
37 For example, NAI, DFA, 366/1/32, London, Iremonger to Horan, 10 February 1960. Following the branch's establishment, the initial offers of accommodation from the NUI Club and the Irish Club were declined owing to their determination to 'remain independent of other Irish groups'.
38 O'Hanrahan papers, 'Tuairim – London, report by chairman, Michael O'Hanrahan, AGM', 29 March 1963; Rudd papers, chairman, Seán O'Sullivan, to ambassador, 24 May 1965, Frank K. Lee, Secretary, 1916 Commemoration Committee, to organisations involved in committee, 'Report of the 1916 Commemoration Committee', March 1966.
39 Roy Johnston, 'Independence, partition and the emigrants', *An Occasional Bulletin*, 4 (1961), 4–5; *Hibernia*, March 1964. See *Irish Times*, 16 May, 1–3 September 1960, for Jackson's paper.
40 *Hibernia*, March 1964.
41 For example, Rudd papers, Scully to Boland, 21 October 1959, 25 January 1960, '*Tuairim* Central Council, report of General Secretary to Council of *Tuairim*', 17 December 1959, 'AGM', 18 June 1966; *Irish Times*, 3 October 1960; www.yeats-sligo.com accessed on 1 July 2008. Also Peacocke papers, 'Speech by Peacocke, National President of *Tuairim*, to inaugural meeting of Waterford branch', 17 November 1970; Institute of Public Administration, *Yearbook and diary* (Dublin: Institute of Public Administration, 1973), p. 129. The *Yearbook* in 1970, 1971 and 1972 also contained descriptions of Tuairim. The Waterford branch, which had lapsed in 1965, was restored in 1970 before its final demise in 1973. See Hederman O'Brien papers, 'Council', 1958–59; interview with Michael D. Higgins, Galway, 17 February 2006; Tomás Finn, 'Priests, politics and poetry: *Tuairim* in Limerick, 1954–75', *History Studies*, 7 (Limerick: University of Limerick, 2006), 15–30, for insights into the Belfast, Galway and Limerick branches.
42 For example, *Irish Times*, 8 May, 16 December 1967, 14 December 1968, 6 December 1969, 5 February, 30 October 1970, 23 April 1971, 27 March 1973. See also Rudd papers, 'Report of development sub-committee of Dublin branch'; *Irish Times*, 9 January, 3, 5 March 1971.
43 Franklin O'Sullivan was the driving force behind the society in the late

1960s but he resigned on reaching forty in 1970. See *Irish Times*, 22 May 1969. See also minutes of committee meetings of Tuairim's Dublin branch, 12 November 1965, 17 May, 12 October 1966, 8 January, 26 June, 13 November 1967; *Northern Standard*, 8 September 1967; *Irish Times*, 12 November 1966, 9 September 1967, 14 June 1968; Peacocke papers, 'Report of Dublin branch, 1970', minutes of meeting of Tuairim National Council, 28 November 1970; Xavier Carty, *Government and people: a creative dialogue: a report of the 1969/70 communications conference* (Dublin: Tuairim, 1970). This publication placed the branch £150 in debt but it was claimed that this would be recovered once the pamphlets were sold. See *Cork Examiner*, 7 June 1973; *Irish Independent*, 7 June 1973; *Irish Times*, 7 June 1973 for the decision to disband the Dublin branch.

44 For example, *Hibernia*, January 1937, Autumn, November 1954, February, September 1955, July–September 1956. See also interview with Kilroy, 26 May 2005; Brown, *Ireland*, p. 223; Garvin, *Future*, p. 184. Both Kilroy and Garvin stated that the Knights of Columbanus had published the periodical. While the periodical reflected the interests of the Knights, the only occasions on which the organisation was mentioned seem to have been in 1937 and 1939, when it was praised. There was no suggestion of a link between them, which was probably due to the Knights' secretive nature.

45 DDA, McQuaid papers, Tuairim file, McQuaid to Apostolic Nuncio, 23 January 1965. See also interviews with Barrington, 19 May 2005, and Kilroy, 26 May 2005; *Hibernia*, September 1959. The Fine Gael TD Declan Costello and Alexis FitzGerald had recently established the *National Observer*, and the *Plough* was a socialist paper. *Hibernia* became a private limited company with Kilroy and Smith as well as Seamus Grace, who already wrote for the periodical, and Peter Walsh, a lecturer at Edinburgh University, joining Clancy on the board. See *Irish Times*, 4 May 1957. The failure to establish its own newspaper prompted the society to publish pamphlets.

46 *Catholic Herald*, 24 June, 8 July 1961. Michael O'Hanrahan responded that while Tuairim could not claim credit for inspiring *Hibernia*, many of its members wrote articles and the society had a deep respect for the paper. Also interviews with D'Arcy, 21 May 2005, and Kilroy, 26 May 2005. D'Arcy went to Magee College in late 1960. For *Hibernia*'s subsequent history see John Horgan, *Irish media: a critical history since 1922* (London: Routledge, 2001), p. 96.

47 *Irish Democrat*, October 1958. See also Minutes of committee meetings of Tuairim's Dublin branch, 20 June, 8 November 1966. In 1966, *Hibernia* requested 'some sort of tie-up' with Tuairim. This does not appear to have occurred. Pamphlets were, nevertheless, advertised in *Hibernia*, while the London branch's *An Occasional Bulletin* had advertisements for the periodical.

48 For example, NAI, DT, S16247, 'Protestants: boycott in Fethard-on-Sea, County Wexford', *Irish Press*, 26 June 1957; *Irish Independent*, 29 June 1957; *Irish Times*, 29 June 1957; *The Standard*, 29 July 1957, *Free Press*, 5 July 1957; Irish Press, 8 July 1957. See also interviews with Barrington, 19 May 2005, and Kilroy, 26 May 2005. Kilroy, as Secretary of the Catholic Truth Society, had kept him informed of the hierarchy's reaction. He was critical of the

boycott to McQuaid. See also Tim Fanning, *The Fethard-on-Sea boycott* (Cork: Collins Press, 2010), pp. 142–3; Daithí Ó Corráin, *Rendering to God and Caesar: the Irish churches and the two states in Ireland, 1949–73* (Manchester: Manchester University Press, 2006), pp. 94–7, 186–8. See *Irish Times*, 14 January 1965, 1, 22 February, 24 May, 17 December 1966; *Limerick Leader*, 16 April 1966, for reports of Tuairim meetings at which Vatican II was discussed.

49 Keogh, *Twentieth-century Ireland*, p. 240.

50 DDA, McQuaid papers, Tuairim file, Fr. Edward McElroy to McQuaid, 19 February 1963, McQuaid to McElroy, 21 February 1963. McElroy had been invited to speak to the London branch. He had noted that their discussions attracted a good number of Irish university students and young Catholic and Protestant professionals. See also McQuaid to Apostolic Nuncio, 23 January 1965. McQuaid thanked the Apostolic Nuncio for being 'good enough to interrogate me on Tuairim on the occasion of the report of the ecumenical meeting in the Irish Times'. He noted that he had not dealt with the topic for some time and so was not very helpful when the Apostolic Nuncio called upon him. After consulting his notes, he, however, wrote a letter in which went into some detail about the society. This followed on from a report of Tuairim's meeting on Christian unity in the *Irish Times* of 21 January 1965.

51 DDA, McQuaid papers, Tuairim file, M. B. Crowe to Ardle, secretary, 2 February 1965. The file contains literature relating to Tuairim's activities in late 1964 and early 1965.

52 Cooney, *McQuaid*, p. 398. See also *Irish Independent*, 10 April 2006.

53 *Irish Times*, 1 February 1964. See also Rev. Canon C. M. Gray-Stack, 'The Church of Ireland and Christian unity', and Enda McDonagh, 'The Roman Catholics and Unity', *An Occasional Bulletin*, 7 (1963), 4–5. See *Irish Times*, 15 December 2001; Cooney, *McQuaid*, p. 387; J. V. Luce, *Trinity College Dublin: the first 400 years* (Dublin: Trinity College Dublin Press, 1992), p. 196. Boland, the future head of the Public Trustee Office in London, and David Thornley worked both for Catholic and ecumenical interests within Trinity.

54 *Hibernia*, 25 September 1959.

55 DDA, McQuaid papers, Tuairim file, Patrick Farrell, Correspondence Secretary, to McQuaid, 4 March 1970, Reverend Secretary to Farrell, 6 March 1970.

56 *Irish Times*, 30 November 1964, 25 May 1965.

57 John Whyte, *Dáil deputies: their work, its difficulties, possible remedies* (Dublin: Tuairim, 1966). See also minutes of meeting of committee of Dublin branch, 20 April 1966; Thomas Garvin, 'The strange death of clerical politics in University College Dublin', *Irish University Review*, 28:2 (1998), 308–14 for an account of the circumstances leading to Whyte's leaving UCD.

58 For example, *Hibernia*, June 1963. See also Barry Desmond, *Finally and in conclusion: a political memoir* (Dublin: New Island, 2000), 38, 118, 131, 142–4, 146; Michael Gallagher, *The Irish Labour Party in transition, 1957–82* (Dublin: Gill and Macmillan, 1982), pp. 143, 212, 217, 228; Michael D. Higgins, 'Dr David Thornley, TD: an intellectual in Irish politics' in Thornley (ed.), *Unquiet spirit*, pp. 153–64; Thornley (ed.), *Unquiet spirit*; Tomás Finn, review

of Thornley (ed.), *Unquiet spirit, Journal of the Galway Archaeological and Historical Society*, 61 (2009), 228–30. See David Thornley, 'Political Prospects', in Adrianus Vermeulen, Paul Jackson, Colum Gavin Duffy and David Thornley, *The European challenge: its social, legal and political prospects* (Dublin: Tuairim, 1963), pp. 26–36.

59 NAI, DFA, 366/1/32, Iremonger to Horan, 16 December 1959. See also NAI, DFA, 366/1/32, London, 'Memo regarding Tuairim symposium', possibly by First Secretary Frank Coffey, 13 May 1960. Following its first meeting in May 1960, it was claimed that the society could 'set a headline for other organisations in Britain'. See also *Irish Times*, 10 October 1960, 18 May, 2 June 1961. See *Irish Times*, 2 May 1961 for an article by Michael McInerney in which he praised Tuairim's 'penetrating study of many problems'.

60 NAI, DFA, 366/1/32, Coffey to Horan, 10 May 1960. See NLI, 'Special article on new English–Irish dictionary', Weekly Bulletin of the Department of External Affairs, 449 (7 September 1959). Also Máire Cruise O'Brien, *The Same Age as the State* (Dublin: O'Brien Press, 2003), pp. 203, 213.

61 NAI, DFA, 2002/19/70, London, 'Report of second AGM', 2 May 1962. For further information on Tadhg Feehan, the author of this report, see Daly, *Slow failure*, p. 315.

62 NAI, DFA, 2002/19/70, London, note appended to Iremonger to Secretary of Department of External Affairs, 17 May 1962. This was a handwritten note followed by what seems to be Coffey's signature.

63 NAI, DT, S13373D, Relief of distress abroad measures taken by Ireland, 'Memorandum: National Hungarian relief fund: submitted on behalf of Tuairim', 4 November 1956; interviews with Barrington, 19 May 2005, and Kilroy, 26 May 2005. Tuairim also contacted the Minister for Defence, Seán McKeown, and other members of the government and opposition as well as Cardinal D'Alton, Archbishop McQuaid and the editors of the Sunday newspapers.

64 *Irish Times*, 6 February 1958. Though Costello did not specifically mention Tuairim's name, he seems to have had the society in mind. See also *Irish Times*, 29 January 1958 and 21 November 1959.

65 *Irish Times*, 12 February 1958.

66 See Maurice Manning, *James Dillon: a biography* (Dublin: Wolfhound Press, 1999), pp. 317, 324–76. See also interview with Barrington, 19 May 2005. Invited to a meeting at which Costello spoke on the 'Just Society', Barrington ended up defending the TD against his own party leader, James Dillon. See FitzGerald, *All in a life*, pp. 67–9; *Irish Times*, 26 February, 2 May 1964; T. F. O'Higgins, *A double life* (Dublin: Town House & Country House, 1996), p. 189; David McCullagh, *The reluctant Taoiseach: a biography of John A. Costello* (Dublin: Gill and Macmillan, 2010), pp. 2–4, 375–83.

67 *Irish Times*, 6 February 1958. See also *Irish Times*, 21 August 1963. In one of a series of articles in 1963, Thornley claimed that a third of people did not vote in the 1961 general election. See *Irish Times*, 6, 10, 12, 14 February 1958 for more correspondence to the newspaper. Another Tuairim member, Michael O'Hanrahan, was one of those who wrote.

68 For example, interview with Declan Costello, Dublin, 14 June 2005; Minutes of committee meeting of Tuairim's Dublin branch, 1 May 1968; *Northern Standard*, 8 September 1967.
69 See *Irish Times*, 10 April 1964, 9 March 1974; Dáil Éireann Debates, vol. 220, col. 744, 'Military services pensions – private members' business', 2 February 1966; Whyte, *Dáil deputies*. In the Dáil, Ryan stated that the pamphlet was just another reason to be grateful to the society. At Tuairim's meeting, he also stated that political indifference was an indictment of politicians.
70 Dáil Éireann Debates, vol. 176, col. 1577, 'Committee on Finance – vote 3, Department of Taoiseach', 21 July 1959. Lemass argued that Tuairim and others encouraged 'thought on national problems by debate and study'. He claimed that their 'activities [were] greatly helping to increase understanding of the country's possibilities and opportunities'. See also *Irish Independent*, 26 November 1957. Lemass spoke at a private dinner of a study weekend that dealt with export problems. He did not speak to the society on any other occasion. See also *Irish Times*, 8 February 1964. Thornley was to speak to Fianna Fáil's Comh Comhairle in Dublin on 'The practice of politics' on 9 February. Lemass, as president of the committee, seems to have been the instigator of this seminar. The vice-presidents of the committee were the ministers Seán MacEntee and Charles Haughey.
71 NAI, DT, S16603/B63, Tuairim general, *Irish Times*, 29 November 1963. MacEntee claimed that O'Higgins's 'propaganda speech' attacked the government for inadequate provision of healthcare. MacEntee, having read a report of the meeting from the *Leinster Express*, mistakenly believed that the meeting had recently been held. See *Irish Times*, 28 September 1963; *Irish Press*, 27 November 1963. See also minutes of committee meeting of Tuairim's Dublin branch, 8 November 1966; *Irish Times*, 23 February 1963. The society's concern to ensure that it was perceived as neutral between the political parties is reflected in these minutes, which state that it would invite politicians such as Declan Costello and Noel Browne to a meeting where Donogh O'Malley was the intended speaker. For more on Tuairim's contribution to debate on health policy see Anthony Coughlan, *Aims of social policy: reform in Ireland's social security and health services* (Dublin: Tuairim, 1966); *Irish Independent*, 28 September 1963, 20 April 1964, 22 May 1965; *Irish Times*, 29 November 1963, 18 April 1964, 22 May 1965.
72 For more on Franklin O'Sullivan and Tuairim's criticism of Fianna Fáil see Frank Callanan, *The Literary and Historical Society, 1955–2005* (Dublin: A. & A. Farmar, 2005), pp. 25, 51; interview with Franklin O'Sullivan, Dublin, 13 May 2005; minutes of committee meetings of Tuairim's Dublin branch, 26 June 1967, 27 May 1969; *Irish Times*, 6 June 1973. On the occasion of the disbandment of the Dublin branch in 1973, its chairperson, Francis Xavier Carthy, while emphasising that Tuairim had been 'non-party political', welcomed the new coalition government, claiming that it contained many of the people who had advocated 'the very ideas that Tuairim was trying to put across'. See also *Clonmel Nationalist* and *Munster Tribune*, 24 October 1962. For perceptions of Fianna Fáil see Finn, 'Priests, politics and poetry', pp. 18, 28;

interview with Barry Desmond, Dublin, 11 May 2005. See also Gallagher, *Labour*, pp. 51, 70–1, 91–7; Manning, *Dillon*, pp. 348–9. Charles Haughey was already a controversial figure at this stage.
73 Kurzman and Owens, 'Sociology of intellectuals', p. 81.
74 O'Dowd (ed.), *Intellectuals*, pp. 1–2, 6. See also Murphy, '"A wider perspective"', pp. 247–64; Richard Rose, *What is Europe? A dynamic perspective* (New York: Harper Collins College, 1996), pp. 37–44.
75 For example, Richard H. Pells, *The liberal mind in a conservative age: American intellectuals in the 1940s and 1950s* (Middleton: Wesleyan University Press, 1989); George H. Nash, *The conservative intellectual movement in America since 1945* (Wilmington: Intercollegiate Studies Institute, 2006). Also Hugh Wiltord, 'American Labour Diplomacy and Cold War Britain', *Journal of Contemporary History*, 37 (January 2002), 45–65.
76 Interview with Barrington, 19 May 2005; Barrington, *Uniting Ireland*, pp. 3, 22. See also interview with Dermot Kinlen, Dublin, 11 April 2005. Kinlen, a former High Court judge and Tuairim member, recalled that he and Barrington also admired Daniel O'Connell's belief in 'people power'. See D. George Boyce, *Nineteenth-century Ireland: the search for stability* (Dublin: Gill and Macmillan, 2005), pp. 45, 52, 78–84, 115–18.
77 *An Occasional Bulletin*, 1 (1960). See also *An Occasional Bulletin*, 2 (1960), 1; http://library-2.lse.ac.uk/archives/handlists/Fabian/Fabian.html accessed on 24 July 2008. The Fabian Society was established in 1884.
78 Brian Harvey, 'Does Ireland need more think tanks?', *Administration*, 49:4 (Winter 2001–02), 89–100.
79 Michael D. Behiels, *Quebec since 1945* (Toronto: Copp Clark Pitman, 1987), p. 25. See also Robert Bothwell, *Canada and Quebec: one country, two histories* (Vancouver: UBC Press, 1998), pp. 105, 124–5; John A. Dickson and Brian Young, *A short history of Quebec* (Montreal: McGill-Queen's University Press, 2000), p. 284.
80 Behiels, *Quebec*, pp. 27, 41. See Garvin, *Future*, pp. 214–15 for his comparison of Quebec and Ireland.
81 For example, Lee, *Ireland*, p. 577; www.publicinquiry.ie accessed on 23 July 2008; www.tascnet.ie accessed on 31 July 2008. See also Harvey, 'Think tanks', pp. 96–9; John Horgan, *Noel Browne: passionate outsider* (Dublin: Gill and Macmillan, 2000), pp. 189–91.

2

Representation and reform: Tuairim, the government and the Oireachtas

Tuairim argued for a thorough overhaul of the state's administration and its political institutions. Ireland's development needed to be planned, according to the society, and the way policy was formulated fundamentally reformed if the state was to respond effectively to the major challenges of this period. The existing culture within governmental circles inhibited sustained intellectual analysis. Tuairim's proposals were intended to address this: they would, if implemented, alter the whole system of government and its relationship with the Oireachtas and with the people. The proposals originated from Tuairim's initiative, but the society also responded to particular government decisions, as in the case of its consideration of the electoral system and its proposal to create a new body within the Department of Finance. Professor Patrick Lynch, an influential thinker, was central to the views that Tuairim put forward for administrative, economic and political reform. The atmosphere at meetings at which he and other individuals including politicians spoke contrasted with the hostility between the political parties in the Dáil. While many recognised as critical the contribution made by Tuairim, the nature of the debate on the political system highlighted the difficulties for an independent society attempting to influence policy. This chapter is concerned with the society's role in generating debate in this area and the impact of its arguments for administrative and political reform.

Tuairim, politics and the economy

Tuairim sought a more consensual form of democracy in Ireland. Its members argued that the rules and procedures of the Oireachtas needed to be reformed so that it would be less adversarial and more accountable; they also called for the government to be more inclusive, and for individuals and groups in Irish society to be given a role in policy formulation. Tuairim's examination of the government's proposals in relation to the electoral system was critical to the question of how the Oireachtas operated. This led the society to put forward suggestions for reforms designed to increase the efficiency of the Oireachtas and the effectiveness of its members. In challenging Irish political culture and questioning the adversarial system of government, Tuairim anticipated many of the subsequent criticisms made of the Irish political system. The Dáil, in particular, has been criticised by many academics for its weakness in ensuring that the government was held accountable. Though Ireland's parliamentary system contains features of both the Westminster and consensual models of democracy, the Dáil's adversarial style and its weakness are reminiscent of and indeed have been strongly influenced by the Westminster system of government. 'Civil war' politics reinforced the tendency of the Westminster model of democracy towards strong government and a weak parliament. The major difficulty was that it was not in the government's interest to reform the Oireachtas. To do so would give more power to the opposition and make it more difficult for the government to implement its programme. This adversarial system, which was reflected in and exacerbated by the dominance of the nationalist cleavage and bitterness from the civil war, enabled two disciplined political parties, Fianna Fáil and Fine Gael, to dominate Irish politics. During the first decades of independence, both parties, while in government, centralised power and limited the opposition's role in parliament; this was particularly true of Fianna Fáil under Eamon de Valera, which was in power for the longest period. The Dáil's weakness has to be seen in the context of a strong political party system and the desire on the part of the government to retain power. While the parties gave stable government to the country, and their commitment to democracy was rarely threatened, the distrust between them meant that the Oireachtas was unsuited to holding governments to account. For example, Tuairim pointed out how little discussion there was in parliament on important matters such as the Buchanan report (1969).[1]

Tuairim's proposals for the reform of political structures were all the more pertinent given the government's ever-expanding role in terms of intervention in the economy and of tackling the emerging problems in society. Donal Barrington, Miriam Hederman O'Brien, David Thornley and John Whyte published articles on the nature of Irish democracy in *Hibernia*.[2] Thornley and Whyte as well as Franklin O'Sullivan stressed the need for reform to the Oireachtas so as to enable the state to respond effectively to pressing economic and social problems. Their target was Ireland's political culture, a culture that has been characterised by nationalism, authoritarianism and conformism. It mirrored the nature of society, the powerful position of the Catholic Church and the constituency-based system of politics operating in the country. To convince politicians of the need for reform was to overcome such obstacles and the resistance of individuals who had dominated the state since independence; the reality was that there was little support within the political establishment for a new approach to how deputies conducted their business.

In 1965 in his pamphlet *Ireland: the end of an era?*, Thornley criticised the political parties for their lack of attention to social and economic matters. The consequence of this was the limited amount of time that the Dáil seemed to give to matters of national interest. Thornley stressed the importance of communicating new issues to the electorate and questioned who was making the important decisions in the state. The reality, Thornley claimed, was that a minority of civil servants and government ministers ruled the country and the rest of the deputies concentrated on dealing with the concerns of their constituents. He referred to the first and second programmes of economic development as the 'most important political events of the last decade' but argued that they pointed to the real possibility of democratic politics becoming a 'sideshow to the business of government'.[3] Thornley had made an important point: the political system appeared to be disconnected from the process which created the new economic thinking. This had been highlighted by the first *Programme for economic expansion*, the government white paper which had primarily been the brainchild of T. K. Whitaker, the Secretary of the Department of Finance. It also was, however, the culmination of the ideas that produced a new policy direction from the state in response to the economic malaise of the 1950s.[4]

From 1951 to 1961, over 400,000 people left Ireland. While emigration had been a recurring theme in Irish history, the 1956 census revealed that people were leaving from throughout the country and was not only from the west as previously. It was as if the 'Vanishing Irish', discussed in a well-known book by Fr. John A. O'Brien published in 1954,[5] would become a self-fulfilling prophecy. Furthermore, unemployment was also increasing while real national income rose by a mere 8 per cent. The contrast with the 40 per cent income rate increases in continental Europe and 21 per cent in the comparatively unsuccessful British economy only served to emphasise the sense of crisis in Ireland. The apparent inability of successive governments to respond in an effective manner contributed to the all-pervasive atmosphere of gloom and the unprecedented electoral volatility at that time. The 1954 report of the Commission on Emigration, for instance, did not result in a policy of economic development, while the actions of both the Fianna Fáil and the second inter-party government exacerbated the balance of payments difficulties of 1952 and 1956.[6]

From independence onwards, the state had pursued a policy of fiscal conservatism, with the cautious attitude of the dominant Department of Finance emphasising the need for balanced budgets. Though this remained the case after the change of government in 1932, the free trade outlook of Cumann na nGaedhael was, following the Great Depression of

1929–32, replaced under Fianna Fáil by a commitment to protectionism and self-sufficiency. The 'search for autarchy' was reinforced by World War II. These policies were designed to preserve a rural way of life and to build up a native industry behind tariff walls. Factories were, however, small-scale and dispersed throughout the country, which made them ill-equipped to compete against larger and more efficient industries in other countries, most especially in Britain. Furthermore, the belief that a vibrant agriculture would drive the Irish economy was misplaced; there was a lack of markets at home and abroad for such produce. Alternative rural sources of employment such as forestry, tourism and fishing were under-developed, though there were some improvements particularly in relation to the latter, when in 1958, Erskine Childers, Minister for Lands, announced a new policy at a Tuairim weekend.[7] Emigration was, however, the consequence of the lack of employment; people were, generally, unable to find alternatives to agriculture in industry.[8]

Childers' proposals constituted part of the new economic thinking which began to emerge following the end of World War II. The establishment of the Industrial Development Authority in 1949 and the state's first capital budget in 1950 seemed to signify a conversion to Keynesian economics. Córas Tráchtála (the Irish Export Board) was created in 1951, export tax reliefs were introduced, and rules outlawing foreign ownership of companies were relaxed in 1956; together with Whitaker's *Economic development* in 1958 these represented landmarks for the Irish economy. Whitaker's *Economic development* and the subsequent *Programme for economic expansion*, were particularly important. A response to the pervasive atmosphere of despair emanating from the economic crisis, the documents both consolidated the changes that had been made and played an important role in defining the future direction of the state's policy. *Economic development* indicated that the Department of Finance had moved away from its traditional orthodoxy and was committed to economic planning. This had been associated with communism and, therefore, was viewed by many individuals within the Catholic Church with suspicion.[9] Whitaker's insistence that expenditure should be for expansionist rather than social purposes was more questionable, however, for deficiencies in the provision of housing, social and health services were a feature of the following decade. Nevertheless, during the five years of the programme's duration, 1958–63, GNP rose by more than 4 per cent, twice the targeted growth.[10]

Tuairim responded to these developments; most particularly, it provided a platform from which influential individuals examined *Economic development* and the future remedy it proposed for the economy. The state's commitment to opening up the economy, during the late 1950s and particularly following the accession of Seán Lemass as Taoiseach in 1959, entailed attracting companies from abroad as the country moved away from protectionism towards free trade and from an agricultural to an industrial society.[11] This, combined with Ireland's involvement in negotiations for a free trade area in 1957–58, which led to an application for membership of the EEC in 1961, involved a re-orientation away from the isolationism of World War II and the immediate post-war period towards a realisation that the country's future lay within Europe. Lemass also desired to incorporate representative trade union and employer organisations in national planning and intended that the civil service should play a constructive role in the formulation of policy. In 1966, the government appointed the Services Organisation Review Group, which became known as the Devlin Commission, to consider the organisation of departments of state and semi-state bodies.[12] This helped to address the criticism Tuairim and others made of the civil service; more immediately, the society aimed to convince the government that the Department of Finance needed to be centrally involved in planning the economy.

Planning for economic development

Tuairim's pamphlet *Planning for economic development* (1959) was partly a reaction to Whitaker's 'Grey Book', as *Economic development* was occasionally called. More fundamentally it represented an examination of the state's economic policy and its public sector. Tuairim's publication emanated from a study weekend in Greystones, Co. Wicklow, on 11–12 April 1959, at which it invited a number of prominent individuals to present papers. Professor Patrick Lynch of UCD, Professor Charles Frederick Carter of Queen's University Belfast and Dr Tom Walsh, the Director of An Foras Talúntais (the Agricultural Institute), discussed past mistakes and put forward recommendations for the future. Lynch's and Carter's papers formed the basis of the subsequent pamphlet, published that November. Influential figures in terms of government policy, they had been involved in the Capital Advisory Committee, which from 1956 advised the government on the economy, thus forming an important part of the background to *Economic development*. Furthermore, they had both been consulted in the preparation of that document.[13] In this context, it was significant that these individuals agreed to speak and publish their articles with Tuairim. Lynch had previously praised Tuairim in the course of an article on the economy in *Studies* and may have facilitated Carter's participation at the weekend.[14] The fact that their papers were also published in *Administration*, the Irish Public Administration's journal, however, diminished the impact of the pamphlet.[15] Nevertheless, they were originally read to the society, and Tuairim's publication of them would have brought them to a wider audience.

Both papers, namely Lynch's 'The economics of independence' and Carter's 'A problem of economic development', welcomed Whitaker's *Economic development* and developed some of its ideas. Lynch and Carter were also, at times, critical of that document. They thus went further than much of the earlier commentary, which praised it. The papers complemented each other: Lynch focused on completely discrediting past thinking, assessing what was necessary in the future and discussing the part that public sector had to play, while Carter provided a valuable insight into the defects of the civil service and the reforms that would be necessary if it were to formulate as well as implement progressive policies. The pamphlet began with Lynch's reference to the 'Sinn Féin myth [which] assumed that Irish political independence implied economic independence', which in turn meant self-sufficiency.[16] Lynch asserted that contrary to this myth, Irish economic history, particularly emigration, had illustrated that political, geographical and economic boundaries did not coincide. Irish people, he wrote, had by leaving Ireland ensured that those who remained were able to afford a higher standard of living than otherwise would have been possible. Similarly, he dismissed the myth that unification of the island would end all of Ireland's economic problems and instead insisted that the Irish and British economies were interdependent and that this had to be recognised through closer economic association between the two countries. This, he noted, could even be a prerequisite for membership of the Common Market. He claimed that the efficiency, level of education and technical knowledge of both industry and agriculture would be raised only if their future were planned. Regarding agriculture, he was critical of traditional attitudes, which could result in a farmer leaving his farm to a son who was less well endowed intellectually than another sibling. Lynch stated that a new type of farmer was needed if agriculture's economic status was not to result in the workers being considered second-class citizens, a remark that illustrated the potential for conflict between farming and industrial interests. In relation to the public sector, he maintained that it made an important contribution to national economic development but that it needed to be included in a comprehensive plan, which would also indicate the role to be played by private enterprise. For Lynch, the state would have to play a greater, not smaller, role if the economy was to develop.

Carter, meanwhile, was an Englishman who had developed an intimate knowledge of Ireland. He pointed to certain characteristics of his host country, suggesting that people in Ireland were 'not afraid of Socialism; or (to be more accurate) you are very much afraid of being *called* socialists but not of acting in some respects like socialists'.[17] Referring to Whitaker's 'noble effort' to assess the state of agriculture, Carter noted that his report contained much less information on other sectors of the economy. The most valuable part of Carter's paper was his assessment of the Irish civil service: it was deficient in regard to gathering the information necessary to decide the type of investment required, weak in its assessment of information and almost totally inadequate in regard to the preparation and execution of specific projects. He argued that an effective planning system was necessary to ensure that a programme of properly thought-out projects was prepared in advance. These would then await the opportunity to be implemented in their order of priority. Increased expenditure on training civil servants, market research and the sciences would also prove beneficial; this would ensure that the best advice would be available to the government as well as to the country. Carter's most significant recommendation was that a planning division needed to be established within the Department of Finance. It would maximise the probability that investment decisions would be 'taken on rational economic grounds…and without undue delay'.[18] The division would be responsible for the final form in which proposals would come before government ministers. Tuairim recommended the pamphlet and particularly Carter's suggestion as a constructive step towards better governance in the state.

Reactions to the study weekend and pamphlet

Lynch's and Carter's papers provoked a considerable reaction, particularly at Tuairim's study weekend but also afterwards in the Oireachtas and in newspapers and periodicals such as *Hibernia*, *Administration*, *Christus Rex*, the *Spectator* in England, and the *Irish Times* and the letters pages of that newspaper.[19] The comments reflected the suspicion with which many regarded the state; Lynch's and Carter's suggestion that the government needed to become more active was greeted with scepticism but there was at the same time an increasing awareness of the need for a new departure. The *Irish Times*'s editorial, for example, welcomed the 'note of stark realism', 'penetratingly wise remarks' and 'revolutionary theme[s]' put forward by the speakers. It claimed that their papers represented 'one of the most heartening features of a new attitude to our economic problems'.[20] More forcefully, Brian Inglis, the editor of the *Spectator*, claimed that ten years previously people would not have argued 'that political independence can only be retained on the grounds of renouncing economic independence'.[21] Most significantly, Lynch's and Carter's papers came to the attention of members of the Oireachtas. Speaking in the Dáil in 1962, Noel Browne, then a member of the National Progressive Democrats, quoted Lynch's paper in his defence of the public sector, while in 1959 in the Seanad, UCD's Professor of Economics, George O'Brien, claimed that Lynch had made a significant contribution to new economic thinking.[22] Lynch's and Carter's papers encouraged others to respond positively to the challenges of this period. Carter's paper, in particular, prompted the Director of the Institute of Public Administraion, T. J. Barrington, Donal's brother, to examine in *Administration* in 1959 what was required of the civil service if it was to be in a position to formulate and implement projects for the benefit of the Irish economy.

As previously noted, many individuals resisted an increased role for the state. One of the most prominent of these was Jeremiah Newman, the Professor of Sociology at St Patrick's College, Maynooth, and the future Bishop of Limerick. In a letter to the *Irish Times*, Newman, who was concerned about the consequences of Lynch's proposals for the Catholic Church, questioned whether Lynch believed that the church's influence should be limited to faith and morals and confined to the private sphere. Denying that this had been his view, Lynch called on people in authority, lay and ecclesiastical, to seek reform through constructive criticism. In a similar vein, others strived to ensure that the traditional Catholic and rural way of life was protected. The former Professor of Sociology at Maynooth and the editor of the periodical *Christus Rex*, Peter McKevitt, was one such person. His main concern was the future fate of the small farm, traditionally seen by nationalists as the backbone of the nation. McKevitt argued that rather than the lack of enterprise, as Lynch suggested, the main causes of the failure of private enterprise in Ireland were a high level of taxation and the other conditions for which the government had been largely responsible.[23]

Some of these points had already been made at Tuairim's study weekend. The discussion that followed the papers illustrated that the *Irish Times* was at least partly correct in its suggestion in 1960 that since 1956, 'a healthy and informed controversy on matters of realistic principle' had developed between different individuals. Specifically, the newspaper referred to Lynch and, without naming them, 'various members of Tuairim'.[24] These individuals were to the fore in putting forward a new basis for government policy. Donal Barrington went so far as to argue that Lynch's and Carter's papers 'represented a revolutionary departure in Irish economic thinking'.[25] Barrington wrote in *Hibernia* in May 1959 that many individuals at Tuairim's study weekend believed that state planning would undermine individual initiative. Furthermore, he noted that many thought that the civil service was ill equipped to plan the economy. Lynch and Carter, on the other hand, argued that the success of individual state bodies such as the Electricity Supply Board had illustrated that the public sector could be effective in this area, but that because the problems in the Irish economy had proved so intractable a plan was necessary. There was a consensus at the weekend that such a plan should distinguish between the public and private sectors of the economy and that the state should encourage private enterprise. Louis

Smith, the Economic Adviser to the NFA, for instance, spoke in favour of 'more freedom and a greater strength of responsibility' for each individual sector of the economy,[26] with each one planning its own area.

Lynch and Carter hoped despite such views that all the actors – state, industry, agriculture and the employees working in these sectors – would co-operate in the future. They argued for joint consultations between the government, the NFA and employer and trade union organisations. This vision of involving such bodies in the decision-making process was one that Seán Lemass as Taoiseach shared. A consensus was emerging among individual politicians, civil servants and other influential figures on the need for a new departure, and the main speakers at Tuairim's weekend reflected this in their papers. Lynch, Carter and Walsh, who referred to the research conducted by his institute, each agreed that past economic policies had failed, that the economy and its individual sectors had to be planned and that there was a need for shared thinking between agriculture and industry.

Influence of *Planning for economic development*

In his foreword to the pamphlet, Barrington claimed that Lynch's and Carter's papers contained 'original and startling ideas'. He continued: 'some of [these ideas] have been accepted by the government and have become part of its policy'.[27] That was certainly true of Carter's paper. Specifically, his recommendation that an economic planning branch be established in the Department of Finance was hugely influential. Later that year – in September 1959 – an economic planning branch was set up. On 3 June, Lemass, then Tánaiste, had suggested to the Minister for Finance, Jim Ryan, that an outline of that organisation be put forward for the government's consideration.[28] Following a meeting and exchange of correspondence between Whitaker and Carter, a memorandum that included an account of the latter's views was produced. Lemass and Ryan agreed that the organisation should be set up in the Department of Finance. As Carter had recommended, that body would seek, examine and assess new projects for state investment. The economic development branch, as it was called, was to be staffed mainly by economists. Furthermore, it was suggested that the services of 'external economic advisers' such as Carter and Lynch should be retained.[29] This was an indication of how well regarded these individuals were by senior officials in the Department of Finance and by their minister. In December 1959, Ryan described Carter as an 'economist of the highest rank' and Lynch as 'one of the ablest and most active of our younger economists'.[30]

Lemass maintained, however, that economists' advice should be sought only following the prior authorisation of the government. This reflected his determination that the government would remain in 'full control' of policy[31] and underlined his belief that while representative groups would be included in a 'new economic partnership', it was the government that would lead such an arrangement.[32] Furthermore, Lynch and Carter were not representative of any interest group and would not be involved in the corporatist-style arrangement that Lemass was to introduce after he became Taoiseach. Lemass's resistance to the idea that intellectuals should be directly involved in policy formulation may have reflected what Tom Garvin has described as an 'impatience with "academic" research', which in turn emanated from 'a certain anti-intellectualism'.[33] While his attitude to a future role for Lynch could be contrasted with that of the former Taoiseach, John A. Costello, Lemass's view of Tuairim and, for that matter, Lynch indicated that more than many other politicians, he was interested in new ideas – that is, as long as he remained in control of policy. Lemass was not prepared to devolve power from the centre. To prevent any possible 'misunderstanding', civil servants would not 'on their own initiative' discuss government policy with 'persons outside of the public service'.[34] On the other hand, the Department of Finance was crucial to the future Taoiseach's strategy. The establishment of an economic development branch was important in facilitating the change from a protectionist economy to a commitment to Ireland's membership of a free trade organisation. This illustrated not only that the case for planning had been accepted but that the Department of Finance was to be at its centre. Providing a forum for these views, Tuairim played a subsidiary yet important role in facilitating debate and influencing attitudes to economic planning. The case for administrative reform made by Carter and Lynch, while beginning to be recognised, had, nevertheless, to await the establishment of the Devlin Commission in 1966 before it was directly tackled.

Proportional representation

Unlike its views on economic policy, Tuairim's pamphlets in relation to political reform seemed more likely to irritate than to influence the government. This was certainly the case with regard to the means by which TDs were elected. Twice, in constitutional referenda in June 1959 and October 1968, Fianna Fáil governments proposed replacing proportional representation by means of the single transferable vote (PR-stv) with the first-past-the-post electoral system. On both occasions, they were unsuccessful. Tuairim's contribution to debates in this area was in the form of its pamphlet *P.R.: for or Against?* (1959), articles in newspapers and journals and both private and public meetings, through which the society examined various electoral systems and the arguments put forward by the government and the opposition. While Tuairim sought to remain neutral, the society, on balance, favoured the existing system. During the 1960s, Tuairim's David Thornley and Garret FitzGerald continued to doubt whether a single party would in the future achieve an overall majority.[35] They believed that PR-stv was to a large degree responsible for the increased likelihood of coalition or minority governments in the future as well as the focus that politicians had on constituency issues. Thornley argued that the consequences of the way in which the Oireachtas operated would be increased apathy and poor government as new policies and a proper left–right divide failed to emerge. Legislative activity was overshadowed by constituency affairs, an argument that was further developed in John Whyte's pamphlet in 1966. These views reflected dissatisfaction with the electoral system and the extent to which controversy over the issue re-emerged in the aftermath of the 1961 and, particularly, the 1965 general elections. For his part, FitzGerald repeated much of the approach of Tuairim's pamphlet, which had been produced in 1959 by a research group of which he had been part.

The proposal to change the electoral system was first announced by the Taoiseach, Eamon de Valera, in October 1958. De Valera claimed that, as in other countries, proportional representation (PR) led to a multiplicity of parties and government instability in Ireland. In his view, the only alternative available to Fianna Fáil was coalition governments, which he claimed were ineffective. In contrast, it was argued that the first-past-the-post electoral system would promote the development of a two-party system and ensure that the electorate would decide who would form the government rather than it being a matter for post-election bargaining. Fine Gael and Labour rejected these claims and countered with arguments about proportionality and fairness. Fearing that they would at least initially fare badly under the government's proposal, they emphasised that the first-past-the-post system would disenfranchise minorities and could encourage subversive action against the state from those denied representation in the Oireachtas. Fine Gael challenged the government to compromise: retain the transferable vote in single rather than multi-member constituencies. Concerned at its future election prospects once de Valera was no longer its leader, Fianna Fáil insisted, however, that its proposal should be put to the people. The opposition also questioned the government's timing with regard to the referendum and its motives, and urged that a commission should be established to examine the electoral system. During the Oireachtas debates, which lasted from November 1958 to May 1959, each side attempted to gain an advantage by using past speeches by its opponents to support its case. The national newspapers were also divided, with the *Irish Times* and the *Irish Independent* defending the existing electoral system and the *Irish Press*, which was connected to Fianna Fáil, naturally supporting the government.[36] The contrary nature of the arguments was the context in which Tuairim began its examination of the electoral system and the proposed alternative.

In December 1958, during the ongoing Oireachtas debates, Tuairim's recently established Cork branch suggested that the society should consider the arguments for and against PR. Consisting of both Cork and Dublin branch members, the research group which followed was the first to have its findings published in pamphlet form. This was the only occasion on which two branches co-operated to this extent. Twelve members were, however, clearly considered to be an unwieldy number for a research group, and henceforth, groups consisted generally of about half that number. The group was, despite Cork's objections, dominated by individuals such as Donal Barrington, Garret FitzGerald, Ronan Keane and its chairperson, Frank Winder, all from the Dublin branch. This highlighted the fact that Dublin was and continued to be the dominant branch in the society. In this context, its influence was reflected by Tuairim's members in the capital producing and, in January 1959, sending a memorandum to members of the government including the Taoiseach, Eamon de Valera.[37]

The memorandum explained the reasons why the research group preferred the alternative vote. It was an attempt to persuade the government to change the question it was were putting to the people in the referendum. The group believed that retaining the alternative vote or the transferable vote in single-member constituencies would remove the possibility that a minority of the people would elect a government. This was one of its strongest arguments and part of the basis on which it challenged de Valera. The group also claimed that the alternative vote would facilitate the realisation of the government's own objective, that, is the promotion of 'stable Governments by encouraging the formation of a two-party system in which a single-party Government capable of carrying through its policy would be faced by an effective opposition capable of forming an alternative Government'.[38] It argued that the government's proposal, if adopted, would in actuality defeat its stated objective of ensuring that there would be an effective opposition. Governments with large majorities would, according to the group, result from the first-past-the-post electoral system. In Irish circumstances, this could mean that the opposition would not be in a position to offer an alternative government. The evidence it adduced for this argument was first-preference votes in recent general elections. It predicted that at the next election Fianna Fáil would under the proposed system gain a large majority while there would be a small and fragmented opposition. Faced with such a result, the opposition parties would agree to tactical electoral pacts, which would entail each withdrawing its candidate from certain constituencies in order to avoid a split in the non-Fianna Fáil vote. Thus weakened, Fine Gael and Labour would inevitably produce coalition governments, which one of the main criticisms that Fianna Fáil had of PR. The research group thus rejected the government's claim that the first-past-the-post system would provide 'incentives...to [parties to] amalgamate to form an "Opposition Party"'.[39] Retaining the transferable vote in single seat constituencies would, on the other hand, favour the two largest parties and produce a two-party system. The research group claimed that Fine Gael would thus be in a position to resist pressure to form electoral pacts with smaller parties. As considered later in this chapter, the memorandum did not, however, convince de Valera.

The most notable feature of the research that the group conducted was its discussions with politicians and other public figures. These highlighted Tuairim's ability to respond to a divisive issue in an independent fashion. Those who spoke with the society included Brian Lenihan and Lionel Booth from Fianna Fáil, the opposition TDs Michael O'Higgins from Fine Gael and Seán Casey from Labour, Clann na Poblachta's Seán MacBride, his former colleague Noel Hartnett, a member of the National Progressive Democrats, and Senator Patrick Quinlan, a professor at UCC, as well as the former politician and Managing Director of the Abbey Theatre, Ernest Blythe. Other prominent individuals who met Tuairim's research group were Enid Lakeman, the Research Secretary of the Electoral Reform Society in Britain,[40] Basil Chubb, Owen Dudley Edwards and Cornelius O'Leary, each a respected academic in his field. The meetings, held in private mostly in Dublin but also in Cork, were in the format of discussions or interviews between the research group and the individual. Lenihan and Booth, unsurprisingly, defended the government's proposal while Casey, Hartnett, MacBride, O'Higgins and Quinlan criticised it. The fact that the political parties willingly nominated individuals to speak to the research group suggests that they viewed this to be in their interests, as they seemed to believe that the society could influence the referendum result.

As some of the individuals who were most active during the referendum campaign, Lionel Booth, Ernest Blythe and Enid Lakeman shed light on the nature of the opposing arguments. Blythe was outspoken in his support of the referendum and at least privately critical of Tuairim and particularly Garret FitzGerald for his lack of awareness of the integrating effect of the first-past-the-post system; the proposed system would greatly enhance the prospects of a two-party system and hence stable government. While Booth, one of the few Protestant TDs in Fianna Fáil, was similarly adamant that the referendum should be passed, he, according to Ronan Keane, was 'uneasy and defensive' when questioned by Tuairim.[41] The issues that made Booth uncomfortable were the claims that PR could appeal to northern unionists and Fianna Fáil's statements that Britain had introduced PR into Ireland. These factors highlighted the confusion caused by such arguments and the consequent need for an objective study of the merits of each electoral system. The reality was that by 1929 the Unionist government had, in fact, replaced PR with the first-past-the-post system and that it fared better under that system. Nevertheless, PR was clearly better for minorities. In relation to how Ireland came to have this electoral system, there had, prior to independence, been a demand for PR, and it had had many prominent advocates including Arthur Griffith. By 1921, it was not only on the statute books but had also been endorsed by a significant section of the nationalist community. Despite this, Booth was one of the more articulate speakers on the government's behalf. He argued that the four Protestants TDs were not reliant on the electoral system, a point with which the research group seemed to agree.[42] More controversially, Booth claimed that PR led to instability and in this he clashed, on a number of occasions, with proponents of PR, especially Lakeman.

Lakeman wrote many letters to Irish newspapers and spoke to a number of individuals including Tuairim during the referendum campaign. She made an impact upon the research group. According to Keane, the book she wrote with James Lambert, *Voting in democracies*, influenced him and provoked one of the many debates within Tuairim's research group. When Keane commended Lakeman's argument regarding the unfairness of the first-past-the-post system, FitzGerald countered, however, that the function of an electoral system was to establish a government; he was concerned about the future prospects for stable government under PR-stv.[43] Such comments as to the fairness and purpose of an electoral system were central to the debate during the referendum.

As previously noted, Tuairim's pamphlet preferred PR-stv to the first-past-the-post system. This reflected the weight of the arguments that the group heard during the course of its research, the literature on electoral systems and the members' own views.[44] Before drawing any conclusions, the group gave a brief overview of the history of PR in its pamphlet and examined the reasons why it was introduced into Ireland, and how and where it operated, prior to considering other electoral systems. It explained that the Irish form of PR was not strictly proportional and that it in fact favoured the larger parties. While PR-stv was regarded as the fairer of the two systems, the research group was more circumspect in judging which gave more effective government. In response to claims that PR was responsible for the 'failure of democracy in Germany and Italy and the rise to power of Hitler and Mussolini', it argued that other factors had been more important.[45] It maintained that the relationship between the electoral system and the number of political parties was more complex than many opponents of PR believed and cited examples where it did not appear to affect the number and the strength of the parties.

Reflecting its determination to remain objective, Tuairim's research group did not favour strongly one side or the other. It noted that the existing electoral system had not resulted in an increase in support for small parties. Whether that would remain the case was, it claimed, impossible to demonstrate, as it was a political judgement. Thus the pamphlet left it to the readers to decide for themselves on the basis of the merits of the arguments presented. Similarly the research group failed to put forward views in relation to the quality of TDs under the alternative systems or the effectiveness of coalitions, which, given the difficulty of securing an overall majority under PR and the future probability of electoral pacts under the first-past-the-post system, the pamphlet argued, were increasingly likely whatever the electoral system. Its members, however, dismissed claims that gerrymandering of constituencies would be possible under the proposed system. The research group also rejected the view that coalitions were undemocratic: it argued that 'detailed examination of the voting from 1948 to 1957 shows that the people…know how to use P.R. to obtain the *results* they wish to obtain'.[46]

The consequences of the first-past-the-post system seemed to be the crucial determinant in the research group's preference for PR-stv. As previously noted, it gave great weight to the possibility that a government could have the support of only a minority of the electorate. Irish people, it argued, would view the eventuality of a party securing power in that situation as a serious flaw. Like the opposition, it claimed that this could increase the appeal of subversive organisations. Furthermore, the proposed system tended to produce large majorities and depleted oppositions. The increased instability it produced was the result of 'violent swings', a consequence of the small number of 'safe seats' in the country.[47] As in its memorandum, it claimed that electoral pacts would result. Its conclusion, like much of the pamphlet, was tentatively stated. Nevertheless, the research group made it clear that it did not consider the proposed system the best alternative. It argued that the government should have established an independent commission to advise it on which system it should offer to the people.

Influence of Tuairim's memorandum and pamphlet

The research group's views were welcomed and criticised as well as ignored by politicians. Other prominent individuals thought that Tuairim had made a valuable contribution to the referendum debate. The *Irish Times*, unsurprisingly, praised the memorandum and claimed that Tuairim was an 'admirable organisation'.[48] It also published from 20 to 25 April 1959 a series of articles by Prionsias MacAonghusa, a Tuairim member, which contained a bias in favour of the existing electoral system. The government appeared, as already noted, less keen on Tuairim and its views. Shortly after sending its memorandum to the Taoiseach, Eamon de Valera, it challenged him with regard to a statement he had made in the Seanad to the effect that the transferable vote in single-member constituencies 'produces exactly the same results – not quite in the same way, but exactly the same results – as the system of multi-member constituencies'.[49] No response was forthcoming to the request that the statement be explained. He may have been unhappy that Tuairim's memorandum had not, as the research group had promised, remained confidential. His decision not to respond was, nevertheless, indicative of his approach to both Tuairim and to opposition to his plans. He tolerated the society but did not encourage its questioning attitude and would have been unsympathetic to its ideas. Similarly, he did not engage in Oireachtas debates on the merits of retaining the transferable vote. Apart from that oblique response in the Seanad, his only other statement on the matter was to claim in the Dáil that the system could be unfair, and he gave an example demonstrating that a candidate with a minority of votes could be elected. It was a technical argument which neither Tuairim nor the opposition found convincing. The reality is that they are very different systems. The transferable vote in single-member constituencies is a sophisticated version of the majority system, while the transferable vote in multi-member constituencies is based upon proportionality.[50]

De Valera's failure to respond is likely to have influenced Tuairim's view of the government's motives. Donal Barrington's criticism of the question the government was putting to the people could hardly have been stronger at a meeting organised by the Dublin Institute of Catholic Sociology Debating Society. His comments stood in marked contrast to the even-handed approach evident in the society's pamphlet. The sole non-politician present, Barrington, shared the platform with the Minister for Lands, Fianna Fáil's Erskine Childers, Fine Gael's Declan Costello and the former leader of Clann na Poblachta, Seán MacBride, the former Minister of External Affairs in the first inter-party government (see Figure 6). Reflecting his dismay, Barrington claimed that there was 'an element of hypocrisy in Fianna Fáil propaganda which said: "Let the people decide" when in fact Fianna Fáil had "rigged" the question presented to the people'.[51] He argued that the people should have been able to examine whether it was preferable to retain the multi-member or single-member constituency, the first-past-the-post system or the transferable vote or a combination of these systems. Tuairim and Barrington were questioning why the government refused to consider alternative systems. It seemed to him that Fianna Fáil did not want the best electoral system for the country but the one under which it would secure the utmost electoral advantage. Barrington, himself a member of Fianna Fáil, thus displayed the independence of mind that was sought from all

6 Speaking at a debate on PR in 1959 were (left to right) Donal Barrington, Erskine Childers, the chairperson, Rev. Gabriel Bowe, Seán MacBride and Declan Costello.

individuals involved in Tuairim. His attitude was interesting in that in an earlier article in *Hibernia* in October 1958 he had appeared to have been slightly more sympathetic to the referendum proposal. Any doubts as to the benefits of PR were, however, dispelled after he studied the matter as part of Tuairim's research group or indeed following the government's failure to engage with the society.

Nor could Barrington's assertion have improved the government's view of Tuairim. It is, nevertheless, difficult to estimate the extent to which de Valera's antipathy towards Tuairim was shared by other members of Fianna Fáil. Jack Lynch, then the Minister for Education, was one who also seemed to distrust the society. According to Tuairim's Diarmuid Ó Cearbhaill, Lynch regarded Tuairim as hostile to the government; while the evidence that does exist is limited, Ó Cearbhaill, then a civil servant in the Department of Finance, was well placed to comment. Lynch's portrayal of the damage that PR could inflict on the nation certainly points to Tuairim's failure to influence the minister. His closeness to de Valera may have been a factor in his questioning the society's independence; Lynch could not at any stage be said to be on good terms with the society.[52] As for the rest of the government, a Tuairim document noted that Fianna Fáil thought that the pamphlet gave too much credence to its opponent's arguments.[53] It seems that the government was at least concerned and perhaps weary of the society and its intentions.

There was a significant contrast between, on the one hand, the attitude of de Valera and Lynch, and on the other, that of Lionel Booth, a backbench government TD. While Tuairim seemed to irritate de Valera and Lynch, Booth embraced the opportunity to debate. Having spoken to Tuairim's research group, he said in the Dáil that he was 'particularly interested in the pamphlet'.⁵⁴ He noted that it had been sent to all the deputies. Like many deputies, Booth nevertheless sought to use Tuairim's arguments to support his own view; he pointed to its 'very fair comment' that the Irish system of PR was becoming less proportional. The government was, he claimed, merely following Tuairim's logic in attempting to replace PR-stv with the first-past-the-post system. His conclusion was that this was necessary to avoid the disintegration inherent in PR and as such was the only option open to Fianna Fáil. Naturally, the opposition deputies had a different viewpoint. In contrast to Booth, who referred to Tuairim's pamphlet on only one occasion, the Labour Party leader, William Norton, and Clann na Talmhan's Michael Donnellan cited it a number of times. Donnellan noted that the research group provided an 'honest case for and against P.R.',⁵⁵ and he pointed to its claim that a political party could under the proposed system be elected by less than a majority of the people. He quoted the group's examples of recent British general elections to support his allegation that it was in fact a gerrymander by Fianna Fáil. Donnellan's attitude can be explained by the threat that he and his party faced under the straight-past-the-post system. His statements go some way towards explaining why the smaller parties and the majority of independents were so determined in their opposition to Fianna Fáil during the referendum campaign.

Individuals on both sides of the house, namely Norton, Donnellan, Booth, and Francis Loughman and Pádraig Faulkner of Fianna Fáil, referred to Tuairim's pamphlet. Labour, in particular, was vociferous in its support for PR. Norton, for example, attacked Booth's views and, like Donnellan, questioned Fianna Fáil's motives. He quoted at length from Tuairim's 'interesting' pamphlet, its 'sensible observations' and the 'careful survey' it made in relation to European democracies before World War II,⁵⁶ as well as to the unknown consequences of the first-past-the-post system. These quotations brought the forthright response from Loughman that all the deputies had read the pamphlet. Loughman, it seems, was not nearly as impressed with it as was Booth. Like de Valera and Lynch, he was probably much more representative of the Fianna Fáil party. Such partisanship was similarly evident in a speech by Faulkner: he claimed that PR made it impossible for both post-war Germany and Italy to deal with the problems to which Tuairim had referred.⁵⁷ Norton praised, however, the way in which the 'competent and non-impulsive research group' 'rightly and prudently' brought into the public the arguments for and against the abolition of PR.⁵⁸ In response to a ruling from the Leas-Cheann Comhairle, he noted that it was a pamphlet by Irish authors and argued that it was therefore proper that such quotations were placed on the record. These, he said, contrasted with the quotations from books by the Minister for External Affairs, Frank Aiken, and the Minister for Health, Seán MacEntee. Furthermore, Norton maintained that the research group's case for proceeding cautiously was most appropriate to Irish conditions.

These Dáil speeches, particularly Norton's, indicate that Tuairim's pamphlet impacted on the political mainstream during the referendum campaign. Part of the reason why more individuals did not refer to it was simply that it was published after the majority of the debate had taken place. The absence of any comments, notably from Fine Gael, also reflected Tuairim's attempt to remain objective; Alexis FitzGerald, an important intellectual in that party, argued that the pamphlet was too balanced, its 'conclusions...hesitant'.[59] Fianna Fáil, as already discussed, had a similar attitude. Norton, the Labour leader, whose party felt most threatened by the proposed system, acted in marked contrast to the two biggest parties. He clearly felt that Tuairim's arguments strengthened the case in favour of PR. This was an indication that, at least in relation to political matters, Labour was the party that was most sensitive to Tuairim's views.

Norton, the *Irish Times* and at least one academic praised the research group's objectivity, which had been criticised by most politicians. Writing in *Hibernia*, Professor J. L. McCracken of the History Department, Magee College, Derry, described the pamphlet as 'cogent and judicious...designed to impart factual information, to stimulate clear thinking and, in so far as it attempts to influence opinion, to do so by an appeal to reason rather than emotion'. As Tuairim's pamphlet itself noted and McCracken confirmed, it was more likely to appeal to the 'intelligent reader' than to the ordinary person.[60] Therein lay the society's problem in attempting to influence public opinion. By its nature, Tuairim appealed to the intelligentsia. This attitude led to the pretentious statement about the readership of the publication: many individuals, including the group's members, thought that the majority of people would vote on party lines, perhaps indicating the relative political immaturity of the nation. Nevertheless, 4,000 copies of the pamphlet were sold,[61] which was a significant figure. It is likely that it influenced the way in which some of these individuals voted. The Tuairim member and later Labour Party TD Barry Desmond certainly believes that to be the case: he argued in an interview that Tuairim had a considerable impact on the first referendum. The individuals who bought the pamphlet were among those most likely to accept the research group's appeal not to regard it as a party-political issue. In the event, on 17 June, the majority of people kept the presidential election and referendum separate. They voted in favour of retaining PR as well as for the election of de Valera as President. The votes in Cork and Dublin were crucial in the retention of the existing electoral system. It is therefore reasonable to suggest that the society influenced the outcome of the referendum: Tuairim was at its strongest in these cities and the pamphlet was published in late April, a short time in advance of the referendum. While other factors such as the position of the newspapers and the trade unions' support of PR would have been more important in determining the result, Tuairim made a considerable impact; this was reflected in the reaction to its pamphlet from parts of the political establishment.

Tuairim may also have had a long-term impact in influencing individuals and consequently the result of the second referendum on this topic in 1968. In addition to the active role played by current and former members during this campaign, the society provided a forum for members of the government and opposition to put forward their views. At a meeting of the Limerick branch, Fine Gael's T. F. O'Higgins claimed there appeared to be 'something sinister in Fianna Fáil's determination to repeat…the same proposition' and to refuse to consider the alternative vote.[62] This reflected the determination of the opposition and many other individuals, who on this occasion were much more forceful in their support for the existing system. Basil Chubb attempted, however, to be even-handed: he argued that it was difficult to see the Irish people, who were used to the fairness of the existing system, 'easily accept…the distorted majorities and minorities and the capricious results of the straight vote'.[63] During the course of the Dáil debate, the Minister for Local Government, Kevin Boland, nevertheless quoted Chubb's statement that Ireland could 'survive the straight vote'.[64] This was hardly a ringing endorsement of the government's proposal. Chubb made his most significant impact when he and David Thornley demonstrated the vagaries of the proposed system on television: they estimated that under it Fianna Fáil could win over ninety seats at the next general election. This referendum pointed to the continued influence of the pamphlet and the society through individuals such as Thornley, Garret FitzGerald and Barry Desmond. Pertinently, their actions and those of others involved in Tuairim again raised questions about the society's independence; this was a difficulty that was implicit in the nature of the society.

Dáil deputies

During the 1960s, Tuairim, through Thornley and John Whyte in particular, challenged the indifference towards reform of the Oireachtas. The society made a number of recommendations designed to improve the democratic process and the way in which the government, public services and the political system operated. Tuairim felt that the future of Irish democracy could be threatened if these changes were not implemented. This was a question that had hitherto rarely been considered; a notable exception to the lack of concern for democracy and how it operated was J. L. McCracken's

Representative government in Ireland, which examined the function and history of the Dáil from 1919 to 1948. Thornley and Whyte saw the need not only to bring this up to date but to provide a basis for a more accountable and effective system of government. While McCracken had provided biographical information on TDs, he only partly considered how well the Dáil performed and its deputies did their work. Whyte and Thornley as well as Basil Chubb had begun to fill this void. Thornley had been the inspiration behind the establishment of a research group while Whyte wrote up the subsequent pamphlet's findings and constructed its statistical tables. In a more systematic attempt to find information on Dáil deputies, the research group, established in October 1963, examined old newspapers and consulted members of the political parties and journalists. The pamphlet *Dáil deputies: their Work, its difficulties, possible remedies* (1966), as its name implies, focused on the work of the Dáil and its members.[65]

Yet, the research group's most significant innovation in relation to Irish politics was the questionnaire that it sent to TDs, which revealed much information that hitherto had been unknown. Controversial questions such as the quality of Dáil deputies could now be addressed, and it was also possible for the research group to compare its findings from the 1961 and 1965 elections with McCracken's from 1944 and 1948. Tuairim's pamphlet was to provide a useful model for political scientists in the future. The research group asked deputies questions about themselves, the difficulties they faced and their views on possible remedies. Of the 141 deputies circulated, 73 responded,[66] including 38 members of Fianna Fáil, 27 from Fine Gael, 6 from Labour and 2 from the independents and minor parties. Information on deputies' education, their other occupations and their backgrounds was secured. Some of the changes in the deputies' profiles were in line with general developments in society and thus to be expected. This was particularly true of the rise in their educational level and the decrease in their average age. In relation to the former, the proportion of deputies with a university or professional training had increased while the number with only primary-level education had fallen considerably. The link between deputies and their local constituency had become even more important with the decrease in the numbers from the revolutionary generation. Many deputies, for example, lived in their local constituencies, served on their local council, had been involved in sport, were related to sitting or former deputies or combined some or all of those routes to the Dáil. The research group concluded that in this respect, the parties had much in common. Fianna Fáil, on the other hand, provided its deputies with the greatest assistance in relation to correspondence and election expenses.

The most important part of the pamphlet related to the nature of a deputy's work. In their replies, deputies stressed the amount of time they devoted to addressing the grievances of constituents. They claimed that they were compelled to deal with the individual concerns of their constituents because their re-election depended on it. It was the apparent imbalance between constituency and legislative matters that the research group was anxious to address. Many of the deputies thus rejected a suspicion among the public that they deliberately encouraged a belief that people could get public benefits only through them. On the contrary, they claimed that they would prefer to spend more time on their parliamentary work and put forward a number of suggestions in order to ensure that they could properly scrutinise legislation and help shape public policy.

The deputies' proposals were considered before the research group made a number of recommendations that were designed to reduce the burden of constituency work and to improve the efficiency of the Dáil. Whereas the value of constituency work had been questioned in newspaper articles written by Thornley and Whyte, the research group was more balanced in its approach. In rejecting the rather startling argument of some deputies that such work as correspondence and meetings with constituents and civil servants should be prohibited, it recognised that this work had its place. The group argued that a network of citizens' advice bureaux should be established. They also called for better facilities for deputies, including free secretarial facilities and, in the longer term, an office for each deputy. Consideration was also given to reorganising the Dáil on a committee basis and to the argument from six deputies (five from Fianna Fáil) that they should be paid a sufficient amount to make them independent of other sources of income. This highlighted the extent to which many deputies continued to be part-time parliamentarians, a factor which made it more difficult for deputies to contribute to legislation and for the Dáil to hold the government to account. Tuairim's focus was on improving facilities within the Dáil; the society thus helped to initiate a debate on parliamentary reform. Many of the proposals that it first put forward in its pamphlet have, indeed, since been introduced.[67]

The society also considered the effect that multi-seat constituencies had on constituency service. This was an issue that was rarely discussed. Like Tuairim's 1959 memoranda, its pamphlet on Dáil deputies favoured the single transferable vote in single rather than in multi-member constituencies. In addition, the latter research group argued that constituency service was the only means by which candidates of the same party could differentiate themselves from their party colleagues in multi-member constituencies. More recently, this view has provoked debate among both politicians and members of the academic community.[68] Tuairim thus helped to initiate a debate on the electoral system and the need for reform to the Dáil.

Tuairim's influence on democratic reform

The extent to which Tuairim stimulated an interest among Oireachtas members in Dáil reform has yet to be determined. Deputies were at the very least aware of Whyte's pamphlet: Fine Gael's Richie Ryan, for example, praised Tuairim's 'most interesting paper' in the house in 1966.[69] Furthermore, fifty-nine of the seventy-three deputies who replied to Tuairim's questionnaire put forward possible remedies to problems in the Dáil; this suggests that a minority of members were interested in reform. It was well known: 1,000 copies of the pamphlet were sold, and its publication and contents were reported in the *Irish Times*. The Labour Party's Barry Desmond went as far as to suggest that the 'genesis'[70] of his party's policy during the late 1960s was found within the Tuairim pamphlet. He was certainly well placed to influence the future nature of that policy. A memorandum published by Labour in 1968 made a number of recommendations, including the establishment of a Dáil standing committee to debate the committee stages of bills and estimates, a permanent committee to deal with semi-state bodies and reform of the house's rules. The memorandum sought to promote the efficiency of the Dáil and to enable its members to participate more constructively in the work of the house. As such, it had similar objectives to Tuairim's research group. Its proposals were, however, both broader in their reach and more specific. It was thus somewhat ironic that Desmond recalled that Tuairim's pamphlet was 'very radical, regarded as being very daring'.[71] While that was perhaps the case given the meagre facilities available for deputies during this period and the resistance to reform among the political establishment, Tuairim's recommendations were cautious when compared with Labour's. But then Desmond had been a member and so was clearly a sympathetic observer; furthermore, reform was clearly in Labour's interests: because it was the smallest party, and given that the two largest parties dominated governments, a more consensual Dáil would have given it increased influence. It was more striking that it had taken the party so long to put forward such a policy. Tuairim was radical and daring in that it had been the first to put forward proposals; Labour developed Tuairim's recommendations further. Tuairim now sought to ensure the momentum that had been built up was not lost.

During this period, further calls for reform of the Oireachtas were heard at Tuairim events. For example, Declan Costello argued for an ombudsman, Basil Chubb a committee system and Kadar Asmal, a lecturer in Trinity, a permanent Law Commission, while a future Supreme Court judge, Catherine McGuinness, urged women to become more active in politics.[72] Tuairim's success in attracting such notable individuals was reflected in the creative society series which it organised in 1969–70. During that year, the society organised meetings and weekends with a common theme, its aim of facilitating the full participation of each person in Irish life. Its communications conference held at the Royal Dublin Society, Ballsbridge, Dublin, on 13 and 14 December 1969 marked the culmination of its desire for meaningful debate within the country and its parliament and epitomised Tuairim's attempts to bring people from different backgrounds and vocations together to discuss the country's problems and its future development.

Tuairim reported the conference's proceedings in its final pamphlet, *Government and people: a creative dialogue* (1970). This claimed that it was the 'first time in the history of the State that delegates from so many different types of organisation had come together for the purposes of communication'.[73] It was, indeed, a significant occasion which demanded much time and effort in organisation. Representatives of the political parties, the civil service, the judiciary, local government, state-sponsored bodies, the churches, the press and a range of professional and voluntary bodies, including of course a number of Tuairim members, were present. Overall, the pamphlet named 183 people who attended the conference. These included the Tánaiste and Minister for Health, Erskine Childers, and Senators Neville Keery and Peggy Farrell of Fianna Fáil, the leader of the Liberal Party in Britain, Jeremy Thorpe, the future ministers Richard Burke and Garret FitzGerald of Fine Gael, and the Labour Party's Flor O'Mahony and its Public Relations Officer, James Devine. The future President of Ireland, Senator Mary Bourke, the Governor of the Central Bank, T. K. Whitaker, the foremost advocate of reform in relation to local government, T. J. Barrington, the President of the NFA, T. J. Maher, and another future minister, Michael Woods of Tuairim, were also in attendance. The conference was divided into a number of sessions, each examining a specific area and chaired by prominent individuals; of these Patrick Lynch and the General Secretary of the Vocational Teachers' Association (VTA), Charles McCarthy, had already been involved in Tuairim.[74]

Civil servants in attendance included the Secretary of the Department of Labour, Tadhg Ó Cearbhaill, James Dolan of the Department of Finance and Tomás Ó Floinn, the Assistant Secretary of the Department of Education. Generally reluctant to speak in public, many departments had taken their lead from the Department of Finance. The initial view of Charlie Murray, the secretary of that department, was that Finance should give the conference '"a wide berth"'.[75] The minister, Charles Haughey, was said to be 'even less enthusiastic'.[76] Haughey was dismissive of both Tuairim and the proposed changes to the way in which the government operated. He was representative of the view of many within Fianna Fáil: they did not believe it was in their interests, as opposed to the country's interests, to support reform of the Oireachtas. This followed from what Muiris

MacCarthaigh has called the 'tendency of incumbent administrations to maintain the institutional status quo'.[77] The attitude of civil servants was due to their determination not to interfere with the principle that the minister, as the head of the department, was accountable for the decisions of her or his department. Civil servants were, in turn, responsible to their own departments, which, as MacCartaigh has commented, 'reinforces the political neutrality and anonymity of the civil service'.[78] The inherent difficulties in ensuring that they were accountable for the quality of their decisions were, accordingly, rarely discussed in public. No reason was given for the Department of Finance's change of heart in relation to the conference. It may simply have been a recognition that given the size of the conference and those that were to attend, it would have seemed incongruous for the department not to be represented. It may also be significant that Murray had, according to Tuairim's Diarmuid Ó Cearbhaill, in the past been open to Tuairim and was one of the few civil servants to engage in public debate.[79]

Many departments were, however, unrepresented at the conference, perhaps partly because they were frequently criticised in the media. Those who did attend were articulate in defence of the civil service. Ó Floinn responded to criticisms of the Department of Education from David Martin of Macra na Feirme as to the content of the national school curriculum. Tadig Ó Cearbhaill was more constructive in his arguments: he claimed that there would not be resistance from the civil service to its members speaking in public. Ó Murchadha of the Department of Defence stated, however, that civil servants had no policy of their own and wished to be seen as 'their Ministers' officers rather than advisers'.[80] He added that they could speak only in the name of their minister. These statements were, on the whole, defensive and obscured at least part of the truth: civil servants did not, as Dolan in Finance argued, merely 'present dispassionately the pros and cons of any particular project'.[81] The reality was that because ministers usually accepted the views put before them, the civil servants played an important part in defining the policy of the country. Nevertheless, the most significant speech by a civil servant during the conference was from Dolan. This was partly because he was the first to contribute and thus broke through the tradition which prevented civil servants from speaking in public, but also because it was in response to a strong attack from Garret FitzGerald. FitzGerald criticised what he believed to be the civil servants' overly robust protection of their minister. Dolan accepted that the minister's speech could be 'sometimes stilted'. He denied, however, that the civil servants' refusal to speak in public diminished the quality of their decisions or was due to 'moral cowardice'.[82] Dolan and his colleagues argued that this was the system which governed civil servants, and one over which they had no control. While this could be said to have been partly true, the speeches of Dolan and his colleagues betrayed a lack of imagination when discussing the public service and the country's problems.

The conference represented a progressive step in addressing administrative reform and was recognised as such. Patrick Lynch, in his concluding remarks, congratulated Dolan, remarking that it was 'of inestimable advantage to civil servants themselves to speak in public in a way which enables people to judge the kind of advice they contribute towards the formation of public policy'. He pointed to T. K. Whitaker's 1956 speech to the Statistical and Social Inquiry Society, which he claimed 'disposed dramatically of the absurd myth that anonymity was necessarily a virtuous feature of the public service'.[83] Lynch and others have seen this speech as a watershed in the Irish government's economic policy; it certainly highlighted the significant contribution that civil servants could make to public discourse. The conference served a useful purpose in demonstrating how this concept could work in practice and thus challenging the civil service's traditional anonymity. Crucially, it also illustrated that the quality of the decisions made by civil servants could be judged. While the number of occasions for them to speak in public increased, no formal mechanisms for ensuring civil servants were accountable were put into place for some time.

Many ideas to improve communications between the government and people were discussed at the conference. Indeed, a criticism implicit in remarks in Tuairim's pamphlet and by individuals in attendance was that some, like a recommendation for a press council and for access to the Oireachtas, were not developed into concrete proposals. Given that there were so many individuals present this was to an extent inevitable, and it was the main reason why it was decided that Tuairim should have a report written and submit it to a further meeting in 1970. Effectively Tuairim's pamphlet, this included excerpts from the speeches of Erskine Childers and Jeremy Thorpe. Having praised Ireland's PR electoral system in a wide-ranging speech, Thorpe also referred to disaffection in a number of Western countries and made a number of recommendations such as decentralisation and the increased use of referenda, measures which were intended to help ensure that democracy worked and that it facilitated creative dialogue.

Yet Childers's speech was confined to the formulation of government policy within Ireland. Though he has been viewed as a reforming minister, his attitude reflects the complacency that existed among parts of the government and the political elites. Many of the delegates were surprised that Childers seemed content with existing structures for communication between government and people, and they pointed to extra-parliamentary protests, apathy, lack of discussion between the government and sectional groups and the lack of debate within political parties as evidence of discontent with the political system. Childers claimed, however, that there would be 'anarchy' if the parties fragmented and argued that decisions had to be made by the 'authoritative majority'.[84] As if shaken from his lethargic attitude, Childers conceded that there was a 'need for a grass roots communications system from the parish level right up to the government'. Childers's colleague Senator Neville Keery, on the other hand, saw the need for wider reform, specifically arguing for live radio and television coverage of the Oireachtas. He did, nevertheless, agree with Childers on the value of political parties: while appealing for more people to join the parties, he recognised the need for genuine dialogue between them and the electorate.

There was at the conference a widespread impatience with the government over the lack of participation of voluntary and professional organisations in the formulation of policy. Parents and farmers, to name two groups, felt excluded from a role in policy formulation by the Departments of Education and Agriculture. This, in part, reflected the discontent that farmers and those involved in education felt at the state's policy approach, but also what they perceived to be their lack of influence. Though Lemass, as previously noted, involved representative bodies in national planning, he and his successor, Jack Lynch, remained in control of the policy process. A further consequence of the discussions that did take place was that they alienated other organisations and individuals who had not been invited. Given rising expectations and industrial unrest, and a government increasingly active in a range of economic and social areas, many individuals felt that the absence of an overall vision for the country was deeply damaging.

It was as if David Thornley's warning, in his 1965 pamphlet *Ireland: the end of an era?* had come to fruition; as if the consequence of the way in which the Oireachtas operated was increased apathy. The frustration with parliament was reflected in the call by Myles McSwiney for the establishment of an organisation, similar to the Academy of Democratic Institutions in the USA, to discuss national problems. It was to be the task of further delegate conferences to ascertain how this would work in practice. In particular, what form would parliamentary democracy take and how was it to be reconciled with greater vocational participation in the decision-making process? More immediately, while the government was viewed as the main obstacle to 'creative dialogue', some such as Franklin O'Sullivan and Mary Cannon of Tuairim also argued that increased professionalism and co-operation from and between voluntary organisations were necessary for them to be truly effective. This suggests that the lack of consultation was due not merely to government's reluctance to engage with those outside their immediate circle but also to the inability of interest organisations to represent the people.

Change happened slowly; as part of the response to the economic crisis of the 1980s, the 'social partners' – farmers' organisations, trade unions and business groups – came to have a 'role in defining the broad economic approach of the state'.[85] That solution did not, however, overcome the dilemma to which FitzGerald had referred: how to integrate the 'parliamentary bodies at national level with the voluntary bodies at local bodies'.[86] Charles McCarthy felt that communication between government and people could improve through increased local autonomy, decentralisation and regionalisation. Having argued previously in his book *The distasteful challenge* for the democratisation of not only the institutions of state but also all the structures of society, McCarthy viewed reform of local government as one means by which power would be given to the people; it was an area, particularly the finance thereof, which Tuairim had previously considered.[87] Despite indications in the early 1960s that the society would influence government policy in relation to local government, the trend since independence towards increased centralisation continued throughout this period. Resistance to change and especially the devolution of power was very strong. There would, in the words of T. K. Whitaker, 'always be a need for the public administration to quantify and discuss all the aspects… which were to be the subject of major policy decisions'.[88] If at Tuairim's conference there was a general consensus among those present; including Whitaker, as to the need to improve the means of communication, there was also a determination from within the political system that the establishment of national priorities would remain the responsibility of the government.

Tuairim's hopes for reform to the public sector were also undermined at events it organised. A summary of such views, the 1970 pamphlet recommended that the Devlin report should be adopted 'with certain reservations', and the Buchanan report 'subjected to further discussion'.[89] These reports, having advocated radical changes in the structures of government and the future planning of the country, received some criticism at Tuairim's meetings. The assumptions upon which Buchanan was based were questioned, while it was claimed that Devlin did not address the intellectual standard of the civil service. Patrick Lynch, Charles McCarthy and T. J. Barrington were much more positive at the conference: Lynch and Barrington argued for devolution of power to the regional and local area while McCarthy called the 'concept behind [the Devlin report] "excellent"'.[90] Tuairim's pamphlet reflected the variety of views that the society heard. It indicated that there was far from universal support for these reports, which when combined with political difficulties led the government to distance itself from the Buchanan report in particular. In the event, the report was treated with indifference by the political establishment and with it Ireland's long-term economic development.[91] Devlin was less controversial and more successful, with the Department of the Public Service, for example, being established on 1 November 1973. There was then, at least, an increased awareness of the need to reform the institutions of state, but they were very different opinions as to how exactly to proceed.

Tuairim recognised that if democratic structures were to be improved, there was a need for concrete proposals to be put before the government. Some of these were, of course, contained in the pamphlet *Government and people*, which was sent to Jack Lynch in March 1970. Lynch, then the Taoiseach, had previously received a report of the conference from Senator Neville Keery, who had been present. Keery, who regarded the conference as a 'success' and pointed to 'the range and depth of the discussions', argued that Fianna Fáil's National Executive should be represented in 'considerable strength' if and when Tuairim held another meeting.[92] He was, however, the sole member of Fianna Fáil to be represented at the next meeting in Dublin in April 1970. This considered the pamphlet and the resolution that those present – representatives of community, vocational and professional bodies – were to put before the government. At the meeting, chaired by Franklin O'Sullivan, serious charges against the government were made and a demand for reform was put forward in the strongest terms. These organisations viewed with 'grave concern [how] little impact' they had made on 'political decision-making' and urged the government to 'enable these bodies to take an effective part in the formation of public policy'.[93] Those in attendance recommended that committees of the Oireachtas should be established and should meet representatives of these organisations. Furthermore, they argued that the procedures of the Dáil and Seanad should be amended so that they would have more time to discuss matters of national importance. Government departments needed to be more transparent and participation in local government widened. The resolution seemed to make little impact on the government, for which it was not an immediate priority. Lynch replied that the government would 'give due weight to the views expressed in the resolution' in the context of its examination of the changes required following upon the Devlin report.[94] This suggests that the government responded only once the need for change could no longer be ignored. Tuairim, however, persisted; the government's response encouraged the society to consider which reforms were necessary.

Tuairim established a study group to examine how its proposals would affect the Oireachtas. It considered how the people who worked in these houses needed to adapt and the ways in which the institution related to professional and vocational bodies and to the general populace. The group, which held twelve meetings under the chairmanship of O'Sullivan, met from October 1970 to June 1972. It included a number of politicians, such as Neville Keery, Richard Burke, Barry Desmond and T. J. Fitzpatrick, a Fianna Fáil TD; three other high-profile individuals, T. J. Barrington, T. J. Maher and Tom Walsh, were also involved. The attendance of politicians suggests that resistance to reform was being broken down slowly and that the society had the goodwill of parts of the political establishment. It also gave Tuairim an insight into and access to members of the Oireachtas that was unusual for the time. This is confirmed by the fact that, with the permission of the Chief Whip and the chairperson of Fianna Fáil, in June 1971 Keery and Fitzpatrick sent a questionnaire, prepared by the study group, to each deputy in their party.[95] Similarly, Burke and Desmond sent questionnaires to members of their respective parties. All three parties were content to co-operate with Tuairim on this matter.

Tuairim's parliamentary study group attempted to, in its words, counter the 'drift from democracy' and put an end to the situation where matters were increasingly discussed and decided outside the Oireachtas.[96] Included in the 'useful, practical suggestions' that TDs had proposed were the reform of Dáil procedures to improve how the house spent its time as well as improved research and secretarial facilities for deputies.[97] The group proceeded to recommend the establishment of a permanent committee system to cover each area of government. Furthermore, it argued for longer sitting hours for the Oireachtas, for debates to be shown on television and reform of the house's 'out-of-date rules of order' so as to increase opportunities for members of the opposition to contribute to policy.[98] While this represented a considerable progression from the proposals put forward in Tuairim's 1966 pamphlet, the study group repeated John Whyte's earlier recommendation that citizens' advice bureaux be established.

The government finally began, around 1970, to view parliamentary reform with greater urgency. It established the Informal Committee on Reform of Dáil Procedure in 1971. This was to examine parliament and its procedures, and it was probably in part a reaction to the anger expressed at Tuairim's conferences by what were after all influential individuals in society and respected voluntary and professional organisations. The disquiet of such individuals and those involved in the parliamentary study group at the increasing irrelevance of parliament was striking. It seems that the society and many of the individuals who spoke at its meetings thought that the inadequate nature of the Oireachtas had led to a crisis of confidence in the state's democratic structures. Tuairim was much more forthright in its views and solutions in the early 1970s than in the 1960s. While the conference and the parliamentary study group can be seen as developing the views put forward by John Whyte and David Thornley, the involvement of many influential individuals strengthened the conviction that far-reaching reforms were necessary.

Tuairim and the pressure it exerted were not, however, the principal factors in the government's finally taking some steps to address this issue. According to Keery, the new-found urgency was due to events in connection with Northern Ireland (presumably the outbreak of the 'troubles' and the arms trial in the south) and an already heavy legislative programme that during 1970 had placed the Dáil under considerable pressure. The need to respond to the apparent inability of parliament to cope in the face of such a crisis led to the establishment of the Informal Committee on Reform of Dáil Procedure, to which Labour and Fine Gael nominated David Thornley and Richard Burke. It was to examine Dáil procedure, while Neville Keery was one of only two people to forward their views to the committee.[99]

Tuairim's parliamentary study group was quite radical in the proposals it put forward, especially in comparison to those from the Informal Committee on Reform of Dáil Procedure, which mostly dealt with relatively minor matters. The committee was, nevertheless, the first forum since the foundation of the state in which the Oireachtas had thoroughly examined the procedures of parliament. It seems to have eased some of the concerns that were expressed at this time. However, it did not examine the relationship between the Oireachtas and state-sponsored bodies and the broadcasting of Dáil debates. At a Tuairim meeting in Cork, Thornley criticised its failure to consider another issue, that of better research facilities for opposition members. Moreover, also speaking to the branch, the Lord Mayor of Cork, Seán O'Leary, referred to the disregard, even contempt, with which central government treated local government and commented that 'there could not be an effective opposition unless the Government of the day wants one'.[100]

Meanwhile, the Informal Committee on Reform of Dáil Procedure recommended that more bills be taken in Special Committee, which was a welcome suggestion. Other proposed reforms included new procedures for Question Time and further suggestions designed to improve the efficiency of the Dáil. These were all proposals that had been advocated by Tuairim. The society had, of course, gone much further in the range of issues it considered. Not only was Tuairim the first to consider this matter in detail, but its contribution was recognised as critical by influential individuals and professional and vocational bodies. Politicians were more reticent; here too, however, some perceived its role as crucial. The society had at the very least placed the issue in the public domain. More than that, Tuairim had made a significant contribution to the debate on parliamentary reform. While there does not seem to be any evidence to suggest that Tuairim influenced directly the government or the committee it established, the ideas it put forward had gained a widespread acceptance among many individuals including some politicians.

It was left to the 1973–77 Fine Gael Labour coalition government to implement the majority of the proposals of the Informal Committee on Reform of Dáil Procedure. It may have been significant that it was a government that consisted of the former Tuairim members Garret FitzGerald and Barry Desmond that finally tackled the issue of Oireachtas reform. The long-term influence of Tuairim in this matter was highlighted when Desmond, then the Labour Party Chief Whip, criticised the committees his own government had established and put forward proposals similar to those that had previously been recommended by Tuairim and his own party.[101] It was not until Desmond was a minister in Garret FitzGerald's 1982–87 government that a comprehensive committee system was established. Given that proposals for reform of the Oireachtas were first advocated two decades earlier, the frustrations of Desmond and other members of the society were understandable. The system evolved further with social partnership during the late 1980s, giving social partners and more recently voluntary organisations a voice which, in turn, has led to many decisions being made outside parliament. The weakness of mechanisms of accountability has remained despite improvements since the 1990s to the parliamentary system, local government and the public service. An imbalance between central and local government and, it seems, a greater gap between state and society than exists in most Western countries have been the result of resistance to reform from the political system.[102]

Conclusion

Tuairim argued that reform of the state's institutions was critical if the country was to meet future economic and political challenges. The consideration it gave to the way policy was formulated, the electoral system, the role of the Oireachtas and how it interacted with citizens influenced the political mainstream. Tuairim's clearest influence in this area was in facilitating the establishment of the economic development branch in the Department of Finance and thus recognition of the importance of economic planning to Ireland's future. But the reluctance of the political establishment to implement wider reforms to the system of government meant that the structures were not put in place to ensure the long-term development of the country. Yet Tuairim's examination of the electoral system and arguments for changes to the government and parliament led it to co-operate with political parties, professional and vocational organisations and even civil servants. The civil service was, however, hesitant and, generally, defensive in its approach. Equally politicians seemed to be wedded to the adversarial system of government. Nevertheless, through the 1969 'Government and people' conference, meetings and study groups, Tuairim provided a platform on which members of the political establishment and others debated the efficiency of governmental institutions. Moreover, the 1959 referendum on the electoral system indicates that the main political parties were aware that the society could influence public opinion. The evidence suggests that Tuairim impacted upon the political mainstream and had an effect on the referenda on that question. It also points to a contrast in attitudes between the government and the opposition. The society's attempts during the 1960s and early 1970s to persuade political parties that it was in their interests to reform the Oireachtas also met with considerable resistance, particularly from Fianna Fáil. Nevertheless, the political establishment did respond, albeit slowly, to the need for reform. In contrast to the two main political parties, Labour's interest in a more consensual form of politics made it most amenable to Tuairim's views. This is reflected in the arguments that the party made regarding the need for Oireachtas reform as well as during the debates leading up to the first referendum. Though this added to the momentum for change, Seán Lemass's insistence in 1958 on retaining full government control of the policy process was an indication of how deep was the commitment to centralised decision-making. Jack Lynch was, in that regard, little different from his predecessors. A reluctance to engage with intellectuals and others outside their immediate circle remained as disillusionment with the political system became acute in 1970. Although some progress has been made, reform of parliament continues to be a long-term process. While Tuairim can certainly be said to have increased the momentum for reform and to have confronted the apathy this issue faced from the public, this continues to be a problem that confronts citizens in our day. The adversarial nature of politics and the fact that the way in which the Oireachtas operated directly affected politicians' interests meant that it was and continues to be a particularly difficult area for a voluntary society such as Tuairim to influence.

Notes

1 Michael Gallagher, 'Parliament', in Coakley and Gallagher, *Politics*, pp. 211–38; Muiris MacCarthaigh, *Accountability in Irish parliamentary politics* (Dublin: Institute of Public Administration, 2005), pp. 41–51, 65–72.
2 For example, *Hibernia*, June 1958, June 1961, April, May, November, December 1964, June, November 1965, 16 January 1976; *Irish Times*, 3 May 1964.
3 Thornley, *Ireland*, p. 17. The text also appeared in the *Irish Times* from 1 to 3 June 1964. See *Irish Times*, 19–24 October 1964 for a series of articles entitled 'Irish government observed' by Thornley and Chubb. See also Michael Gallagher and Lee Komito, 'The constituency role of Dáil deputies', in Coakley and Gallagher (eds), *Politics*, pp. 265–6.
4 See Bradley, 'Changing the rules', pp. 105–17; Ronan Fanning, 'The genesis of economic development', in John F. McCarthy (ed.), *Planning Ireland's future:*

the legacy of T. K. Whitaker (Dublin: Glendale, 1990), pp. 74–106; *Programme for economic expansion* (Dublin: Stationery Office, 1958); T. K. Whitaker, *Economic development* (Dublin: Stationery Office, 1958).

5 John A. O'Brien, *The vanishing Irish: the enigma of the modern world* (London: W. H. Allen, 1954).

6 See Daly, *Slow failure*, pp. 178–9; Tracey Connolly, 'The commission on emigration, 1948–1954', in Keogh, O'Shea and Quinlan (eds), *The lost decade*, pp. 87–104; Cormac Ó Gráda, *A rocky road: the Irish economy since the 1920s* (Manchester: Manchester University Press, 1997), pp. 25–9; Cormac Ó Gráda, 'The Irish macroeconomic crisis of 1955–56: how much was due to monetary policy?' *Irish economic and social history*, 25 (1998), 52–80. See also Daly, *Social and economic history*, p. 163.

7 See Finn, 'The influence of *Tuairim*', pp. 134–41.

8 For example, Keogh, *Twentieth-century Ireland*, pp. 88–90; Cormac Ó Gráda and Kevin O'Rourke, 'Irish economic growth, 1945–88', in Nicholas Crafts and Gianni Toniolo (eds), *Economic growth in Europe since 1945* (Cambridge: Cambridge University Press, 1996), pp. 388–421. See also Ronan Fanning, *The Irish Department of Finance, 1922–58* (Dublin: Institute of Public Administration, 1978).

9 For example, '*Economic development*', in Basil Chubb and Patrick Lynch (eds), *Economic development and planning* (Dublin: Institute of Public Administration, 1969), pp. 100, 114; Ferriter, *Transformation*, pp. 463–4, 467; J. J. Lee, '*Economic development* in historical perspective', in McCarthy (ed.), *Planning Ireland's future*, p. 122; Gary Murphy, 'From economic nationalism to European Union', in Girvin and Murphy (eds), *Lemass*, p. 31.

10 See *Economic development*, pp. 2, 206–9; Paul Bew and Henry Patterson, *Seán Lemass and the making of modern Ireland, 1945–66* (Dublin: Gill and Macmillan, 1982), p. 113; Garret FitzGerald, *Planning in Ireland: a PEP study* (Dublin: Institute of Public Administration, 1968), p. 23.

11 For example, Ó Gráda, *A rocky road*, pp. 114–16, 146–7, 168–71. Many including the government continued to view agriculture as the most important sector within the Irish economy.

12 Fanning, *Finance*, pp. 558–9, 602, 604; Chubb and Lynch (eds), *Economic development and planning*, pp. 302, 348. See also John Horgan, *Seán Lemass: the enigmatic patriot* (Dublin: Gill and Macmillan, 1997), pp. 219, 228–35; Murphy, ' "A wider perspective"', pp. 252–64.

13 *Economic development*, pp. 8, 226; NAI, DT, S16474A, Cabinet Committee on Economic Development – up to April 1960, 'Memorandum for the government: programme for economic expansion – follow-up procedure', 27 November 1958, James Ryan, Minister for Finance to Taoiseach, Eamon de Valera, 1 December 1958. See also Fanning, *Finance*, pp. 507, 516; *The Guardian*, 2 August 2002.

14 Patrick Lynch, 'Comment on foregoing article, the Irish economy viewed from without by C. F. Carter', *Studies*, 46:182 (Summer 1957), 145–7. Lynch claimed Tuairim reflected 'an encouraging recognition by some university graduates of the need for struggle against the intellectual inertia which still

paralyses action in too many fields'. See Donal Barrington, 'Foreword', in Patrick Lynch and C. F. Carter, *Planning for economic development* (Dublin: Tuairim, 1959); *Irish Times*, 13 April, 7 November 1959; *Hibernia*, May 1959. Lynch's article was also published in the *Irish Times* in three instalments from 25 to 27 May 1959.
15 Patrick Lynch, 'The economics of independence: some questions of Irish economics', in Lynch and Carter, *Planning*, pp. 1–18, and C. F. Carter, 'A problem of economic development', *Administration*, 7:2 (1959), 91–118; T. J. Barrington, 'The next necessary thing', *Administration*, 7 (1959), 119–41; Chubb and Lynch (eds), *Economic development and planning*, pp. 128–76.
16 Lynch, 'Independence', p. 3.
17 Charles Carter, 'A problem of economic development', in Lynch and Carter, *Planning*, p. 20.
18 Ibid., pp. 26–7.
19 Peter McKevitt, 'Planning, notes and comments', *Christus Rex*, 13 (June 1959), 214–17; *Hibernia*, May 1959; *Irish Times*, 13, 15, 17 April, 28, 29 May 1959; *The Spectator*, 5 June 1959; Barrington, 'The next necessary thing', pp. 119–41.
20 *Irish Times*, 13 April 1959.
21 UCD, AD, P24, Blythe papers, 2482, 804, 'Brian Inglis, "Irish notebook", *The Spectator*, 5 June 1959'.
22 Seanad Éireann Debates, vol. 51, col. 287, 'Finance bill', 15 July 1959; Dáil Éireann Debates, vol. 198, col. 301, 'Transport bill', 28 November 1962.
23 McKevitt, 'Notes and comments'. See Patrick J. Corish, *Maynooth College, 1795–1995* (Dublin: Gill and Macmillan, 1995), pp. 315–16, 348, 467 for further information on McKevitt. For the exchange between Newman and Lynch see *Irish Times*, 15, 17 April 1959.
24 *Irish Times*, 8 April 1960.
25 Barrington, 'Foreword', in Lynch and Carter, *Planning*.
26 *Hibernia*, May 1959.
27 Barrington, 'Foreword', in Lynch and Carter, *Planning*.
28 NAI, DT, S16673A, Economic development: establishment of organisation in Department of Finance, Ryan to Lemass, 10 July 1959, Secretary, Department of Finance, T. K. Whitaker, to Secretary, Department of Taoiseach, Maurice Moynihan, 18 September 1959, 'Memorandum entitled Economic development – Department of Finance organisation'. NAI, DT, S16673A, Economic development, Department of Finance organisation, Ryan to Lemass, 10 July 1959. See also NAI, DT, S166066B, Economic development schemes 1956–, *Irish Press*, 1 October 1960.
29 NAI, DT, S16673A, Economic development: establishment of organisation in Department of Finance, 'Memorandum', p. 6.
30 NAI, DT, S16474A, Economic Development, Ryan to Taoiseach Eamon de Valera, 1 December 1958.
31 Ibid., Lemass to Ryan, 2 December 1958.
32 Murphy, *Promised Land*, p. 305.
33 Tom Garvin, *Judging Lemass: the measure of the man* (Dublin: Royal Irish Academy, 2009), p. 182.

34 NAI, DT, S16474A, Lemass to Ryan, 2 December 1958.
35 See *Irish Times*, 19–22 August 1963, 15, 16, 19 April 1965; Thornley, *Ireland*, pp. 3, 17. See also *Irish Times*, 1–3 June, 19–24 October 1964.
36 Manning, *Dillon*, p. 321; Cornelius O'Leary, *Irish elections, 1918–1977: parties, voters and proportional representation* (Dublin: Gill and Macmillan, 1979), pp. 46–58. See Garret FitzGerald, 'P.R.: the great debate', *Studies*, 48:189 (Spring 1959), 1–20; Gallagher, *Labour*, pp. 35–8.
37 NAI, DT, S16514E, Third amendment of the constitution bill, 1958, Frank Winder to Eamon de Valera, 31 January 1959. See UCD, AD, P24, Blythe papers 1468, 1473, Barrington to Blythe, 18 February 1959; *Irish Times*, 13, 23 February 1959. The memorandum was circulated privately to the members of the government, the executive of the Fianna Fáil party and a number of other individuals including Ernest Blythe. The *Irish Times* was aware of its contents. See also Tuairim Research group, *P.R.: for or against?* (Dublin: Tuairim, 1959), foreword. The other members of the research group were Patrick Fitzgerald, Deirdre O'Donovan, Ronan Brocklesby, Richard Dennis, Maurice Gaffney, and from Cork, Patrick Daly, Dermot Hare and Dermot Moloney. See also Hederman O'Brien papers, 'Council', 1958–59. *Tuairim*'s Council resolved the difficulties in relation to the membership of the research group.
38 NAI, DT, S16514E, Third amendment, 'Memorandum on the proposed referendum by the Tuairim research group on proportional representation', p. 2.
39 Ibid., p. 3. The group claimed that under the first-past-the-post system, there was no more incentive to agree on policy than under PR-stv, when some agreement on policy is necessary to encourage the electorate to give their second and third preferences to other opposition candidates.
40 See E. M. Syddique, 'Lakeman, Enid (1903–1995)', www.oxforddnb.com/view/article/63221 *Oxford Dictionary of National Biography* (Oxford: Oxford University Press, 2004) accessed on 8 October 2008. See also Tuairim, *P.R.*, foreword; UCD, AD, P24, Blythe papers 1469, Frank Winder to Blythe, 14 May 1959. The group met others like Professor Denis Gwynne, Dr Seamus Fitzgerald, Kennedy Roche and the Cork Executive of the Labour Party.
41 Interview with Ronan Keane, Dublin, 24 May 2005. See also Garret FitzGerald, 'P.R.'; UCD, AD, P24, Blythe papers, 1468, 1473, Barrington to Blythe, 18 February 1959, Blythe to Dr F. A. Hermes, 17 April 1959. Barrington claimed that Blythe's views would be all the more valuable because he was unlikely to agree with the research group.
42 Tuairim, *P.R.*, pp. 17–18, 21. The group wrote that Protestants could lose a seat in the Dun Laoghaire Rathdown constituency, where Booth was a TD. It claimed that the parties might select a Catholic rather than a Protestant as was more likely under the current system. See also O'Leary, *Elections*, pp. 5–11, 49, 53; Richard Sinnott, 'The rules of the electoral game', in Coakley and Gallagher (eds), *Politics*, p. 107.
43 See *Irish Times*, 31 January, 11 May 1959; *Irish Independent*, 10 May 1959; Desmond, *Finally*, pp. 201–3; FitzGerald, *Reflections*, pp. 91–6. See also UCD Archives P39, Fine Gael papers, 51, Lakeman to chairman, Research Group

on Proportional Representation, Tuairim, 5 December 1958. Lakeman wrote to Winder, asking to meet the research group. See *Irish Times*, 11 December 1958. Deirdre O'Donovan, on behalf of the group, wrote to the *Irish Times* seeking the views of informed persons and bodies on the proposed change to the electoral system. See also Enid Lakeman and James D. Lambert, *Voting in democracies: a study of proportional electoral systems* (London: Faber and Faber Limited, 1959).

44 For example, FitzGerald, 'P.R.', pp. 17–20; *Irish Times*, 4, 9, 13, 18 December 1958, 3 February, 28 April, 13 June 1959, 19 April 1965; interview with Maurice Gaffney, Dublin, 9 June 2005; O'Leary, *Elections*, pp. 56, 69. Basil Chubb and Kennedy Roche both said that they favoured the existing system. The one exception appeared to be Cornelius O'Leary, who defended the first-past-the-post system. See also Tuairim, *P.R.*, p. 22; James Hogan, *Election and representation* (Cork: Cork University Press, 1945). According to the group's members, the only individuals who influenced their views were James Hogan, Lakeman and, ironically, given his strong support for the prosposed system, Blythe.

45 Tuairim, *P.R.*, pp. 6–7. The pamphlet referred to Germany and Italy in the period following World War I and France after World War II, and noted that despite having PR-stv, both Malta and Tasmania had a two-party system.

46 Ibid., pp. 10, 20. Italics in original text. It was argued that the government's proposal to establish a commission to decide electoral boundaries meant that gerrymandering was not an issue.

47 Ibid., pp. 13, 20. The group contrasted Ireland with Britain, where it claimed that there were about 200 safe seats each for Labour and the Conservatives.

48 *Irish Times*, 13 February 1959. See also *Irish Times*, 17 February 1959. Having thanked the newspaper, Winder stressed that the group had not yet completed its study.

49 Seanad Éireann Debates, vol. 50, col. 886, 'Third amendment on the constitution bill, 1958', 19 February 1959. See NAI, DT, S16514F, Third amendment, Rúnaí Príobháideach, Department of Taoiseach to Winder, 5 March 1959. An acknowledgement was sent. At the bottom of the letter, a handwritten note stated that the matter was mentioned to the Taoiseach and that the 'question of any further action may be deferred for the moment'.

50 Sinnott, 'The rules of the electoral game', pp. 110–12. See Dáil Éireann Debates, vol. 172, cols. 1287–9, 'Third amendment on the constitution bill, 1958', 28 January 1959. De Valera used imaginary figures for three fictitious candidates, A, B and C, to illustrate his case. The Minister for Defence, Kevin Boland, put forward similar arguments earlier in the Dáil. See Dáil Éireann Debates, vol. 171, col. 1295, 'Third amendment on the constitution bill, 1958', 2 December 1958, and also FitzGerald, 'P.R.', pp. 7, 14–15.

51 *Irish Independent*, 16 February 1959. See also *Hibernia*, October 1958; interview with Barrington, 19 May 2005. Barrington stated that while there was a case to be made against the existing electoral system, he remained a PR man.

52 NAI, DT, 2003/16/273, Tuairim general, Frank Daly, chairman of the Cork branch, to Lynch, 22 November 1967, Runaí Peasanta, Department of

Taoiseach to Franklin O'Sullivan, 8 September 1967. Lynch, despite many invitations, appears to have spoken to the society on only one occasion; that was to the Cork branch in October 1967. See *Irish Times*, 1 May 1959 for a speech by Lynch where he strongly argued in favour of the proposed electoral system. See also T. Ryle Dwyer, *Nice fellow: a biography of Jack Lynch* (Cork: Mercier Press, 2001), pp. 30, 41–2, 55; interview with Diarmuid Ó Cearbhaill, Galway, 12 December 2003.
53 O'Hanrahan papers, MacErlean, 'On Tuairim'. This document claimed that the 'two political camps complained that it leaned too far towards the other side: a criticism, it was felt, which crowned the effort'.
54 Dáil Éireann Debates, vol. 174, col. 1629, 'Third amendment on the constitution bill, 1958', 5 May 1959.
55 Ibid., cols. 1992, 1996, 13 May 1959.
56 Ibid., cols. 1657, 1658, 5 May 1959.
57 Ibid., col. 1707, 6 May 1959.
58 Ibid., cols. 1660–1, 5 May 1959.
59 Interview with Barrington, 19 May 2005. See Patrick Lynch and James Meenan (eds), *Essays in memory of Alexis FitzGerald* (Dublin: Incorporated Law Society of Ireland, 1987). See also UCD, AD, P39, Fine Gael papers, 83, 'Tuairim pamphlet'.
60 *Hibernia*, June 1959. See J. L. McCracken, *Representative government in Ireland: a study of Dáil Éireann, 1919–48* (London: Oxford University Press, 1958); Tuairim, *P.R.*, foreword. See also *Irish Times*, 28 April, 15 May 1959; O'Leary, *Elections*, pp. 49–58; Tuairim, *P.R.*, p. 23.
61 O'Hanrahan papers, MacErlean, 'On *Tuairim*'.
62 UCD, AD, P39, Fine Gael papers, 128 (23), 'T. F. O'Higgins, TD speaking at Tuairim discussion at "The referendum – the people's choice", Wednesday 4 September 1968, at the Intercontinental Hotel, Limerick, 8pm'. See also *Cork Examiner*, 24 February 1968. The Parliamentary Secretary to the Ministry for Fisheries and Agriculture, Don Davern, spoke to the Cork branch.
63 *Irish Times*, 20 April 1968. During the mid-1960s, Chubb was on Tuairim's mailing list. See also interview with Desmond, 11 May 2005. Desmond claimed that Tuairim's pamphlet had a long-term impact on Thornley and Chubb and their television programme in 1968. See Gallagher, *Labour*, p. 75 for Thornley and Chubb's prediction. See also *Irish Times*, 19–22 August 1963, 19–24 October 1964. See Dáil Éireann Debates, vol. 233, col. 1091, 'Third amendment of the constitution bill', 26 March 1968; Seanad Éireann Debates, vol. 77, col. 885, 'Electoral (amendment) bill', 10 April 1974. Bobby Molloy, the Fianna Fáil TD, noted Thornley's preference for the alternative vote while John Horgan, then a Labour Party senator, referred to Tuairim's PR pamphlet. See also *Irish Times*, 10 May, 21 October 1968.
64 Dáil Éireann Debates, vol. 236, col. 645, 'Referendum (amendment) bill', 9 July 1968.
65 Whyte, *Dáil deputies*, pp. 1–2. The pamphlet noted that, unlike many other countries, Ireland lacked a reference book on the composition of the Dáil. This was a difficulty that McCracken had also recorded. The other members

of the research group were Carmel Kelly, a science teacher at Alexandra College, Aubrey McElhatton, an accountant and lecturer in economics, John Glynn, also an accountant, and Peter Doyle, a graduate student. One journalist who was particularly helpful to the research group was the political correspondent of the *Irish Times*, Michael McInerney. See also See Basil Chubb, '"Going about persecuting civil servants": the role of the Irish parliamentary representative', *Political Studies*, 11:3 (1963), 272–86.

66 Whyte, *Dáil deputies*, pp. 3–4. The questionnaire was sent to 141 deputies. As two seats were vacant and a questionnaire was not sent to the Ceann Comhairle, this was slightly less than the full Dáil strength of 144 seats. Urban deputies were more responsive than those from rural areas. The political affiliation of the two deputies from the independents and minor parties was not specified because it was promised that the information given would remain confidential. The 52 per cent response rate compared favourably to the 28 per cent who responded to the 1963 questionnaire of British MPs by the *Observer* of London. See also Brian Farrell, 'The Dáil deputies: "the 1969 generation"', *Economic and Social Review*, 2:3 (1971), 312, 25; Brian Farrell, 'Ireland: from friends and neighbours to clients and partisans: some dimensions of parliamentary representation under pr-stv', in Vernon Bogdanor (ed.), *Representatives of the people? Parliamentarians and constituents in Western democracies* (Aldershot: Gower Publishing Company, 1985), p. 243.

67 A Citizens' Information Board was established in 2000 to provide information about public services to citizens: www.citizensinformationboard.ie, accessed on 5 December 2008. Each deputy has also been given an office and secretarial assistance. See also MacCarthaigh, *Accountability*, pp. 239, 95; Whyte, *Dáil deputies*, pp. 16–19.

68 For example, Gallagher and Komito, 'The constituency role of Dáil deputies', p. 258. See Michael Laver, *A new electoral system for Ireland?* (Dublin: Policy Institute and All Party Oireachtas Committee on the Constitution, 1998); MacCarthaigh, *Accountability*, pp. 97–152. See also Sinnott, 'The rules of the electoral game', pp. 120–2.

69 Dáil Éireann Debates, vol. 220, col. 744, 'Military services pensions – private members' business', 2 February 1966.

70 Interview with Desmond, 11 May 2005. See also Minutes of committee meetings of Tuairim's Dublin branch, 14 December 1965, 17 May, 8 November 1966, 8 January 1967; *Irish Times*, 28 January 1966.

71 Interview with Desmond, 11 May 2005. See NAI, DT, 2002/8/320, Parliamentary reform, 'Proposals for the reform of parliamentary procedure in Dáil Éireann, Parliamentary Labour party', 30 October 1968. See also Desmond, *Finally*, pp. 24, 28–38; Gallagher, *Labour*, pp. 67–103; John Horgan, *Labour: the price of power* (Dublin: Gill and Macmillan, 1986), p. 82.

72 *Irish Times*, 20 January, 28 October 1967, 20 March 1968. Asmal was a long-term political activist who helped found the British and Irish anti-apartheid movements. After the fall of apartheid in 1994, he became a minister in the African National Congress government.

73 Carty, *Government and people*, p. 3. See also Peacocke papers, 'Address by

Franklin O'Sullivan, Vice-President, Tuairim and chairman, Dublin branch to Cork branch of Tuairim', 4 September 1969; minutes of committee meetings of Tuairim's Dublin branch, 25 June 1968, 27 May 1969.
74 Carty, *Government and people*, pp. 2, 26. Also present were Tomás Roseingrave, the national Director of Muintir na Tíre, John H. Harbinson, the President of the Institute of Engineers of Ireland, Myles McSwiney, the General Secretary of the Royal Institute of Architects of Ireland, and Rev. Bro. Eamon O Beachain, FMS, the Headmaster of Moyle Park College, Clondalkin, Dublin, as well as Tomás Breathnach, the chief of the Rural Economy Division of Foras Talúntais, who replaced Dr Tom Walsh, its Director who was ill. Walsh, along with the other chairmen, had given helpful advice in advance of the conference. See T. J. Barrington, 'Big government and local community', *Christus Rex*, 24 (July 1970), 200. Barrington referred to Tuairim's pamphlet as evidence of the need for reform of the political system. See also *Hibernia*, August, September 1961, 24 May 1974. In New Delhi in 1961, McCarthy, an active member of the trade union movement, joined representatives of nearly eighty countries at the World Confederation of Organisations of the Teaching Professions. He was Secretary of the Committee on Technical and Vocational Education, which was established as part of the confederation, and as General Secretary of the VTA from 1956 to 1972 he attended various international conferences.
75 NAI, DFA, 2002/19/70, London, 'Handwritten note regarding invitation to communications conference which Tuairim organised for 13/14 December, 24/11/1969'. This was one of a number of handwritten notes debating whether civil servants should attend Tuairim's conference. Carty, *Government and people*, pp. 46–7. Apart from those previously noted, the civil servants in attendance included John C. Horgan, the chairperson of the Association of Civil Servants, Mr P. Ó Murchadha, the Assistant Secretary of the Department of Defence, John Whelan, a principal officer in the Department of Finance, Mr J. J. O'Keefe, also a principal in the Department of Industry and Commerce, the information officers Gearóid O'Sullivan of the Department of Labour, Eibhlis MacCurtain of the Department of Posts and Telegraphs and Patrick MacHale of the Department of Social Welfare, Mr S. P. Bedford, Assistant Secretary of the Revenue Commissioners, and Dr D. Murphy of the secretariat of the National Science Council. Mr D. M. Candy, Meath County Manager and President of the County Manager and City Managers Association, represented local government.
76 NAI, DFA, 2002/19/70, 'Handwritten note, 2/12/1969'.
77 MacCarthaigh, *Accountability*, p. 73.
78 Ibid., p. 21.
79 Interview with Ó Cearbhaill, 12 December 2003. See also interview with Desmond, 11 May 2005.
80 Carty, *Government and people*, p. 35. See also ibid., pp. 3, 47; NAI, DT, 98/6/501, Tuairim: general, Taoiseach's private secretary to Taoiseach, 4 September 1969, Franklin O'Sullivan to the Taoiseach's Private Secretary, 4 September 1969, Replies from Taoiseach Private Secretary, 8 September;

NAI, DFA, 2002/19/70, London, 'Handwritten note, 2/12/1969'. Representatives of all government departments were invited to attend. The pamphlet referred to the absence of representatives of the Departments of Justice, Agriculture and Local Government and the Government Information Bureau. The Taoiseach, Jack Lynch, and the Minister for External Affairs, Patrick Hillery, were also invited but said they were unavailable. The Department of Agriculture would not attend because An Foras Talúntais would 'be there in force'. The pamphlet noted that representatives of the universities and many trade unions were also absent.

81 Carty, *Government and people*, p. 15.
82 Ibid., pp. 15–16. FitzGerald withdrew 'cowardice' and replaced it with 'misplaced loyalty'.
83 Ibid., pp. 50–1. For further discussion of the value of Whitaker's speech, see Mary E. Daly, *The spirit of earnest inquiry: the Statistical and Social Inquiry Society of Ireland, 1847–1997* (Dublin: Statistical and Social Inquiry Society of Ireland, 1997), p. 153; Fanning, *Finance*, pp. 502–3. See also Patrick Lynch, 'Administrative theory and the civil service', *Administration*, 4:4 (1956–57), 97–116, and 'The economist and public policy', *Studies*, 42:167 (Autumn 1953), 256–60. Lynch was already arguing in the early 1950s for civil servants to speak in public.
84 Carty, *Government and people*, pp. 8–9, 12, 15–16.
85 Murphy, *Promised Land*, pp. 15–18. See also MacCarthaigh, *Accountability*, p. 83.
86 Carty, *Government and people*, p. 34.
87 See Finn, 'The influence of *Tuairim*', pp. 114–16. Tuairim organised a weekend conference in 1961 at which an alternative system of local taxation was put forward. Its proposals came to the attention of Seán Lemass and the Minister for Local Government, Neil Blaney, who, despite wishing to introduce reforms, did not overcome the difficulties that were involved. See also Charles McCarthy, *The distasteful challenge* (Dublin: Institute of Public Administration, 1968).
88 Carty, *Government and people*, p. 30.
89 Ibid., p. 5. See *Irish Times*, 27 September, 17 November 1969. See also Daly, *Buffer state*, pp. 471–3; Daly, *Slow failure*, pp. 248–55; Fanning, *Finance*, pp. 558–9.
90 Carty, *Government and people*, p. 45.
91 See Daly, *Slow failure*, pp. 248–55. See also NAI, DT, 98/6/501, the Secretary, Department of Taoiseach to Patrick Farrell, Correspondence Secretary of the Dublin branch, 31 October 1969, Response, 5 November. The Secretary of the Department of the Taoiseach said he was unavailable to attend Tuairim's seminar on the Buchanan report. Farrell asked that the matter be sent to other members of the department. A handwritten note, dated 6 November 1969, stated that no action was necessary.
92 NAI, DT, 2003/16/263, Tuairim: general, Neville Keery to Lynch, 31 December 1969. Jack Lynch and Fianna Fáil's General Secretary, Tommy Mullins, had received a report of the conference from Keery, who on the

nomination of the national executive represented the party. See also Francis Carty to the Taoiseach, reply, 18 March 1970. Lynch wrote that he looked forward to reading the pamphlet. Neville Keery's papers are in UCC. See, for example, Neville Keery papers, University College Cork, Special collections, Press release, Box no. 43, Topic files: women, youth, transport, Tuairim, Taca, sundry correspondence issues related C, 'Paper on the role of political parties by Senator Neville Keery to Tuairim conference on government and people – creative dialogue at RDS [Royal Dublin Society]'.

93 NAI, DT, 2003/16/263, Tuairim: general, Patrick Farrell, Correspondence Secretary to the Taoiseach, 'Resolution', 25 April 1970; *Irish Times*, 27 April 1970. See also Keery papers, 'Tuairim to all representatives in attendance at Tuairim conference held at RDS, Ballsbridge, Dublin, on 13/14 December 1969'. Tuairim suggested that the conference could be an annual event.

94 NAI, DT, 2003/16/263, Tuairim: general, Rúnaí Príobháideach, Department of Taoiseach to Patrick Farrell, 21 May 1970, Patrick Farrell to the Taoiseach, 12 June 1970.

95 Maurice Manning papers, Tuairim file, letter from O'Sullivan; NAI, DT, 2003/16/263, Tuairim: general, Fitzpatrick and Keery to members of Fianna Fáil parliamentary party. A handwritten note, dated 19 July 1971, to the Taoiseach stated, 'You will hardly wish to answer these questions but you may wish to see them.' See also Barry Desmond papers, Tuairim file, letter from Barry Desmond, 21 June 1971; Maurice Manning papers, Tuairim file, Dublin branch, 'Press release', 14 June 1972. The Tuairim members Francis Xavier Carty, Ian Hart, Mary C. MacCarthy, P. J. McEvoy, Kathleen O'Higgins, Mona Stanton and Michael Woods were all part of the study group. See Séamus Ó Cinnéide, 'Dr. Ian Hart – an appreciation', *Administration*, 28:1 (1980), 3–5. Ian Hart worked in the Economic and Social Research Institute. He was an important figure in the study group. Sadly, he died in 1980, aged forty.

96 Manning papers, Tuairim file, Dublin branch, 'Press release', 14 June 1972, from Francis Xavier Carty, National President and chairperson of the Dublin branch of Tuairim.

97 Manning papers, Tuairim file, Letter from Ian Hart, 22 February 1972.

98 Manning papers, Tuairim file, Dublin branch, 'Press release'. They also called for deputies' salaries to be linked to those of public servants and for the reorganisation of the Seanad to make it a truly vocational institution, representative of national and professional organisations.

99 NAI, DT, 2002/8/320, Parliamentary reform, Oirechtas committee: a suggestion for an experiment in 1971, 'Paper by Neville Keery', 6 January 1971. Keery sent his paper both to Jack Lynch and the Chief Whip, David Andrews. Desmond O'Malley was the committee chairperson; its other members were David Andrews, Richard Burke, Hugh Byrne, Frank Carter, Patrick Cooney, Joe Dowling, Tom Fitzpatrick, James Gallagher, Augustine A. Healy, Michael O'Kennedy, Michael O'Leary and David Thornley. See NAI, DT, 2004/21/365, Report of informal committee on reform of Dáil procedures.

100 Finnegan papers, undated newspaper, most probably *Cork Examiner*. Speaking at the same meeting, the chairperson of the committee, Des O'Malley, did not comment on the Dáil. Instead, he focused on the Seanad, criticising how its members were nominated. John A. Murphy chaired the meeting.
101 Desmond papers, Tuairim file, Barry Desmond, *The houses of the Oireachtas – a plea for reform* (Dublin: Leinster House, 1975). See also MacCarthaigh, *Accountability*, pp. 77, 80–2.
102 Katy Howard and Muiris MacCarthaigh (eds), *Recycling the state: politics of adaptation in Ireland* (Dublin: Irish Academic Press, 2007).

3

North and south: Tuairim and a divided island

Tuairim contributed significantly to a reassessment of nationalist attitudes in relation to Northern Ireland. While Tuairim's views impacted most directly on southern thinking, the society also attempted to influence unionism. Tuairim, however, was closer to nationalists. In this regard, the extent to which there was interaction between the society's members and northern nationalists was impressive. Tuairim's two pamphlets challenged the traditional nationalist attitude that maintained that Ireland was one nation and that Britain was responsible for partition. These publications reflected the society's ideals and hopes for a new relationship between nationalists and unionists. The context in which the pamphlets were written illustrates how radical they were for Ireland in the late 1950s. The pages that follow consider the extent to which the society challenged the orthodoxy of the time and paved the way for better relations between the two communities on the island. As well as producing the pamphlets, Tuairim's members wrote several articles relating to Northern Ireland in the current affairs periodical *Hibernia*, while its meetings addressed subjects such as the nature of the opposition within Northern Ireland, the wisdom of the Irish government's Northern policy and north–south co-operation. The meetings also reflected the different opinions that were held by Tuairim's members. These included those with traditionally republican interpretations and those attempting to break down the sectarian divide within Northern Ireland. Certain Tuairim members' involvement in distinct organisations such as the Connolly Association, the Irish Association and National Unity illustrated this diversity of views. The different contexts in which the society's members held these beliefs highlight how emotive a topic Northern Ireland could be and the obstacles to an independent society influencing public policy that existed in Ireland at this time.

Traditional views of partition

Tuairim's pamphlets *Uniting Ireland* (1958), written by Donal Barrington, and *Partition today: a northern viewpoint* (1959), by Norman Gibson, challenged orthodox nationalist views and attempted to explain unionist fears. The lack of understanding between the two states and the two communities within Northern Ireland was reflected in the ongoing refusal of the southern government, during the 1950s, to recognise the government of Northern Ireland. The stated objective of the southern government's policies was a thirty-two-county independent republic. However, the emphasis placed by southern politicians on the Catholic and Gaelic nature of the southern state alienated northern unionists. Nationalists' belief in the evils of partition was perhaps most apparent in the border campaign conducted by the Irish Republican Army (IRA) from 1956 to 1962. The high level of emotional support for the IRA's actions, in both the north and the south, added to the difficulties for the more moderate Anti-Partition League in Northern Ireland. Nationalists suffered discrimination from both the local and the central authorities, were divided over whether to take their seats in the Northern Ireland parliament and were alienated by Unionist governments, which reflected the wishes of the majority and emphasised the Protestant nature of the state.[1]

Certain individuals were, nevertheless, seeking better relations between north and south as well as between the two communities within Northern Ireland. Desmond Fennell's *The northern Catholic: an inquiry*, published in 1958, argued that the ineffectuality of the Anti-Partition League was making the need for a new departure increasingly clear to many nationalists. Fennell, who had attended some Tuairim meetings and became a controversial commentator on Northern Ireland, welcomed the new thinking, which, he claimed, was beginning to emerge within the northern Catholic community.

In relation to southern nationalism, the traditional nationalist understanding of Northern Ireland was questioned by both Michael Sheehy, a young Catholic, and Ernest Blythe, a former government minister from an Ulster Protestant background. Blythe, who during his youth developed a passion for Irish, had a distinctive position in relation to unionism since the 1920s. His book *Briseadh na teorann* ('The smashing of the border'), written in 1955 in Irish, recognised that 'partition existed not because of the British but because of the northern Protestants'.[2] Sheehy also criticised the Irish government's policy on partition. He wrote that unionists had profound reasons for not agreeing to a united Ireland and called for the south to adopt more realistic policies. The fact that the Northern Ireland Prime Minister, Lord Brookeborough, was positive about Sheehy's book may have militated against its receiving a favourable press in the south. Blythe's writings, on the other hand, seemed to make an impact upon those in positions of influence. While nationalists north and south had thus begun to question the effectiveness of their approach, Garret FitzGerald noted in *Studies* in 1956 that indifference and lack of understanding were the dominant features of relations between the neighbouring states.[3]

Unionists insisted that co-operation with the southern government was conditional upon its recognition of the constitutional status of Northern Ireland. Their actions were motivated by the threat that they perceived as being posed by the southern state and by the northern minority, combined with their religious, economic and cultural fears of being incorporated into a predominantly Catholic state. These concerns were reflected in the hard-line position of Lord Brookeborough, whose policies resonated with the Protestant nature of the state. On the other hand, Brian Maginess, a minister in successive Northern governments, believed that the 'Unionist party needed to develop a broader and more inclusive conception of the Union which would appeal to…Catholics'.[4] The historian Henry Patterson has, however, argued that in supporting 'a more inclusive Unionism' Maginess misunderstood nationalist attitudes and threatened to undermine the basis of support for the Ulster Unionist Party (UUP). Similarly, when, at a conference at Garron Tower in 1958, George B. Newe, the Secretary of the Northern Ireland Council of Social Welfare, appealed to Catholics to co-operate with Protestants for their mutual benefit, he, like Maginess, was heavily criticised by his own community. This illustrates the strength of the sectarian divide in Northern Ireland. Thus when Cardinal D'Alton put forward a detailed a plan to end partition, the lack of enthusiasm from unionists was unsurprising. Moreover, its prospects and provisions received a similarly lukewarm reception from Eamon de Valera.[5] As in the relations between the two states, an atmosphere of suspicion and distrust was prevalent between unionists and nationalists. This was the context in which Tuairim attempted to contribute to a better understanding between the two communities, and between north and south.

Uniting Ireland

Uniting Ireland was the first pamphlet that Tuairim published. Though it appeared in *Studies* in December 1957, a fact that diminished its novelty, Tuairim by publishing the pamphlet brought the views therein to a wider public. Donal Barrington wrote his study in reaction to the IRA campaign then underway and to Frank Gallagher's book *The indivisible island*. Gallagher, a journalist and historian who was close to the Taoiseach, Eamon de Valera, reiterated the traditional nationalist understanding of the relationship between Ireland and Britain that was prevalent during the 1950s. His was an influential account, which has been described as being 'for many years orthodoxy for Irish nationalists, north and south of the border'.[6] Barrington criticised this nationalist orthodoxy and in so doing aimed to explain Unionist fears. He said that to this end, prior to its publication, he sent drafts of the pamphlet to Norman Gibson, a northern economist. In support of his argument, Barrington's pamphlet referred to 'the official historian' of the Orange Order, Robert Mackie Sibbett, a Presbyterian and a 'deeply religious man', who had written a number of books on the Orange Order.[7] Barrington thus attempted to illustrate the 'vital importance of the religious factor underlying Partition'. Unlike Gallagher's traditional view, Barrington's claim was that partition was the result of the divisions within Ireland rather than the machinations of the British government.

Barrington focused on unionists rather than the British government as the reason behind the establishment and continued existence of Northern Ireland. While he accepted that there was discrimination in Northern Ireland, he claimed that the reason behind it was a unionist determination to ensure that Catholics did not get 'any political or economic power', which in turn emanated from the unionist view of northern nationalists as 'disloyal'. Even though Barrington had used examples of discrimination from Gallagher's book, he was critical of his use of language and especially his references to 'free Ireland', which, Barrington argued, implied that the 'North is unfree or enslaved'. For Barrington, the logical consequence of such 'propaganda' was the IRA's campaign. He claimed that successive Irish governments had used similar language since independence and that that they were at least partly responsible for the deaths that had resulted from that violence. Barrington wrote:

> The logical follow-through from such propaganda is a resistance movement. If the North is 'occupied territory' held in subjection by a 'British army of occupation', one need not be surprised if the young men of the North rise in arms against the invader or if the young men of the South go to the assistance of their Northern fellow-countrymen.

Certainly, the first inter-party government and the Fianna Fáil opposition were not blameless, for the propaganda campaigns of the late 1940s heightened expectations for the ending of partition, which while unfulfilled led people to take matters into their own hands.[8]

A new nationalist approach was necessary, 'a policy of persuasion'. Barrington argued that new policies were needed to reduce the tensions between north and south and between nationalists and unionists within Northern Ireland. This, he hoped, would 'create an atmosphere in which a unity of wills can grow'. The south first had to end its coercionist policies, and in return unionists should dismantle the system of discrimination in operation and reform the electoral system. Nationalists had to respect the wishes of the majority of the people of Northern Ireland, which was to remain part of the United Kingdom. Barrington was thereby one of the first people to articulate the principle of consent, which maintained that a united Ireland would not become a reality until that was the desire of a majority of people within Northern Ireland. In truth, he went further and urged the Irish government to give the same guarantee as the British government had under the terms of the Ireland Act in 1949: that there could not be unity without the consent of the parliament of Northern Ireland.[9] He proceeded to outline a number of steps that needed to be taken, not least by northern nationalists, if a 'unity of wills' would be created. The first was for the Northern minority to dissolve its existing political organisations and support the Liberal and Labour Parties in Northern Ireland. Then he called for the Catholic clergy, and specifically Catholic organisations such as the Ancient Order of Hibernians, to desist from playing a part in politics. He was also critical of voluntary and sporting associations for introducing politics into their organisations. In that context, he urged an end to the Gaelic Athletic Association's ban on foreign games. His wish was for increased co-operation between unionists and nationalists in all areas of Irish life.

Barrington's aim was to demonstrate that 'Irishmen can live in peace and can solve their problems in a spirit of friendship'. More than that, he called for people to be tolerant of differences and for 'a new Irish culture and a new form of nationalism' that would embrace all traditions and religions on the island. Such inclusive language was quite radical for Ireland in the late 1950s. It was within this context that it praised the Young Irelanders and Thomas Davis. Barrington also quoted from the *Belfast Telegraph* and the poet John Hewitt. The latter was to illustrate the absurdity of denying 'the title of Irishman to a man whose people have been living in Ireland since before the "Mayflower"'. Both were interesting choices, one being a liberal unionist newspaper which in the late 1950s advocated reform and, unusually, was read by both nationalists and unionists, and the other a poet who along with other members of the literary community in Northern Ireland 'provided an alternative Protestant version of Northern culture' to that offered by the unionist government.[10] While Hewitt's vision of a regional Northern Ireland sought to 'transcend sectarian division(s)', the reality was that along with many individuals from a Northern Protestant background, he lacked a full understanding of Catholics. Nevertheless, such diversity, along with the *Belfast Telegraph*'s calls for a more inclusive society, was to an extent subversive of the official unionist belief, which viewed the state in exclusively Protestant terms. In this context, it was clear that it would be a long time (Barrington suggested fifty years) before there was 'mutual trust and understanding' between unionists and nationalists. Barrington recognised this and described Cardinal D'Alton's plan as 'premature'. Rather than discussing proposals for a united Ireland, he called on the south to concentrate on improving relations with the northern state and between the two traditions on the island.

Partition today: a northern viewpoint

Having put the case for a new nationalist policy, Tuairim and Barrington invited Norman Gibson to set out his views, that is, those of a Northern Protestant who supported the constitutional position of Northern Ireland. Gibson, a lecturer in economics at Queen's University, spoke at a Tuairim meeting in Dublin in September 1958, and his pamphlet *Partition today: a northern viewpoint* was published in January 1959. This was not the first occasion on which he spoke at a meeting in Dublin. In 1957, he delivered a paper to the Statistical and Social Inquiry of Ireland, and shortly afterwards he was invited to lunch by the Secretary of the Department of Finance, T. K. Whitaker. As the years passed, Gibson continued to show an interest in the whole of Ireland, and his views were, it seems, increasingly sought after in Dublin and London. For instance, in the early 1970s, he was a member of the Northern Ireland Commission, which advised the Secretary of State for Northern Ireland, William Whitelaw, on matters affecting Northern Ireland.[11]

Gibson's pamphlet examined the divisions within Northern Ireland and outlined the manner in which he desired politics to develop on the island. He claimed that an alliance between religion and politics was the real cleavage, that the division existed between those who supported and those who opposed the constitution, the 'Partitionist' and 'Anti-Partitionist'.[12] The southern government had, for Gibson, exacerbated the divisions in northern society. To make amends, it should recognise the constitutional position of Northern Ireland. He was also critical of northern governments, which he believed had contributed to the alienation of the Catholic minority. Gibson, nevertheless, felt that there were reasons to be optimistic about the future of Northern Ireland. He welcomed Barrington's pamphlet as a 'striking contribution' and hoped that it would provide the basis for future Irish policy; in a similar vein, he claimed that Maginess and Newe (who in 1971 became the first Catholic to be appointed to the northern government) had been constructive in their approach.[13] As previously noted, the respective communities had, however, dismissed such pleas for tolerance. The limited influence of liberal members of the UUP, as well as the reaction from nationalists to calls for a new departure, was an indication of the lack of contact and understanding within Northern Ireland. Gibson was, nevertheless, hopeful that attitudes would change and provide the basis for a new society.

Unionist policy, according to Gibson, was motivated by fear of the 'exclusiveness of Roman Catholicism', a point underlined by his claim that the Catholic Church attempted to 'augment its own authority with the authority and power of the State'. Furthermore, the place of the Irish language in the southern education system was criticised, as was the 'myth that Ireland can not become a nation unless Irish is generally restored'. The partitionists feared that in a united Ireland they would be in a minority against a large Catholic party which permanently held office. Gibson suggested that partitionists were also afraid of the 'narrow, sectarian, exclusive [and] anti-British' nature of Irish nationalism. His claims about the nature of the southern state underline the sense of alienation that even a sympathetic Northern Protestant could feel towards the southern state. By referring to the Economic Survey of Northern Ireland, published in 1957, he demonstrated that the dependency of that state on the British economy highlighted the difficulties that would face a united Ireland.[14]

Having laid out the basis of the differences between the two sides, Gibson outlined new policies that he believed should be adopted. Regarding the government of Northern Ireland, he called for 'a policy of free and voluntary integration of the people of Northern Ireland'. He hoped that such a policy would bring the Catholic community into the mainstream of social, political, economic and cultural life and 'destroy the sectarian link between politics and religion and all the bitterness it entails'. He wanted the party system to be characterised by social and economic rather than constitutional issues, and hoped that a situation would exist in the future where a person's religion would no longer be of crucial importance. The first step necessary was the establishment of an impartial inquiry into allegations of discrimination. He felt that the Irish Association for Cultural, Economic and Social Relations would be a suitable body to undertake such an inquiry. The association, of which he was a member, was a 'non-party and non-sectarian association with the aim "to make reason and goodwill take the place of passion and prejudice in Ireland, north and south"'.[15] Gibson, unlike at least some Northern Protestants, thus acknowledged the possibility of discrimination in Northern Ireland.

Gibson also recognised that nationalists were concerned about the Mater Catholic Hospital in Belfast. As a result of the Health Services Bill in 1947, which proposed that 'all voluntary hospitals be taken over by a government-appointed Hospitals Authority', a controversy had developed over the control and funding of the hospital: among those who protested at the 'confiscation of Catholic property' was Archbishop D'Alton.[16] The government relented, and while it allowed it to remain outside the scheme, the hospital did not receive any financial assistance from the state. Gibson suggested that a compromise could be found whereby Catholics would 'safeguard their medical ethics' and the state would fund the cost of running the hospital. Acknowledging that he went beyond what the majority of Northern Protestants were prepared to concede, he stated that many partitionists would be critical of the pamphlet. Attempting to be even-handed, however, he defended the government's record on education. Nationalists objected to the unequal financing of the schools while unionists countered that except for the cost of the building of the schools, the same provision was made for all of them. Because Catholics insisted on their children being educated in Catholic schools, these schools were independent of the local authority and were not financed to the same extent as other schools. Gibson referred to the journalist Desmond Fennell's *Northern Catholic* in support of his view that education was an issue for Catholics to solve among themselves.

Gibson's pamphlet claimed that an integration policy was the only alternative open to the Unionist government; such a policy would force those against partition to change southern society in order to make it more attractive to northern Protestants. Existing policies, on the other hand, would only 'Perpetuate...bitterness and divisions [and] give some justification to the gun-men and their sympathisers'. He stressed that the 'use or threat of force or its passive acceptance' would not alter this position; if nationalists really wanted a united Ireland, they had to realise that unionists would not live in a society where rights that were valuable to them were illegal or unconstitutional. Gibson maintained that the south had to ensure that the 'essential pre-conditions of mutual trust and confidence' were present before any proposal for a united Ireland would be considered. He hoped for 'closer economic co-operation and integration with the Republic' [and stressed that that should] 'not...be dependent on the removal of the Border'. While his interest in Ireland as a whole was unusual for someone from his background, he acknowledged later that in the late 1950s his understanding of the roots of the conflict was incomplete. That is reflected in the pamphlet, which, as he admitted, lacked 'an appropriate understanding or exposure to the historical context of Ireland'.[17] Gibson accounted for this failure by reference to his own education, stating that, at Portora Royal School in Co. Fermanagh, the only Irish history he learnt was that which was incidental to British history. This lack of an appreciation of the history of north or south also helps to explain the limited reassessment of traditional unionist literature on Northern Ireland.

To an extent, reading Barrington's and Gibson's pamphlets together provided balance as well as a way forward for better relations between the two traditions on the island. Barrington, a nationalist who wished for a united Ireland, discussed the reasons why partition existed and sought to develop an understanding of unionism while Gibson explained contemporary unionist fears.[18] Tuairim's first two pamphlets challenged traditional nationalist and unionist views of Northern Ireland, put forward new policies which it hoped would be adopted by the governments north and south of the border and by northern nationalists and argued for a pluralist society that would be inclusive of all traditions and religions.

Unionism

Tuairim's attempts to reach across towards unionism met with mixed success. Certainly, Gibson's pamphlet does not seem to have made an impact on the Unionist government. Nevertheless, individuals from a northern Protestant background continued to speak to Tuairim. These meetings pointed to the conciliatory attitudes of the early and mid-1960s and later to the extent to which relations with nationalists had deteriorated. A feature of the former period was the hopes for increased north–south co-operation, as expressed by Henry Clark, one of the younger, progressive Unionist MPs, at a meeting of the London branch on 27 March 1963 and by the increasing confidence among unionists, as reflected at a meeting of the Cork branch in 1966. Clark's speech in 1963 was a sign of a new unionist attitude and the hopes that existed for better relations with the south; this optimism was particularly evident following the emergence of Terence O'Neill as the likely candidate to replace Lord Brookeborough as Prime Minister. Clark, a graduate of Trinity and a frequent visitor to the south, claimed that 'there was no reason why there should not be full co-operation across the Border at every level'.[19] He warned, however, that people needed a more realistic attitude regarding the border and claimed that 'co-operation will come only when leaders in the North are respected in the South and vice-versa'.[20] Such hopes facilitated the Lemass–O'Neill meetings in 1965. Another feature of this era, the increasing confidence among some unionists, was reflected in the acceptance by John Taylor, a member of the Ulster Unionist executive and a future MP, of an invitation in 1966 to speak at a televised symposium, organised by the Cork branch. This meeting also illustrated the ambitious nature of the society. With speakers throughout the island, including Austin Currie, a Nationalist Party MP, and Taylor, who declared that he 'is an Irishman, proud to be British', it was an event that the *Irish Times* described as 'thoroughly absorbing'.[21] Taylor, one of the first unionists to travel south, nevertheless reflected the changing nature of unionism, for he has since the 'troubles' generally been seen as a hard-line politician. Before the situation deteriorated within Northern Ireland, the Tuairim members Donal Barrington, Richard Dennis, an accountant, and David Thornley had from the late 1950s met individuals such as Taylor.[22] While in the long term such attempts failed to make a significant impact, they played an important, if subsidiary, role in improving relations with unionism during the 1960s.

Clark and, perhaps, Taylor were not the only moderate unionist politicians whom Tuairim contacted. In 1970, Dick Ferguson, a Stormont MP for a brief period, was to contribute to a planned Tuairim pamphlet, *Towards a Northern policy*. This was to be written by the Fine Gael Senator John Kelly, with another contribution by the newly elected independent MP for Derry, John Hume. Kelly, also a member of Tuairim as well as a professor of constitutional law at UCD, was implacably opposed to republicanism and also sympathetic to the difficulties faced by unionism. Kelly, more than most southern politicians seemed to be able to examine the conflict from the unionist viewpoint. Meanwhile, Hume was actively working towards the establishment of a new political party and shortly thereafter became the deputy leader of the Social Democratic and Labour Party (SDLP), and Ferguson, a barrister, who was a member of both the Northern and the southern bar, joined the Alliance Party in March 1971. Ferguson shared with the other politicians and Tuairim the hope that there would be an agreed settlement in Northern Ireland, even voting with nationalists on various civil rights issues. In January 1970, however, he became ill and left active politics.[23] His ill health may have been the reason why the proposed pamphlet never came to fruition. The episode indicates the ability of Tuairim to build up contacts and its modus operandi in a particularly difficult context. It would have been a significant example of politicians from opposite sides of the divide attempting to overcome their differences. On the other hand, the failure of this project highlights the limits of the society's influence, particularly in relation to unionism.

Reaction to *Partition today: a northern viewpoint*

The reaction to Gibson's pamphlet pointed to the limited contact between the two traditions on the island. The *Irish Times*, the *Irish Press* and *Hibernia*, as well as an article by Ernest Blythe in the *Sunday Independent*, each reported the contents of *Partition today: a northern viewpoint*.[24] While they recognised that Norman Gibson's views were unusual, they all reflected a lack of familiarity with unionism. The *Irish Press* went so far as to misrepresent Gibson in its report; it gave the impression that he was in favour of an end to partition. Its use of the term 'Six Counties' in describing Northern Ireland was in accordance with the usual practice of the *Irish Press*, for it served to convey concisely the irredentist nature of nationalist rhetoric. The newspaper did, however, record Gibson's view that partition would not end in the immediate future, and that the southern government 'should recognise the government of Northern Ireland and guarantee to respect the wishes of the Northern majority'.[25] In a similar vein, an unidentified reviewer in *Hibernia* seemed to indicate that nationalists were continually inviting unionists to explain their concerns. Almost contradicting herself or himself, the reviewer then admitted that public discussion of Northern Protestant 'fears' which seemed 'strangely unreasonable' might be a good idea.[26] The reviewer claimed to be acting in a similar manner to Tuairim in that he or she was seeking to understand Gibson's views. The tone and content of the review, however, suggested hostility to unionism, though because of the unusual nature of Gibson's views, it did display some insight in hesitating to refer to him as a unionist. The review was at its most conciliatory in accepting the validity of Gibson's economic arguments and criticisms of southern nationalism. It dismissed, however, his fears for a Protestant's freedom to practise his religion in a united Ireland and argued that there was not nearly as much of a difference on moral issues between north and south as Gibson had claimed. It ended on a positive note, declaring that Gibson's proposal for an objective inquiry into allegations of discrimination was a 'very considerable step forward'. Most surprising was 'An Irishman's diary' in the *Irish Times*, which suggested that Gibson had 'little new to say'. While acknowledging the impact that Tuairim was making on 'socially-conscious citizens' and claiming that the pamphlet would 'arouse a good deal of comment from both sides of the border', it argued that the society should commission a pamphlet from 'representative Southern Protestants [which] might open a few Northern eyes' to the conditions in this part of Ireland.[27]

Ernest Blythe's article in Irish in the *Sunday Independent* on 25 January 1959 was arguably the most significant. Blythe argued that everyone should be grateful to Tuairim for discovering one aspect of the truth; heretofore this had been hidden from many nationalists. He praised the society for publishing the pamphlet, which he believed represented something new. Blythe thought that there had never before been a unionist opinion as friendly or as clear as that from Gibson. Gibson, he wrote, was unusual in that he supported the existence of the border and hoped for equality for Catholics. Given that Blythe urged people to listen to unionists' views, it was, however, ironic that he failed to note Gibson's argument that an Irish-speaking Ireland would, rather than facilitating unification, impede such a development. Blythe's view was that unless the language became the vernacular over a large part of the country there could be no end to partition. While Blythe was perhaps less guilty than the other reviewers, he also failed to consider Gibson's argument in its entirety. All these articles indicate that there were different levels of misunderstanding among nationalists regarding the strength and nature of unionist opposition to a united Ireland. This reflected the limited contacts taking place between nationalists and unionists during the 1950s. Gibson himself stated that many unionists would have felt that a policy of integration with the nationalist community was 'fraught with danger'.[28] The reaction he recalled to his views on RTÉ television and radio and on discussion programmes in Northern Ireland during the late 1960s and the 1970s certainly suggests that they were not welcome among loyalists. While Gibson may have been unusual in attempting to explain unionist fears to a southern audience, he was, however, not alone in expressing radical views. Like those of the *Belfast Telegraph* and members of the Irish Association, Gibson's arguments were contrary to that of the unionist establishment, which viewed the state in exclusive terms. In comparison to Gibson's views, however, which had a limited impact on public opinion, Barrington's work helped to instigate a debate on nationalism.

Barrington as an 'innovator'

The extent to which Donal Barrington's pamphlet was novel has been contested in academic circles. Originally, in his influential book *Interpreting Northern Ireland*, John Whyte put forward the view that in 'switching the thrust of nationalist policy from trying to induce the British to leave Ireland and trying to induce the Protestants to join in a united Ireland', Barrington was an 'innovator'. Another historian, Daithí Ó Corráin, has, however, maintained that Blythe, rather than Barrington, was the real 'pioneer'.[29] Ó Corráin claimed that Blythe was the first to recognise that unionists rather than Britain were the real opponents of Irish unification. Certainly, Blythe and, indeed, Michael Sheehy had questioned traditional nationalist views before Barrington. Barrington's approach, nevertheless, differed from Sheehy's in that the latter focused on southern attitudes while the former also proposed new policies for nationalists and unionists in Northern Ireland. While Ó Corráin was correct that Blythe, earlier than both Barrington and Sheehy, had attempted to explain the unionist position, he failed to acknowledge that there were significant differences between Blythe and Barrington in regard to northern nationalism and, particularly, the Irish language.

These were reflected in a memorandum that Blythe wrote on the views that Barrington had expressed. Blythe firstly welcomed Barrington as one who explained the realities of Irish reunion in a sober and candid manner. He thus acknowledged Barrington's efforts to generate a more conciliatory attitude towards unionism. Barrington was, he wrote, correct that the policies pursued in the south 'have been calculated to buttress and perpetuate partition'.[30] However, he, disagreed with Barrington's criticism of the same southern politicians who pursued these policies. The intellectual elite in society, he suggested, also had to bear some of the responsibility, and he regretted that they had not the 'public spirit and penetration to enable them to speak say twenty years ago as Mr. Barrington has spoken tonight'. An indication of the influence that Barrington's pamphlet possibly had was Blythe's reference to one 'able young journalist [who remained unidentified] who agrees rather generally with the views expressed by Mr. Barrington'. Blythe called for the development of a healthy public opinion and for people to think about the problem that Barrington had clearly put before them. Despite their differences, which will be examined presently, Blythe's praise of Barrington and Tuairim, given his past career and continued high profile, was significant.

Blythe criticised, however, what he perceived as Barrington's lack of awareness of the importance of the Irish language for the 'the survival of the nation'. He argued that if Ireland 'worked for national re-union along the lines...suggested by Mr. Barrington we should only be repeating the error by which political leaders of the nineteenth century led the country straight to partition'.[31] Convinced that Protestant opposition to a united Ireland was the inevitable result of the Anglicisation of Ireland that took place in the nineteenth century, Blythe claimed that the Irish nation was deficient and stated that the loss of the Irish language was the 'prime cause of politico-religious segregation and subsequently...partition'.[32] As previously noted, for Blythe, the language was of critical importance to ending partition. Barrington, on the other hand, mentioned the language only once in his pamphlet and did not see a role for it in the context of Northern Ireland.[33] Instead, he called for a pluralist society that would embrace all traditions and religions. He was implicitly challenging the belief, as expressed by Blythe and prevalent among nationalists, at least in official circles, that the Irish language was vital to the future of the country. Barrington's opinion contrasted with the traditional view that attempted to justify the twin aims of the language revival and reunion. In this regard, Blythe has been castigated by Clare O'Halloran, a historian, for the 'unreality' of his arguments; Blythe claimed that the revival of the Irish language was 'not only compatible with but also necessary for progress towards unity'.[34] Given unionist identification with British culture, they were alienated, and partition accordingly entrenched, by the aspiration that the Irish language become the vernacular.

In that context, it is somewhat misleading to view Blythe as a revisionist with regard to nationalist understanding of partition. One can conclude that Blythe's writings contained elements of both the emerging nationalist view and traditional rhetoric. Barrington's and Blythe's different positions on the Irish language as well as the Northern minority, which will be discussed later, perhaps explain why John Whyte choose the former rather than the latter as an example of the reassessment then underway. Certainly, in the long term, it is clear that with regard to southern policy, Barrington's and indeed Michael Sheehy's views were more influential. Considering that an Irish-speaking Ireland was not even feasible in southern Ireland, it certainly was not realistic in relation to the entire island. Daithí Ó Corráin has suggested that Blythe has been overlooked because much of his writing was in Irish. Barrington praised, however, Blythe's 'efforts to inculcate a deeper understanding of the partition problem' but seemed unaware of Sheehy's writings on Northern Ireland.[35] The timings of Barrington's and Sheehy's respective publications may have contributed to their immediate impact or lack thereof. Sheehy's book, published in 1955, came at a time when irredentist language dominated the nationalist view and preparations were being made by the IRA for its border campaign, which began in the following year. Barrington's pamphlet was published, however, in 1958 when, partly as a consequence of the IRA campaign, nationalists north and south were beginning to question their approach to Northern Ireland.

Reaction to and influence of *Uniting Ireland*

The reaction to *Uniting Ireland* illustrates not only the strength of traditional nationalist and unionist views but also the emergence of more conciliatory nationalist views both north and south of the border. The sole unionist response to Barrington's pamphlet highlights unionist suspicion of initiatives originating in the south. Robert Babington, a barrister, who was to be elected to the Northern Ireland parliament in 1969, condemned Barrington's pamphlet as a 'new' plan that aimed to undermine unionists. The *Irish Times*'s headline over a speech by Babington to Young Unionists in Co. Down read 'North "will have none" of any Unity Plan'.[36] For Babington, the 'battle-cry is the word "tolerance"' which was being used to end the 'Union of Great Britain and Northern Ireland'. He outlined the steps of Barrington's 'new' plan; the first was to 'recognise the position of the Northern Ireland Government'; the second to 'bring about the conditions whereby the peoples and Governments are to co-operate in cultural and economic matters'. Finally, Babington claimed that once the necessary goodwill existed, Ireland would simply re-enter the British Commonwealth in return for a united Ireland. He was, however, adamant that unionists were not interested in a united Ireland. Babington's was a monocultural Northern Ireland that had little or no room for other traditions: he claimed that the government had 'a magnificent record of tolerance towards our political enemies' and maintained that 'We in Ulster, with our Protestant and Unionist Government...should not weaken our position by seeking to be regarded as tolerant'. Thus Babington strongly rejected co-operation between the two communities within Northern Ireland or between the two traditions on the island. The suspicion with which he viewed Barrington's pamphlet underlines the siege mentality that unionists possessed, particularly when confronted with southern initiatives. For southerners, the difficulty was that Babington was correct insofar as Barrington wanted a united Ireland. It thus seemed safer to unionists for them to presume that Barrington's 'new' plan was really as irredentist as all the rest had been in the past. While Babington's language might have been extreme, it nevertheless reflected the position of the Northern Ireland government. During the late 1950s, its Prime Minster, Lord Brookeborough, refused to co-operate with nationalists, north or south of the border.

The reaction to *Uniting Ireland* was more mixed among nationalists; it provoked both warm approval and outright rejection while it was welcomed as an important development by the newspaper *The Times* in London. The *Irish Times*'s editorial described the pamphlet as 'memorable' and as 'a very thoughtful and intelligently presented plea'.[37] The paper stated that after thirty-five years reunification was more of a remote possibility than ever and claimed that Barrington's plea was for the south to do something practical to convince northern unionists of southern sincerity. The editorial proceeded to ask, 'What better policy has been put forward?' It argued that while Barrington's proposal represented a gamble, it was a worthwhile one and should be taken. A leading article in *The Times* in London was also supportive, stating that it would 'be a happy day for both islands if that sensible document is accepted by all concerned'.[38] The newspaper quoted from Barrington's pamphlet to illustrate how he undermined assumptions underlying Irish nationalism. A letter from Senator Thomas Lincoln Mullins to the London *Times*, however, indicates that such traditional beliefs remained prevalent within government circles. Mullins, a member of the Dáil from 1927 to 1932, a senator from 1957 to 1973 and the General Secretary of the Fianna Fáil party, wrote to that newspaper to refute both its article and particularly Barrington's pamphlet. He claimed that Barrington applied different standards of justice to Irish nationalists, Irish unionists and the British government. Barrington's pamphlet did indeed state that he judged Irish nationalists by a higher standard than unionists because the former claimed to speak for all the people of Ireland. Therefore he argued that nationalists must pursue policies that united rather than divided the people on the island. Mullins did not accept this and criticised Barrington's pamphlet because in his view, arguing that Britain was 'not to be condemned if in the pursuit of her interests she stops short of exterminating the Irish people'.[39] The senator reiterated the traditional nationalist argument that maintained that Britain was responsible for partition; he denied that any Irish government had ever used coercion against the people of Northern Ireland and claimed that there was no democratic basis for partition. He maintained that a nationalist majority in Northern Ireland did not exist, because of gerrymandering of electoral areas. Mullins, like many nationalists, thus exaggerated the extent of discrimination.

In demanding that Britain declare that it had no interest in the partition of Ireland, Mullins, however, raised an important issue, which had been overlooked by Tuairim. The lack of clarity over Britain's long-term objective in Northern Ireland and whether or not it had a selfish interest there only served to further alienate the two communities from each other. In a similar vein to Mullins, a review in *Christus Rex* in 1958 claimed that Barrington, in his 'well-known' pamphlet, had 'buried his head in the sand and is pretending there are two forces in the country – the Catholic majority and the Protestant minority'.[40] It insisted that it was the British government that was responsible for partition and that Barrington's pamphlet was 'in direct contradiction of the facts'. A united Ireland would, it maintained, automatically result from British withdrawal. Unhappily, Barrington had, it was claimed, given voice to recent southern policy in that he wished to rewind the clock back to before 1914 in the hope that Britain would grant Home Rule to a united Ireland. This exacerbated the situation: the government's 'spinelessness has emboldened the Unionists in their cry of "Not an Inch", and…caused a section in the Republic to take up arms and flout the authority of the lawful government'.[41] Though this was a traditional nationalist viewpoint, the reviewer had a point in that a change in government policy can be traced to this time.

There is, despite Mullins's views, evidence to suggest that Barrington's pamphlet influenced thinking within government circles. A new approach, which aimed to create better relations with Northern Unionists rather than to persuade Britain to leave Northern Ireland, emerged in 1957. In this context, it is significant that the pamphlet and the reviews thereof in the *Irish Times* and *The Times* in London, along with two further speeches by Barrington reported in the *Irish Times* and significantly, the *Irish Press*, are in a government file entitled 'Partition: Government policy' and dating from 1957 and 1958. The report in the *Irish Times* was of a speech, 'Specific suggestions for improving relations in Ireland', to the Irish Association in February 1958, in which Barrington effectively repeated much of the argument in his pamphlet. He also claimed that it would be counter-productive to argue that predominantly nationalist territories in Northern Ireland should be handed over to southern Ireland, thus challenging a nationalist belief that was found within certain sections of the governing Fianna Fáil party. The southern government, Barrington claimed, should 'formally…guarantee [the] territorial integrity of Northern Ireland', and in return, Unionists should introduce reforms.[42] His intention was to promote a process under which all sides would compromise and co-operate on important issues. It was only then, he argued, that trust and understanding would begin to exist and could grow between the different traditions on the island. Barrington thought that the situation demanded immediate action, for if an agreement was not reached within the next two to three years, the opportunity could be lost because the successors to de Valera and Brookeborough would not be have the 'stature' to make the necessary concessions.[43]

Barrington developed his arguments further for an address entitled 'Towards a better Ireland' that he gave to the Left Review Group in Belfast in September 1958. In this speech, briefly discussed here but explored further later in this chapter, he called for a new form of northern nationalist organisation. The meeting was reported in the traditionally irredentist *Irish Press* on 26 September 1958. This was significant because although it did not mean that the newspaper was changing its position it was an indication of the extent to which the orthodox nationalist understanding was beginning to be questioned. It also showed that Barrington's opinion extended to those beyond the relatively liberal circles represented in the *Irish Times*'s readership. His speech argued that if better relations were to develop in Ireland, there would have to be 'self-restraint and sacrifice from the three parties primarily concerned – the Northern Protestants, the Northern Catholics and the South'.[44] He recognised the difficulties involved, in that his call for 'a sustained and vigorous effort within each party by those elements which believe that Irishmen should live in peace together' implied that there was considerable resistance to better relations from within each side. Regarding northern Protestants, he urged them to recognise that the nationalist objective of a united Ireland was a legitimate aspiration and that northern nationalists had genuine concerns, and he repeated Norman Gibson's call for an impartial inquiry into nationalist allegations. He again called on both northern and southern nationalists to accept the will of the majority within Northern Ireland and stated that the southern government should also do its utmost to end the IRA border campaign and 'educate its own people into a better understanding of the whole partition problem'.

Barrington's speech prompted the *Irish Times* to call for '*de jure* as well as *de facto*' recognition of Northern Ireland.[45] On 26 September 1958, the paper's editorial referred to Barrington as 'a pioneer of the doctrine that the political *status quo* must be accepted if peace is to come to Ireland and the hope of eventual unity is not to be abandoned forever'. Admitting that the border did exist could, it suggested, facilitate the emergence of 'a new spirit of tolerance', which might hasten the day when a united Ireland would become a reality. Furthermore, on 8 August 1958 the *Irish Times* claimed that the *Belfast Telegraph* had independently come to the same conclusion as Barrington. The *Belfast Telegraph*'s view was that the south should recognise Northern Ireland in return for an end to all forms of discrimination against the nationalist minority. This government file shows that Barrington was part of a rethinking of the nationalist approach to Northern Ireland, a process in which the government was engaged.

Among politicians, the emergence of new thinking on Northern Ireland and Tuairim's influence thereon was not confined to the government. A motion put forward by Professor William B. Stanford of Trinity College Dublin and debated in the Seanad in January 1958 illustrated the impact that the society had upon the wider political establishment. Stanford proposed a government commission to consider the promotion of social, economic and cultural co-operation between north and south. He referred to Barrington's 'very striking and encouraging article' in support of his motion.[46] The senator quoted from the section on education with particular reference to the lack of co-operation between his own college, Trinity, and UCD, especially when compared with the fact that unionist and nationalist students attended Queen's University Belfast. He concluded that anyone who had not read the pamphlet should do so and claimed that it was 'a most salutary and sensible article'.[47] The Fine Gael senator Anthony Barry supported the motion and also insisted that everyone should read Barrington's pamphlet. Similarly, the Trinity senator Owen Sheehy Skeffington spoke in favour of the motion and recalled that he had 'read with admiration the paper of Mr. Barrington…I think he writes with courage and with charity, and with great clarity of vision about a problem which some people in this country do not dare to look at in an unimpassioned way'.[48] He proceeded to provide a summary of Barrington's pamphlet and agreed with the need for a new policy in relation to Northern Ireland. Both Sheehy Skeffington and Stanford were fulsome in their praise of the pamphlet. It certainly seemed to have influenced Stanford's thinking in relation to co-operation between the universities within Dublin. Neither senator could, however, be said to have been within the mainstream of politics. On the other hand, Barry, who stated that he was very impressed by the pamphlet, had been a founding member of Fine Gael and was a member of the Dáil from 1954 to 1957 and from 1961 to 1965.[49]

Speaking in the debate for the government, Eamon de Valera, however, agreed with the concerns as expressed by some of the speakers with regard to the potential of a government commission. Favouring a joint north–south commission, he thought that the Northern Ireland government would not agree to one which was established in Dublin. Furthermore, he argued that initiatives from individuals and societies rather than the state had a better chance of success. While he emphasised that the government was anxious that there should exist the maximum amount of co-operation between the two parts of Ireland, he did not see how this could become a reality. He explained that in terms of the economy, Northern Ireland was part of the United Kingdom and so free trade agreement between the two parts of Ireland would have to involve Britain. In that case, he was concerned that without tariffs, Ireland's industries would be 'smothered in their infancy [in the face of] the developed power of Britain's industrial machine'.[50] It was clear, at least in de Valera's mind, that there were many difficulties to be overcome before better relations could exist. The fact that he failed to see any way forward was partly due to these problems, which were considerable, but also to his longevity in power and his mindset in regard to free trade and Northern Ireland. Rather than viewing these as challenges to be overcome, he seemed committed to protectionism and unclear as to how relations with unionists could be improved. Referring to the possible co-operation of economic, social and cultural groups, he said, 'I would welcome such a coming-together, but how to start it or get it going is the question.' At that point, Stanford withdrew the motion. The senator, however, urged government departments to take some action. Indeed, Stanford's motion prompted ministers to 'agree that North and South faced similar economic problems and that consideration should be given to inter-governmental discussions'.[51]

Donal Barrington's pamphlet could, in this way, be said to have influenced, government policy, albeit indirectly. This was particularly true since it was Seán Lemass's Industry and Commerce Department that called for this cabinet decision prior to the debate in the Seanad. Lemass, who was aware of Tuairim's pamphlet, had, according to Michael Kennedy, been behind calls to develop north–south economic links at least since 1956.[52] While de Valera also supported co-operation between north and south, Lemass actively sought ways to improve the economy, and within the government he was the main advocate of increased contact between the two states. The new approach, which was most apparent after Lemass became Taoiseach in 1959, facilitated the 1965 meetings between Lemass and the relatively moderate Prime Minister of Northern Ireland, Terence O'Neill. Lemass saw increased co-operation as a step towards membership of the EEC and, unlike de Valera, who hoped that it would end partition, viewed an improved relationship only as a means to unification in the longer term.

In 1969, the future President of Ireland Erskine Childers claimed that Barrington's pamphlet 'had changed thinking on the subject and had been an important factor leading to the meetings between Mr. Lemass and Captain O'Neill'.[53] As a minister in successive Fianna Fáil governments, Childers was well placed to comment. He had been to the fore of calls for increased co-operation leading up to the Lemass–O'Neill talks. Childers's statement certainly suggests that the pamphlet influenced his thinking. In relation to the rest of the government, Barrington stated that Lemass had the pamphlet discussed at a meeting of the Fianna Fáil party's National Executive. While the meeting was 'adjourned without a decision', Barrington believed that Lemass agreed with the document. As previously noted, Lemass, as Taoiseach, followed a more conciliatory policy towards unionists than his predecessors. He was, however, already thinking on the lines advocated by Barrington. The pamphlet may have reinforced Lemass's belief as to the need for a new approach to Northern Ireland. That some within governing circles respected Barrington's views is illustrated by his claim that he was chairman of a Fianna Fáil think tank on Northern Ireland in the early 1970s while Jack Lynch was Taoiseach.[54] Furthermore, according to Barrington, his pamphlet sold 10,000 copies.

Barrington's influence may also be seen in the foreword to a paper he gave to the Irish Association in 1970 and an editorial in the *Irish Times* in 1964. The Irish Association claimed that Barrington's article 'produced radical re-thinking in the Republic that led to the Lemass–O'Neill talks'.[55] The newspaper juxtaposed Barrington with politicians who failed to speak the 'truth' in relation to Northern Ireland. It maintained that this task 'has been left to courageous and clear-headed individuals like…Donal Barrington', noting that 'Politicians have admitted in private that they dare not say such unpopular things in public, even if they believe in them'.[56] This statement implied that since the late 1950s the views of some politicians in relation to Northern Ireland had changed, even if they were unwilling to state these in public. From the evidence thus presented, namely the number and kind of references to Barrington's pamphlet, it can be adduced that in terms of influencing government policy and public debate, the pamphlet was significant.

More recently, comments from current and former politicians have confirmed that Barrington's pamphlet impacted on the political mainstream. Two members of Tuairim, Fianna Fáil's Michael Woods and Fine Gael's Garret FitzGerald, have retrospectively claimed that it had a major influence on nationalist views. Woods suggested that the roots of the Good Friday Agreement could be traced to Barrington's pamphlet, while FitzGerald describes it as the 'first major challenge to traditional irredentist anti-partitionism'.[57] Thus it is clear that politicians from various political parties and independents were aware of Barrington's ideas. The majority were supportive of its contents. Even those, such as Mullins, who disagreed were provoked to respond; this served to highlight further the existence of the pamphlet. Most of these individuals seemed, however, already to be aware of the need for a new approach towards Northern Ireland.

This suggests that the pamphlet confirmed rather than altered their view. Nevertheless, there is sufficient evidence to argue that Barrington's ideas impacted upon the members of the Oireachtas and influenced those in positions of power; most significant evidence is that from the late 1950s, the period in which Tuairim's pamphlets were published and when irredentist attitudes were still to the fore in nationalist Ireland. By the 1960s, several years after Barrinton's pamphlet appeared, there was a more tolerant climate. Thus the extent to which the pamphlets, particularly Barrington's, were discussed during the late 1950s by various newspapers and politicians was impressive. It can, therefore, be concluded that Barrington's views reached a wide spectrum of opinion and influenced intellectual debate and policy formulation within Ireland. The extent to which that was the case with northern nationalists is as yet unclear.

Northern nationalism

Barrington's criticism of the Northern Nationalist Party formed part of the debate on the future approach of northern nationalists. David Kennedy, a lecturer in history at St Malachy's College in Belfast, noted that Barrington's suggestion that nationalists should 'permeate other parties, Liberal or Labour, has commended itself to some [nationalists] because of the discredited position in which Nationalism finds itself'.[58] Barrington was, however, criticised for this point by Kennedy in an article in *Christus Rex* in 1959, and more generally in 1958 in a letter from Dr Pearse O'Malley, a consultant and Honorary Secretary to the Mater Hospital. O'Malley wrote to Barrington that his proposal contained within it 'an inevitability about tragedy [as Barrington had accepted] injustice as a basis for co-operation', while Kennedy claimed that the pamphlet 'abandons the Northern Nationalist'.[59] Both O'Malley and Kennedy were strong defenders of northern nationalism. O'Malley argued that Barrington had committed a fundamental error in that unionists, because of the discrimination for which they were responsible, were not 'worthy of respect and tolerance', and Kennedy believed that the implication in Barrington's proposal was that nationalists should '*loyally* accept' the northern government, the British crown and unionist ideology.[60]

O'Malley wrote, however, that Barrington's pamphlet was the 'best and most serious contribution' on the subject that he had seen for some time, while Kennedy acknowledged Barrington's statement that nationalists should adopt the new policy only if the Unionist government agreed to certain reforms like an end to gerrymandering and the introduction of PR. Though Kennedy did not believe that unionists would agree to this proposal, he noted that Barrington and Blythe differed in relation to the northern minority and the Irish language. Kennedy thought that, unlike Blythe, Barrington recognised that his suggestion caused considerable difficulties for nationalists; Kennedy claimed that this was the reason why he made it conditional upon reciprocal moves by the Unionist government. He might have pressed his case regarding Barrington's differences with Blythe even further had he been aware of Barrington's arguments during his address to the Left Review Group in Belfast in September 1958.

The most striking change in Barrington's ideas since his pamphlet was published was in relation to northern nationalists; he argued that they should not 'abandon their political beliefs and become Unionists, but that they should work constructively and persuasively, within the limits prescribed by the Northern Constitution'.[61] This implied recognition that a new form of nationalist organisation was necessary within Northern Ireland. While Barrington was supportive of new initiatives by northern nationalists, it is unclear what prompted this apparent change in attitude. Firstly, it may be noted that even in the pamphlet his concern was for a new departure rather than steadfastly supporting the Liberal and Labour Parties. It also seems unfair to argue the location of the speech was a factor, since he was generally forthright in his views. It is most likely to have been the result of his own reasoning, the reaction from individuals such as O'Malley and Kennedy, and discussions he had with contacts he had built up as a result of the 'several visits' he made to Belfast in order to establish a Tuairim branch in the city.[62]

Similarly to Barrington, Kennedy called on nationalists to lead their own political party. The nationalists also maintained that such a party should be publicly committed to Irish unity and that only constructive political activity would ensure that political violence would end. This in turn raises the question of the attitude of Tuairim's members to violence. While Barrington was clearly opposed to its use, some other members, as will be discussed later, were more ambiguous in their views. In general, Kennedy's article underlines the tensions, within southern policy, between attempting to persuade unionists to co-operate with the south and retaining links with northern nationalists. It was a tension implicit in Seán Lemass's policy during the early 1960s and was, according to John Horgan, his biographer, reflected in the alienation of northern nationalists. For present purposes, Barrington's pamphlet and Kennedy's article as well as Fennell's inquiry each point to an increasing disillusionment with the Nationalist Party during the late 1950s.

The future nature of northern nationalism was clearly exercising the minds of Barrington and other members of Tuairim. This was reflected in a meeting in Dublin in 1966 at which a number of high-profile individuals were invited to debate the future of northern nationalism, including

Gerry Fitt, the republican Labour MP for West Belfast, Austin Currie, the Nationalist Party MP for East Tyrone, Paddy Gormley, the Nationalist Party MP for mid-Derry, and John Hume.[63] Given that the majority of the members of the society were from a nationalist background, it was understandable that Tuairim, throughout this period, remained closest to moderate nationalists and that these were the individuals that it was most likely to influence. The diverse nature of northern nationalism during the 1960s and the fact that the society was predominantly a southern organisation, however, increased the difficulty of influencing developments within Northern Ireland.

It was the members of Tuairim's Belfast branch that were most active in this regard. The society failed, however, to make an impact in Northern Ireland. Since 1958, there had been considerable difficulties in attracting a sufficient number of members in the city. A Tuairim branch in Belfast was finally founded in 1960. The problems surrounding its establishment seem to have arisen at least partly from the society's decision, on advice from unidentified individuals in Belfast, that the branch should have the same number of individuals from each community. It is likely that one of these people was James Scott, a Catholic from a unionist background.[64] Scott was also a member of the Irish Association, and, with Barrington, was largely responsible for the establishment of the branch. Scott and another member of the Belfast branch, Michael McKeown, a teacher and journalist, however, became convinced of the need to establish another organisation to confront the Nationalist Party. Because Tuairim was independent of political parties and as an organisation was not committed to a specific policy, it was an unsuitable vehicle with which to attempt to directly alter the politics of Northern Ireland; this in turn highlights the limits of the society's influence. Writing in *Hibernia* in August 1959 in response to a request from the editor, Frank D'Arcy, McKeown called for northern nationalists to recognise the constitutional position of Northern Ireland and to establish a properly structured political party to work for reform within that system. Acting independently of Tuairim, Scott and McKeown founded National Unity in 1959. It criticised the informal nature of the Nationalist Party and committed itself to the principle of consent. Unusually for an organisation which consisted mainly of young professionals, National Unity also appealed to Protestants. Tuairim's support for the organisation is reflected in the fact that Donal Barrington, Garret FitzGerald and other members travelled to Northern Ireland to speak at its meetings during the late 1950s and early 1960s. Similarly, those within Irish government circles saw the emergence of National Unity as a positive development, especially in comparison with the Nationalist Party. Divisions between the two Northern organisations meant, however, that attempts to create a new nationalist political party during the 1960s failed. The SDLP, which was established in 1970, effectively replacing the Nationalist Party as the main opposition, did, though, retain many of the features of National Unity, including its commitment to the principle of consent.[65]

Barrington had, of course, been one of the first people to enunciate this principle in his pamphlet. Even though his and Tuairim's influence in promoting more conciliatory attitudes was more indirect with regard to northern nationalism, these ideas were thus becoming more prevalent on both sides of the border. The society had interacted with many individuals within Northern Ireland and contributed to debates that informed future developments on the island. The establishment of the SDLP indicated that, by the early 1970s, more pragmatic attitudes existed towards unification. McKeown was pleased that the SDLP was 'an open constituency party dedicated to reunification by political means [which meant that] one of the fundamental purposes in the creation of National Unity had been realised'.[66] His decision not to become a member of the SDLP reflects, however, his disillusionment with politics and especially the prospects for reform within Northern Ireland.

The Northern Ireland Labour Party

Many of the individuals who were optimistic about Northern Ireland had during this period looked to the Northern Ireland Labour Party (NILP), and two very different sources of evidence suggest that Barrington's pamphlet may have had some influence on this party's thinking. The NILP's change in approach contributed to its relative success: in the 1962 election it succeeded in not only retaining the four seats it had won in the 1958 general election, but also increasing its vote. In this regard, both Paddy Devlin, a member of the NILP and later the SDLP, and the Connolly Association, a Marxist republican organisation that had been established in London in 1938, claimed that Barrington's writings had impacted upon the party. The Connolly Association argued that British imperialism was responsible for partition. Its newspaper, the *Irish Democrat*, claimed that the NILP was 'playing with the ideas of…Barrington (to get rid of the border by accepting its permanence)'.[67] Unlike Barrington, who argued that Ireland should accept partition and co-operate with Unionists, the association aimed to 'discredit Ulster Unionism in Britain through exposing the discriminatory practices which occurred under the Stormont regime'.[68] The association also considered the NILP an obstacle to its objectives because it accepted the constitutional status of Northern Ireland and was 'only half-hearted on the civil rights abuses'.[69] Though an unfriendly witness, the association is likely to have had an insight into the NILP's motivations since it campaigned for equal civil rights for nationalists and its aim was to convince the British labour movement of the justness of its view. Barrington's suggestion that Catholics support the party as a means to end the sectarian divide would have been attractive to some of its members.

There had always been those who believed that a solution to the problem of Northern Ireland would come only once the Protestant and Catholic working classes were united. Their influence began to reassert itself during the 1950s, and was reflected in the support the party received from Catholics as well as Protestants at the 1958 and 1962 elections. Paddy Devlin was one person who was committed to securing votes from across the divide. According to Barrington, Devlin claimed that the pamphlet 'persuaded him to take a different course and look for a peaceful solution'.[70] Devlin's view was that there would be no peace without a 'unified working class, ultimately asserting conventional left-right politics'.[71] Devlin did not, however, mention Tuairim in his autobiography. Furthermore, by the time Barrington's pamphlet was published, Devlin already seemed committed to social and economic issues rather than the constitutional question which was central to the politics of Northern Ireland. It is thus likely that Devlin's comment was more an indication of how widely read the pamphlet was than an illustration of influence in regard to his thinking. While the *Irish Democrat*'s statement suggests that the ideas found within Barrington's article contributed to the NILP's new approach, further evidence to confirm that Tuairim had such an impact does not seem to exist. In any case, there remained a tension within the party between the need to retain its Protestant working-class vote and to build up its Catholic vote. Connected to this were the differences that existed in the attitudes of individual NILP members towards partition.[72] Given the continued dominance of the constitutional question, the reality was that the NILP struggled; alternative viewpoints had limited electoral success during these years.

A multiplicity of views

Tuairim, nevertheless, continued to promote a new approach to Northern Ireland through meetings it organised in the 1960s and early 1970s. This included providing a platform for minority parties to put forward their views. One of the most radical individuals who spoke to the society, specifically the Dublin branch, was the chairperson of the Liberal Party, the Rev. Albert McElroy, an Old Presbyterian minister at Newtownards. This invitation showed quite a lot of imagination in that the Ulster Liberal Party was a 'radical, non-sectarian alternative' to unionist and nationalist politics during this period.[73] At the meeting, McElroy claimed that while the Unionist Party had to bear the majority of the blame for the sectarian basis to local politics, Protestant and Catholic religious leaders also had responsibility for the situation. He accused Christian leaders: 'To have permitted and even encouraged the identification of Unionism with Protestantism and nationalism with Catholicism was a disservice to Christianity.'[74] McElroy elaborated on his views in an interview with Barrington for *Hibernia* in December 1962. He was a true radical: his vision was of a united Ireland that would evolve from the Common Market and eventually into world government.

The effect that the EEC would have on Ireland was a topic to which Tuairim returned. Ernest Blythe and Tomás Mac Giolla, the President of Sinn Féin, the political wing of the IRA, were just two of those who presented their viewpoints at Tuairim's meetings. In Dublin in 1968, MacGiolla, who shared the platform with Leyton Pratt of the Liberal Party, claimed that Ireland would cease to be independent and that the 'real question of Ireland's entry into the Common Market is Can Ireland remain a nation?'[75] Ireland was, he claimed, 'the laughing stock of the world' for it was increasingly being controlled by Britain, a situation that would be exacerbated by joining 'that consortium of fallen empires known as the EEC'. Meanwhile, Ernest Blythe, speaking at the same Tuairim meeting as Albert McElroy, stated that 'he did not believe entry into the Common Market would end the border'.[76] Blythe not only disagreed with McElroy, but also attacked a prevalent belief within Ireland: that membership of the EEC would lead to the unification of the island.

While both McElroy and MacGiolla put forward radical, albeit very different, views, neither of their parties was likely at this time to alter fundamentally the political party system of Northern Ireland. Sinn Féin alienated even sympathetic observers, such as Prionsias MacAonghusa, a broadcaster with RTÉ as well as a Tuairim member, with its abstentionist policy. Tuairim's members were, generally, more moderate than that in their views, particularly in the early 1960s. While it was an exaggeration to suggest, as James Scott did, that the sectarian divide was breaking down, many believed that a new attitude was emerging during the late 1950s and early 1960s. Scott's ideal of vibrant liberal parties on both sides of the border may, however, have drawn a response from Donal Barrington, who attempted to put forward a more realistic policy that the existing government could adopt.[77] From even a cursory inspection of publications, it is thus clear that there were many individuals and groups dissatisfied with traditional unionist and nationalist politics: these included Tuairim, National Unity, the Liberals and most significantly, in electoral terms, the NILP, but also others such as the Irish Association.

Many members of Tuairim, including Donal Barrington, Garret FitzGerald, John Whyte, James and Olive Scott, Enda McDonagh, Declan

White and Franklin O'Sullivan, shared with those involved in the Irish Association a concern to help foster a better understanding of the different traditions on the island. Indeed, Barrington and McDonagh were respectively presidents of the Irish Association from 1978 to 1980 and 1988 to 1991. Barrington spoke to the organisation on two occasions: in 1958 as previously noted, and again in 1972. The President of the Irish Association, Edmond Grace, claimed that Barrington's latest address to the association, *Council of Ireland in the constitutional context*, was 'remarkably well thought out and stimulating'.[78] By late 1972, it had become reasonably clear that some form of a council, with members from both north and south, could be part of a future accommodation. Barrington's paper put forward a formula for the council which, he hoped, could secure the agreement of everyone on the island. He argued that it was the 'only body which could solve the security problem' in Ireland and ensure that the 'same basic law on human rights' existed in both states.[79] If the Council of Ireland was part of a new settlement, he suggested, it should be presented to the people of the island, north and south, in a referendum. This paper contained some radical proposals, further illustrating Barrington's active concern that a solution should be found to the divisions on the island. For instance, he worked, behind the scenes, with the SDLP and the Irish government during the 1975 Constitutional Crusade. Tuairim's meetings also discussed possible solutions to the conflict as well as recent divisions between nationalists in Northern Ireland and the parties south of the border.

Speaking on 'A New Ireland' to Tuairim's Cork branch in 1972, Garret FitzGerald, the Fine Gael spokesperson for Finance (see Figure 7), claimed that there were differences between the three main southern parties and the SDLP. Specifically, these, according to FitzGerald, were over the latter's policy document 'Towards a New Ireland'. FitzGerald, a consistent advocate of the principle of consent, stated that they related to the 'proposal for joint sovereignty and for immediate declaration by Britain on unity'.[80] According to newspaper reports, the extent to which there were differences between Fine Gael and the SDLP was unclear. FitzGerald's misgivings certainly did not result in a public rift within Fine Gael or between Fine Gael and the SDLP, as was the case within the Labour Party and between the latter and the SDLP. The differences between the SDLP and Labour centred on the views of the combative Conor Cruise O'Brien, the Labour Party's spokesperson for Northern Ireland. O'Brien claimed that the 'South's continued claim to the reunification of the country served as a "standing justification for bigotry in the North"' and that 'talk about "unity" at the present time was "futile"'.[81] This, combined with what was perceived to be a critical review of O'Brien's recent book *States of Ireland* by John Hume and statements by Paddy Devlin and Ivan Cooper condemning O'Brien, served

7 Val Finnegan, Margaret Hurley and Garret FitzGerald (left to right) spoke at a Tuairim meeting in Cork in 1972.

to re-ignite divisions in the Labour Party; this was particularly noticeable in the case of O'Brien and Tuairim's David Thornley.

This was not the first time that Thornley's republicanism resulted in him clashing with O'Brien on Labour's northern policy. The striking contrast between Thornley's and FitzGerald's attitudes on Northern Ireland and especially the IRA underlines the extent to which there was a diversity of views within the society. Whereas Thornley visited the Mater Hospital when the IRA's Seán MacStiofáin was on hunger and thirst strike in 1972, and in Easter 1976 attended an illegal Sinn Féin march that the government had banned under the Offences against the State Act,[82] FitzGerald claimed at the Tuairim meeting in Cork that the southern government had not done enough to counter to the IRA. Though Thornley's behaviour during this period was perceived to be increasingly erratic, his view that the IRA was a product of Irish history and had to be included in any future settlement was more nuanced than many understood. The IRA had been in ceasefire mode since 1962 but had reorganised itself and, in December 1969, signalled a new phase which emphasised the physical force tradition. That was in response to attacks on Catholics, which had been triggered by the civil rights marches. The IRA was criticised for having been unable to protect the Catholic community. This led to intense debates as to its future direction, culminating in its split in December 1969 and a renewed military campaign in 1970. The 'troubles', as they became known, involved increasing violence from both the IRA and loyalists and a heightening of the security response from the Stormont government, whose inability to deal effectively with the deteriorating situation ultimately led to the implementation of direct rule in 1972.[83]

That was the context for the SDLP's proposals and FitzGerald's response: his main point was that Ireland had 'not done enough to convince even a Northern Protestant of the utmost goodwill that they were serious in trying to preserve Irish lives north of the border'.[84] In a critique of the governing Fianna Fáil party's policy, FitzGerald stated that the south needed to show Britain that it was serious about the creation of a society in which Northern Protestants could live comfortably. Attempts to reform Irish law and constitution, not least by FitzGerald himself, have since met with mixed success. Despite different views as to what kind of society there should be in the southern state, mainstream nationalist opinion in relation to Northern Ireland had changed significantly since the late 1950s. It had evolved from an anti-partitionist stance that misunderstood Unionism and thought that British withdrawal from Northern Ireland would result in a united Ireland to a point where, by the early 1970s, most people accepted that change in the constitutional status of Northern Ireland could not occur without the consent of a majority of its people.[85] This was partly the result of the increased violence within northern society since the late 1960s and the consequent attempts of individuals like FitzGerald to ease tensions. It also reflected the efforts, over the longer term, of people such as Tuairim's Donal Barrington and FitzGerald to change southern attitudes.

Appeals for moderation seemed, however, to have little effect. In May 1970, in response to the emergence of increasingly hard-line opinion throughout Ireland, and following the dismissal of two government ministers for allegedly using government money to import arms for the IRA's use and the resignation of a third in sympathy, Tuairim released a statement to the newspapers. It reflected the society's frustration at the apparent lack of change in southern attitudes. Tuairim claimed that the country's 'greatest lack of achievement was failure to adopt a mature and objective attitude' towards Northern Ireland.[86] The society described as 'political hypocrisy' the refusal to grant de jure as well as de facto recognition. Despite Fine Gael's and Labour's acceptance of the principle of consent, traditional views continued to be prevalent, particularly within Fianna Fáil. Tuairim hoped that changes to Irish society and to the constitution would ease tensions throughout the island. The society argued in its statement that rather than being, as some would claim, a 'sell-out', recognition would represent 'a bargain...[as it] would ease tension, encourage co-operation and purchase a vast amount of goodwill at the small cost of threading on a few out-dated unrealistic toes'. It criticised the lack of consideration that had been given to the most important recommendations, particularly the proposal from the Oireachtas committee on the Irish Constitution to change Article 3.[87] Tuairim stressed that a majority within Northern Ireland were in favour of its current constitutional position and claimed that this would increase if full civil rights were granted to the minority, becasue a united Ireland would entail a reduction in living standards, for those who were from Northern Ireland. Not for the first time, Tuairim urged Irish people to 'make sacrifices in our own society' if 'we' genuinely wished there to be a united Ireland. Included in these 'sacrifices' was an end to religious control of educational and hospital services. That reference and its claim that Ireland would in any case be better off without those things went further than Tuairim had gone previously and were an indication of the society's dissatisfaction, even impatience, with southern attitudes and was reflected in its statement, which represented a radical call to politicians and others in positions of influence to adopt more conciliatory attitudes and policies.

Enda McDonagh, who had also expressed concern at the nature of society and the increasing violence in Northern Ireland, attempted to understand those, such as Miriam Daly, who supported the armed struggle. Miriam, née McDonnell, took the surname of her second husband, James Daly, after her first husband, Joe Lee, died. During a visit to Belfast in the 1970s, McDonagh challenged James and Miriam Daly's sympathy for the use of violence. Living in Belfast since the late 1960s, Miriam, a former member of the then-defunct London branch, had in 1972 briefly been in the SDLP, but later in the 1970s became involved in the more radical Irish Republican Socialist Party (IRSP), the political wing of the Irish National Liberation Army.[88] Loyalists killed her in 1980. Daly's life illustrates how during the early 1970s individuals could be radicalised through events in Northern Ireland. As a member of the London branch in the 1960s, she appears to have had much more moderate views; for instance, she remained aloof from the Connolly Association.

The Connolly Association

The decision of Tuairim's London branch to maintain a distance from the Connolly Association reveals much in relation to the Irish diaspora during this period. While their viewpoints were fundamentally different and there were class differences, some Tuairim members, including Roy Johnston,

Joy Rudd, Des Logan and Leslie Daiken, were members of both organisations; Daiken, a Jewish writer, was on its 'fringe', but Rudd, Johnston and Logan were heavily involved in the association.[89] Once a Tuairim branch was established in London, Rudd's and Logan's energies were, however, increasingly directed to that society, whereas Johnston, who was later involved in efforts to politicise the IRA, concentrated on the association. Logan, 'a good literate working-class intellectual', fell out with the driving force behind the association and the editor of the *Irish Democrat*, Desmond Greaves, over Tuairim. According to Johnston, he, Rudd and Logan wanted the society to be cultivated as a 'focus of support for Irish issues'; they differed, however, from Greaves, who was dismissive of Tuairim and 'Irish originating intellectuals' in general. Since the association appealed for the support of the Irish community in Britain, this seemed counter-productive. It, nevertheless, explains Greaves's refusal to engage in a debate with Gibson and the *Irish Democrat*'s description of Rudd as 'one of the stalwart members of Tuairim London'; Greaves also refused to acknowledge that she was also a member of the association.[90]

Reflecting Greaves's view, the *Irish Democrat* described Tuairim as the 'Cawstle Cawtholic Tuairim outfit', stating that it had been involved in 'anti-national brainwashing'.[91] In May and June 1959, it dismissed Norman Gibson's pamphlet as 'Unionist propaganda' and Donal Barrington as the 'chief of the "get rid of partition by accepting it" brigade'. Barrington, in particular, was criticised by the newspaper as a supporter of imperialism and accordingly partition. It claimed that the literary company that a person kept revealed a lot about her or him; Barrington wrote in *Hibernia* alongside Douglas Hyde, a lecturer on Communism in the Dublin Institute of Catholic Sociology, whose attacks on the association were 'seemingly endless'.[92] Hyde had complained that the organisation, which he saw as communist, had misappropriated the name of Connolly. Hyde, a former communist who became a respected member of the Catholic Church, saw communism and Catholicism as mutually exclusive and the association as detrimental to the faith of Irish immigrants in Britain. Many people within the Catholic Church, including Rev. Michael O'Neill, shared this view. O'Neill, of the Order of St. Columban and a friend of Tuairim's John Boland, viewed the organisation as pro-communist and a 'strong advocate of an alliance between Irish Communists and other Irish parties'.[93] Responding to a letter from O'Neill, Boland wrote that the members were concerned that 'a pink shadow may fall over the London branch'.[94] The sensitivity of O'Neill's information comes across in the correspondence with Boland, as does the latter's desire that Tuairim would in no way be seen as communist. Reflecting such anxiety, Boland noted that Tadhg Feehan in the Irish Embassy in London had 'promised to look into the matter on our behalf'.

It all pointed to Tuairim's concern with ensuring that it would continue to be viewed as a respectable organisation and thus in a position to influence intellectual debate and policy formulation in Ireland. The friendly terms that the society enjoyed with the religious Challoner Club, of which Boland was a member, underlines Tuairim's determination to remain aloof from the association. It was Greaves, however, who remained the main obstacle to better relations.

Tuairim's insistence on its independence and its modus operandi meant that greater co-operation was in any case unlikely; the society provided a platform for individuals to put forward their views or for those from different traditions to argue their case. Reflecting Tuairim's openness to alternative opinions, Boland encouraged Roy Johnston to read a paper to the society. Johnston, while open to the idea, replied that his view 'runs against the Tuairim brand of integrationism'.[95] Boland assured him that the society was no more than 'a platform for any reasoned point of view which makes for informed opinion' and asked him for an article for the branch's *Occasional Bulletin*. Johnston agreed and wrote 'Independence, partition and the emigrants' for the fourth *An Occasional Bulletin*, published in May 1961. Calling for large-scale state investment in the Irish economy, the article had as its most controversial part his argument that the Irish in London should direct their efforts towards the unification of Ireland. In relation to people from Northern Ireland, Johnston suggested that while they might find unification 'traumatic for a short period…at least the question could be decided genuinely between Irishmen'.[96] A comment on the front of the *Bulletin*, presumably by its editor, Fergus Pyle, stated that Tuairim's members might not be in complete agreement with Johnston's views. Pyle, a future editor of the *Irish Times*, argued that it would be unfortunate if they were, as Tuairim aimed to stimulate debate and the article was published with the intention of provoking discussion. The *Occasional Bulletin* had previously claimed that the society's first two pamphlets, by Barrington and Gibson, 'attracted wide attention as the most realistic contributions to this subject in recent years'.[97] While encouraging Johnston to write the article, Boland himself disagreed with Johnston's thesis; he stated, however, that 'Tuairim is a society for the expression of opinion and his article put forward a point of view that has a certain degree of support in the Society'.[98] Nevertheless, the majority of the society's members shared Boland's hope that there would in the future be better relations between the two communities. The Connolly Association, on the other hand, attempted to undermine unionism and was not interested in Ireland's present state. There were thus fundamental differences in the message and the methods of the association and Tuairim. This diversity of views was also reflected in *Hibernia*.

Hibernia

At the invitation of its editor, Tuairim's Frank D'Arcy, Donal Barrington, James Scott and Michael McKeown all wrote articles in *Hibernia* in the late 1950s and early 1960s. These attempted to explain the different traditions on the island, articulate the need for conciliatory attitudes in relation to Northern Ireland and, most importantly, influence nationalist attitudes. During the late 1950s, Barrington and Scott, in particular, advocated a new policy which was designed to break the link between politics and religion. The majority of McKeown's writings, on the other hand, came after 1965. McKeown was then the periodical's 'Northern Correspondent' and, in contrast to his article calling for a new form of nationalist organisation in 1959, reflected his apathy with politics and the increasing tensions within Northern Ireland. Typical of the earlier more optimistic articles was Scott's first, published in June 1958, in which he commented that while 'the gulf between Unionists and Nationalists is too deep…a substantial number of people, both Catholic and Protestant, are looking for a less hidebound, more liberal and up-to-date alternative'. Scott, a constant critic of the Nationalist Party, realised, however, that there were significant obstacles in the way of progress, particularly from what he viewed as the lack of leadership in the existing party system. His writings were indicative of the questioning mindset that Tuairim sought but also reflected his unusual religious background. He simultaneously criticised past Catholic attitudes and argued that the church should provide real leadership in the future. Scott also called for toleration of diverse views and claimed that the way forward was for nationalists to accept partition, end 'their self-imposed segregation' and fully co-operate with unionists.[99] Similarly to Tuairim's pamphlets, he put forward an inclusive argument that envisaged a true sense of community throughout Northern Ireland. There were, however, differences with Barrington, who thought that Ireland could rejoin the Commonwealth only in the context of reunification. Despite positive signs in these articles, responses to Scott and Barrington underlined the continued strength of traditional arguments. Individuals who replied to Scott's direct challenge to the IRA and Barrington's review of new thinking in relation to Northern Ireland also illuminated the motivations of the IRA as well as the depth of unionist opposition to a united Ireland.[100]

In contrast to the earlier optimism, the increasing prevalence of hard-line views was reflected in *Hibernia* during the late 1960s and early 1970s. Michael McKeown reflected the concern, even impatience, among nationalists at the lack of progress. His writings suggested that events in Northern Ireland made it increasingly difficult to put forward moderate opinions. On 26 May 1972, McKeown, in criticising the IRA, claimed that its attacks were sectarian and remarked that 'the ordinary volunteer is quite happy to strike at Protestant institutions simply because they are Protestant'. This comment was cited by the outspoken critic of the IRA, Conor Cruise O'Brien in support of his argument that *Hibernia* was 'sympathetic to Sinn Féin-IRA'.[101] While McKeown was sympathetic to nationalists' plight, the evidence, contrary to O'Brien's implied view, suggested that he was hostile to the IRA.

The episode, nevertheless, involved him in a controversy that illustrated that certain opinions in *Hibernia* had become radicalised in relation to Northern Ireland. John Mulcahy, then the editor and owner of the periodical, was much more amenable to republican views than Frank D'Arcy. As if to illustrate this point, he became involved in an acrimonious exchange with O'Brien and Tuairim's John Kelly. Similarly to O'Brien, Kelly maintained that events in Northern Ireland were turning reasonable individuals such as the '*Hibernia* belt...into conscious or sub-conscious militants'.[102] The article was prompted by an attack on a speech that Kelly had made in defence of unionism, in which he claimed that the approach of *Hibernia* and others was incompatible with democracy and the rule of law and would only further divisions with unionists without improving the situation for the northern nationalists. These clashes with the media resulted from the concern of politicians such as Kelly and O'Brien that the attitudes found within the periodical, along with similar ones elsewhere, would only exacerbate an already bloody conflict in Northern Ireland as well as divisions within Irish politics and their respective political parties.

The case made by Kelly and O'Brien is supported by the tone and content of some of Prionsias MacAonghusa's articles in *Hibernia*, which suggested ambivalence towards the use of violence. In separate pieces in 1971, for example, he questioned whether force was necessary to end 'British imperialism' and refused to condemn an attack on the British navy.[103] MacAonghusa's criticism of the republican movement's abstentionist policy suggested that he was, however, committed to democracy. While apparently sympathetic to the motives of the IRA, he did not see the conflict which Kelly had claimed to exist between democracy and an ambivalent attitude towards the use of violence. His republicanism is illustrated in his writings, which also reflected the radicalisation of journals such as *Hibernia* and generally of Irish public opinion in relation to Northern Ireland during this period. This highlights the extent to which southern politicians had failed to educate people about the reality of the divisions within northern society as advocated by Tuairim since the late 1950s. Overall, a significant contrast existed between many of the articles that appeared in *Hibernia* in the early 1970s and those of the late 1950s and early 1960s. In the same way as the former reflected the deteriorating situation of the early 1970s, the writings of Barrington and Scott suggested that a more conciliatory attitude was emerging in the late 1950s and early 1960s. These articles also pointed to the links that existed between Tuairim and *Hibernia* during the earlier period and the increasingly limited influence the society had upon the journal once its editorship and ownership had changed hands in 1968.

Conclusion

'Passionate moderation', part of a title of a Tuairim meeting in 1970,[104] is an apt description of the society's attitude to Northern Ireland. Tuairim challenged the traditional nationalist view in its first two pamphlets, in articles in *Hibernia*, at its meetings and through the contacts that the society had built up from the 1950s. Tuairim's pamphlets, in particular, provoked a significant reaction in newspapers and periodicals. The evidence indicates that Tuairim influenced southern nationalist attitudes. In this regard, the difficulty of isolating the extent of Tuairim's influence is considerable. The society's contribution was, particularly in relation to Northern Ireland, enmeshed with those of other individuals and organisations in debates. Furthermore, Tuairim played a significant role both through the direct involvement of its members and through its writings in the examination of Northern nationalism's future course of action. The evidence also underlines the society's failure, however, to make a noteworthy impact on unionism. This illustrates the difficulties that Tuairim faced in influencing the nature of Northern Ireland and symbolises the increased polarisation of that society from the late 1960s. Reflecting its frustration at the deteriorating situation, Tuairim's statement of 1970 wondered if there really was a '"silent majority" on both sides of the border'.[105] The change from the optimism that was expressed by Tuairim members during the late 1950s and early 1960s illustrates the extent to which communal antagonisms had resurfaced. Even if the society had helped to change the terms of the debate by the early 1970s, the similarities with the views Tuairim expressed in the late 1950s was depressing in that the society was again calling for moderation in relation to Northern Ireland. Nevertheless, the willingness of individuals from different traditions to engage with Tuairim reflected the high regard in which the society was held. Tuairim thus served a valuable purpose in contributing to a more complete understanding of the divisions on the island. Furthermore, its meetings highlighted questions that went to the core of whether Irish people really wanted a united Ireland. It is also clear, however, that there was a wide range of viewpoints within Tuairim. Involvement in diverse organisations such as National Unity, the Irish Association and the Connolly Association was not incompatible with membership of Tuairim. While all members of Tuairim attempted to contribute to a solution of the divisions within the island, their conception of the problem differed and their objectives occasionally clashed. Not all of Tuairim's members agreed with the society's attempts to build bridges across the community divide and thus provide a future basis for peace and justice on the island.

Epilogue:
Tuairim and the Good Friday Agreement

Individuals such as Garret FitzGerald and Michael Woods suggested that Tuairim had a significant impact on nationalist views and even on the 1998 Good Friday or Belfast Agreement; this raises the question of to what extent the content of that and other documents have elements in common with the society's approach. A perusal of the Sunningdale Agreement, the New Ireland Forum Report, the Anglo-Irish Agreement, the Framework Documents and the Downing Street Declaration, in addition to the Good Friday Agreement, indicates that a frequent theme within these documents is the principle of consent, of which Tuairim was an early advocate. Similarly, a rejection of violence is common to Tuairim's approach and to these agreements. Tuairim also advocated changes to the Irish Constitution and in particular to Articles 2 and 3, which were the basis of the southern claim to the whole island of Ireland. In 1970, Tuairim recommended that Article 3 be altered, while Donal Barrington's approach was that there could be a change in these articles only in the context of an overall agreement. He subsequently went further, arguing in his articles in *Administration* that in the event of an agreed settlement, there should be a new Irish Constitution and that such an agreement should be put to referenda in both parts of the island. This effectively was what occurred. Articles 2 and 3 were amended in a referendum in Ireland on 22 May 1998, the same day as the Good Friday Agreement was accepted by the people of Northern Ireland. Barrington had in early 1973 also discussed the concept of a Council of Ireland and in that context called for a new police force and the adoption of the European Convention of Human Rights by the two states in Ireland. Both the 1973 Sunningdale Agreement and the 1998 Good Friday Agreement included councils as well as the convention, while an independent commission established as part of the Belfast Agreement considered the future of police.

Most striking was the recognition by nationalist political parties, north and south, that rather than the British presence, it was the clash between nationalist and unionist identities that was at the core of divisions in Northern Ireland. The 1984 New Ireland Forum Report was significant in this regard. These agreements echoed Tuairim's call for reconciliation between the different traditions. It was, furthermore, increasingly accepted that there needed to be significant changes in southern as well as in northern society. From the late 1950s, Tuairim had been advocating a more pluralist society in the south in the interests of better relations with unionists. Significantly, this was explicitly recognised by a Fianna Fáil government in the Downing Street Declaration in 1993. Of course, new elements, including the nature of the overall relationship between Britain and Ireland, were introduced in this agreement. The Framework Documents in 1995 included and built upon these parts of the Downing Street Declaration. These were the ideas that formed the basis to the subsequent Good Friday Agreement, which could in some ways be seen as the culmination of a process begun in the late 1950s. This is not to argue that Tuairim directly influenced these developments. Nevertheless, the extent to which the ideas put forward by the society and its members were subsequently found within the agreements between some or all of the Irish government, the British government and the unionist and nationalist political parties upon the island is striking.

Notes

1 Gillian McIntosh, *The force of culture: unionist identities in twentieth-century Ireland* (Cork: Cork University Press, 1999), pp. 221–3. See also John Bowman, *De Valera and the Ulster question, 1917–1973* (Oxford: Oxford University Press, 1989), pp. 286–8; Keogh, *Twentieth-century Ireland*, pp. 229–30; Enda Staunton, *The nationalists of Northern Ireland* (Dublin: Columba Press, 2001), pp. 186–90, 200, 221.

2 John Whyte, *Interpreting Northern Ireland* (Oxford: Clarendon Press, 1991), p. 119. See Ernest Blythe, *An appeal to leaders of nationalist opinion in the North: a memorandum written in 1957* (Dublin: Elo Publications, 1997); UCD, AD, P24, Blythe papers 70, 'Memorandum in regard to policy on north-east Ulster, prepared by Blythe', 9 August 1922. See also Daithí Ó Corráin, '"Ireland in his heart north and south": the contribution of Ernest Blythe to the partition question' in *Irish Historical Studies*, 35:137 (May 2006), 63–4; Clare O'Halloran, *Partition and the limits of Irish nationalism: an ideology under stress* (Dublin: Gill and Macmillan, 1987), pp. 100–5. See Maye, Brian, 'Blythe, Ernest', *Oxford Dictionary of National Biography* (Oxford: Oxford University Press, 2004), www.oxforddnb.com/view/article/52525, accessed on 12 December 2008. See also Michael Sheehy, *Divided we stand: a study in partition* (London: Faber and Faber, 1955); Garvin, *Future*, pp. 147, 205. See Desmond Fennell, *The northern Catholic: an inquiry* (Dublin, Mount Salus Press, 1958), pp. 12, 15. Fennell's inquiry was an extended version of a series of articles published by Fennell in *The Irish Times* from 5 to 10 May 1958. See also correspondence with Desmond Fennell, 24 April 2006; Whyte, *Northern Ireland*, p. 137. Fennell wrote many books that both supported and questioned traditional nationalist views.

3 Garret FitzGerald, 'Irish economy north and south', *Studies*, 45:180 (Winter

1956), 373–88. See Viscount Brookeborough, *Why the border must be: the Northern Ireland case in brief by the Northern Ireland government* (Belfast: Stormont Castle, 1956), http://cain.ulst.ac.uk accessed on 20 December 2008.
4 Henry Patterson, 'Brian Maginess and the limit of liberal unionism', *Irish Review*, 25 (1999/2000), 96, 101–2, 106–9. See also *Irish Press*, 5 February 1958.
5 *Irish Press*, 9 March 1957. See NAI, DT, S9361F, Partition government policy December 1955–February 1957, *Irish Times*, 5 March 1957, *Irish Independent*, 16 March 1957. D'Alton's proposal was from an interview by a journalist, Douglas Hyde, in *The Observer* on 3 March 1957. For Newe see *Irish Times*, 12 August, 30 December 1958; Michael McKeown, *The Greening of a nationalist* (Dublin: Murlough Press, 1986), p. 95.
6 Whyte, *Northern Ireland*, p. 118. See Bowman, *De Valera*, p. 76; John McGarry and Brendan O'Leary, *Explaining Northern Ireland: broken images* (Oxford: Blackwell Publishers, 1996), p. 428; Frank Gallagher, *The indivisible island: the history of the partition of Ireland* (London: Gollancz, 1957).
7 Barrington, *Uniting Ireland*, p. 4. Unless otherwise stated, the quotations that follow in this section are from Barrington's pamphlet. See R. M. Sibbett, *The sunshine patriots: the 1798 rebellion in Antrim and Down* (Belfast: GOLI Publications, 1997), which was reprinted from Sibbett's *Orangeism in Ireland and throughout the Empire*. Sibbett was appointed the official historian of the Orange Order in 1926 and in 1938 finished his two-volume history of the Orange Order, *Orangeism in Ireland and throughout the empire, from 1688 to 1938*. He also wrote *On the shining Bann* in 1928. He died in 1941. Barrington also quoted from speeches in the *Strabane Weekly News* and another speech from a unionist politician, Erne Cecil Ferguson, who was appointed the Crown Solicitor for Co. Fermanagh by the Northern government in 1956.
8 Bowman, *De Valera*, pp. 286–8; Keogh, *Ireland*, pp. 229–30. This policy, highlighting partition at each international opportunity, was subsequently known as the 'sore-thumb' of partition.
9 The terms of the 1949 Ireland Act were that 'Northern Ireland remains part of His Majesty's dominions and of the United Kingdom and it is hereby affirmed that in no event will Northern Ireland or any part thereof cease to be part of His Majesty's dominions without the consent of the Parliament of Northern Ireland'.
10 McIntosh, *The force of culture*, pp. 3, 181. See also Andrew Gailey, *Crying in the wilderness: Jack Sayers, a liberal editor in Ulster, 1939–69* (Belfast: Institute of Irish Studies, Queen's University Belfast, 1995), pp. 180–5; Frank Shovlin, *The Irish literary periodical, 1932–1958* (Oxford: Clarendon Press, 2003), pp. 156–83.
11 Whyte, *Northern Ireland*, p. 160. Gibson was a member of the National and Economic Social Council in Ireland in the 1970s and with Dermot McAleese contributed to the report of the New Ireland Forum. See also interview with Gibson, 30 August 2005; *Irish Press*, 9 January 1959; *Irish Times*, 6 September 1958; Brian O'Connor papers, '*Tuairim* document, 1958'. Gibson completed his Ph.D. in economics at Queen's University Belfast in 1959. This had involved him in visiting banks throughout the island. From the late 1950s,

Whitaker showed an interest in Gibson's research on the economy and politics of Northern Ireland. See Daly, *Social Inquiry*, p. 154. Gibson, in his paper to the Statistical and Social Inquiry of Ireland, argued that the Central Bank would have to be given 'greater control over the monetary system' if Ireland was to develop an 'expansionary economic policy'. Describing the paper as 'controversial and outspoken', Patrick Lynch 'believed that it provided "a means of educating public opinion on real issues rather than on phantom prejudices"'.

12 Norman Gibson, *Partition today: a northern viewpoint* (Dublin: Tuairim, 1959), p. 1. The quotations in this section, unless otherwise stated, are from this pamphlet.
13 Ibid., p. 3. According to Gibson, Maginess had called for recognition and toleration of differences and increased co-operation between the two communities. Gibson believed that Maginess had thus given 'a gentle reprimand to those who through their actions and pronouncements sow discord'. See Barrington, *Uniting Ireland*, p. 8; *Irish Times*, 10 November 1959.
14 Gibson, *Partition today*, p. 10. Gibson argued that Northern Ireland would be making considerable economic sacrifices, which the south failed to realise, if it were to agree to a united Ireland. This can be seen as a response to the nationalist view that partition harmed Ireland economically and that a united Ireland would prosper. See also Gailey, *Crying in the wilderness*, p. 48.
15 Paul Bew, Kenneth Darwin and Gordon Gillespie, *Passion and prejudice: nationalist / unionist conflict in the 1930s and the origins of the Irish Association* (Belfast: Institute of Irish Studies, Queen's University Belfast, 1993), p. vi; interview with Gibson, 30 August 2005. While Gibson had for a couple of years from 1956 been a member of the Unionist Party, he was never again to be a member of a party. As an academic with an active interest in the politics and economy of both parts of Ireland, he thought that an attachment to a political party would impose an inappropriate constraint on what he could say. Instead, he devoted his energies to the Irish Association.
16 Whyte, *Church and state*, p. 150. See also Gibson, *Partition today*, p. 11; interview with Gibson, 30 August 2005. Gibson claimed that even noting 'nationalist support for the Mater Hospital [would have been seen as]…a betrayal of the Unionist Protestant side'. See McKeown, *Nationalist*, p. 34. Terence O'Neill, the Prime Minister of Northern Ireland, integrated the hospital into the health services.
17 Interview with Gibson, 30 August 2005. Gibson claimed that he learnt as much or as little about Britain in Canada as he did about Britain in Ireland. See also Whyte, *Northern Ireland*, p. 148; McGarry and O'Leary, *Northern Ireland*, p. 96. See also interview with Gibson, 30 August 2005.
18 Gibson, *Partition today*, foreword. Barrington claimed that some would find 'Gibson's views to a degree complementary' to those found in his pamphlet. See also O'Hanrahan papers, MacErlean, 'On *Tuairim*'. This document stated that it was 'indicative of Tuairim's scope and purpose that these statements on Partition, so opposite and yet complementary, could be published under its auspices'.

19 *Cork Examiner*, 4 April 1963. See also *Sunday Review*, 7 March 1963; Michael Kennedy, *Divisions and consensus: the politics of cross-border relations* (Dublin: Institute of Public Administration, 2000) p. 193.
20 *Cork Examiner*, 27 March 1963.
21 Rudd papers, Tuairim, 'Cork branch report, 1964/65 season'; *Irish Times*, 19 November 1964. See also *Irish Times*, 22 April 1963, 11 March 2008.
22 For example, interviews with Barrington, 19 May 2005, Cian O'Carroll, Limerick, 3 December, 2005, and Enda McDonagh, Maynooth, 24 June 2005. Barrington met Taylor in Michael Duggan's house in Dublin, probably in 1963. Duggan was a member of the Dublin branch. James Deegan, who had also been involved in Tuairim, invited Taylor to Dublin. See Kennedy, *Divisions*, pp. 196–7; *Hibernia*, May 1964. Duggan and Richard Dennis, both members of Tuairim, were involved in the young Fine Gael group who met Young Unionists in 1963. Thornley also met unionists during the late 1950s and early 1960s. See *Hibernia*, 25 July 1975. In this letter, Thornley implied that he visited republican elements in Northern Ireland in the early 1970s. The radical nationalism that he expressed during that period had, however, rarely been articulated in earlier years. He was generally more moderate while in Trinity, where his colleagues T. W. Moody and Basil Chub may have influenced him.
23 For example, George Drower, *John Hume: peacemaker* (London: Victor Gollancz, 1995), p. 51; correspondence with Rebecca Black, Policy Unit, Ulster Unionist Party, 2 May 2006; Paddy Devlin, *Straight left: an autobiography* (Belfast: Blackstaff Press, 1993), p. 97. See *Hibernia*, 4 February 1972. In 1972, Ferguson claimed that 'another solution must be found, not in a United Ireland, but in a New Ireland'. An MP from 6 November 1968 to 26 January 1970, Ferguson was appointed Queen's Counsel (Northern Ireland) in 1973, and was chair of the Northern Ireland Mental Health Review Tribunal from 1973 to 1984, Irish State Counsel in 1983 and, in England, Queen's Counsel in 1986 and chair of the Criminal Bar Association from 1993 to 1995. I am grateful to Rebecca Black for this information. See also *Hibernia*, 2 July 1976. Barrington criticised a *Hibernia* report that disapproved of the call of sixteen southern barristers including Barrington to the Northern bar. As a 'reciprocal gesture of friendship', Ferguson initiated the process whereby barristers could practise in both jurisdictions in 1969. See *Hibernia*, 14 November 1975. The editor, John Mulcahy, went so far as to suggest that John Kelly found it 'easier to associate with Northern Protestants than Northern Catholics'. See also Peacocke papers, 'Agenda *Tuairim* national council', 20 February 1970. The pamphlet was the first to be published by the Limerick branch. See Finn, 'Priests, politics and poetry'. The branch had published a booklet, *Castle poets*, in 1966.
24 *Irish Press*, 9 January 1959; *Irish Times*, 13 January 1959; *Hibernia*, February 1959; *Sunday Independent*, 25 January 1959. Blythe's article was entitled 'Tuairim on Tuaisceart' ('Tuairim on the north'). I would like to thank Tonaí Ó Rudaidh for assistance in translating the article.
25 *Irish Press*, 9 January 1959.

26 *Hibernia*, February 1959. The reviewer also claimed that Gibson was 'novel' in that he recognised partition to be a 'problem' while the pamphlet was the first 'Northern Unionist' view of partition, 'written at the invitation of a representative Dublin Group'.
27 *Irish Times*, 13 June 1959. The article, however, also claimed that Gibson was unusual for his generation.
28 Gibson, *Partition today*, p. 11. See also interview with Gibson, 30 August 2005. Threatening phone calls were made to Gibson's home during this period. Gibson claimed that he had been seen as a 'bit of a retrograde on the Unionist side' in the late 1960s. He had no links with Tuairim at that stage. Appointed an economics lecturer at the University of Manchester, he had been out of Ireland since 1962. Upon his return following his appointment in 1968 as head of the Economics Department at the recently established New University of Ulster, he became active in media circles.
29 Ó Corráin, 'Ireland', p. 80. See also Whyte, *Northern Ireland*, p. 120.
30 UCD, AD, P24, Blythe papers 1880, 'Mr. Barrington's lecture, comment on lecture by Donal Barrington apparently on Partition, the situation in Northern Ireland and the policies of southern politicians towards the South, c. 1960s', p. 1. The quotations that follow are from this document.
31 Ibid., pp. 9, 13. Blythe also claimed that Barrington had 'taken the official historian of the Orangemen [R. M. Sibbett] of whom incidentally I have never heard a little too seriously'.
32 UCD, AD, P24, Blythe papers 1773, 'Confidential notes on the Pomeroy, Armagh and Omagh incidents', p. 13–14.
33 Barrington, *Uniting Ireland*, p. 5. Barrington acknowledged that 'the identification of nationalism with Catholicism was facilitated by the virtual loss of the Irish language in the…nineteenth century'.
34 O'Halloran, *Partition*, pp. 171–4.
35 *Hibernia*, July 1958. See also *Irish Times*, 2 February 1957. Blythe spoke to a meeting of Tuairim's Dublin branch in 1957.
36 *Irish Times*, 6 February 1958. The quotations in this paragraph are from the *Irish Times*. See also Brian M. Walker, *Parliamentary election results in Ireland 1918–92: Irish elections to parliaments and parliamentary assemblies at Westminster, Belfast, Dublin, Strasbourg* (Dublin: Royal Irish Academy, 1992), p. 80. See *Hibernia*, 16 January 1976 for an account of Babington and his lineage. He became a judge in 1973.
37 *Irish Times*, 7 January 1958.
38 *The Times*, 30 December 1957.
39 Ibid., 6 January 1958.
40 P. Houlihan, 'Uniting Ireland: notes and comments', *Christus Rex*, 13 (December 1958), 73. See also interview with Gibson, 30 August 2005. Gibson criticised Britain for its lack of concern about the divisions in Northern society and the relative economic poverty of Northern Ireland. See Barrington, *Uniting Ireland*, p. 7; Gibson, *Partition today*, p. 2. Gibson wrote that the situation would be even worse if British troops left Northern Ireland while Barrington, having referred to Britain's share of the responsibility for

partition, stated that troops were present in accordance with the wishes of the majority of the people of Northern Ireland.
41 Houlihan, 'Uniting Ireland', p. 73.
42 NAI, DT, S9361G, Partition: government policy, co-operation on social, economic and cultural matters, March 1957–December 1958, *Irish Times*, 28 February 1958. Barrington also welcomed Lemass's plans for increasing trade within Ireland. See also NAI, DT, S10585C/62, Partition: statements, resolutions etc by Northern Ireland groups and individuals. Gibson's pamphlet can be found in this government file.
43 *Irish Times*, 28 February 1958. It was, however, closer to the truth that progress had to wait until de Valera and Brookeborough left active politics in 1959 and 1963, respectively.
44 NAI, DT, S9361G, Co-operation, *Irish Press*, 26 September 1958.
45 *Irish Times*, 26 September 1958.
46 Seanad Éireann Debates, vol. 48, cols. 1387, 1390, 'Motion: co-operation between twenty-six counties and six counties', 29 January 1958. Stanford stated that he deliberately excluded political co-operation because he did not foresee the prospect of co-operation between the two states in that sphere.
47 Ibid., cols. 1390–1. See also Barrington, *Uniting Ireland*, p. 20. Barrington wrote that contact between students of different traditions in Queen's University was 'fostering an increasingly enlightened approach to Northern politics'. He criticised how little contact took place between the two universities in Dublin, especially since each year many nationalist students attended UCD and many unionist students were in Trinity. It was argued that increased interaction between these students could bring Irishmen together. This foreshadowed some of the arguments that were implicit in Tuairim's pamphlet *University College Dublin and the future*, which is discussed later.
48 Seanad Éireann Debates, vol. 48, col. 1405.
49 Barry was a senator from 1957 to 1961. See also the RTÉ television programme *Dynasties*, 3 May 2006. The Barry family owns Barry and Co. Ltd., a tea company. Anthony was also the first of three generations who served as Lord Mayor of Cork and were members of the Dáil. His son Peter was the Minister for Foreign Affairs at the time of the Anglo-Irish Agreement.
50 Seanad Éireann Debates, vol. 48, cols. 1414–5, 'Co-operation', 29 January 1958. Ibid., col. 1411. Senator O'Quigley foresaw difficulties in keeping political considerations separate from possible discussions on co-operation in economic, social and cultural matters.
51 Kennedy, *Divisions*, p. 169; NAI, DT, S16272A, Co-operation. See also Kennedy, *Divisions*; Bowman, *De Valera*, p. 286; Horgan, *Lemass*, pp. 252–83.
52 Michael Kennedy, 'Towards co-operation: Seán Lemass and north–south economic relations, 1956–65', *Irish Economic and Social History*, 24 (1997), 42–61.
53 Carty, *Government and people*, p. 10.
54 Interview with Barrington, 19 May 2005. See also Dermot Keogh, *Jack Lynch: a biography* (Dublin: Gill and Macmillan, 2008), p. 403; Horgan, *Lemass*, p. 210; McCullagh, *Reluctant Taoiseach*, p. 390. Keogh states that Barrington

was on a 'Rapporteurs Committee' following Fianna Fáil's defeat in the 1973 general election. Michael Woods was also a member. In addition, Barrington was, according to McCullagh, with John A. Costello and John Kelly, the Supreme Court judges Brian Walsh and John Kenny, and others, a member of a group of legal experts that was established in 1966 to advise the all-party committee on the Irish Constitution.

55 Irish Association, *Council of Ireland in the constitutional context* (Dublin: Irish Association, 1972). The association's President, Edmond Grace, wrote the foreword.
56 *Irish Times*, 23 March 1964.
57 FitzGerald, *Reflections*, pp. 176–7; interview with Michael Woods, Dublin, 25 May 2005. It is significant that many Tuairim members recall Barrington's pamphlet more clearly than any other when asked about the society.
58 David Kennedy, 'Whither northern nationalism', *Christus Rex*, 13 (October 1959), 283. See also *Hibernia*, July 1958: Barrington had argued that Northern nationalists needed to 'facilitate the growth of new political organisations which will reflect the economic interests of the people of Northern Ireland and [would benefit both] Catholics and Protestants'.
59 Kennedy, 'Nationalism', p. 276; NUI Galway, Special collections, T4/3/24, O'Malley archive, Lyric Theatre [Belfast], O'Malley to Barrington, 29 January 1958. Kennedy welcomed the attention Barrington drew to the harm that southern pressure and propaganda were doing to the prospects of unity while O'Malley claimed that the pamphlet would encourage a 'more tolerant and constructive attitude'. See also David Kennedy, 'Catholics in Northern Ireland', in Francis McManus (ed.), *The years of the great test, 1926–39* (Cork: Mercier Press, 1967), pp.138–49.
60 *Irish Press*, 26 September 1958. Kennedy was either unaware of Barrington's speech to the Left Review Group in Belfast or alternatively may have already sent his article to *Christus Rex*. See also Ó Corráin, 'Ireland', pp. 75, 80. Ó Corráin stated that it was Blythe's 'dismissal of several issues' such as gerrymandering and discrimination that led to criticism by both Cahir Healy, the veteran northern MP, and Seán Lemass. At the same time, Blythe argued that northern nationalists should recognise Northern Ireland and end the sectarian politics that they practised. Ó Corráin noted that Barrington was aware that northern nationalists had legitimate grievances.
61 Kennedy, 'Nationalism', p. 278; NUI Galway, Special collections, T4/3/24, O'Malley archive, Lyric Theatre, O'Malley to Barrington, 29 January 1958
62 Hederman O'Brien papers, 'Council', 1958–59; Rudd Papers, 'Tuairim newsletter no. 5'.
63 Minutes of committee meetings of Tuairim's Dublin branch, 5 April, 17 May, 6 December 1966. What discussions that did take place do not appear to have been recorded in the national newspapers despite the fact that Tuairim wrote to them in advance of the meeting. This seems strange given that the 'publicity' the society received was according to the Dublin branch's minutes 'excellent'. The one exception was the *Irish Times*; this may have reflected the consideration that newspaper was increasingly giving to political, social and

economic issues and the fact that Tuairim was not perceived to be as radical as previously it had been. In reality, however, as all the newspapers continued to report the society's activities, it most probably points to a lack of interest in Northern Ireland. See also interviews with Mona Stanton, Dublin, 12 May 2005, and Brian Geary, Limerick, 3 December, 2005; Rudd papers, 'Tuairim Dublin notice, notice of meeting'; Minutes of committee meeting of Tuairim's Dublin branch, 19 November 1968.

64 *Hibernia*, October 1958. Scott was 'brought up under a modified system of fosterage with a north Louth Republican farming family'. See also James Scott, 'Thoughts of the conversion of Ireland', *The Furrow*, 4:11 (1953), 615–18. See also Hederman O'Brien papers, 'Council', 1958–59; Rudd papers, 'Tuairim newsletter no. 5'. Scott had in 1958 established a Catholic and Protestant undergraduate society in Queen's University. This group had asked for association with Tuairim, which thought that its foundation was an 'important development'.

65 Ian McAllister, 'Political opposition in Northern Ireland: the National Democratic Party, 1965–1970', *Economic and Social Review*, 6:3 (April 1975), 361; McKeown, *Nationalist*, pp. 17–22, 31–3. The National Democratic Party, which was established after a failed convention in 1965, retained from National Unity the conviction that unity could come about only through the principle of consent. Apart from McKeown and Scott, members of National Unity included Tuairim's Garret FitzGerald and John Mee. See FitzGerald, *All in a life*, p. 64; *Irish Times*, 20 December 1997. In his newspaper column (ibid.), FitzGerald calls McKeown and Scott 'forward-thinking nationalists'. The committee minutes of the Dublin branch from 2 March 1964 state, however, that a negative reply was given to an invitation to speak at a National Unity meeting. No reason was given. Considering the society's previous co-operation with National Unity, it is more likely that no one was available to speak rather than that there was an unwillingness to do so. It is also possible that the society did not have the same interest in this as Barrington and FitzGerald. See also Horgan, *Lemass*, p. 270; Staunton, *Nationalists*, p. 233; *Hibernia*, May 1961.

66 McKeown, *Nationalist*, p. 88.

67 *Irish Democrat*, August 1959. See also *Irish Democrat*, June 1959, July 1962. See Simon Prince, 'The global revolt of 1968 and Northern Ireland', *The Historical Journal*, 49:3 (2006), 851–75.

68 Anthony Coughlan, *C. Desmond Greaves, 1913–1988: an obituary essay* (Dublin: Irish Labour History Society, 1990), p. 7.

69 Seán Redmond, *Desmond Greaves and the origins of the civil rights movement in Northern Ireland* (London: Connolly Publications, 2000), p. 9. See also Bob Purdie, *Politics in the streets: the origins of the civil rights movement in Northern Ireland* (Belfast: Blackstaff Press, 1990), p. 71.

70 Interview with Barrington, 19 May 2005.

71 Devlin, *Straight left*, pp. 69, 70, 78; *Hibernia*, 1 March 1974. Devlin left the Irish Labour Party and joined the NILP in 1960. The move of party was due to his view of the respective parties' potential.

72 Finn, 'The influence of *Tuairim*', p. 196. Samuel Watt, who was also in Tuairim, was one party member who contemplated unification. See *Irish Times*, 9 April 1963; McGarry and O'Leary, *Northern Ireland*, p. 157. See also Terry Cradden, 'The left in Northern Ireland and the national question: the democratic alternative in the 1940s', *Saothar*, 16 (1991), 35–47; Aaron Edwards, *A history of the Northern Ireland Labour Party: democratic socialism and sectarianism* (Manchester: Manchester University Press, 2009).
73 Purdie, *Streets*, p. 73.
74 *Irish Press*, 3 November 1962. See also *Hibernia*, December 1962; UCD, AD, P24, Blythe papers, 1518, 1489, McElroy to Blythe, 5, 10 October 1962.
75 *Cork Examiner*, 23 March 1968. See also minutes of committee meeting of Tuairim's Dublin branch, 6 February 1968.
76 *Irish Press*, 3 November 1962. See also McGarry and O'Leary, *Northern Ireland*, pp. 277–8; Kennedy, *Division*, p. 179; Horgan, *Lemass*, p. 343. Lemass thought that the EEC would help to bring about a united Ireland. See also Donal Barrington, 'After Sunningdale', *Administration*, 24:2 (1976), 256. Barrington claimed that while the EEC would not bring unity, it would make the problem irrelevant.
77 *Hibernia*, 3 June 1960. See also *Hibernia*, July 1961, September 1962, June 1958. Scott argued for a new radical party which would support a return to 'external relations' with the Commonwealth.
78 Edmond Grace, 'Foreword' to Irish Association, *Council of Ireland*. Grace sent the paper to 'members of the legislatures, leaders of opinion as well as members' of the Irish Association. The full series of papers on 'Ireland in the constitutional context' appeared in *Administration*. Gibson contributed three papers, 'Constitution building in Ireland', 'Political possibilities for the people of Northern Ireland' and 'Note on financial relationships between Britain and Northern Ireland'; See also Rev. Dr Eric Gallagher, *Inter-denominational trust* (Dublin: Irish Association for Cultural, Economic and Social Relations, 1973); interview with Declan White, Dublin, 8 June 2005; Bew, Darwin and Gillespie, *Passion and prejudice*, p. 113; correspondence with Jean Whyte, 9 May, 2005. Jean is the late John Whyte's wife; they were also members of PACE (Protestant and Catholic Encounter).
79 Donal Barrington, 'Council of Ireland in the constitutional context', *Administration*, 20:4 (1972), 43–5. See *Hibernia*, 21 September 1973. See also Finn, 'The influence of *Tuairim*', pp. 217–22.
80 *Cork Examiner*, 21 October 1972; *Irish Press*, 21 October 1972; *Irish Independent*, 24 October 1972. FitzGerald was the Minister for Foreign Affairs from 1973 to 1977. His book *Towards a New Ireland* may have acted as an impetus for Tuairim to organise this meeting. See Whyte, *Northern Ireland*, pp. 121–2. See also Austin Currie, *All hell will break loose* (Dublin: O'Brien Press Ltd., 2004), p. 199; Devlin, *Straight left*, pp. 185–6; Paul Routledge, *John Hume: a biography* (London: Harper Collins Publishers, 1997), pp. 118–19.
81 *Irish Independent*, 6, 10 October 1972; Conor Cruise O'Brien, *States of Ireland* (London: Granada Publishing, 1979). John Hume described Cruise O'Brien's book as 'a case in defence of Unionism', *Irish Independent*, 16 October 1972.

See also *Irish Independent*, 13, 16, 17, 22, 26 October 1972; *Cork Examiner*, 26 October, 4 November 1972; Conor Cruise O'Brien, *Memoir: my life and times* (Dublin: Poolbeg Press, 1998), pp. 338–40; Devlin, *Straight left*, pp. 187–8; Desmond, *Finally*, p. 145. Cruise O'Brien would have fundamentally disagreed with the SDLP's call for a British declaration in favour of unity.

82 *Hibernia*, 4 June 1976; *Irish Times*, 28 April 1976; Gallagher, *Labour*, p. 212. Thornley also said that if he was sent for trial before the Special Criminal Court, he would refuse to recognise it. See also *Hibernia*, 27 June, 25 July 1975; Thornley, 'Labour'. A profile of Thornley claimed that he attacked Cruise O'Brien in 1971 for what he saw as a 'deviation from the traditional association of Labour and Republicanism'. He had also stated that the party had been insufficiently nationalistic in 1963. In 1975, he explained that his Republicanism came from his parents and an 'academic affection' for Pádraig Pearse. See Michael D. Higgins, 'Dr David Thornley, TD: an intellectual in Irish politics', in Thornley (ed.), *Unquiet spirit*, pp. 153–64. Higgins described Thornley's attitude as both critical of the IRA and defensive of its right to be heard. See also Desmond, *Finally*, pp. 83, 141, 144–5.

83 Thomas Hennessey, *A history of Northern Ireland, 1920–1996* (Dublin: Gill and Macmillan, 1997), pp. 162–8. The British Army arrived in August 1969, following an upsurge in violence.

84 *Cork Examiner*, 21 October 1972; *Irish Press*, 21 October 1972.

85 *Irish Press*, 21 October 1972; FitzGerald, *All in a life*, p. 91; FitzGerald, *Reflections*, pp. 93–7, 177–8. The *Irish Press* stated that the principle of consent was 'in tune with the feelings of all parties in the Republic'. According to FizGerald, Fine Gael and Labour adopted the principle in 1969. Fianna Fáil did not, however, formally adopt it until 1993. See also Keogh, *Twentieth-century Ireland*, pp. 356–7, 369–73; McGarry and O'Leary, *Northern Ireland*, pp. 49, 101, 131–3.

86 The quotations in this paragraph are from an article in the *Irish Times* of 22 June 1970.

87 Peacocke papers, Tuairim Press release, 20 June 1970. Tuairim's President, William Peacocke, issued this statement. The other recommendation that the statement referred to was the deletion of the special position of the Catholic Church from Article 44. Peacocke claimed that the report had been unsuccessfully 'used as a wedge with which to abolish Proportional Representation'. See Keogh, *Twentieth-century Ireland*, pp. 265, 296, 437–8.

88 *Hibernia*, 3 July 1980. Daly was also involved in welfare work for republican prisoners. See David McKittrick, Séamus Kelters, Brian Feeney and Chris Thornton, *Lost lives: the stories of the men, women and children who died as a result of the Northern Ireland troubles* (Edinburgh: Mainstream, 1999), p. 831. Daly resigned from the IRSP in the late 1970s. See also interviews with McDonagh, 24 June 2005, and Barrington, 19 May 2005. Barrington, then a High Court judge, was among those who attended her funeral. He received criticism for doing so from some quarters.

89 Correspondence with Roy Johnston, 8 June 2005; 13 June, 15 December 2005; *Irish Democrat*, November 1961; interview with Seán Redmond, Dublin,

8 August 2005. See Ray Rivlin, *Shalom Ireland: a social history of Jews in Ireland* (Dublin: Gill and Macmillan, 2003), p. 186 for further information on Daiken. See also Ed Moloney, *A secret history of the IRA* (New York: W.W. Norton and Company, 2002), p. 57; Roy H. W. Johnston, *Century of endeavour: a biographical and autobiographical view of the twentieth century in Ireland* (Carlow Tyndall Publications, in association with Dublin: Lilliput Press, 2006); e-version, *A century of endeavour: a father and son overview of the 20th century*, private source 2005. Johnston stated that Rudd also supported the efforts to politicise the IRA. Please contact Dr Johnston by email (rjtechne@iol.ie) should you wish to access his e-book.

90 *Irish Democrat*, November 1966. See also correspondence with Roy Johnston, 13 June 2005. Johnston stated that Greaves would have been dismissive of Rudd largely because she was a woman but also because she was a Tuairim supporter. He claimed that Greaves did not believe anything good would come of Tuairim. See also Johnston, *Century of endeavour*, p. 1968.
91 *Irish Democrat*, 10 October 1960, May, June 1959.
92 Ibid., October 1958. See also ibid., August 1959; *Hibernia*, February, June 1959.
93 *Hibernia*, April 1962.
94 Rudd papers, Boland to O'Neill, 1 July 1961. See also Rudd papers, O'Neill to Boland, 30 May 1961.
95 Ibid., Boland to Johnston, 27 February 1961, Johnston to Boland, 1 March 1961. See also ibid., Boland to Johnston, 20 March 1961.
96 Roy Johnston, 'Independence, partition and the emigrants', *An Occasional Bulletin*, 4 (1961), 5; *Irish Press*, 18 May 1961.
97 *An Occasional Bulletin*, 2 (1960).
98 Rudd papers, letter by Boland, 10 September 1961.
99 *Irish Independent*, 24 February 1959; *Hibernia*, September 1961, July 1962. See *Hibernia*, July 1961, August 1962; *Irish Times*, 25, 30 January 1969. The collection of the Nationalist MP Cahir Healy at the Public Record Office of Northern Ireland contains a number of letters written between 1960 and 1965 in which Healy defends the Nationalist Party against Scott's criticism. See also *Hibernia*, July, August 1958, September, October 1958.
100 Scott wrote an 'open letter' in which he appealed to the IRA to direct its energies to more worthwhile causes than 'murder'. There followed a brief correspondence with three individuals who claimed to be active in the organisation. Barrington's approach was slightly different: he criticised those engaged in the use of violence in Northern Ireland as 'pathetic' but also wrote that the 'failure in Ireland has been the failure of a whole people to adapt its thinking to changing circumstances, and the result has been to throw up a new generation whose ideas are forty years out of date'.
101 O'Brien, *States*, p. 271. O'Brien did not claim that McKeown supported Sinn Féin-IRA, although the implication was present. See McKeown, *Nationalist*, pp. 112, 125. McKeown interviewed Daithí Ó Connaill, the Chief of Staff of the IRA. McKeown believed that the risks of such people not being heard and thus not taking responsibility for their actions were greater than the risks of

them being heard and justifying their actions. The *Republican News* criticised McKeown for his 'hostility to the Republican movement'. McKeown, who stopped writing for *Hibernia* in 1975, was annoyed with the manner in which his articles were edited. He seems to have disagreed with the direction the periodical had taken.

102 *Hibernia*, 10 September 1971. See also ibid., 14 November 1975. According to *Hibernia*, Kelly was an 'implacable critic of republicans and the romanticisation of conflict'. His opposition to republicanism resulted in him repeatedly criticising the Fianna Fáil party. See Horgan, *Broadcasting*, p. 134; FitzGerald, *Reflections*, pp. 176–7; FitzGerald, *All in a life*, pp. 91, 97–8, 102. See also *Irish Times*, 22 May 1973; *Hibernia*, 25 May, 8 June 1973. O'Brien maintained that 'quite a number of your contributors and past contributors' had been members of Sinn Féin and thus supportive of the Official IRA. He did not name any of these individuals.

103 *Hibernia*, 28 May, 30 April 1971. See ibid., 19 February, 14, 28 May, 25 June 1971. See also ibid., 8 June 1973. O'Brien identified MacAonghusa as a republican, thus suggesting that he was also sympathetic to Sinn Féin. MacAonghusa wrote a column in *Hibernia* from 1969 to 1971. See Horgan, *Broadcasting*, pp. 87–8, 177–8; *Hibernia*, 13 July 1971; *Irish Times*, 30 January 1971; www.rte.ie/news/2003/0928/macaonghusap.html, accessed on 7 October 2008. See Hennessey, *Northern Ireland*, pp. 171–3. The controversy regarding whether the republican movement should end its policy of parliamentary abstentionism contributed to the IRA's split in December 1969 and Sinn Féin's split in 1970.

104 Minutes of committee meeting of Tuairim's Dublin branch, 24 June 1970; see Chapter 1 n. 11.

105 Peacocke papers, Tuairim press release, 20 June 1970.

4

Discourse and discord: Tuairim's challenge to the conservative consensus on education and childcare

Tuairim advocated radical reforms to primary, post-primary and third-level education as well as to the system of childcare in Ireland. Increased investment in primary and post-primary schools, an end to divisions between the different strands of education and a third-level sector where both UCD and Trinity would play a full part in the future of the country were among the recommendations made by the society. Tuairim's vision was of a more integrated system of education for all individuals including those children in full-time care. This was radically different from that of the Department of Education, which maintained that the state had a limited role in education and childcare, while the Catholic Church considered these areas within its sphere of influence. Tuairim's views resulted in its being regarded with hostility by elements of the political and religious establishments. That was certainly the case with the Dublin branch after the publication of its pamphlet on university education. This is the first pamphlet examined in this chapter. A consideration of its influence on policy formulation is followed by an assessment of the Dublin branch's pamphlet on primary and post-primary education and its impact, along with that of the London branch's publications on education. Finally, the London branch's pamphlet on the institutional care of children and its influence will be examined. An analysis of the London branch answers the question of why it had a different perspective from Tuairim in Ireland. The pamphlets and the reaction they provoked also reflect the changing nature of debates in relation to education and childcare during this period. As the 1960s progressed, the government increasingly considered reforms in areas where the Catholic Church had a vested interest. Though this chapter indicates that Tuairim's pamphlets impacted upon the political mainstream, it also highlights the difficulties the society faced in attempting to influence such a sensitive area of public policy.

Conservative consensus

Tuairim claimed that increased investment in educational facilities was crucial for Ireland's economic and social development as well as 'its spiritual and cultural needs'.[1] The education and childcare systems were organised on denominational lines, with the emphasis on the spiritual and cultural role of education dominating the government's policy since independence. Primary and post-primary schools, in particular, were designed to meet the spiritual needs of the population and to promote the national aspiration that Irish become the vernacular of the country. The state's attitude was reflected in the Council of Education, appointed by the government in 1950, whose reports on primary and secondary schools in 1954 and 1960 rejected proposals for reform and indicated a complacency regarding the existing educational system.[2] The dominant viewpoint in Irish society supported the influence of the Catholic Church in this area. This was underlined in the priority given by the state and the Catholic Church to primary and secondary schools to the detriment of vocational education. While the post-primary education system consisted of both secondary and vocational schools, the greater emphasis on the former was due to the larger numbers which they educated, but came about also because the Catholic hierarchy was suspicious of the secular and relatively independent nature of the vocational educational system. In any event, the Catholic Church, despite such concerns, was highly influential in vocational as well as primary and secondary education. The vocational schools were intended for the weaker students, who were generally limited to two years' education and were not prepared for the main second-level examinations, the Intermediate and Leaving Certificates, and hence were unable to proceed to higher education. This reflected a certain snobbery that associated technical education with the lower classes in Irish society.[3]

This remained the orthodoxy up to the late 1950s. A notable challenge to the consensus in this area was the Irish National Teachers' Organisation's *A plan for education*, published in 1947. Calling for changes to how Irish was taught, a raising of the school-leaving age and the co-ordination of the different strands of education, this report was dismissed and ignored by government and vested educational interests. Increasing criticism of the educational system during the 1950s, partly in reaction to the Council of Education's report, however, challenged this complacent attitude. Foremost in this were Professor John O'Meara of the Latin Department at UCD and Seán Ó Catháin of the Education Department also at UCD. O'Meara's pamphlet *Reform in education* and Ó Catháin's articles in *Studies* criticised the curriculum and advocated a reduction in the time allocated to the teaching of Irish and Latin. The methods used to teach Irish were increasingly questioned during the late 1950s. This criticism, combined with recognition of the connection between education and economic development, led to calls for reforms and increased state investment. For instance, in 1959 Patrick Cannon, the President of the Federation of Catholic Lay Secondary Schools, and in 1960 a teacher, T. J. McElligott, writing in the *Irish Times*, criticised the education system and contrasted the expenditure by the Irish state with the expenditure by Britain and Northern Ireland.[4] The demands facilitated certain reforms by the government, including an end to the ban on married women teachers in 1958, but more important was the background to the dramatic and sustained initiatives of the 1960s.

Similarly, in line with its general approach, the government did not wish to intervene in industrial schools, reformatories and other institutions which were also under church control. Reformatories had been established in Ireland after 1858, and the first industrial school followed in 1869,[5] in response to the inadequacy of existing provisions for delinquent children. For them to succeed, it was critical that Catholic objections were met. The Catholic Church, which was already active in this area, assumed responsibility for the management and maintenance of industrial schools for Catholic children. Unlike the situation in England, which during the twentieth century introduced reforming legislation and made determined efforts to keep families intact, in Ireland industrial schools and reformatories seemed to provide a solution for children in need of care. Once committed, many children remained in these schools until they were sixteen. Upon being released they had little idea of how to look after themselves, and at least some migrated to England. Revelations of physical and sexual abuse during the 1990s, but particularly as revealed by the Ryan report in 2009, have illustrated that many of these institutions were not only seriously inadequate, but also potentially deeply damaging to their inmates. While the extent to which church, state and society had knowledge of this abuse has been a controversial subject, it is now generally accepted that all to different degrees were complicit in subjecting children to abuse. The state provided the legal and financial framework within which the schools operated, and the church the personnel that ran them, and at least some sections of society were aware that the care provided in these institutions was inadequate. With exceptions such as criticism by the Department of Education from 1939 to 1945 of the conditions in the schools, and certain reservations expressed in the 1936 government-commissioned Cussen report in relation to the nature of education the children received, there was general satisfaction with the system. Institutions reflected a class divide in which children from less propitious circumstances were perceived as defective and a public morality that made it difficult to question the suitability of their facilities.[6]

Like the education system, the system of childcare began to be questioned during the 1950s. In the case of industrial schools and reformatories, it was the system, but not the Catholic Church, which tended to be criticised in articles in *Studies* and *Christus Rex*. The Rev. Cecil Barrett, the Director of the Catholic Social Welfare Bureau, M. McCauley, a member of the Adoption Board, and Ann Kenny, who compared facilities in a children's home in London with those in an Irish institution, claimed that these institutions should be 'a last resort'.[7] Similarly, the Joint Committee of Women's Societies and the Social Workers, the Joint Committee on Vandalism and Juvenile Delinquency and the Commission of Youth Unemployment argued for reform. Calls were made for more assistance to keep families together, for existing large-scale institutions to be replaced with smaller homes and for the provision of alternatives such as foster homes and adoption, as established by the Adoption of Children Act passed by the Dáil in 1952.

Such views anticipated those in Tuairim's pamphlet and made at its meetings. The society tended to be most pointed in its criticism of the system. Foreshadowing an article he wrote in *Studies* in 1963 as well as parts of the London branch's pamphlet in 1966, James O'Connor, a barrister, speaking at a meeting of the Dublin branch in 1959, was particularly critical of industrial schools and the length of detention of many of its inmates. He went further in his article: he argued that the system had 'serious defects'; in many cases, he claimed, the children's court was 'left with no alternative' but to place those before it in institutions.[8] Moreover, 'rigid and severe' discipline and 'lack of contact with the opposite sex' often led to 'violent and irresponsible' reactions when children were released from these schools and 'to a degree of sexual maladjustment in the inmates'. The Department of Education continued, however, to defend the system. Notwithstanding that, the Ryan report maintains that a 'consensus' was emerging from 1965 as to the need for reform.[9] Reviews of Tuairim's pamphlet by the Department of Education and Fidelma Clandillon, an inspector of boarded-out children in the Department of Health, indicates that the society was part of this new perspective; significantly they also indicate that civil servants were, at the very least, aware of the pamphlet. Meanwhile, religious orders managing the schools were intent on continuing to operate the system, a point emphasised by their requests for more rather than fewer children in response to a decrease in the number committed by the courts during the 1950s. Though this remained the primary concern for some orders during the 1960s, the system of funding was increasingly under pressure with the decline in numbers; it is also the case that some orders responded to the more liberal society and introduced smaller-scale homes for children, thus reflecting best practice. More generally, these reforms echoed the changes within the education system.

University challenge

As with the institutional care of children and with primary and post-primary education, the origins and divisions within the university sector in Ireland reflected the divisions generally within Irish society. Trinity College, which was exclusively Protestant until the late eighteenth century, continued to be associated with the Church of Ireland in the nineteenth century and during part of the twentieth. It was the only university in Ireland from 1592 to 1845, when, the Queen's Colleges were established in Cork, Galway and Belfast.[10] The Catholic Church deemed these institutions unsuitable because they were non-denominational. This question led to a clash between the Young Irelanders and Daniel O'Connell and their competing interpretations of what constituted the Irish nation. The Young Irelanders viewed the new colleges as an 'essential part of creating a real Irish nation' whereas O'Connell, who needed the Catholic Church's support for his political campaigns, opposed the 'Godless' colleges.[11] Established in Dublin in 1854, the Catholic University was a response to the demand for Catholic higher education. In 1908, it became part of the federal National University, which consisted of UCD, UCC and University College Galway (UCG); the latter two replaced the colleges in Cork and Galway.

The university was dominated by a Catholic ethos from its foundation. This Catholic sense of identity was very much reflected in the ideals of Michael Tierney, the President of UCD from 1947 to 1964. Tierney, who had strong links with the Fine Gael party, and Archbishop McQuaid were close allies throughout this period. They both emphasised the Catholic nature of UCD and were hostile to Trinity. In return for 'co-operating with the archbishop's wishes' with respect to UCD, Tierney was able to rely on McQuaid's support in a number of areas including the future location of the college. The increased numbers of students attending UCC, UCG and, in particular, UCD were creating significant pressures for space within all the colleges. After experiencing frustration in seeking sites around Earlsfort Terrace, its existing location, Tierney became convinced that the only solution was for UCD to move to Belfield. His vision was of a 'Catholic and independent university' situated at Belfield.[12] Almost immediately after he became president in 1947, Tierney's determination to overcome all challenges saw him become the driving force behind UCD acquiring property by the Stillorgan Road. In this, the Department of Education was one of his main supporters.

Tuairim's pamphlet *University College Dublin and the future* (1960) challenged the wisdom of UCD's proposed move. It followed discussions in the government and between the government and UCD's authorities on the move to Belfield as well as increasing resistance from within and outside the university to such plans. As part of that opposition, Tuairim argued for increased co-operation between UCD and Trinity and was fundamentally opposed to Tierney's and McQuaid's ideals for the future of the university sector. The latter two saw the universities as rivals and thought that any new relationship between them would be disadvantageous to UCD. This view was partly due to Tierney's belief, which would have been shared by McQuaid, that Trinity was threatening UCD's fair share of the country's resources. Furthermore, Tierney's nationalism emphasised the Catholic nature of the nation and dismissed the past achievements of the Protestant ascendancy. His views reflected his admiration for Daniel O'Connell; the corollary of this was his rejection of Thomas Davis and the Young Irelanders. This contrasted with the Davis type of nationalism that Tuairim advocated; the society's openness to individuals from both colleges and all religions would have irritated Tierney. The president did not easily tolerate individuals or organisations that were opposed to what he saw as the college's best interests. Because many of Tuairim's members were students in UCD and active in various societies, such as the Literary & Historical Society (L & H), during the late 1940s and early 1950s, they were aware of Tierney's methods. His presidency was notorious for rows with students, the banning of societies meetings, in particular those of the L & H, and the censoring of college publications. Many individuals resented his autocratic style and questioned the secrecy surrounding the proposed move to Belfield. These controversies underlined the need for a commission to examine the future needs of UCD and higher education in general. They also reflected Tierney's personality, which was emblematic of the paternalistic culture in Ireland at this time. Deterioration in relations with many individuals including Donal Barrington replaced the earlier optimism following the election as president of someone who was after all a man of serious intellect.[13] This was particularly the case in the aftermath of the publication of the *Report of the Commission on Accommodation Needs of National University of Ireland* (1959) and Tuairim's pamphlet *University College Dublin and the future*.

Tuairim questioned the divisions between the Dublin colleges; to this end, the society encouraged discussion on the future of university education between individuals from the two Dublin colleges at a study weekend in Glendalough in March 1957. With limited co-operation and few contacts between the two colleges during this decade, Tuairim thus provided a valuable opportunity to examine issues such as the financing of the third-level sector and UCD's proposed move to Belfield. Professor T. W. Moody of the History Department and J. K. Hudson, the Appointments Officer, represented Trinity while Garret FitzGerald, a member of Tuairim who in 1955 as a correspondent with the *Irish Times* had written a number of articles on university education, and Roger McHugh, a lecturer in English, a member of UCD's governing body and a senator from 1954 to 1957, were from a UCD background. The question of the number of foreign students attending Irish universities was one controversial issue addressed by FitzGerald. Trinity claimed that the reason for its high number of foreign students was the church's ban on Catholics attending the college, an argument that was, however, later rejected by the Commission on Higher Education (this was established in 1960 to examine the whole sphere of third-level education). The reality was that an unhealthy rivalry for finance and students had developed between UCD and Trinity. This was partly due to the ban and the consequent need for alternative courses for Catholics in UCD but also because of the attempts by the new Provost, A. J. McConnell, to integrate Trinity more fully into Irish life.

At the study weekend, McHugh, a long-term opponent of Tierney, called for 'a unified policy on financial endowment' rather than the practice of each college putting forward 'conflicting claims' which were then easily resisted by governments.[14] He pointed to the tensions between the different colleges, with those in Cork and Galway fearing that there would be grave implications for them if UCD moved to Belfield and became independent. Their concern was that if UCD received the resources to move to a new site, it would become so powerful that their position would decline. Tierney and his supporters within UCD, on the other hand, thought that the Cork and Galway colleges were undermining the Belfield case. Referring to the divisions with Trinity, McHugh commented that the segregated nature of the university sector was contrary to the national interest. He warned that it would be difficult to make progress towards a united Ireland if 'we allow fortified frontiers between our universities'. Comparisons between Northern Ireland and the nature of the two universities in Dublin were common in this period. Frank Winder, who had studied in both UCD and Trinity, reflected Tuairim's hopes for increased co-operation in this sector; he stressed the need for a commission to examine the whole question of university education in Ireland, a call that was supported by those who attended the weekend. The debate continued in the letters pages of the *Irish Times* in March and April 1957. Responding to the news that college fees for students would be increasing from the following October, McHugh argued that 'every alternative to the raising of fees should be thoroughly examined' including 'abandoning the Belfield project...which...seems both uncertain and expensive'.[15] Winder agreed, commenting that 'none of the major problems [in the third-level sector] could be considered in isolation'.[16] He claimed that in the context of the country's 'comparative poverty', the idea of one university spending 'millions of pounds on an entirely new college for itself [was] almost incredible' and described the project as a 'great white elephant'. A letter from the Tuairim member Gerard Quinn, a lecturer in economics at UCD, however, supported the assertion of Thomas E. Nevin, the Professor of Experimental Physics, that the 'facts regarding Irish university education are thoroughly well known'.[17] He shared Nevin's reluctance to have a commission examine the college's proposed move.

Arguments continued over the extent to which there was public accountability for the Belfield project, the cost involved, the amount of space available in the city centre, and whether a commission was needed. McHugh foreshadowed some of the ideas expressed in Tuairim's pamphlet, including the view that the college should remain in the city and build 'up instead of out'.[18] Donal McCartney, in his study of the college, has claimed that 'some of the points…influenced' the calls by the government ministers Seán MacEntee and Jim Ryan for a commission.[19] McCartney may well be correct in that the letters from McHugh and Winder contained similar views to those in the memoranda by the two ministers. The letters controversy, certainly, left the wisdom of UCD's proposed move to Belfield open to question and illustrated that Tuairim and Winder were part of a larger opposition to Tierney and his plans for the college. That also included individuals such as John O'Meara, the Professor of Latin at UCD, who argued for 'some union' between the two colleges.[20]

The UCD President had, however, been remarkably successful in convincing the government of the merits of his views in relation to university education. One exception was the Minister for Health, Seán MacEntee, who had serious misgivings about the Belfield project. In 1957, after the Minister for Education, Jack Lynch, pressed for government action on the decision by the previous inter-party government for the college to move to Belfield, MacEntee wrote a memorandum against the proposed relocation. He repeated some of the arguments that he and others had previously made and MacEntee claimed that a 'practical effort at decentralisation' should be attempted and consideration should be given to providing further resources for the universities in Cork and Galway rather than for UCD.[21] He further stated that the college could do more to explore possible sites around Earlsfort Terrace and stressed the need for a commission. In this way, MacEntee, like McHugh, made at least some of the arguments that were later put forward by, among others, Tuairim. On the other hand, Lynch, supporting UCD's plans, argued that the college could not continue at Earlsfort Terrace and repeated the view put forward by many supporters of the proposed move that a commission could only 'draw attention to facts already known'.[22] MacEntee's views contrasted with Lynch, and with those of Eamon de Valera and the majority of the government of which he was a minister as well as the attitude of the two inter-party governments of 1948–51 and 1954–57. Furthermore, there were few attempts by either Fianna Fáil or the inter-party governments to improve the relationship between UCD and Trinity. The Department of Education certainly did not wish to integrate Trinity more fully into Irish life and remained steadfastly behind UCD's proposed move to Belfield. Faced, however, by the Ministers for Health and significantly, Finance, Lynch had little choice but to accede to their demand for a commission. The commission on the accommodation needs of the National University of Ireland was established in 1957 to inquire into the accommodation needs of the three colleges of the university and whether it was preferable to transfer UCD to Belfield or for it to remain in the city centre.

Tuairim was severely critical of the commission and its findings. Chaired by Mr Justice Cearbhaill Ó Dálaigh and including a number of businessmen such as J. J. Davy, Joseph Wrenne and Aodhogán O'Rahilly, it was the first commission to examine any area of higher education since independence and represented a belated response to the significant pressures on the colleges. Because it viewed each college as 'virtually an independent institution', the commission examined UCD's needs independently of those of UCC and UCG.[23] It claimed that its terms of reference excluded a consideration of co-ordination between the different colleges or indeed between the colleges and Trinity. Tuairim criticised this interpretation, as did O'Rahilly, who in his reservation to the main report argued that because UCD was 'utterly overcrowded', and Trinity was 'struggling to keep open by taking in foreign students', amalgamating the colleges and rationalising their courses was the only possible solution to the university problem in Dublin. The majority of the commission's members, however, attached considerable importance to the maintenance of the 'physical unity of [each] college'. They claimed that without this unity, students and staff from different faculties would not be in a position to meet and thus one of the most important functions of a university would be lost.

In relation to UCD, the commission emphasised the overcrowding at Earlsfort Terrace and argued that there was insufficient room for the buildings required in that or the surrounding area. The majority of its members maintained that the 'only alternative solution was to transfer the entire College to a new site'. They thus accepted Tierney's case that the best site available was the 250 acres acquired by the college authorities at Stillorgan Road: it offered 'a final solution to the College's accommodation problem'. Tuairim challenged this and many of the commission's other findings, including the costs involved in the proposed move. Similarly to Tuairim, O'Rahilly argued that the cost of the move would 'be nearer to £10 million than to £5 million'.[24] With the exception of O'Rahilly, the commission accepted the college's figures and indeed its case for a move to Belfield. UCD's authorities responded with a brochure, *University College Dublin and its building plans*, which retold the story of the college's efforts to acquire sites and of its new location. Rather than supporting the proposed move, Tuairim insisted, however, that parts of the brochure actually illustrated the argument that the college should remain in the city centre, including the college's claim that a new relationship between it and Trinity would be possible in the future. However, the college maintained that 'no arrangement short of complete fusion could have a bearing on the problem'.[25] The government subsequently decided that, subject to the approval of the Dáil, the college should move to Belfield. Despite continued reservations from Finance, the Minister for Education, Patrick Hillery, intended to seek the approval of the Dáil in the spring of 1960 for the transfer of the college to Belfield.

While Tuairim was unaware of the existence of concerns regarding the proposed move within the government, it was at this point – December 1959 – that the society produced its pamphlet in a stencilled format. It made the most significant case for UCD's remaining in the city centre. Having repeated some of the points that had previously been made by individuals such as Roger McHugh in public and Seán MacEntee in private, the society further developed these ideas, putting the arguments forward in a much more comprehensive manner. At seventy-four pages, including appendixes, it was the largest pamphlet produced by Tuairim. During the six-month period following the publication of the commission's report, the research group, which had as some of its most important members Donal Barrington, Frank Winder and Ronan Keane as well as Mary O'Reilly, an architect, examined that report, newspapers, and the college's arguments and accounts as well as publications like those by the University Grants Committee in Britain. In this way, they compared the situation in Ireland with that in certain universities in Britain as well as some in continental Europe. The pamphlet was published in January 1960 after calls to do so from those who had read it in its original format. This is an indication of the gravity with which Tuairim's members viewed the future of the third-level college. After all, the majority of the members of the research group who produced the document were graduates of UCD, with Harold Clarke the 'token Trinity Protestant'.[26] Its membership contrasted significantly with that of the commission, which consisted mainly of businessmen. In comparison to Tuairim's research group, which counted an architect among its members, the commission relied on the external advice of Raymond McGrath, the chief architect in the Office of Public Works.

The research group argued that the proposed move to Belfield was both 'undesirable and unnecessary', and believed that it would have 'grave consequences both for the College and the City'.[27] The pamphlet stated that the commission had not properly examined the factors involved and the consequences of a move from the city centre. As previously noted, it shared Aodhogán O'Rahilly's view that the commission had taken a 'narrow view of the terms of reference'; in effect it had provided an incorrect answer to a 'purely artificial question'. Tuairim's research group argued that the commission had examined the needs of each college in isolation: it was as if each one only served its immediate community and no other institutions of higher learning existed in the country. The reality, according to the pamphlet, was that there was unnecessary duplication of faculties between, for example, UCD and Trinity. Focusing on Dublin, the research group believed that significant savings were possible if UCD remained at its present site. On the other hand, it feared that co-operation would be impossible if the college moved to Belfield. Arguments relating to wasteful duplication and savings later came to the fore in the context of the debate surrounding the proposed merger of UCD and Trinity in 1967. In this way, the pamphlet underlined the need for a thorough examination of the higher education sector. The research group, however, mentioned the other institutions only insofar as they facilitated its argument that UCD should remain in the city centre.

Tuairim suggested a number of solutions to UCD's needs in the city centre; these included the purchase of land close to the college's present location and the use of the houses of the Oireachtas or government departments. The pamphlet argued that sufficient suitable sites were available in the area surrounding St Stephen's Green. In this regard, the research group was very critical of the college authorities for abandoning attempts at expanding in its present location. It claimed that opportunities to buy sites had been missed; as much as 23 acres could be acquired in the immediate term, which would even meet the commission's calculations for the amount of land required. Tuairim's pamphlet criticised the commission for the 'misleading comparisons' it made with other universities and argued that Dublin had many advantages as a location in comparison with other cities such as Manchester and Birmingham in England or Copenhagen and Aarhus in Denmark. The research group also wrote that the commission had underestimated the costs of raising the standards of the college to those of a modern university and that there would be significant consequences for the colleges in Cork and Galway if a large amount of money was spent on UCD. Both Tuairim and the commission, however, called for the establishment of a university development committee; they also warned that all the funds necessary would have to be made immediately available if it were decided that the college should move to Belfield.[28]

The research group and commission also diverged on whether there should be a limit to the number of students in a college. To ensure that the 'contact of minds from different disciplines, which is such an important aspect of university education', an institution should not, according to Tuairim, contain more than 5,000 students. Having opportunities for staff and students from diverse faculties to meet and discuss various issues was also an important consideration for the commission and the college authorities. While both planned for 5,000 students, however, neither saw the need to limit the student population to that number. On the contrary, their view was that the only solution to the college's accommodation needs was one that would allow for ample room for the future expansion of the college. The research group, on the other hand, stated that 23 acres was more than adequate for the college's present and future requirements. In the case of the student population increasing further, more facilities should be provided in Cork and Galway and new colleges should be established in, for example, Limerick. While nobody wished to see universities become too big, changes in Irish education and society resulted in the number attending UCD reaching 10,000 in 1969. Accordingly, in this regard, Tuairim's pamphlet may be seen as somewhat short-sighted. Yet few people in 1960 predicted the huge increases in the number of students going on to third-level education in Ireland. Furthermore, at least some members of Tuairim retained a belief that contact between students and staff is essential to the nature of a university; this, they maintained, would be lost once colleges became too large.[29]

Perhaps the most significant disagreement between the research group and the commission was over the latter's failure to recommend the use of compulsory purchase powers; this was central to the question of whether it was possible for UCD to remain in the city centre. The commission argued that the 'disturbance to homes and business would be too great'; its aversion to the use of these powers, apparently shared by the government,[30] reflected the attachment that Irish people had to the ownership of property. Tuairim's pamphlet, on the other hand, claimed that the disruption to commercial and residential property would be minimal, and that in any case, the university should be given priority over businesses and homes; the 'disruption to the life of the College, and the damage to its place in the community, caused by the proposed move would be so great as to far outweigh the objections to granting such powers'.

Tuairim's pamphlet further criticised the commission on a number of other matters: for miscalculating the amount of land already available to the college, exaggerating the quantity required and dismissing buildings of over two or three stories. In relation to the latter point, the commission argued against tall buildings, partly on the advice of Raymond McGrath, the chief architect of the Office of Public Works. McGrath 'favoured groups of two or three storied buildings' for a university and thought that high buildings would be too expensive; in any case the commission argued that 'in the Iveagh Gardens [they] would be out of character with existing buildings and the surrounding neighbourhood'.[31] These were important factors in the commission's decision. On these issues, Tuairim was in a minority. While the research group did not comment on the cost of high buildings, it disagreed that they would be unsuitable for the area or for a university and gave examples to support its arguments. It also stated that many of the buildings in the vicinity surrounding the college required reconstruction or replacement; in any future development, the needs of higher education should be considered paramount. UCD, it was argued, could not be considered in isolation: it was 'a problem of town planning in a most important area of the capital'. The alternative to a 'detailed development plan for the area' was its 'gradual disintegration'.

The research group claimed that the move would present serious difficulties to both staff and students; each discipline would suffer from the loss of access to facilities located in the city centre. It fundamentally disagreed with the commission as to the extent of the inconvenience caused by the move; the fact that the majority of the college's teaching hospitals were located in the north of the city meant that there was a 'very strong case for retaining the Medical School in the city centre'. In a postscript to the pamphlet, the research group was highly critical of the college authorities and particularly saw as a 'wasteful duplication' of resources its assertion that 'a town centre will be needed for the very important work of evening courses'. In that way, the pamphlet used the college's own arguments, including its claim that UCD was the successor to Newman's College; rather than making the case for a move, Tuairim believed this strengthened the arguments for the college remaining in its present location. The research group, and many others, feared that following a move to Belfield, the college could 'become progressively more divorced from the community, and in failing to serve the country as it should, may become sterile and inward looking'.

Tuairim placed a great emphasis on the value of the cultural and educational centre of the capital, which it believed would weaken and fragment if the college left the city centre. The research group argued 'that the whole complex of Government, university, cultural and educational establishments should be considered as a whole and no one aspect of it (such as the needs of UCD) can be properly studied without taking into consideration all the factors involved in the planning of this area'. Included in the area, which extended from St Stephen's College to College Green, were UCD, Trinity, the College of Surgeons, the College of Physicians, the National College of Art, the Institute for Advanced Studies, the Irish Academy, the Catholic Central Library, the Institute of Architects, the Society of Antiquaries, the National Library, the National Museum, the National Gallery, a number of schools and university hostels, hospitals, several professional bodies, state agencies, government departments and the houses of the Oireachtas. This was the most appealing aspect of the pamphlet. The research group argued that a move from the city centre would lessen the effectiveness of the college and undermine both its usefulness to the public and the contribution it could make to the future of the country.

In December 1959, the research group sent the earlier stencilled form of the pamphlet to the Taoiseach, ministers and parliamentary secretaries. The pamphlet itself seems to have been forwarded to most, if not all, individuals inside the Oireachtas as well as to many outside it, and it appears alongside the college's brochure *University College Dublin and its building plans* in a government file. The choice facing the members of the government was thus clear: whether to proceed with the college's preference and the commission's recommendation and move to Belfield or to retain UCD at Earlsfort Terrace. These were two fundamentally different visions for the future of the college. Tierney and UCD's authorities were solely concerned with the future of UCD, whereas the research group wished to see an examination of the whole higher education sector and a development plan for the city centre, of which the college was a part. According to Tuairim's Donal Barrington, the central issue was that the society wanted to 'create a great cultural capital of Dublin where the students of North and South [would] mix together and create a true Republic for the people of Ireland whereas [Michael] Tierney and the Department of Education…and the Archbishop of Dublin wanted to create a Catholic University to get [the students] away from the evil influences of the secular city'.[32] Frank McDonald supports this view and argues that UCD's move was part of Archbishop McQuaid's greater plan for 'a great Catholic axis…in the suburbs, counterbalancing the pernicious orbit of Trinity and the Protestant teaching hospitals in the city centre'.[33] The assertion that McQuaid had such a scheme in mind has, however, been dismissed by McCartney. Both accept that McQuaid supported Tierney's plans and favoured the college's new site. This was at least partly because it would allow more space for student hostels. Tuairim, on the other hand, maintained that its 'ideal, a quadrangular type of development' in the city centre would mean that the students and staff would be in closer contact with one another as well as the public than if the buildings were spread throughout Belfield.

Reaction to and influence of
University College Dublin and the future

Tuairim's pamphlet received much support and made a considerable impact inside and outside the Oireachtas. The research group claimed that it was 'widely accepted as an outstanding contribution towards a solution of [UCD's accommodation] problem'. Included in those who praised it were the *Irish Times* and *Hibernia*. The London *Times* also reported its contents. This was the second occasion on which this newspaper commented on a pamphlet published by the society.[34] Of these articles, the editorial in the *Irish Times* was the most favourable; it declared that the pamphlet was a 'convincing document' and that the decision to move UCD was 'unnecessary' and had been made on 'insufficient grounds'.[35] The editorial hoped that the government would quickly put in place a 'co-ordinated plan of development' for UCD, the institutions of technology and Trinity. Similarly, *Hibernia* claimed that the public interest demanded that the college authorities respond to the criticisms of them in the 'crisp Tuairim report'.[36]

Others were not so pleased with the pamphlet. Speaking at an NUI symposium with Tuairim's Donal Barrington and UCD's Professor Thomas E. Nevin, Senator Patrick M. Quinlan, the Professor of Mathematical Physics at UCC and a supporter of the Catholic university system, was, according to the *Irish Press* of 22 January 1960, sympathetic to his fellow college's plans. The presence of Barrington and Nevin was an indication that Tuairim had come to be seen as one of the most significant opponents to the proposed move. UCD's L & H society, in one of its periodic disputes with Tierney, perceived Tuairim as Tierney's enemy and at one of its meetings passed the motion 'that this house welcomes the Tuairim memorandum concerning Belfield...by an overwhelming majority'.[37] Speaking at the symposium, Nevin, one of the most outspoken defenders of the move, outlined UCD's needs, and its previous attempts to secure sites before warning that with the exception of the Arts and Commerce faculties, the college's difficulties were such that it could collapse within two years. Elsewhere, in a letter to the *Irish Independent*, the college Registrar and future President, Professor Jeremiah Hogan, claimed that the opponents of the move were either obstructionists or unaware of the problems involved. Tuairim's research group countered that it expected Hogan to respond to its arguments 'rather than attack their bona fides or intelligence'.[38]

These letters were part of a larger exchange which included Roger McHugh; it was referred to in the debate that was simultaneously taking place within the Dáil. McHugh stated that his views were similar to those expressed by Tuairim. Indeed, he is likely to have influenced Tuairim's members at the 1957 meeting of the society. McHugh proceeded to criticise the statement by the Fine Gael TD Patrick McGilligan in relation to Trinity: McGilligan saw UCD as the Catholic University and claimed that the two colleges were incompatible. The former Minister for Finance hoped that there would be no integration between UCD and Trinity and that the possibility thereof would not be mentioned again for at least fifty years.

McHugh thought increased co-operation would save a lot of taxpayers' money. He was particularly critical of McGilligan's suggestion that there was 'no alternative between "amalgamation" of UCD and TCD and segregation of "people among whom there could be no unity"'.[39] Patrick Byrne, also a member of Fine Gael, quoted McHugh's view of McGilligan. Byrne commended Tuairim and was sympathetic to the call for increased co-operation between the two colleges. The difference in views between the two members of the same party reflected a clash in the attitudes of different generations of UCD graduates. The younger Byrne was willing to accept Trinity as an important Irish institution whereas McGilligan, who was originally from Derry, would have been influenced by memories of arguments from the nineteenth and early twentieth centuries; past divisions within higher education, especially those prior to the establishment of the National University, continued to cast a long shadow.

The reaction of members of the government to Tuairim's views varied from hostility to curiosity. Maurice Moynihan, the secretary to the government, was pleased to receive the postscript to the memorandum from the research group while a member of the Department of Finance requested that she be sent a copy.[40] The response it had provoked, as well as Seán MacEntee's misgivings, seems to have forced the government to examine its contents. However, when the Taoiseach, Seán Lemass, requested that the Minister for Education, Patrick Hillery, have the memorandum considered, only one outcome was likely. In a detailed critique of Tuairim's pamphlet,[41] the Department of Education maintained that the research group had underestimated the difficulties of building the university in the city centre and, at times, contradicted its own arguments. The department's memorandum stated that the advantages of sites such as the Harcourt Street station were exaggerated and that the cost of remaining at its present location could well prove to be higher than that of moving to Belfield. It stated that the main reason why the commission rejected high buildings was the price thereof, a matter that the research group had neglected to mention. In relation to compulsory purchase, the memorandum argued that the pamphlet was 'uninformed and unconsidered', as the use of this power would involve significant disruption to industrial, commercial and domestic properties. The department also claimed that the college was not as dependent on part-time lecturers as the research group suggested and that Tuairim had exaggerated the difficulties for students and departments; the memorandum challenged a number of the research group's statements, at least one of which was made in a dogmatic fashion.[42] Certainly, in criticising the commission's plans and challenging the college authorities, Tuairim's research group, particularly considering the relative youth of its members, displayed a striking confidence in the merits of its views.

The department had different priorities from Tuairim: educational and cultural interests should not, it said, be given precedence over equally important claims from administrative, commercial and industrial areas. In relation to the 'cultural and educational complex', the memorandum 'observed that all the cultural and educational institutes in the area have a separate and distinct life of their own which in no way depends on their proximity to (or distance from) University College, Dublin'. The department pointed to the 'slight and occasional' contacts between undergraduate students from UCD and Trinity. Increasing the quantity and quality of these contacts was, however, one of the main reasons why Tuairim wanted the college to remain in the city centre.

Co-operation between UCD and other third-level institutions was not a consideration for the department. It remarked that UCD was a very different organisation from the institutes of technology. There were even greater obstacles to better relations between it and Trinity; these included issues of 'Control of these facilities, the financing of their provision [and] the organisation of courses in the two colleges'. The department, nevertheless, commented that the difficulties were not insuperable; the college's new location in Belfield 'need not constitute a barrier to such co-operation'. This was somewhat disingenuous given that the department had not, because of the church's ban, attempted to improve relations between the two colleges. In this regard, the memorandum referred to the increasing numbers of students from Dublin attending UCD and stated that attendance at Trinity was 'a matter of conscience'. It claimed that the students could not be expected to attend the colleges in Cork or Galway when there was already a college in their own city; rationalisation of facilities could occur only if both UCD and Trinity removed the same departments. The department's response thus reflected its view that Trinity was unsuitable for Catholics.

Perhaps the strongest argument in the memorandum concerned the need to be able to provide for the college's future needs. The department pointed to how much the college had grown in the past, claimed that there should be room for unforeseen expansion and dismissed the argument that the college had to be limited to 5,000 students. The department stated that the research group had contradicted itself in that it argued against the duplication of facilities in much of the pamphlet and proceeded to 'consider further duplication, by the establishment of other university colleges.' It concluded that the move to Belfield offered a 'satisfactory and final solution to the College's accommodation problem without disturbance to business, administration, etc., and ensures that the current problem will not again arise'.

A thorough examination of Tuairim's pamphlet, the memorandum legitimately criticised the research group on some points. In particular, the

8 The ministers Brian Lenihan, Charles Haughey, Erskine Childers and Patrick Hillery (left to right) outside government buildings in 1965.

pamphlet seemed to underestimate the difficulties involved in the college's remaining in the city centre, and the limit placed on the number of students in a college appeared impractical. The department itself could, however, have been criticised for not tackling unnecessary duplication of facilities within university education and for having ignored the changes that were taking place within Trinity. Overall, it underlined the department's determination that UCD would move to Belfield. In effect, Tuairim's pamphlet seems to have changed little, for the department proceeded with its original plan to have a Dáil debate in early 1960 (see Figure 8 for a photograph of Hillery and other government ministers).

Patrick Hillery, a medical graduate of UCD, brought the matter to the Dáil on 23 March 1960. Delivering an overview of the history of UCD's accommodation problems with particular reference to the recent rapid increase in student numbers and the likelihood of a continuance of that upward trend, Hillery argued that there was 'no reasonable alternative' to the move to Belfield.[43] That Tuairim had been in his view unreasonable was, as discussed later, the obvious implication. Hillery's speech elaborated on many of the arguments in the department's critique of Tuairim's pamphlet, praised the commission and strongly supported its recommendations. He rejected the possibility that there should be some form of integration or amalgamation between UCD and Trinity, basing his argument on of Article 42 of the Irish Constitution: the 'State shall not oblige parents in violation of their conscience and lawful preference to send their children...to any particular school designated by the State'. Indeed, he went on to argue against any kind of arrangement between any of the four colleges in the present time or, it seems, in the future. This was an interpretation with which Donogh O'Malley disagreed when advocating a merger between UCD and Trinity, both during the Dáil debates and as Minister of Education in 1967. O'Malley, who had good relations with Tuairim, described its research group as an 'excellent body'. He quoted the figures in the pamphlet; this was by way of illustrating the difficulty of realising the hope, as expressed by Hillery and others, that everyone in the country would have the opportunity to access university education. The different views of O'Malley and Hillery, particularly regarding Trinity, reflect the changing nature of public opinion during this decade. But they also point to the fact that O'Malley was a more liberal and charismatic individual than the cautious Hillery. Their attitude towards Tuairim underlines this distinction.

The opinion of the members of the Oireachtas was on the whole in favour of the move to Belfield. Nevertheless, several members on both sides of the Dáil and Seanad, even some of those who supported the minister, complimented Tuairim on its pamphlet. Fine Gael's James Dillon defended the society's right to speak on the subject against those who resented its 'intrusion' and who described its members 'as nothing but "nosey-parkers" and mischief makers'. Some individuals criticised Tuairim for not having published the pamphlet while the commission was sitting. Many within UCD shared these views and were reproved by at least one Dáil deputy for statements that implied that one could not even refer to an alternative. The research group's response to such criticisms was that it was impossible to make an 'informed submission' any earlier, that is, while 'the detailed facts...were not available to the public'.[44] Nevertheless, Fianna Fáil's Vivion de Valera and Fine Gael's Patrick Byrne, both of whom favoured the move, thought that its pamphlet had arrived 'too late' to influence the decision.[45] De Valera elaborated on the reasons why he rejected Tuairim's 'interesting document', which he had read with a 'great interest and a good deal of sympathy'; he favoured the commission's report because it would have had the greater resources and the 'expert advice available [to it] would at least be as good as the volunteer advice available in the Tuairim report'. The crucial factors that led him to support the move to Belfield were the extra space available, his belief that the college could not be united in one site if it remained in the city centre and his opposition to the use of the power of compulsory purchase. Moreover, the pride he shared with other UCD graduates, such as Patrick McGilligan, James Dillon and Patrick Hillery, in that college's tradition and his view that Trinity had a different tradition caused him to reject proposals for integration between the two institutions. Patrick Byrne's attitude was different; while he supported the move, he argued for increased co-operation between UCD and Trinity. He 'was impressed by the case' that Tuairim made and shared Dillon's concern that it should not be seen as 'nosey-parkers'. Byrne went further and claimed that everyone was 'indebted' to Tuairim and praised its 'disinterested zeal and… altruism'. He also referred to Tuairim's place in the country; because the organisation consisted of educated individuals, he argued, its members had a 'duty to society', a role to play as 'leaders of society', and he challenged them to become involved in politics and seek election to the Dáil.

Unlike Byrne, some individuals seemed convinced both by Tuairim's pamphlet and by the case for a new relationship between UCD and Trinity. The National Democratic Party's Jack McQuillan dismissed the suggestion that the future of the university sector did not concern Tuairim; the society represented the state's 'younger generation', and given that it was 'non-political', its 'very excellent booklet' should have helped members from all sides of the house.[46] He feared, however, that the move was a '*fait accompli*', and that it would make better relations between UCD and Trinity all the more difficult. There was a fundamental clash between McQuillan's opinion of the value of Trinity and that of Patrick McGilligan, Vivion de Valera and Patrick Hillery, which McQuillan criticised. Even more controversially, his colleague Noel Browne, one of the few Trinity graduates in the Dáil, called for 'non-denominational Universities'.[47] Browne proceeded to criticise the authorities in both UCD and Trinity and what he referred to as their sectarian attitudes. He praised Tuairim for the trouble to which it had gone to prepare a 'comprehensive document', a 'magnificent report' and the 'simple, inconvertible facts' that could now be used by each deputy.[48]

Other individuals referred to Tuairim while expressing disquiet at the move to Belfield. These included Gerald Boland and Lionel Booth, who was also a Trinity graduate, Fine Gael's Tadhg Manley and the independent George Edward Russell. They focused on the merits of the two locations, Belfield and Earlsfort Terrace. Boland and Manley were convinced by Tuairim's pamphlet; the former claimed that the case made by the research group was 'almost unanswerable'.[49] Boland, a former minister, believed that this was particularly true in relation to the possibility of high buildings at the Iveagh Gardens. This was a point with which Booth agreed. He wondered if the cost of high buildings was as high as Hillery suggested, criticised the lack of recent efforts to provide sites in the city centre and claimed that the college could have entered into negotiations with some of the schools mentioned in Tuairim's pamphlet. Similarly, Russell was not convinced that the move was necessary; the whole area of higher education needed first to be considered. Whatever one's views were in relation to the matter, he claimed, each deputy should be grateful to Tuairim 'for offering constructive criticism and alternatives to the plans of the College authorities'.[50] On the other hand, Fine Gael's Seán McKeown was unconvinced by the pamphlet. In the end, there was little doubt but that UCD would move to Belfield. The opposition political parties, Labour and, in particular, Fine Gael, supported the government. Noel Browne was the only deputy who was recorded as being opposed to the move. Nevertheless, the records of the Dáil debate, which lasted a number of days, reveal that Tuairim's pamphlet made a considerable impact; many individuals were sympathetic with its contents. This was perhaps more true of Fianna Fáil than of Fine Gael, the latter being consistent supporters of the plans of the UCD's authorities throughout this period.

Since the move to Belfield was not discussed in the Seanad until January 1961, there was little surprise that many senators shared the view of some TDs that it was a *fait accompli*. Nevertheless, some senators spoke against the proposed move and praised Tuairim. As in the Dáil, individuals from both sides of the house commended the society for its efforts. Patrick Crowley, an independent, speaking in support of the college's present location, paid tribute to the 'excellent case' made by the research group and the 'painstaking care and great labour' which it had shown in making an 'invaluable contribution' to public debate on the matter.[51] Responding, Fine Gael's Anthony Barry spoke in favour of a merger between UCD and Trinity and praised Tuairim for its 'public spirit'; he claimed that the society was a 'fine example of intelligent citizenship'. Fianna Fáil's Seán Ó Donnabháin referred to Tuairim's pamphlet to support his contention that there were plenty of sites available in the city centre. Similarly, the liberal senator Owen Sheehy Skeffington applauded the 'trouble, care and moderation with which they express their view' and the 'eminently clear way' in which the research group had put the pamphlet together. His was perhaps the most interesting contribution to the debate. Despite the appeal of the central educational area and his wish to be associated with the tributes that were being paid to Tuairim, he believed that it had made a fundamental error; its claim that 5,000 had to be the maximum number of students in a college had, he believed, given 'away their whole case'.

Professor Michael Hayes and John O'Donovan, both of UCD, and Patrick Quinlan of UCC also strongly favoured the move to Belfield. Hayes, a long-term supporter of Tierney and his plans, spoke of the frustration at what he and others in UCD believed to be the obstructionist attitude of those who opposed the college's plans. The concern of those intimately involved with UCD's authorities at Tuairim's pamphlet was reflected in Hayes's claim that the individuals who wrote it could, if they had wished, have met Michael Tierney, Jeremiah Hogan and Professor Pierce Purcell of Engineering; the research group, however, 'did not want to hear the facts'.[52] As if to underline his displeasure with Tuairim, at no stage during his speech did Hayes actually state who wrote the pamphlet. In this he was in the majority in that his view of the society was governed by his preference as to the college's future location. There were, however, exceptions to this trend: the research group was praised by individuals who favoured the move as well as by some of those who were opposed to it; many referred to the society as having made a positive contribution to public debate and to Tuairim as a beneficial force in the country. The contrary viewpoint was reflected in the refusal of the college authorities, Archbishop McQuaid and members of the political establishment to remain open-minded in relation to the college's future location.

Tierney and McQuaid were both delighted with the government's decision that UCD should move to Belfield. The corollary of this was their view of Tuairim. Tierney was, according to Donal Barrington, outraged by the pamphlet and by Barrington's views as expressed at the symposium. Barrington thought that the episode cost him the position of Chair of Constitutional Law in UCD.[53] Given that Tierney was antagonistic towards those who argued against what he perceived as the college's best interests, he may well have acted in such a manner. There certainly was a contrast between Tuairim's relations with UCD's authorities and those of Trinity. According to McQuaid, Frank Mitchell, the Registrar of Trinity, facilitated a Tuairim discussion on education. McQuaid's support for the Belfield project and suspicion of both Trinity and Protestants in general were to the fore in his views of the society. His secretary, Leon Ó Cuinnleain, noted that the archbishop would remember 'the failure of [Tuairim's] move to keep the College in skyscrapers in Earlsfort Terrace'; perhaps of even greater concern to McQuaid was the fact that many of the society's members were against the church's ban on Catholics attending Trinity.[54] Furthermore, McQuaid, in a letter to the Apostolic Nuncio, claimed that Tuairim's views in relation to university education were 'ignorant and disloyal'. To add insult to injury, Tuairim's members were unaware that they were ignorant of Catholic teaching and had been disloyal to the Catholic Church. This, in turn, highlights the struggle between conservative attitudes and the increasingly pervasive liberal values during these decades.

During the Dáil debates on UCD's proposed move to Belfield, Patrick Hillery announced that a commission would be established to examine the whole area of higher education in the country. The need for such a commission was a matter on which both the supporters of and opponents to UCD's move to Belfield agreed. Among those who suggested individuals to serve on the commission was Seán MacEntee. Reflecting his own misgivings regarding the Belfield project, he proposed that Frank Winder, Patrick Lynch and Garret FitzGerald should be considered for membership, arguing that they were part of the 'progressive elements' in the country, represented an industrial economic outlook and would support increased facilities for scientific education and research.[55] His fear was that the interests of the Catholic Church, which he believed saw scientific education as dangerous to the faith of the laity, would otherwise dominate the commission. Significantly increased provision for the sciences was, he claimed, necessary to bring Ireland into line with other states in Northern Europe and America and for the country to meet the demands of the modern world. In this regard, he wrote that Frank Winder as a representative of the scientific community and the 'emancipated, younger' generation should be considered. MacEntee's respect for Winder and the society was further highlighted with his comment that Winder represented the 'independent, body of graduates who are associated with Tuairim'. For MacEntee, this further strengthened the case for his inclusion in the commission. The minister's doubts regarding the Belfield project seem to have been reinforced by Tuairim's pamphlet. While his support for Tuairim and Winder must be seen in that context, it was nevertheless indicative of the regard in which certain members of the government held the society.

Hillery's reply to MacEntee, on the contrary, revealed a deep suspicion and hostility to Winder and Tuairim. The minister attacked the research group: Hillery argued that it had 'taken a wholly negative attitude'; its preference was 'in effect to postpone the whole issue and to take a few more years having another look at it'.[56] This attitude was prevalent among the strongest supporters of UCD's move and was to an extent understandable given the amount of time that had lapsed since the Belfield project was first mooted. Hillery, however, went further and questioned the motives of 'these "progressive elements"'; he concluded that their wish was for the government to challenge the Catholic Church's view of higher education. He reiterated his support for the church's belief that a Catholic should not be forced to attend a non-Catholic institution. Hillery thus accepted the view that the National University was a Catholic university whereas Trinity was unsuitable for Catholics. His cautious nature meant that he was undoubtedly influenced by the steadfast support that the Department of Education gave to the Belfield project. Whereas MacEntee had displayed an independence of mind, Hillery defended the church and argued that it had done much for the sciences. While Hillery deserves credit in that he did more for the university sector than most, if not all, of his predecessors, his hostility to

Tuairim highlights the resistance to an alternative viewpoint among large parts of the establishment.

In the event, the Commission on Higher Education agreed that Trinity was a valuable Irish institution and that it wished to integrate itself fully into the life of the country. Its main recommendation was that the National University of Ireland should be dissolved and each of the three colleges be established as on independent university. Therefore, if this recommendation was accepted, the country, would, in addition to Trinity, have three universities, two of them in Dublin. On 18 April 1967, the Minister for Education, Donogh O'Malley, announced that the government had, however, decided that there would be one university in Dublin, consisting of both UCD and Trinity. The new university would be 'multi-denominational, with the fullest mutual respect and recognition for all denominations of students'.[57] In response, the *Sunday Independent* pointed to Tuairim's research group and its ideal of a 'great cultural complex running right through Merrion Square and linking up with T.C.D.', while *Confrontation*, the publication of the most radical UCD students, criticised the idea of the move to Belfield; it claimed that the opposition to the suburban location 'reached its most articulate point in the Tuairim pamphlet'.[58] This was a further indication of how widely read the pamphlet had been. As for the proposed merger, it was not realised, although discussions between representatives of UCD and Trinity facilitated an end in 1970 to the Catholic Church's ban on Catholics attending Trinity and thus that college's acceptance as a fully Irish institution. The Catholic hierarchy also responded to the more liberal climate of the late 1960s, in which the ban was becoming irrelevant and was increasingly ignored. There remained, however, much rivalry between the colleges, despite an agreement for limited rationalisation of facilities in 1970. While UCD and Trinity did not go as far as envisaged in O'Malley's original proposal, the colleges had evolved significantly from the hostile relations evident at the time when Tuairim published its pamphlet. The society had advocated reforms that were unpopular at that time. Despite continued opposition from the hierarchy and from within the universities, the need for a new relationship between the colleges had been recognised by the government. This transformation in the state's policy approach was perhaps most evident in relation to primary and post-primary education.

Tuairim's publications on primary and post-primary education

As with the university pamphlet, Tuairim's research groups were, at least in part, responsible for *Educating towards a united Europe* and *Irish education*. These were published in quick succession in September and October 1962.

During the course of their examination of the education system, interesting tensions emerged between the London and Dublin branches. The London branch's research group, established in January 1961, consisted of Joy Rudd and Miriam Daly, both of whom were involved in education, as well as Pat Crowley, an engineer. They were solely responsible for *Irish education* while the Dublin branch's pamphlet, *Educating towards a united Europe*, emanated from a study weekend in Greystones in November 1961. The Dublin branch's pamphlet was the result of the joint efforts of its research group, which included the teachers Marie Hynes and Mary Hogan as well as Máire Mullarney, a future advocate of numerous causes including home education, and the Irish section of the AEDE, an organisation established in Paris in 1956 to help 'foster…a European civic spirit'.[59] At the weekend, representatives of the AEDE and the research group, along with the playwright Thomas Kilroy who was also the Headmaster of Stratford College, Rathgar, and Charles McCarthy of the VTA, gave papers, which were incorporated into the pamphlet. Significantly, Fianna Fáil's George Colley, a recently elected TD and a future Minister for Education, and representatives of various teaching unions also attended the conference. In addition to providing a platform for discussion of the education system, the event's importance lay in the establishment of the Irish section of the AEDE. With Hynes and Hogan subsequently members of this organisation, it reflected the Dublin branch's active interest in European developments. Tuairim hoped that the new organisation would help 'foster understanding and co-operation' within the fragmented teaching profession.[60]

Hynes and Hogan were also to the fore in the tensions that emerged between the Dublin and London research groups following the publication in May 1961 of an article, 'Irish primary education', in London's *An Occasional Bulletin*. A vigorous critique of education, the piece contained a number of controversial proposals, including the establishment of an institute of education to train teachers, reconsideration of the place of Irish within the education system, the replacement of one- and two-teachers' schools with at minimum four-teacher schools and the creation of parent–teacher organisations. The institute of education would entail the closing of university departments of education and the teacher training colleges, while London's research group's belief that existing one- and two-teacher schools were not educationally or economically viable directly challenged the Catholic hierarchy's preference for small schools, which it believed would better withstand secular influences. It was, however, the tone of some of the language that was the most controversial part of this article, in particular, the reason the authors gave for what they claimed was the 'backward state of Irish education':

It is due primarily to the complacency and apathy of the people. This can be traced to the fear of upsetting the delicate balance between church and state, which is enshrined in the constitution. Churchmen have been reluctant to make constructive proposals lest they appear too dictatorial, politicians loath to change a system, which appeared to be working reasonably well. Friction has been avoided at a heavy price: stagnation in the schools.[61]

The Dublin research group's concerns related to Joy Rudd, who following a visit to Dublin seems to have left the branch with an impression that she would recommend 'non-denominational schools'.[62] At a meeting of the London branch, Rudd had advocated 'the systematic amalgamation of small schools' as well as a school transport system for children to travel to the larger central schools.[63] As if to reassure themselves that she would not recommend non-denominational education, Hynes and Hogan felt it necessary for Hogan to pay a surprise visit to London to attend one of that branch's meetings on education. The relatively radical nature of the London branch will be discussed shortly. For the moment, it suffices to comment that these tensions, at least partly caused by limited contact that was exacerbated by distance between the branches, were quickly overcome. Furthermore, it was never the intention of either research group to recommend non-denominational education.

Both pamphlets concluded that the educational system was deeply flawed and in need of significant reform. The Dublin research group used words such as 'unchanged' and 'stagnant' in referring to education, while the London branch claimed that the attitude to education was 'Victorian'.[64] They both began by tracing the development of the education system and made similar recommendations. These included a decrease in the amount of time devoted to Irish, recognition by the state of teaching experience gained in Britain, and the need for parents' voices to be heard. They also argued in favour of a higher school leaving age, the need for a vocational guidance service and a 'policy formulating body'.[65]

Proposals in relation to a future role for parents were potentially some of the most controversial. As if in recognition of this, the London research group argued for 'informal parents' organisations' which would not 'have any part in the running and organisation of the school',[66] rather than reiterating the view it put forward in *An Occasional Bulletin* that parent–teacher organisations and representatives of the Department of Education should decide the language of instruction in a school. It seems likely that the more conciliatory language reflected the influence and respect in which the society held Maynooth's Enda McDonagh. In response to the *Occasional Bulletin* piece and the subsequent tensions between the research groups, he wrote to Daly that neither 'parents nor teachers [were] ready [for the] immediate setting up of Parent Teacher organisations'.[67]

Tuairim's London pamphlet, nevertheless, reiterated and expanded upon the main proposals contained in the earlier article. It was intended that the institute of education would research problems in education as well as training all teachers. Furthermore, the authors proposed free education and equal opportunity for all children, the provision of subsidised transport, the integration of the education system and, as discussed below, where necessary, accommodation for children in special boarding schools. Indeed, London's pamphlet argued that the existing primary, secondary and vocational systems should be replaced with infant, junior and middle schools and county colleges. The research group claimed that this would have the advantages of including under-privileged children and rationalising the number of schools. Partly in response to criticisms of larger schools, they suggested that these schools could consist of several buildings, some distance apart. These should be centrally organised and share facilities and specialist teachers so that children of similar ages would be taught together in the same class, rather than, as in the current system, one person teaching students of all ages in small schools.

The London branch's proposals were, generally, more comprehensive than those considered by Dublin's research group. Rather than effectively proposing a new system of education, the Dublin pamphlet focused on the existing one and the 'fundamental adjustments [that] could be made without disrupting the system of education'. Without London's level of detail, the Dublin research group argued for increased state investment and a more balanced curriculum that would include modern languages and science subjects and which would alter 'the nationalistic bias of the present history books'.[68] The Dublin pamphlet claimed that young children, in particular, should be taught through the vernacular and that the school leaving age needed to be raised to sixteen. In contrast to the London branch, Dublin's research group gave greater consideration to history and was more definite in the age to which it believed children should remain at school. Furthermore, rather than arguing for the abolition of the university departments of education, the Dublin branch's pamphlet stated that they should be closely associated with a teacher training college. The Dublin group proposed that an institute of educational research, similar to the institute proposed by the London branch, be established to address the perceived lack of work in this area. However, it argued that the institute should co-operate with other interested parties such as the department, the body responsible for formulating policy, the universities, the teacher training colleges and the schools. This was necessary because of the government's perceived abdication of responsibility for the formulation of policy, which resulted from the 'delicate relationship between Church and State'.[69] If less forcefully, the Dublin research group echoed the words of the London branch.

While the Dublin and London research groups shared certain perceptions of the problems in education, they differed significantly in the remedies they put forward. Rather than suggesting that one was more radical than the other, it is perhaps more accurate to argue that Dublin's research group was less critical or controversial and more pragmatic in its approach than its London counterpart. Nevertheless, the London branch's pamphlet was more detailed in the issues it considered and generally more far-reaching with regard to its recommendations. Part of the explanation for these differences can be found in the group's research. Both groups conducted a significant amount of research, including studying legislation and the schools' curricula. However, the London research group directly compared the Irish educational system with Britain's, while the Dublin branch considered it in the context of possible membership of the EEC. The London branch requested and received six copies each of the rules for primary, secondary and technical education and Intermediate and Leaving Certificate examination papers in all subjects from the Department of Education in Dublin and their equivalents from the British government. They also sent over 500 questionnaires to people who had left schools in Ireland since 1956, seventy-one of which were returned and noted that the Crowther report in England had argued for a system similar to the one it proposed.[70]

Thus part of the reason for the London branch's different views was that London's pamphlet reflected to a greater degree the influence of developments in Britain. The research group was in a better position than the Dublin branch to compare the policies of the two countries. This is underlined by the London branch's view of the fate that awaited migrants to Britain. The London research group claimed that the education system left children ill prepared for life: it resulted in the Irish in London showing 'little interest or discrimination in their choice of jobs'.[71] This proved to be a contentious claim and will be further discussed in the context of the reaction to the pamphlets.

As previously noted, the Dublin branch's pamphlet included sections written by Charles McCarthy and Thomas Kilroy as well as representatives of the AEDE, namely its President, M. Alers, the chairperson of the Belgian section of the society, Jean Anthony Strauven and Michael O'Donnell, the treasurer of the Irish branch. Whereas Alers and Strauven were more concerned with the ideals of the AEDE, O'Donnell, who was also a member of Tuairim, focussed on the organisation's methods. Meanwhile, Kilroy supported the research group's call for a 'Central Educational Advisory Authority'[72] and McCarthy developed that argument by proposing that a national body would be representative of not only educational interests but also industry, commerce and agriculture. Kilroy also repeated criticisms of the overly academic basis of the curriculum and condemned pretentious attitudes towards vocational education. His main purpose, though, was to place education in a European context. In this regard, he recommended that there should be increased specialisation or streaming for fifteen- and sixteen-year-olds within secondary schools. Referring to Europe and a UNESCO report, he claimed that the standards in Irish schools were significantly lower than those in countries on the continent.

An influential figure in educational and trade union circles as well as a Tuairim member, Charles McCarthy concentrated on vocational education. Reforms proposed by him included the introduction of streaming and the establishment of regional technical colleges, which would allow its students to continue to higher education. With regard to the latter, he noted the need for both universities and, particularly, the existing third-level colleges of technology to develop their programmes further and welcome students from the different systems of education. Moreover, he argued that it should be possible to move between institutions in both post-primary and higher education. This would mark a significant step towards breaking down the barriers that existed within those levels of education. McCarthy suggested that Kilroy's streaming proposal would facilitate this possibility. Because of the different nature of the post-primary systems, McCarthy, unlike Kilroy, argued that streaming should be introduced following the first year at the vocational school and that a third-year course should be developed for the 'more able students'.[73] This, he claimed, would allow them to proceed to a highly skilled trade or higher education via regional technical colleges while 'a student of lower ability [could] enter industry or [a] less demanding apprenticeship' following her or his completion of two years at the school.

McCarthy, Kilroy and the research group each highlighted a number of anomalies in the education system, and were, in effect, proposing to overcome these through a more comprehensive system of education with increased co-ordination between the different strands. Since they were all to a greater or lesser extent affiliated to one of the systems, however, they did not share the London branch's ideal of a fully integrated system of education. On the other hand, by creating a link with Europe and directing people's attention towards developments on the continent, the Dublin branch put forward its own vision for Irish education. Taken together, the pamphlets made a comprehensive case for reform. While it is the case that many of the proposals such as curriculum reforms and an extension to the leaving age had previously been put forward by other commentators such as O'Meara, Ó Catháin and McElligott, few were as ambitious as Tuairim in the range of issues they addressed and what they recommended.

Reaction to Tuairim's pamphlets

Tuairim's pamphlets received a considerable amount of publicity, both favourable and hostile, in national and provincial newspapers in Ireland. The London branch's pamphlet, in particular, was the subject of a number of critical articles and editorials. Since the Dublin pamphlet was the first to be published, it was, therefore, the first to have its main findings reported. The *Irish Press*, the *Irish Times* and *Hibernia* each highlighted the criticisms that were put forward and recommendations made by various individuals present at Tuairim's study weekend the previous year. The *Irish Press* also noted the comments of Fianna Fáil's George Colley in support of Kilroy's proposal for the streaming of students at the age of fifteen or sixteen. Colley agreed that this was 'desirable' and claimed that some of the 'practical problems' that it would present could be overcome by 'having teachers of specialised subjects alternating between schools in rural areas'.[74] The future minister thus put forward views similar to the proposals of the London branch. Colley also welcomed the Department of Education's initiative in sending representatives to a conference in the USA on modern teaching methods. This illustrates his interest in and awareness of the need for reform in this area. Significantly, attitudes within the department had also evolved, as indicated by the contrast between its decision to send representatives to the conference and its resistance to contact with other educational systems during the 1950s. Crucially, this new approach led to the 'investment in education' survey, which, inspired by the Organisation for European Co-operation and Development, had a profound impact upon education in Ireland. Published in 1965, the report *Investment in education* was commissioned in 1962 by the Minister for Education, Patrick Hillery, and co-written by Patrick Lynch of UCD, William Hyland from the UN's Statistics Office and Martin O'Donoghue, an economics lecturer at Trinity. It proved to be hugely influential, particularly with regard to Colley's determination to ensure that future educational development was effectively planned.[75] In 1961, many of those advocating reform, however, viewed the Department of Education as primarily having an administrative role. The department had provided little evidence to suggest that it would make a more significant contribution to the formulation of policy. This meant that by placing education in the public realm, the Dublin branch's input had been valuable to the evolution of the debate on the education system.

As previously noted, much of the reaction to the London branch's pamphlet was critical. As well as generating articles in national newspapers such as the *Irish Times*, the *Irish Independent* and the *Irish Press*, the pamphlet came to the attention of newspapers outside of Ireland. These included London's *Catholic Herald* and the liberal unionist *Belfast Telegraph* as well as the political organisation National Unity. Furthermore, having sold 2,500 copies within a month of its publication, the pamphlet was discussed in the *Cork Examiner*, the *Limerick Weekly Echo* and the *Sunday Review*. It was the subject of critical reviews in the periodical *Hibernia*, the VTA's journal *Gairm* and the Protestant review *Focus*, and a generally favourable editorial in Cork's *Southern Star* as well as being serialised in the *Roscommon Herald* and discussed by a panel of educationalists on the Irish television programme *Broadsheet*. While many held Tuairim in high regard, there were varying views as to the accuracy of some of the analysis in the pamphlet and, in particular, the results of the research group's investigation into the effects of the education system. In relation to the former point, the *Irish Times* praised the society: its editorial claimed that the Dublin and London branches had published 'two well-thought out sets of proposals'.[76] That newspaper's 'London letter', which, particularly at the beginning, took a major interest in the fortunes of the London branch, 'congratulated' the research group on its 'very fine pamphlet' and claimed that it had shown 'acute penetration when dealing with the Irish in England'.

This view contrasted, however, with that of the Protestant review *Focus* and three London publications, the *Irish Catholic*, *Catholic Herald* and *Times Educational Supplement*, as well as the opinion of the journalist William Newman in the *Irish Press*. They argued that Tuairim's analysis of the Irish in Britain and the statement that the 'typical product of an Irish secondary education is a dreamer, a weaver of fantasies' was not based upon reality: Newman referred to it as 'the rankest balderdash', and the *Irish Catholic* asked wether the members of the research group had 'been dazzled by the lights of the metropolis.'[77] Newman, the *Irish Catholic* and *Focus* each pointed to a range of professionals, businesspeople and volunteers to counter Tuairim's argument. Furthermore, it was claimed that such comments damaged the overall effect of the report and many of its otherwise constructive proposals. On the other hand, the *Irish Catholic* and other publications, such as the VTA's journal *Gairm*, accused the research group of reiterating well-known criticisms of the education system, like the academic bias of the curriculum and the fact that some existing schools were inadequate. It was also argued that the research group's views were at times contradicted by existing evidence. On just this point, *Gairm* defended vocational education against claims that its teachers were poorly educated and that the curriculum in these schools was limited. That there was some truth to both Tuairim's claims and such criticism was indicated by the underdeveloped nature of adult and vocational education and the evidence that *Gairm* put forward in response, including figures for the number of people attending evening courses.[78] The diverse range of newspapers and periodicals commenting on Tuairim suggests that the London branch's pamphlet was well known throughout Ireland and among the Irish community in London. While it was welcomed as a positive contribution by some individuals, others viewed it as overly critical. As much as the wide range of issues it considered, it was the tone of the pamphlet which provoked such a strong reaction among vested interests such as *Gairm* and the Catholic publications.

These criticisms raise questions about the nature of Tuairim in London and Ireland. There was a clear implication, which at times was explicitly stated, that the society was well respected. A recurring feature of the articles in journals and newspapers was disappointment that a group of intelligent young people could make what the *Times Educational Supplement* referred to as 'intemperate' statements.[79] It was in this context and that of its interest in education that *Gairm*, for example, welcomed the fact that the London branch's pamphlet would 'stimulate thought and provoke discussion'. *Hibernia* and the liberal unionist *Belfast Telegraph* expressed the view that at least some of its proposals were, however, unlikely to be implemented. Highlighting the obstacles to reform, the *Belfast Telegraph* questioned whether the London research group's recommendations in relation to the Irish language would make an impact, while *Hibernia* pointed to the probable opposition of the Catholic Church to the proposed middle schools and that of both religious orders and universities to the establishment of an institute of education. The branch had, according to *Hibernia*, been the 'most ambitious [but] least helpful in offering practical suggestions' as to how to implement ideas; it concluded that while there were 'many shrewd observations and…helpful suggestions…the general impression it leaves is one of unreality'.[80]

Responding in the following issue of the journal, Miriam Daly rejected the claim that Tuairim had failed to consider the reality of the Catholic Church's place within the educational system. She countered that the research group's proposed committees were intended to ensure that the parish priest would maintain contact with the school. The reality was, however, that it was unclear how this would operate in practice. Daly reiterated her view that only a comprehensive system of education would 'provide equal opportunities for all children irrespective of the income of their parents' and their geographical location.[81] She called for the vocational system to be extended and claimed that members of all religions had accepted this proposal. The Catholic hierarchy's opposition, however, remained, as the *Hibernia* article suggested, a considerable obstacle to such an extension. The distinction made in private, following the earlier tensions between the research groups, that 'We are not anti-Church education just anti bad church education', would have been too fine for many people.[82] Nevertheless, she and the research group had highlighted a major weakness in post-primary education: the problem, they believed, was the absence of education for children over fourteen years of age in remote areas of the country, the solution was a comprehensive system of education modelled on the vocational system. This foreshadowed Patrick Hillery's proposals in 1963 for a pilot scheme of comprehensive schools. Elsewhere, Joy Rudd also responded to criticisms of the pamphlet, this time in the *Sunday Press*, stating that Tuairim's arguments were, in fact a 'compromise [between small schools and large comprehensive schools] in which existing small schools would be centrally organised, sharing facilities and visiting specialist teachers'.[83] This may have been the case but was perhaps disingenuous in that the research group's proposals marked a radical departure from the current system. In reality, Daly and Rudd had put forward a new basis for the education system: 'expansion into an integrated system of post-primary education' would mean that the state, and not the church, would henceforth have the major responsibility.[84]

Comparisons of the two education pamphlets led the *Irish Times* and the *Southern Star* to claim that the London branch was more 'radical' than Tuairim in Ireland. Both newspapers argued that the reasons why its views seemed more 'utopian' than those in Dublin's pamphlet were that their approach was more theoretical and that 'distance has lent disenchantment'.[85] It was the case that the London branch had a different perspective from that of the members of Tuairim in Ireland. In the previously mentioned letter to Daly, Enda McDonagh argued that the London branch 'would naturally feel freer to take a more radical approach while Dublin people would be more conscious of the amount of progress (small) that could be made here and now and afraid to jeopardise that progress by too extreme criticism'.[86] It is interesting to speculate whether the London members would have been in a position to help produce a similar pamphlet had they remained in Dublin. While it is impossible to answer definitively, it is true that with regard to education Daly and Rudd were two of the more radical individuals in the society. At a Tuairim meeting in Dublin in 1957, shortly before she left, Daly described Irish secondary education as 'denominational and restricted in scope', criticised it as serving a 'small minority' who could afford it and claimed that urgent action was needed to remedy its inadequacies.[87] The fact, however, remains that had she and the others not left, it would have been more difficult to be conscious of developments outside Ireland. Tuairim's members noted that the London branch was in a better position to argue for fundamental reforms. That was certainly true of Daly and Rudd, who were influenced by developments in Britain. There was also a belief that the London branch would have a sense of detachment from Ireland and that it would not be faced with the same pressures to conform as was Tuairim in Ireland. In this regard, it is interesting to note that women dominated both research groups and that it was the female members in Dublin who feared what the London members might recommend. The members of Tuairim in Ireland were then also influenced by the country in which they lived.

Perhaps the most perceptive comment in the publicity regarding Tuairim's London branch was in relation to the research group's mindset. *Hibernia*'s article in November 1962 claimed that the pamphlet threw 'an interesting light on psychological facets of the exile's mind' insofar as the members of the research group were 'class-conscious critics'. The critique of the educational system and of the responsibility ascribed to the middle classes for the deficiencies therein was largely based upon what the research group viewed as the products of the educational system: emigrants and the lower socio-economic classes in Irish society. Tuairim itself was, of course, largely a middle-class organisation. In the context of the concern that the research group professed for poorly educated individuals, while Rudd was an exception, it seemed hypocritical that Tuairim generally should choose to remain aloof from working-class organisations in London.

The differences between Tuairim in London and in Ireland perhaps should not be exaggerated, as there was also a considerable diversity of views between branches and members in Ireland. The most public example of such divisions was the response of the Cork branch to a report of Dublin's study weekend in *Hibernia*. The Tuairim members Rev. Tadhg Ó Murchú, a prominent Irish scholar, and John A. Murphy, a historian, were among those who referred to parts of the research group's paper as 'naïve', 'illogical' and containing a 'high proportion of generalities and inaccuracies' and argued that the group was unaware of the reality within the Irish education system.[88] In particular, the Cork branch claimed in its letter to *Hibernia* that the existing history curriculum followed 'international practice' in that it treated 'national and general history separately, while at the same time correlating the two as far as is practicable'. Most significantly, the branch argued that the research group's solution for the Irish language showed 'scant concern for our "national identity"'. These arguments indicate that certain members of the Cork branch had a very different understanding of the role that education should play in Ireland. In this context, it is interesting to note that unlike the Dublin branch, Cork defended the Council of Education with regard to its view of the place of the Irish language within education. The health of the language was identified as being closely related to that of the country. Therefore the suggestion that it should not have such a prominent position within the education system was seen as threatening to the national project, that of restoring Irish as the vernacular. The place of the Irish language in the country was a controversial topic at a number of Tuairim meetings. Public debate on this issue tended to be dominated by arguments relating to the claim that compulsory Irish should be abolished and by Gaelic revivalists pointing to a symbiotic relationship between it and the welfare of the Irish nation. Marie Hynes and Máire Mullarney rejected such criticism of their pamphlet. Hynes noted that at neither of the occasions on which she delivered the paper had anyone referred to it in the same terms as had the Cork branch. Nor did the Cork branch ask for a copy of the paper, a fact which led Hynes effectively to accuse it of adopting an 'ostrich-like approach'.[89] Each branch thus claimed that the evidence suggested that the other was unaware of the reality within the schools. The views put forward by the Cork branch serve to underline the emotive nature of education. That was particularly the case with regard to the Irish language; such arguments foreshadowed the heated debates thereon during the mid-1960s.

Tuairim, the Catholic Church and the Department of Education

The case that Tuairim put forward for reform in relation to primary and post-primary education probably influenced the Minister and Department of Education. That was despite the hostility with which Patrick Hillery regarded the society following its pamphlet against UCD's proposed move. McQuaid and the Catholic hierarchy, on the other hand, continued to be suspicious of Tuairim. Given that the preservation of the denominational character and management of schools was the church's greatest concern, it is easy to understand the misgivings that some of its members had about Tuairim's proposals. McQuaid was certainly aware that Tuairim had examined the Irish education system. There was a genuine fear on the part of the church that the replacement of small schools with larger ones would result in the death of rural Ireland and the traditional Catholic way of life. Rejecting the London branch's proposals for larger schools in a paper read to the Irish Vocational Association in Sligo in 1965, the Professor of Sociology in Maynooth and future Bishop of Limerick, Jeremiah Newman, claimed that the 'village [had] to be preserved as the proper framework for elementary education, church life and…daily needs'.[90] Because the church had a considerable interest in education, Hillery understandably continued his predecessor's practice of maintaining close relations with the Catholic hierarchy. Furthermore, he was unwilling to proceed with new departures without the latter's agreement.

Hillery, along with his successors George Colley and Donogh O'Malley, has, nevertheless, been seen as a reforming minister. Encouraged by the Taoiseach Seán Lemass, each minister recognised the importance of education for the country's economic and social development. The state's commitment to educational expansion was underlined by Hillery's appointment of the *Investment in education* survey team in 1962 and his announcement in 1963 of a pilot system of comprehensive schools in western areas. It was intended that such schools would provide a broad curriculum and in time be extended to the whole country. As with Miriam Daly and Joy Rudd's arguments, this proposal highlighted weaknesses in the provision of post-primary education, thus making it difficult for the church to resist the scheme. Furthermore, the *Investment in education* report illustrates that increasingly the recommendations in Tuairim's pamphlet, such as equality of opportunity and the integration of the post-primary education, while not fully implemented, were part of the political agenda.

This was the context in which Hillery and David Thornley became involved in a public dispute in 1964. A brief confrontation, it came to the attention of Archbishop McQuaid, who continued to be well informed of attitudes within government circles. The row began with a critical comment by Thornley and Basil Chubb during a series of perceptive articles that they co-wrote for the *Irish Times*. They referred to the *Investment in education* survey team in support of their argument for the need of an overhaul of the machinery of government. In their opinion the investigation was a 'sad reflection upon the total failure' of the department to identify problems and plan the education system effectively.[91] In response, Hillery suggested that rather than using the survey as a 'stick to beat the Department', the authors should have recognised that it was in fact a 'pioneer among the educationally developed countries' in having its education system examined in conjunction with the Organisation for European Co-operation and Development.[92] He claimed that it represented an even greater danger than complacency, that of a 'reluctance…to give any credit to educational effort here and urged Irish political scientists to "grow up"'. If that latter point reinforced the impression from the Belfield debate that Hillery could be overly sensitive to criticism and reflected his occasional combativeness, it was the case that Ireland was, as he claimed, one of the first countries to agree to such a survey. McQuaid later claimed that Thornley was 'guilty of an unjust public attack' that had been 'bitterly resented by the Minister and his officials'.[93] This would, despite Thornley's insistence that the minister should not feel responsible for past inertia, help to explain Hillery's response. A reflection of Thornley's increasing profile and the range of issues he considered, the articles highlighted many issues that needed to be elucidated as well as his interest in education, a matter on which he made a number of contributions following his election to the Dáil. This underlines the long-term impact of Tuairim. More immediately, his conflict with the minister illustrates the ability of some Tuairim members to highlight important issues and indicates that their statements could form the subject of public controversy.

To say that Tuairim was not on the best of terms with the minister and the department in the early 1960s is not to dismiss the possibility that the society may have influenced the formulation of government policy. In that context, the existence among government papers of articles from the *Irish Times*, *Irish Press* and *Hibernia* reporting the contents of the pamphlets indicates that they came to the attention of the government. Seán O'Connor, a senior civil servant in the Department of Education, noted in his book *A troubled sky* that Tuairim's pamphlets received considerable publicity before adding that the government did not react to it. It may be significant that the articles in the government's papers which related to the London research group were in a file concerning that branch rather than with education documents, and this perhaps reflects the fact that the London branch's proposals were too radical and were in the immediate term seen by the Department of Education as being outside the realm of practical politics.

A letter of November 1962 from Seán Lemass to Hillery, nevertheless, suggests that Tuairim could have facilitated educational reforms. The Taoiseach's view was that the government had to respond to the recent criticism of the education system.[94] While Lemass did not specify who was making these comments, the timing of the letter, which he wrote shortly after Tuairim's pamphlets were published, suggests that it was, at least in part, a reaction to the society. Part of Hillery's response was the announcement about comprehensive schools. This, in turn, may have been prompted by the Labour's Party's educational policy, a radical document which had been co-written by the Tuairim member Barry Desmond and published the previous February. Its authorship and content suggest that it was influenced by Tuairim's pamphlets; many of its recommendations, including an integrated system of education, equality of opportunity and free education for all children, provision of larger schools, a transport system, an educational guidance service and the possibility of transfer between secondary and vocational schools, had previously been made by the society.[95]

In the longer term, the London branch's argument that larger schools needed to be established was perhaps of greatest significance. The government's comprehensive school proposal was similarly intended to address the defects of the existing system; it indicates that the Minister for Education and his department were aware of the need for a new type of post-primary school. In this context, it was significant that Hillery and other members of the government attended a meeting of Fianna Fáil's Comh Comhairle in Dublin in 1964 at which Miriam Daly had been invited to deliver a paper. She reiterated the London research group's proposals for post-primary education. While welcoming reforms such as Hillery's attempts to reduce class sizes and the promise of an increased number of scholarships to secondary and third-level students, she was critical of the decision to give building grants to secondary schools, which, she believed, was contrary to the minister's plans for comprehensive schools. The increase in investment in secondary schools, along with the other measures highlighted by Daly, suggests that Hillery was, indeed, a reforming minister. It is also clear that, faced by opposition from a range of interests including the Catholic Church and teaching unions, Hillery remained committed to a gradualist approach and did not fully implement the comprehensive schools concept. Nevertheless, it provided an important precedent for community schools, which were established in the 1970s. Furthermore, the proposal facilitated increased demand for secondary school places; hence Hillery's building grants. The scheme proved to be very popular with sixty-five schools applying for assistance from the time of the announcement in April 1964 to the end of that year. Daly, however, denounced the grants as 'wasteful' and 'iniquitous': they perpetuated a separate system which would mean that secondary education continued to be for those who could afford it and remained 'impractically literary' while vocational educational was 'inhumanly dull' and directed towards the poor and the majority of rural children.[96] The language, which many would have considered intemperate, was typical of London's research group. An editorial comment in the same issue of *Hibernia* noted Daly's reference to objections that the Catholic managers of the 'privately-owned secondary schools' would have in relation to her recommendations. Other criticisms of the branch's proposals came from UCD's Academic Staff Association and the Commission on Higher Education, which, having praised its plan for an institute of education, commented that it would 'cut across' the traditions of Church and state, while the association wrote that Tuairim 'don't care much for the principle of closing the University's Department of Education'.[97] Though no indication was given of the opinions of the minister or the other members of Fianna Fáil of Daly's paper or Tuairim's pamphlets, it is clear that the research group threatened vested interests. While the government's actions suggest that it disagreed with her view or at least was unwilling to tackle such interests, its decision to attend the meeting indicates that it was open to Tuairim's arguments; significantly it also demonstrates that some members of the society had access to the government.

Published in December 1965, the same year in which George Colley became minister, the *Investment in education* report proved to be a watershed in educational policy. Its analysis of the defects of the education system provided the basis for the reforms introduced by Colley and his successor, Donogh O'Malley. The report's identification of the inefficient nature of the education system, particularly the widespread existence of small schools, was the feature that most clearly attracted Colley's attention. The rationalisation of the number of schools and the need for co-operation between secondary and vocational education were foremost on his agenda. Such ideas were common to both the *Investment* report and Tuairim's pamphlet. With regard to the possible influence of the London branch's pamphlet, the members of the influential *Investment in education* survey team were each on good terms with the society. William Hyland regularly met Joy Rudd and other Tuairim members during his time working on the report, while Patrick Lynch spoke to the society on a number of occasions as well as having co-written the 1959 Tuairim economics pamphlet. In addition, Martin O'Donoghue explained the approach of the survey team to a meeting of Tuairim's Dublin branch in February 1966.[98]

As for the government, evidence suggests that Colley may have been influenced by the London branch's pamphlet. Even prior to the publication of the *Investment* report, Colley, speaking at a meeting of Tuairim's Cork branch in November 1965 at which 300 people were in attendance, claimed that the state had to intervene to end the 'uncoordinated building of secondary and vocational schools'.[99] Clearly influenced by the survey, the minister referred to the importance of the recently established development branch in the Department of Education, which had been the *Investment* report's sole recommendation. He said that the branch was examining the needs of post-primary education with a view to ensuring equality of opportunity, and that by 1970 all children would receive some form of post-primary education until they were fifteen years of age. In giving a public commitment to equality of opportunity and the raising of the school leaving age, Colley thus went further than Patrick Hillery, for whom these had been only aspirations. Furthermore, in indicating that it was the state which would initiate, plan and direct future educational developments and co-ordinate the different branches of the post-primary education system, the minister was making an important statement. While Hillery had established that the minister could initiate changes, his rhetoric was more cautious than Colley's. That Colley had used a platform provided by Tuairim publicly to outline the government's role in education indicates that the society was seen as an important conduit through which ministers could seek public support for government policy. It should, however, be added that this was one of a series of speeches at the end of 1965 which the minister gave in an attempt to gain acceptance of the policy of amalgamating one and two teacher schools.

This meeting in Cork, combined with the fact that Colley had previously spoken to the society in 1961, lends credibility to the statement of his brother-in-law, the Tuairim member Jim Doolan, that the minister was aware of and supported the London branch's recommendation regarding larger schools.[100] Whether he had been influenced by its content is, however, unclear. Certainly, the friendly relations that Colley had with Tuairim significantly contrasted with those between the society and his predecessor. Moreover, Tuairim's proposals such as equality of opportunity and free education secured wider acceptance in government circles during his tenure as minister. This was particularly the case following the government's agreement with the scheme of his successor, Donogh O'Malley, for free post-primary education in 1967. With the inclusion of free tuition and a free transport scheme, it proved to be a major success and resulted in greatly increased participation at school. A dramatic initiative, it nevertheless represented a continuation of the policies of his predecessors and a culmination of thinking on education over the previous decade. Perhaps equally important, if more modest, changes were made through the 1960s to the curriculum of both primary and post-primary schools. A reduction in the focus on the Irish language at primary school level and an increased emphasis on oral Irish as well as modern continental languages and science subjects, alongside a common Intermediate Certificate examination for both secondary and vocational schools were significant achievements. Vocational schools, however, could not offer courses for the Leaving Certificate examination until 1969.[101] This, at least partly, explains why they did not benefit fully from free education. Tuairim's influence on educational developments was felt in relation to many of these issues but was most clear with regard to the London branch's proposals and Colley's policy of rationalising the number of schools. It is also the case that even before his tenure as minister, the society's pamphlets provoked a considerable response; these raised awareness of the need for reform as well as future expectations and helped to place education firmly on the political agenda. With the government increasingly active in this sphere, other areas such as industrial schools became more prominent.

Some of our children

It was significant that it was the London branch that also argued that the system of industrial schools and reformatories was damaging to children in full-time care. The branch's second and final pamphlet, *Some of our children: a report on the residential care of the deprived child in Ireland* (1966), like its education pamphlet, was the work of a research group, in this case established in May 1964. Its chairperson was Joy Rudd, who in 1961, in the earlier critique on education in the branch's *Occasional Bulletin*, had referred to the lack of awareness of the numbers committed to industrial schools, the conditions of admission and the unskilled employment that many of its residents gained upon being released from these institutions. Furthermore, the branch's education pamphlet had argued for the need to integrate children in industrial schools into the educational system, because of the inadequacy of the education they received, as indicated by the nature of the work that they subsequently secured.[102]

The research group examining industrial schools also called for children of travellers to be included in the educational system. As a transitional measure, it was proposed that a special boarding school be established for travellers in preparation for the ordinary education system. Though possibly acceptable as a 'starting point', this was a plan of which the Department of Health's Fidelma Clandillon reproved; she argued in her review in 1968 that the boarding schools would 'cut right across the preservation of the family as a unit [and] lead to more deprived children. [Where possible travellers] should go to the local schools'.[103] Clandillon was concerned that boarding schools would remove children from 'the main stream of students in secondary and vocational schools' and would serve only to isolate them from the rest of the community and the local facilities. She also criticised the suggestion that 'existing certified schools and private voluntary Homes should be given the option of becoming National or Vocational boarding schools under the Department of Education, or Children's Homes under the Department of Health', since that would similarly result in children being in boarding schools. In addition, she argued that the schools' principals as well as the children's department would help the students find employment. This point was made in response to the pamphlet's recommendation that a national association for the deprived child should be set up; the research group suggested that this would be responsible for ensuring that each child had someone to visit her or him and would help secure suitable employment on her or his release.[104] Overall, Clandillon, as will be discussed later, accepted the criticism that Tuairim made of the system. Describing the provision of childcare services generally as totally inadequate, the research group claimed that many people would be shocked to hear that the 1908 Children's Act, which had since been replaced in Britain, was still in operation in Ireland. It noted that on 31 March 1965, under this Act, there were 3,419 children in three reformatories and forty-three industrial schools in Ireland.[105]

The research group compared facilities in Ireland with those available in Britain: it claimed that, in contrast to the latter, in Ireland little effort was made to ensure that children remained with their parents. Furthermore, once committed, many of these children remained in the schools until they were sixteen. The group also stated that upon being released these children were unprepared for adult life and that many of them migrated to England. The pamphlet highlighted the lack of welfare officers and childcare workers, the undeveloped nature of the probationary service and the need for proper training for people to fulfil these positions. The research group called for more preventive welfare services, including the provision of assistance upon leaving an institution. It argued that children's sections of local health authorities should be established and should assume guardianship of disadvantaged individuals of under seventeen years of age. A considerable obstacle, however, existed to the 'vesting of parental rights in anyone but the parents [as that was] contrary to the…constitution'.[106] The research group seemed to be on firmer ground when recommending that the schools should after a certain period of time have to give a reason as to why a child had not been discharged. It also suggested the establishment of a 'reciprocal arrangement with England and Wales to supervise young people under 18 who are in care'.

While this part of the pamphlet represented progressive thinking, the most significant recommendations included a new Children's Act and the calls for a subsidiary children's department to be established in, significantly, the Department of Health rather than the Department of Education. The research group claimed that the Department of Health was the most appropriate place for a children's department because it already ran a number of residential homes and supervised boarding-out of deprived children, thus having considerable experience in this area as well as a basis upon which local services could be built. Fidelma Clandillon maintained, however, that this statement was untrue. She argued that it reflected the 'muddled and out-moded thinking' in existence at the time when the pamphlet was published; for instance, the research group was unaware of the distinction between her Department of Health and that of Social Welfare.[107] She accepted, however, that all these homes should be registered with the Children's Department and the pamphlet's call for the establishment of 'substitute homes for children deprived of their natural home'. Particularly welcome was the research group's statement that these homes should be 'small, mixed units of all age groups'. That was perhaps the pamphlet's most important recommendation. The replacement of the existing large-scale institutions with small-scale mixed homes for children of all ages to be funded by the state and staffed by professionals was in accordance with international best practice and was accepted by Clandillon and the Department of Education. Like the branch's education pamphlet, this part had clearly been influenced by contemporary thinking in Britain.

The group had carried out extensive research into childcare in Britain, in addition to its investigation into the historical and legal background of childcare in Ireland and the figures it gave for the number of children in care. The authors of the pamphlet stated that they had visited twenty different childcare facilities and had spoken with and sent questionnaires to a number of former industrial school pupils.[108] Not only did it contact people who had been in these institutions and were involved in childcare, but it also compared different types of institutions in Ireland and Britain. In addition, it corresponded with the Home Office in London and the

Departments of Education and Health in Dublin. The research group made it clear that the residential and educational facilities at the Irish schools were inadequate. For instance, it commented that it was unclear 'what rehabilitative or reformatory work' was possible at the reformatory in Daingean. Its conclusion was that, provided a child was 'physically healthy, well clothed, obedient and can speak Irish, officialdom is satisfied'. That, according to a memorandum by the Department of Education, was a 'cheap and untrue jibe'.[109] The department, though, seemed satisfied with Tuairim's claim that generally children were being 'well cared for…neatly dressed' and that the schools were 'meticulously clean and tidy'.[110] Rather than attaching responsibility to the managers of the schools for the inadequate care provided, the pamphlet actually praised them for doing their best under the circumstances.

That we now know that the conditions within at least some of the institutions were appalling and that the managers and staff were clearly negligent in the care they provided illustrates that this part of the pamphlet was clearly deficient. Most controversially, the research group did not seem to believe contemporary accounts that they had heard of excessive punishments of pupils. It wrote that in the 'absence of verification…they must be treated as hypothetical'. It added, without defining these terms, that it was its view that 'corporal punishment for "sex offences" or alleged "sex offences" is likely to be more harmful to the boy' than the 'misdeed' itself. While both of the London branch's research groups viewed corporal punishment as an inappropriate method of discipline and harmful to its victims, it was reticent in describing what occurred or criticising its perpetrators.

Related to this, the research group failed to record the memories of one of its members, Peter Tyrell, who was a pupil at Letterfrack industrial school from 1924 to 1932. A piece he wrote for the research group, probably in 1964, revealed the brutal conditions inside the school and the treatment meted out by the Christian Brothers. One person particularly, Brother Vale, inflicted indiscriminate physical abuse upon students. Tyrell claimed that during his 'time as a prisoner of war in a German camp, [he] found the…conditions far more humane than in the eight long frightened and miserable years spent in an Irish Industrial School'.[111] Reluctance to incorporate testimonies such as Tyrell's is likely to have been due to an inability to prove their accuracy and possible fear of legal consequences. Having visited the schools, the group may genuinely have also believed that such punishment had diminished in severity and frequency. It seems to have been common practice to ensure that the children were well dressed and the premises thoroughly cleaned, often by the children themselves, for visitors. In the end, the research group clearly believed that personal testimony was insufficient as proof. Such claims gained credibility only in the 1990s when backed by similar accounts. The complaints that were made were dismissed or ignored by the Department of Education.

This all seems to have become too much for Tyrell, who in April 1967 committed suicide by burning himself to death. Suggestions that it was disappointment over his experiences with Tuairim that led him to this course of action need to be considered in the context of all the evidence. His early experiences of the branch from 1964 were certainly encouraging. In letters to Senator Sheehy Skeffington, he wrote that Joy Rudd was 'very nice and capable...sincere and devoted to her work' and that the meeting of the branch in November 1964 at which Maura Hunt spoke was a 'great success'.[112] Rudd and the research group made quite an impression on Tyrell. In a letter he wrote to her, he described everyone as 'wonderful'. Furthermore, Rudd assisted him in having a short article describing his experiences published in *Hibernia*.[113] That he seemed to be on good terms with the society is suggested by the fact that in 1963 he made a donation towards the cost of the proposed pamphlet.

Its timing suggests, however, that this was more out of hope that it would provoke a response by the government than one of a sense of contentment with the final product. The reality is that it is impossible to know his frame of mind. Diarmuid Whelan, in the introduction to Tyrell's manuscript 'Founded on fear', claims that it was likely that he was a 'manic depressive' and that suicide had been on his mind for a long time.[114] Nonetheless, the omission of Tyrell's testimony could have exacerbated any existing instability. He might have been disappointed that Tuairim did not appear to agree with what seems for him to have become an obsession, that of achieving a 'secular education'.[115] His claim that changes would happen in the 'near future [once] thousands of enlightened people' returned home suggest that he had exaggerated expectations for the society and the Irish in London. Tuairim's unwillingness to incorporate his account into its pamphlet highlights the difficulties faced by those attempting to illuminate the reality in these schools. It should, however, be noted that reference to beatings received by boys was unusual for the 1960s. Furthermore, it was significant that Tuairim approached and spoke with former industrial school pupils, who generally had been ignored. The fact that even a sympathetic body found it impossible to publish their stories suggests that the London branch felt restricted in what it could say, perhaps partly by its respectable nature but more by the constraints imposed by contemporary society. Tuairim had put forward recommendations that, nevertheless, represented best practice in childcare. The pamphlet reflected the society's idealism in that it argued that the social problems underlying disadvantaged young people needed to be tackled.

Influence of Tuairim's pamphlet

Government memoranda and the coverage given to Tuairim's pamphlet in newspapers and periodicals suggest that it made an impact upon intellectual debate and policy formulation. Initially, the pamphlet's contents and main recommendations were reported in the *Irish Independent* and the *Irish Times* in January 1966. It subsequently prompted a more analytical piece in *Hibernia*. Describing the work of the London branch as 'detached and objective', Bruce Arnold, a journalist, claimed in May 1966 that its pamphlets had created a deep 'sense of unease' and in relation to childcare a 'picture...of State neglect, inactivity and inefficiency'.[116] That same month, in a series of articles in the *Irish Times* on 'The Young Offenders', Michael Viney, at this point an influential investigative social reporter, called Tuairim's pamphlet a 'painstaking and devastating document'.[117] Subsequently, others such as Helen Binchy of the Social Science Department and Paul McQuaid of the Department of Psychiatry at UCD, in articles in *Christus Rex* and *Studies*, referred to the pamphlet in support of their argument that there continued to be serious defects in this area. While the government-commissioned Kennedy report into reformatories and industrial schools (1970) indicated some progress, serious problems remained. Established by the government in 1967, at least partly as a result of 'Representations...by various groups' and references in the press, the Kennedy report played a critical part in the process whereby these institutions were replaced with a modern, child-centred system.[118]

The Ryan report refers to the importance of Tuairim's pamphlet in the change in government policy. According to Eoin O'Sullivan's paper in the report, many commentators, who were unidentified, felt that the research group had 'hastened the process of change'.[119] Its timing makes it likely that Tuairim played a role in creating an environment that facilitated the establishment of the Kennedy Committee. As to the pamphlet's greater significance, the memoranda of the reformatory and industrial schools branch of the Department of Education and, that of Fidelma Clandillon, who was in the Department of Health from 1948 to 1980, suggest that it influenced the government's thinking. Though the Ryan report notes that an inter-departmental committee had made criticism of the system in 1962, the Department of Education, according to its memorandum, now recognised that the 'entire system' was in need of a major 'overhaul'.[120] Clandillon also claimed that there were 'some sound recommendations in the Report... [and that] everyone concerned with the welfare of deprived children would agree with the view that a new Children Act should supersede the present fragmented legislation and widen its scope'.[121] Open to Tuairim's views, she, as previously noted, accepted the need for small-scale homes as well as the establishment of courses for probation officers and residential childcare officials and agreed that trained staff should work in the homes and that their wages should be commensurate to their qualifications.

More generally, the Department of Education agreed with this assessment. With certain exceptions, however, its memorandum, which was undated and unsigned, was somewhat complacent in its attitude. For instance, in relation to the absence of a probationary service outside Dublin, it was 'unable to say...to what extent their work impinges on the reformatory or industrial schools'.[122] Anxious to defend the system, the memorandum noted that Tuairim's pamphlet had been 'compiled objectively'. The department examined each criticism made by the research group before concluding that the

> majority of faults found within the reformatory and industrial schools system are soundly based and confirmed by my experience. They highlight the necessity for a complete review and overhaul of the entire system...In the whole system the most serious defect in my opinion is the absence of the official after-care machinery.

The contrast with the department's view of the society's university pamphlet could hardly be greater. Though lacking a sense of urgency, the memorandum was significant; it recognised that children 'could be better cared for at less expense to the state without splitting up the family'.

A Dáil debate on the Department of Education's estimates in 1966 and an article in the *Irish Press* the following year were the only public indications that the government was aware of Tuairim's pamphlet. Responding to the minister, Donogh O'Malley, David Andrews, the recently elected Fianna Fáil TD and future minister, referred to the society, while the newspaper claimed that both of the London branch's publications had had 'a considerable impact on aspirations and policy'.[123] Though the standard of care provided was in the view of the Department of Education to be praised, the need for reform had been recognised. The evidence indicates that Tuairim's pamphlet impacted upon the government. While the research group added to the momentum for reform, members of the civil service and the Minister for Education, nevertheless, seem to have already been aware of the need for changes to the system. Fidelma Clandillon's interest in Tuairim's pamphlet was a reflection of the debate as to whether the Department of Health should assume greater responsibility for this area and an indication that her department was giving active consideration to how childcare services should be reorganised. Before Tuairim's pamphlet such concerns had, however, rarely been articulated or acted upon. While the question as how exactly to proceed continued to cause difficulties for some time following the publication of the Kennedy report, Tuairim's arguments were a catalyst in the decision to reform the system of childcare. As part of a wider discussion, Paul McQuaid had in 1971 suggested that, along with Viney's 1966 articles, Tuairim's pamphlet had 'exemplified...A growing and public dissatisfaction with the existing "system"'.[124] Tuairim thus raised awareness of the need for change and helped create a climate conducive to reform.

Conclusion

Tuairim called for increased investment and fundamental reforms in relation to a wide range of educational and childcare facilities. While the society's arguments for greater co-operation in education provoked a strong reaction from vested interests, they facilitated increased activity by the state in this area. In calling for a fully integrated education system, the London branch went further than Tuairim in Ireland. Such calls by both the London and Dublin branches for increased co-operation in education echoed Tuairim's arguments, as discussed elsewhere in this book, for better relations between different sectors of society. Equally, the hopes Tuairim had for a move towards equality of opportunity were reflected in its views in other areas. In regard to education as well as childcare, the London branch was influenced by developments in its host society. The fact that it was the only one to examine industrial schools lends credence to the view that detachment due to the branch's location outside Ireland facilitated its examination of controversial matters. Nevertheless, this pamphlet illustrates that Tuairim felt constrained in what it could say. It seems that though the branch was detached from vested interests and pressures to conform in Ireland, it was partly inhibited in what it wrote. This frustrated Tuairim's attempts to go beyond the conventional wisdom of the period. While the branch had a different perspective from Tuairim in Ireland, the Cork branch's reaction to Dublin's pamphlet points to the existence of a wide variety of views within the society in Ireland. In regard to influencing government policy, the education and childcare pamphlets added to the momentum for reform. Their call for educational reform came to the attention of both the political and religious establishments, while the government accepted the need to plan the provision of primary and post-primary education as well as to overhaul the system of childcare. The pamphlets encouraged the government to implement much-needed reforms. As the 1960s progressed, successive Ministers of Education were increasingly willing to tackle controversial issues and powerful interests, such as the church. This was in contrast to the early part of the decade when the segregated nature of the third-level sector was accepted by the government. Business and private interests as well as the political and religious establishments rejected Tuairim's arguments that the third-level sector should be given priority in any future development in the city. Attempts to improve relations between the Dublin universities during the late 1950s and early 1960s were always likely to be resisted by influential figures. It was also the case that despite Tuairim's concern regarding UCD and the future of higher education, the society's proposals in relation to the maximum size of universities would have inhibited their progression. Thus Tuairim could be said to have miscalculated in regard to higher education. Neither UCD nor the capital city has suffered as Tuairim predicted. While the city centre has advantages as a location, Belfield has resolved the college's accommodation problems. Tuairim, nevertheless, deserves credit in that it articulated its ideal – greater co-operation between the Dublin colleges – at a time when there was little contact between these institutions. The increasingly liberal attitudes of the 1960s changed this; they helped to bring about the full integration of Trinity into Irish life as well as fundamental reforms to primary and post-primary education and to the system of childcare. Tuairim's contribution was to help create a climate of opinion that was conducive to that change and to the transformation in the state's policy approach.

Notes

1 Tuairim London research group, *Irish education* (London: Tuairim, 1962), p. 3. See also Tuairim, *University College Dublin and the future: with special reference to the proposal to transfer University College, Dublin to a new site: a memorandum from a research group of Tuairim Dublin branch on the report of the Commission on Accommodation Needs of the constituent colleges of the National University of Ireland* (Dublin: Tuairim, 1960); Tuairim, *University College Dublin*; Tuairim Dublin branch in co-operation with Irish section of the EADE, *Educating towards a united Ireland* (Dublin: Tuairim, 1962); Tuairim a London branch study group, *Some of our children: a report on the residential care of the deprived child in Ireland* (London: Tuairim, 1966).
2 Department of Education, *Report of the Council of Education: (1) The function of the primary school (2) The curriculum to be pursued in the primary school from the infant age up to 12 years of age* (Dublin: Stationery Office, 1954), pp. 266–92; Department of Education, *Report of the Council of Education: the curriculum of the secondary school* (Dublin: Stationery Office, 1960), pp. 256–82. See also Seán Farren, *The politics of Irish education, 1920–65* (Belfast: Institute of Irish Studies, 1995), pp. 228–2, 238–41; Ferriter, *Transformation*, pp. 349–53, 426–30; Garvin, *Future*, pp. 69, 96–7, 140–1; Lee, *Ireland*, pp. 132–6; Séamas Ó Buachalla, *Education policy in twentieth century Ireland* (Dublin: Wolfhound Press, 1988), pp. 67–8; Whyte, *Church and state*, pp. 16–21, 37–8. See also Adrian Kelly, *Compulsory Irish: language and education in Ireland, 1870s–1970s* (Dublin: Irish Academic Press, 2002).
3 Garvin, *Future*, pp. 97, 136–40, 155. See also Ó Buachalla, *Education*, pp. 63–4, 68–70, 77–9, 275–8, 384.

4 *Irish Press*, 9 January 1959; NAI, DT, S1289D/1/61, Post war planning: education, the Federation of Lay Catholic Secondary Schools, 'Memorandum presented to the Minister for Education on various problems arising in secondary education'; *Irish Times*, 19 April 1960. See Irish National Teachers' Organisation, *A plan for education* (Dublin: Irish National Teachers' Organisation, 1947); T. J. O'Connell, *History of the Irish National Teachers' Organisation, 1868–1968* (Dublin: Irish National Teachers' Organisation, 1968), pp. 365–76; John O'Meara, *Reform in education* (Dublin: Mount Salus Press, 1958); Seán Ó Catháin, *Secondary education in Ireland* (Dublin: The Talbot Press, 1958). Ó Catháin published five articles in *Studies* in 1951, 1955, 1956 and 1957; these appeared as a collection in 1958. See also T. J. McElligott, *Education in Ireland* (Dublin: Institute of Public Administration, 1966).

5 Joseph Robins, *The lost children: a study of charity in Ireland, 1700–1900* (Dublin: Institute of Public Administration, 1980), pp. 297, 303. See also Arnold and Laskey, *Poor Clares*; Diarmaid Ferriter, *Occasions of sin: sex and society in modern Ireland* (London: Profile Books, 2009), pp. 325–33; Ferriter, *Transformation*, pp. 49, 324–5, 392–4, 465, 511–17; Raftery and O'Sullivan, *Children*; Moira Maguire, *Precarious childhood in post-independence Ireland* (Manchester: Manchester University Press, 2009).

6 For example, *Report of the Commission to Inquire into Child Abuse*; Ferriter, *Transformation*, pp. 6, 11–12, 322, 511–14, 589, 737–8; Ferriter, *Occasions*, pp. 329–30; Garvin, *Future*, p. 150; Raftery and O'Sullivan, *Children*, pp. 14–16, 219, 232–4, 317–18.

7 Cecil J. Barrett, 'The dependent child', *Studies*, 44:176 (Winter 1955), 419–28; M. McCauley, 'Our children', *Christus Rex*, 9 (March 1955), 126–33; Ann Kenny, 'The deprived child', *Christus Rex*, 10 (March 1956), 99–114. See Eoin O'Sullivan, 'Residential child welfare in Ireland, 1965–2008: an outline of policy, legislation and practice', *Report of the Commission to Inquire into Child Abuse*, vol. iv, 4.83; Raftery and O'Sullivan, *Children*, pp. 356–7.

8 James O'Connor, 'The juvenile offender', *Studies*, 52:205 (Spring 1963), 80. See *Irish Independent*, *Irish Times*, 7 March 1959. See also *Irish Times*, 19 March 1960, 21 March 1966.

9 O'Sullivan, 'Residential child welfare', 4.83. See also Department of Education, 'Brief commentary on *Tuairim* pamphlet: "Some of our children"'. I would like to thank the Department of Education for access to this document. See also Augusta McCabe, 'The inspection of boarded out children in Ireland – legacy of Fidelma Clandillon', *Irish Social Worker*, 21:1–2 (2003), 22–6.

10 McCartney, *UCD*, p. 2. Technically, the colleges were established in Cork, Galway and Belfast in 1845 while the Queen's University was incorporated in 1850. See also Luce, *Trinity*, pp. 93–4.

11 Boyce, *Nineteenth-century*, p. 80; McCartney, *UCD*, p. 2.

12 McCartney, *UCD*, p. 185. A member of Fine Gael and a former senator, Tierney numbered among his friends John A. Costello, Patrick McGilligan, who was on leave of absence from his position as Professor of Constitutional Law at UCD, James Dillon and Richard Mulcahy, all of whom were members of the two-inter-party governments. See also Whyte, *Church and state*,

pp. 305–7; Cooney, *McQuaid*, pp. 227, 294–6. McCartney, *UCD*, pp. 212, 224, 125–7.
13 Interview with Barrington, 19 May 2005. Barrington initially thought that Tierney's presidency meant that 'Newman's University had arrived'. McCartney, *UCD*, pp. 284–92. See also *Irish Times*, 26 March 1957; *Irish Independent*, 13 May, 4 December 1953, 13 December 1954, 31 May, 1 August 1955; *Report of the Commission on Accommodation Needs of the constituent colleges of the National University of Ireland* (Dublin: Stationery Office, 1959), p. 28, 'Submission from Dr Roger McHugh, UCD', 11 November 1957, 'General statement on the advantages of building on or in the vicinity of the present site of the college made to the commission by Dr Roger McHugh, University College Dublin'. See also Michael Tierney (ed.), *Daniel O'Connell* (Dublin: Browne and Nolan, 1949), foreword, pp. 151–70.
14 *Irish Times*, 11 March 1957; *Irish Independent*, 11 March 1957. See also FitzGerald, *All in a life*, pp. 36, 48–52.
15 *Irish Times*, 21 March 1957.
16 Ibid., 28 March 1957.
17 Ibid., 30 March 1957.
18 Ibid., 30 March 1957. See also ibid., 25, 26, 28 March, 3, 6 April 1957.
19 McCartney, *UCD*, p. 266. See NAI, DT, S13809C, University College Dublin accommodation, *Irish Times*, 25 March 1957. Some of the letters can be found in government files.
20 *Irish Times*, 28 March 1958. See also ibid., 8 December 1958.
21 NAI, DT, S13809C, University College Dublin accommodation, Proposed transfer of UCD to Belfield, Stillorgan Road, 'Department of Health observations on the memo by the Minister for Education', 25 June 1957. See also NAI, DT, S13809C, Accommodation, 'Department of Finance's observations on memo by Minister of Health', 25 June 1957.
22 McCartney, *UCD*, p. 262.
23 *Accommodation needs*, p. 3.
24 Ibid., p. 48. The majority of the commission's members accepted the accuracy of the college's estimate of £6,700,000.
25 NAI, DT, S13809D, University College Dublin accommodation, University College Dublin, *University College Dublin and its building plans* (Dublin: University College Dublin, 1959), p. 18. See also Dáil Éireann Debates, vol. 177, col. 643, 'University College Dublin accommodation requirements', 4 November 1959.
26 Interview with Harold Clarke, Dublin, 15 June 2005. Clarke later became the general manager of Eason's bookshop. Tuairim, *University College Dublin*. The research group also included Franklin O'Sullivan, Patrick Moore, Joseph McCullough, Henry MacErlean and Elizabeth Healy. Barrington, then the President of Tuairim, though not named, was also involved. Patrick Moore had worked in UCD and was in St James Hospital at that time, while Joseph McCullough was an engineer. Elizabeth Healy was in a publishing house, where she wrote and edited a number of books on Ireland including a *Literary tour of Ireland*. Individuals who possibly made a financial contribution to the

cost of the pamphlet's publication included Roger McHugh, John O'Meara, Garret FitzGerald and Paddy Lynch. The pamphlet referred to the report of the British University Grants Committee for the years 1952–57, and to an article by D. W. Brogan which was published in the *Cambridge Journal* in 1952. Other articles that were cited included those by Dermot F. T. Engelfield in *The Tablet* in 1958, P. Callinan in the *Irish Builder and Engineer* in 1959 and William B. Stanford in the *Trinity Handbook* in 1959 as well as a paper by Eric Ashby to a symposium on the design of teaching laboratories in 1958. The pamphlet also contained a map of the city centre that marked the areas currently possessed by the college and others that the research group believed could be acquired.

27 Tuairim, *University College Dublin*, foreword. Many of the quotations in this section are from this pamphlet.
28 Ibid., pp. 26, 56–7; *Accommodation needs*, p. 45. The research group went further than the commission in arguing that the university development committee should cover all the institutions of higher education in the country. See Luce, *Trinity*, p. 183. A Higher Education Authority was established in 1968.
29 Interview with Barrington, 19 May 2005. See also Tuairim, *University College Dublin*, pp. 35, 49–50. The group commented that in spite of less demand for employment for well-educated individuals than in Britain, Ireland already had more students per head of population than Britain. Barrington has argued that UCD is now too large. These views should not be seen as elitist, as the research group was concerned by the 'paucity of scholarships' available for third-level education. Indeed, some members including Barrington had themselves experienced such difficulties during their time in college. See also McCartney, *UCD*, p. 345.
30 *Accommodation needs*, p. 31. See also NAI, DT, S13809B, University College Dublin accommodation, 'Memorandum from inter-departmental committee for the government on proposed transfer of University College, Dublin, to Stillorgan site, 1954'.
31 *Accommodation needs*, pp. 30–1. See also Tuairim, *University College Dublin*, pp. 38–9. See McCartney, *UCD*, p. 229; *Irish Independent*, 14 August 1948. Tierney claimed that 'few would welcome the proposal to "build-up"' in the Iveagh Gardens.
32 Interview with Barrington, 19 May 2005.
33 See also *Accommodation needs*, p. 30. See Frank McDonald, *The destruction of Dublin* (Dublin: Gill and Macmillan, 1985), p. 9. The corollary of McDonald's criticism of the commission was his praise for Tuairim's pamphlet. See also Cooney, *McQuaid*, p. 339; McCartney, *UCD*, pp. 121, 126.
34 *Times*, 8 January 1960. See also *Times*, 30 December 1957.
35 *Irish Times*, 8 January 1960.
36 *Hibernia*, 15 January 1960.
37 McCartney, *UCD*, pp. 294–6. On 12 March 1960, Dermot Ryan, a former auditor who was chairing a meeting of a sub-committee of the society, suggested writing to Tuairim, the press and the Council of Civil Liberties in

relation to what was perceived to be the unfair suspension of a third-year arts student.
38 *Irish Independent*, 19, 23 March 1960. The research group stated that its report was available in newsagents and had been sent to individuals such as Hogan.
39 Dáil Éireann Debates, vol. 180, col. 1169, 'Universities and colleges', 24 March 1960; col. 1417, 30 March 1960; *Irish Independent*, 26 March 1960. See also ibid., 30 March 1960; Dáil Éireann Debates, vol. 180, col. 1417, 'Universities and colleges', 30 March 1960.
40 NAI, DT, S13809D, University College Dublin accommodation, Maurice Moynihan to Frank Winder, 14 January 1960, Moynihan to Secretary of the Department of Education, 16 January 1960, Winder to Moynihan, 21 December 1959. Moynihan wrote that he was glad to receive an extra copy of the postscript to the memorandum. Miss Kelly, in the Department of Finance, requested and was sent a copy of the memorandum and postscript. Winder and Moynihan clearly knew each other, for Winder mentioned the memorandum to Moynihan at a reception at which they met the previous Saturday.
41 NAI, DT, S13809D, University College Dublin accommodation, 'Department of Education's observations on memorandum from Tuairim on report of University accommodation commission', 9 February 1960, Secretary of the Department of Education to Taoiseach's private secretary, 16 February 1960. The memorandum was sent confidentially to the Taoiseach. It was also forwarded to Seán MacEntee. The quotations that follow are from this document. See also McCartney, *UCD*, pp. 240–1. In accordance with precedent, matters in relation to university education were first to be considered by the Minister for Education.
42 NAI, DT, S13809D, University College Dublin accommodation, 'Department of Education's observations on memorandum from Tuairim on report of University accommodation commission', pp. 6–8. The memorandum dismissed Tuairim's view as to the amount of space needed for the science building and challenged its figure for costs. It also claimed that the statement that the college would become sterile and inward-looking was 'highly debatable'.
43 Dáil Éireann Debates, vol. 180, col. 938, 'Universities and colleges', 23 March 1960. See also interview with Keane, 24 May 2005; McCartney, *UCD*, p. 276. Opinions of Hillery's speech differed: many of the deputies congratulated the minister on its quality, but Ronan Keane, who was in the Dáil gallery, was appalled by its poor standard.
44 Tuairim, *University College Dublin*, introduction. See Dáil Éireann Debates, vol. 180, col. 1176, 'Universities and colleges', 24 March 1960. Michael Carty, a Fianna Fáil TD, was critical of the attitude of UCD's authorities. See also *Hibernia*, 15 January 1960.
45 Dáil Éireann Debates, vol. 180, cols. 1407, 1421, 'Universities and colleges', 30 March 1960.
46 Ibid., col. 1478, 31 March 1960.
47 Ibid., col. 1374, 30 March 1960.
48 Ibid., col. 1178, 24 March 1960.
49 Ibid., col. 1479, 31 March 1960.

50 Ibid., col. 1425, 30 March 1960. See also Tuairim, *University College Dublin*, p. 64; interview with Clarke, 15 June 2005. Clarke noted that the High School and Alexandra and Wesley Colleges moved to the suburbs in the 1960s.
51 Seanad Éireann Debates, vol. 53, col. 927, 'Universities and colleges', 10 January 1961. The quotations in this section are from this debate.
52 Ibid., col. 991, 11 January 1961.
53 Interview with Barrington, 19 May 2005. Patrick McGilligan would also have been opposed to Barrington. Rory O'Hanlon was appointed to the position. See also NAI, DT, S13809E, University College Dublin accommodation, McQuaid to Lemass, 1 April 1960.
54 DDA, McQuaid's papers, Tuairim file, Ó Cuinnleain to McQuaid, 23 January 1963, McQuaid to Apostolic Nuncio, 23 January 1965. See also NAI, DT, S13809E, University College Dublin accommodation, McQuaid to Lemass, 1 April 1960.
55 NAI, DT, S16803A, Higher Education Commission of Inquiry 1960, Commission on Higher Education Membership, MacEntee to Hillery, 26 August 1960. The quotations in this section are from this letter. MacEntee wrote that Winder had completed a most distinguished course in UCD and was engaged in important research work. See *Irish Times*, 26 January 2008 for Winder's obituary.
56 NAI, DT, S16803A, Higher Education Commission of Inquiry 1960, Commission on Higher Education Membership, Hillery to MacEntee, 29 August 1960. The quotation that follows in from Hillery's reply to MacEntee. Hillery pointed to the memorandum on Tuairim's pamphlet, which he had sent to MacEntee the previous Christmas. He claimed that the society's ideas did not stand up to such an examination and that it was unfortunate that the memorandum could not be published. The minister also claimed that the scientific community would more than adequately be represented on the commission. His wish to see only one representative of each college ruled out FitzGerald and Lynch, since Professor Edward Keenan of Medicine in UCD was appointed to the commission and Hillery was particularly keen to have Professor T. W. Moody, rather than Winder, represent Trinity.
57 Donogh O'Malley, 'Statement on university education in Dublin', *Studies*, 56:222 (Summer 1967), 121. See *Reports I & II, Commission on Higher Education, 1960–1967* (Dublin: Stationery Office, 1967), vil. ii, p. 439. The London and Dublin branches sent memoranda to the commission. Tuairim's Dublin branch argued that 'the degree of isolation of [Trinity]...from the community is unhealthy for that institution...it [is] important that T.C.D. be better integrated into the Irish university system'. See also Fuller, *Irish Catholicism*, p. 188; Cooney, *McQuaid*, p. 411.
58 *Sunday Independent*, 23 February 1969; UCD AD P22, Robin Dudley Edwards papers, 203 (98), Student publication from 2 December 1968–4 March 1969, *Confrontation: students for democratic action – UCD*, 4 March 1969.
59 Tuairim, *United Europe*, foreword. See *Irish Times*, 26 September 1962; *Cork Examiner*, 2 October 1962. See also Tuairim, *Irish education*, introduction, pp. 27–8; *Irish Times*, 7 December 1961; *Sunday Review*, 21 May 1961. Both

branches established research groups in early 1961. Dublin's decision was in response to recent developments with regard to Ireland's application for membership of the EEC. Towards the end of the pamphlet, information was included on the AEDE. Tuairim, *United Europe*, pp. 2–5, 7; interview with Ó Cearbhaill, 12 December 2003. Alers, without directly naming Tuairim, stated that Ireland, the 'first of the English speaking countries to join...brings us the enthusiastic co-operation of all branches of the teaching profession, through the initiative of a group of young people'. Ó Cearbhaill informed me that as well as being involved in Tuairim and writing a section of the pamphlet, Michael O'Donnell was a future President of Dublin Institute of Technology, while the future Minister for Education John Wilson, a member of the AEDE, was also present at the weekend. See also *Irish Times*, 21 November, 7 December 1961; ibid., 16 November 1967, 1 December 2007, 30 August 2008; and www.esperanto.ie/english/mullarney.htm accessed on 13 November 2008, for information on Mullarney.

60 Tuairim, *United Europe*, p. 7. The research group noted that there were at that time about twelve teaching associations acting independently of each other. See also *Irish Times*, 7 December 1961; interview with Ó Cearbhaill, 12 December 2003; NAI, DT, S1289D/1/61, Education, *Irish Press*, 27 November 1961. See also *Hibernia*, May 1962; minutes of committee meeting of Tuairim's Dublin branch, 18 December 1963. Mary Hogan was Tuairim's delegate to the Committee for Advancement in Education in Ireland.

61 Tuairim research group, 'Irish primary education', *An Occasional Bulletin*, 4 (1961), 1.

62 Rudd papers, Boland to Daly, 18 May 1961.

63 *Catholic Herald*, 2 June 1961. See also Rudd papers, Boland to Daly, 18 May 1961. An article in the *Irish Independent* caused 'mild dismay'. See *Irish Independent*, 17 May 1961 for a summary of the article in the branch's *An Occasional Bulletin*. See also Rudd papers, Boland to Daly, 24 May 1961, Daly to Boland, 21 May 1961. Daly, who thought that a Dublin delegate travelling to London was a 'scream', claimed that the Dublin branch would be 'disappointed' because the paper was 'all very sober stuff'.

64 Tuairim, *United Europe*, p. 7; Tuairim, *Irish education*, p. 2.

65 Tuairim, *United Europe*, p. 7. The quotations in this section are from Tuairim's two pamphlets except where otherwise stated.

66 Tuairim, *Irish education*, p. 29.

67 Rudd papers, Enda McDonagh to Daly, 6 June 1961.

68 Tuairim, *United Europe*, pp. 6, 29.

69 *Irish Times*, 27 November 1961. See Tuairim, *Irish education*, p. 26. London's research group called for new curricula for infant schools for children of 5–7 years of age, junior schools for ages 7–11, middle schools for ages 11–15, and the optional county colleges for 15–18-year-olds. The London branch stated that in some cases, children would be 16 before leaving middle school. See also *Sunday Press*, 4 November 1962.

70 Tuairim, *Irish education*, foreword, p. 37; Pat Crowley, 'Analysis of the view of Irish school leavers', *An Occasional Bulletin*,7 (1963), 2. See also T. L. Jarman,

'Developments in English education in 1959: the year of the Crowther report', *International Review of Education*, 6:2 (1960), 231–4. Tuairim claimed that the 1959 Crowther report argued for junior colleges in England, which the research group stated were similar to its county colleges. The Crowther report recommended that the leaving age be raised to sixteen and part-time education be available up to eighteen. According to Jarman, the report actually used the term 'county colleges' although Tuairim was correct insofar as both called for continued education for this age group. See also NAI, DFA, 2002/19/70, London, Coffey to Secretary, Department of External Affairs, 14 January 1961, Secretary, Department of Education to Secretary, Department of External Affairs, 15 March 1961, Coffey to Secretary, Department of External Affairs, 9 May 1961; Tuairim, *Irish education*, p. 10; Tuairim, *United Europe*, pp. 9–10, 13, 17–18. The Dublin branch's pamphlet cited the UNESCO report on the preparation of general secondary school curricula. It claimed that students over fifteen years of age in much of Europe were offered a choice between three groups – classical languages, modern languages and science and mathematics. The Dublin group also referred to speeches from Michael Tierney in 1927 and Gael Linn's Riobard MacGabhrainn in 1959. See Michael Tierney, 'The revival of the Irish language', *Studies*, 16:61 (March 1927), 1–10. See also *Hibernia*, December 1962; *Irish Independent*, 8 February 1961; Miriam Lee, 'Argument and persuasion', *An Occasional Bulletin*, 5 (1961), 6–8. An article by Daly in *Hibernia* cited the Department of Education's report for 1959–60. She also emphasised the importance of changes to the educational system in advance of membership of the EEC. In additition, the London group regretted that the Irish National Teachers' Organisation's plan for education had not been implemented, while the Dublin branch seemed more positive about recent improvements in education like the abolition of the preparatory training colleges.
71 Tuairim, *Irish education*, p. 8.
72 Tuairim, *United Europe*, p. 21.
73 Ibid., p. 23.
74 NAI, DT, S12891D/1/62, Education, and S1289D/1/61, Education, *Irish Press*, 27 November 1961.
75 Walsh, *Expansion*, pp. 114–61; Garvin, *Future*, pp. 152–3, 157; Horgan, *Lemass*, p. 296; Ó Buachalla, *Education*, pp. 72–4, 281, 284, 315; *Investment in education: report of the survey team appointed by the Minister of Education in October 1962* (Dublin: Stationery Office, 1965).
76 *Irish Times*, 2 October 1962. See also O'Hanrahan papers, Tuairim-London, 'Report by chairman, Michael O'Hanrahan, AGM', 29 March 1963; Tuairim London branch folder: press cuttings, *Irish Press*, 1, 3 October 1962, *Belfast Telegraph*, 2 October 1962, *Cork Examiner*, 2 October 1962, *Irish Independent*, 2 October 1962, *Irish Times*, 27 October 1962, 4 March, 28 June, 3 July 1963, *Irish Catholic*, 4 October 1962, *Catholic Herald*, 6 October 1962, *Southern Star*, 6 October 1962, *Limerick Weekly Echo*, 6 October 1962; *Sunday Review*, 7 October 1962, *Roscommon Herald*, 20 October 1962, *Times Educational Supplement*, 26 October 1962, *Unity Bulletin*, 2 (1962), *Focus*, November 1962,

Hibernia, June 1961, November 1962, *Gairm*, 6 November 1962. No indication was given of the total number of pamphlets sold. Seán MacBride and the Countess of Wicklow praised the London branch's pamphlet at a Tuairim weekend in 1962. See McKeown, *Nationalist*, p. 22. In the second *Unity Bulletin*, National Unity welcomed the 'glare of publicity which has focused on education in the twenty-six counties following the recent publication of two *Tuairim* pamphlets'.

77 Tuairim, *Irish education*, p. 9; *Irish Press*, 3 October 1962; *Irish Catholic*, 4 October 1962.
78 See Tuairim, *Irish education*, pp. 8, 11, 17; *Gairm*, 6 November 1962. Rejecting claims that much of adult education consisted of '"hobby" classes', *Gairm* noted that 56,177 people had enrolled in the last (unspecified) year for which the Department of Education had figures.
79 *Times Educational Supplement*, 26 October 1962. See also *Irish Press*, 3 October 1962.
80 *Hibernia*, November 1962. Also *Belfast Telegraph*, 2 October 1962.
81 *Hibernia*, December 1962.
82 Rudd papers, note by Daly to Boland regarding Fergus Pyle, 15 May 1961.
83 *Sunday Press*, 4 November 1962.
84 *Hibernia*, December 1962.
85 Ibid., November 1962. See also *Irish Times*, 2 October 1962; *Southern Star*, 6 October 1962.
86 Rudd papers, McDonagh to Daly, 6 June 1961. See also *Irish Times*, 31 January 1963. Winder commented in a speech to the Irish Association in 1963 that the London branch had put forward a 'plan for the future development of...education [which although] seemed too revolutionary...to be adopted immediately...indicated the way...Irish education would have to move'. Significantly, he did not refer to the Dublin branch's pamphlet.
87 *Irish Times*, 2 November 1957. See also correspondence with Roy Johnston, 15 December 2005. Rudd later became involved in the Association for Democracy in Europe, the Wolfe Tone Society and the Irish Sovereignty Movement. She also was commissioned to write reports by the Department of Education. See NAI, DJ, 2006/147/4, 'Industrial training for women: European seminar on vocational guidance and training for women: Irish report by Joy Rudd'; Denis O'Sullivan, 'National school terminal leaving and school delay', *Studies*, 62:245 (Spring 1973), 63–74.
88 *Hibernia*, March 1962; see also February, May 1962. Seán Mac Carthaigh also signed the Cork branch's letter. See also *Irish Times*, 4 July 1969, 13, 14 December 1971. At this time, John A. Murphy used the Irish version of his name, Seán A. Ó Murchú. The Cork branch referred to the Council of Education and UNESCO in support of its arguments in relation to the Irish language. See *Irish Times*, 18 January 1958, 26 September 1964, 8 October, 6 December 1966; *Clonmel Nationalist*, 23 April 1960; and *Hibernia*, March, April, May, June 1962 for other Tuairim meetings on the Irish language. See also *Irish Times*, 11 May 1959. At a meeting of the Cork branch in 1959, Seán

Hamilton, the Headmaster of Bandon secondary school, was, however, critical of the limited investment in education in Ireland.
89 *Hibernia*, May 1962. Highlighting the need to consider Irish developments in a European context, Hynes referred to an article in the current issue of *Múinteoir Náisiúnta*, published by the European Cultural Centre in Geneva.
90 *Irish Times*, 9 June 1965. See also Garvin, *Future*, pp. 36–7, and DDA, McQuaid's papers, Tuairim file, McQuaid to Apostolic Nuncio, 23 January 1965. McQuaid wrote that Tuairim had studied and organised discussions on primary and post-primary education and the Irish language.
91 *Irish Times*, 23 October, 26 November 1964. The series was in the *Irish Times*, 19–24 October 1964.
92 Ibid., 21 November 1964. See Walsh, *Expansion*, pp. 62–99. See also Séamas Ó Buachalla, '*Investment in education*: context, content and impact', *Administration*, 44:3 (Autumn 1996), 10–20. Ireland and Austria were the first countries to agree to have their educational systems examined, with many Western European countries following their example.
93 DDA, McQuaid papers, Tuairim file, McQuaid to Apostolic Nuncio, 23 January 1965. For Thornley's contribution as a TD towards debate on education see Dáil Éireann Debates, vol. 255, col. 1093, 'Industrial school detention', 13 July 1971; vol. 274, col. 148, 'Teaching qualifications', 3 July 1974; vol. 298, col. 209, 'National agricultural advisory, education and research authority bill', 23 March 1977; vol. 229, col. 1559, 'Dismissal of teachers', 25 May 1977.
94 NAI, DT, S12891D/2/62, Post war planning: education, Lemass to Hillery, 23 November 1962. It should be noted that there were many press reports in this file following upon the one containing the articles which related to the Dublin branch's pamphlet. See NAI, DT, S12891D/1/62, Post war planning: education, *Irish Press*, 27 November 1961, *Irish Times*, 29 November 1961, *Hibernia*, February 1962; NAI, DT, S16603B/62, Tuairim general, *Irish Press*, 1 October 1962, *Irish Times*, 2 October 1962.
95 Irish Labour History Museum, Dublin, Labour annual reports, 'labour educational policy, appendix: Labour's policy on education', 1963. See also Puirséil, *The Irish Labour Party*, pp. 220, 224, 229; Randles, *Post-primary education*, pp. 125–7. Labour's educational policy was co-written by Desmond and its Parliamentary Officer, Catherine McGuiness. I would like to thank Mr Patrick O'Donnell in the Irish Labour History Museum, who sent me copies of these documents. See also O'Hanrahan papers, Tuairim-London, 'Report by chairman, Michael O'Hanrahan, AGM', 29 March 1963; interview with Desmond, 11 May 2005. O'Hanrahan noted recent statements by the minister and the similarity between the branch's pamphlet and the Labour Party's policy as indications that the research group had been successful in influencing public policy. Desmond argued that education and politics were the two areas in which Tuairim might have had an impact. He sent me a copy of the London branch's pamphlet that he still had among his files.
96 *Hibernia*, March 1964. See also Walsh, *Expansion*, p. 97.
97 *Commission on Higher Education*, vol. ii, p. 199; Rudd papers, Academic Staff Association to Daly, 3 October 1961. The branch sent memoranda to both

these organisations. See also Rudd papers, Barrington to Boland, 30 October 1961; Erskine B. Childers, 'The problem of Katanga', *An Occasional Bulletin*, 5 (1961), 1, 4; Lee, 'Argument and persuasion', pp. 6–8. Following the government's request that copies of the bulletin in which Childers's article appeared be sent to it, Barrington added that that would be a good way of circulating Daly's article, which had called for a more dynamic system of education, 'in the right circles'. The article by Childers, the son of the minister, argued that Ireland needed to develop its own information sources in response to the recent tragic events in the Congo. This, according to Barrington, had 'caused great excitement' in Fianna Fáil.

98 *Irish Times*, 19 February 1966; correspondence with Áine Hyland, 22 July 2005; Lynch and Carter, *Planning*. For discussion of the *Investment in education* report see Walsh, *Expansion*, pp. 114–216.

99 *Irish Times*, 20 November 1965; Rudd papers, 'Report from Cork branch of Tuairim for National Council meeting on 27 November 1965'.

100 Interview with Jim Doolan, Galway, 10 December 2003.

101 See Horgan, *Lemass*, pp. 297–301; Walsh, *Expansion*, pp. 76–7, 140–1, 257–66, 316–17. O'Malley established the regional technical colleges in the late 1960s.

102 Tuairim, *Some of our children*; Tuairim, 'Irish primary education', pp. 1, 2; Tuairim, *Irish education*, p. 22. The other members of the research group that examined industrial schools were Maeve O'Reilly, Randal Kinkead and Maura Hunt. Reflecting the large turnover of members in the branch, others, namely Peter Tyrell, Jeanne Hackett, Brian McCarthy and Mary Campbell, also contributed to part of the work of the pamphlet.

103 Department of Health, Dublin, RM/ARC/0/489709, Fidelma Clandillon, 'Tuairim report "Some of our children"'. I would like to thank Mr Fergal Flynn of the Department of Health for access to this review.

104 Tuairim, *Some of our children*, pp. 48–9. Tuairim proposed that the National Association for the Deprived Child would include representatives of the Departments of Health and Education, employers, trade unions, teachers and managers of the schools. It would have branches throughout Ireland, while the Irish in England were called on to establish an association to assist young homeless immigrants from Ireland. Many of the quotations in this section are from this pamphlet.

105 Ibid., p. 9. The research group also stated that 1,782 were in foster care and that it had been claimed that adoption was limited to children of '"good class" parentage'. The 1908 Children's Act remained in force in Britain until 1933 when reformatories and industrial schools were abolished by the Children and Young Persons Act. In addition to the 1908 Children's Act, the group noted that the other Acts relating to children in Ireland included the 1957 Children (Amendment) Act, the 1926 School Attendance Act and the 1952 Adoption Act. They claimed that there were only six probation officers in Dublin and none outside the capital.

106 Department of Health, RM/ARC/0/489709, Clandillon, 'Tuairim report "Some of our children"'. See also O'Sullivan, 'Residential child welfare', 4.155. The 1989 Health Act resolved this issue.

107 Department of Health, RM/ARC/0/489709, Clandillon, 'Tuairim report "Some of our children"'. Clandillon claimed because the members resided in London, the research group should have been aware of the need for two different ministries and that deprived children should be cared for by a social work department. She recognised, however, that the reports in Britain that made this point had been published after Tuairim's pamphlet.

108 Tuairim, *Some of our children*, pp. 2, 4–18, 23, 25, 28–9, 32, 33, 44. The pamphlet compared the numbers of children in care in Ireland, England and Wales and the amounts paid in respect of a child in care. The research group referred to the period of time spent by boys at Marlborough House. The members made telephone calls to the managers of the institutions and to those in foster care. They visited eleven certified schools and homes, five private voluntary homes, the remand home in Dublin and the Eccles Street hostel. These were compared with a residential school for the mentally handicapped, run by the Department of Health and a voluntary children's home in London. In addition to interviewing former pupils, the group spoke to organisations connected to childcare in Ireland and conducted a survey of Irish boys in English borstals; it received replies from eighteen borstals in respect of 124 boys. It thanked the Home Office for facilitating this survey and the Departments of Education and Health for providing up-to-date figures. The group also referred to the 1936 Commission on Industrial and Reformatory Schools and the 1951 report of the Commission on Youth Unemployment in Ireland, the 1946 Curtis Committee and the 1961 Home Office report on the work of the Children's Department in Britain as well as John Bowlby's book *Childcare and the growth of love* and Donald Ford's *Delinquent child and the community*, published respectively in 1953 and 1957.

109 O'Sullivan, 'Residential child welfare', 4.86.

110 Tuairim, *Some of our children*, pp. 20–2, 29. These statements were made in respect of Letterfrack industrial school and generally of the girls' schools. An exception was Daingean, where the children were said to be 'very shabbily dressed'.

111 Rudd papers, Peter Tyrell, 'Memories of an Irish boyhood, Letterfrack 1925–1932'. This piece was undated.

112 NLI, MS 40/543/11, 12, Owen Sheehy Skeffington papers, Tyrell to Sheehy Skeffington, 29 April, 7 November 1964. Tyrell spoke about Letterfrack at the Tuairim meeting. In a letter to Sheehy Skeffington, he wrote that an Irish priest had said that he agreed with Tyrell. See Maura Hunt, 'Institutional care of the deprived child', in Tuairim, *Some of our children*, pp. 50–4. Discussed at a meeting of the London branch in November 1964, Hunt's paper examined the effects of institutional care.

113 *Hibernia*, June 1964. Tyrell's article described his background, his family's poverty and Letterfrack's physical appearance. The only indication of the brutality he experienced there was when a Christian Brother dispersed a crowd surrounding him and his brothers with a walking stick, which he used to 'beat the back and legs'. Rudd also published a piece editiled 'Children in care' in this edition of *Hibernia*, in which she referred to many of the

deficiencies of the existing system. See also Rudd papers, Tyrell to Rudd, 7 November 1964; Tuairim-London, 'Report by chairman, Seán Ó Súilleabhain, AGM', 29 March 1963. Tyrell, along with John Boland and the historian Cecil Woodham-Smith, made unspecified donations to the cost of the proposed pamhlet. See NLI, MS 40/543/11, Owen Sheehy Skeffington papers, M. Carmel to Tyrell, 26 July 1964. Tyrell's letter enlisted sympathy, if scepticism, from M. Carmel, a teacher in Loreto Convent, Navan, Co. Meath.
114 Whelan, *Founded on fear*, p. xxxiii.
115 NLI, MS 40/543/12, Sheehy Skeffington papers, Tyrell to Sheehy Skeffington, 7 November 1964.
116 *Hibernia*, May 1966. See also *Irish Independent*, 12 January 1966; *Irish Times*, 13 January 1966.
117 *Irish Times*, 4 May 1966.
118 NAI, DT, 98/6/156, 'Memorandum for the government: proposed committee for reformatory and industrial schools', 4 August 1967. See Helen Binchy, 'The role of voluntary agencies: the social services of Ireland today', *Christus Rex*, 21 (July 1967), 259; Paul McQuaid, 'Problem children and their families: assessment and referral for institutional care', *Studies*, 60:238 (Summer 1971), 155. McQuaid also worked in the Mater Misericordiae Hospital in Dublin. See also Arnold and Laskey, *Poor Clares*, pp. 137–40; Ferriter, *Transformation*, p. 559; Raftery and O'Sullivan, *Children*, pp. 364–81; O'Sullivan, 'Residential child welfare'; *Report of the Commission to Inquire into Child Abuse*, vol. iii, 6.45, 8.49.
119 O'Sullivan, 'Residential child welfare', 4.83.
120 Ibid., 4.86.
121 DH, RM/ARC/0/489709, Clandillon, 'Tuairim report "Some of our children"'. See also O'Sullivan, 'Residential child welfare', 4.87.
122 Department of Education, 'Brief commentary on Tuairim pamphlet: "Some of our children"'.
123 Dáil Éireann Debates, 'Office of the Minister for Education: Department of Finance', 1 December 1966; *Irish Press*, 26 May 1967. Andrews merely stated that the society had published a pamphlet on the subject. He hoped that the minister would give greater attention to the matter.
124 McQuaid, 'Problem children', p. 155. See also O'Sullivan, 'Residential child welfare', 4.02, 4.06, 4.105.

5

Sense and censorship:
Tuairim and cultural conservatism

The extreme form of censorship was anathema to Tuairim and its aim of creating a more open society. In attempting to influence public opinion and public policy in favour of changes to the system of censorship, Tuairim invited several individuals, most notably Fr. Peter Connolly, to speak to the society. Connolly, through his speeches and articles, advocated a more sophisticated understanding of literature and film and a relaxation of the censorship laws, and the development of his ideas can be closely followed from the talks he gave at three Tuairim meetings from 1959 to 1966. Other notable individuals who used the forum that Tuairim provided to challenge the system in place included Edna O'Brien, a controversial author who at that time had all of her books banned. In 1966, with O'Brien sharing the platform, Connolly provided a critique of the author's works at a meeting of the Limerick branch to a public divided between support for her and a view that regarded her as a writer of obscene literature. The contrast between the radicalism of the views that Connolly and others put forward at Tuairim's meetings and those of the Catholic hierarchy reflects the extent to which censorship remained a controversial issue in the 1960s. That reforms were introduced in 1967 by the Minister for Justice, Brian Lenihan, raises the question as to what influence Tuairim and Connolly had on this change in government policy. What follows is an assessment of the arguments put forward at Tuairim's meetings, their impact and an analysis of how radical they were for this period.

Cultural conservatism

Censorship, while not unique to Ireland, came to operate in an extreme manner in the Irish case. The system introduced during the 1920s reflected the concerns of a predominantly Catholic country. Its preoccupation with 'obscene' literature, however, existed throughout the Western world at this time. Ireland's response was the Censorship of Films Act in 1923 and the

1929 Censorship of Publications Act. Like books and periodicals, films could be banned for indecency or obscenity. In the 1920s, the legislation met a perceived need for 'stricter control of objectionable publications' and films.[1] This was because the existing law, which was inherited from Britain, dealt, according to Michael Adams, only with material which was of an 'obviously...obscene character'. It did not, for example, keep imported periodicals, particularly from the 'English gutter press', out of Ireland. The legislation in relation to literature, as well as films, was stricter and more inclusive than the previous system. In the context of what was to be censored, the definition of the term 'indecent' was crucial. It was decided that 'the word indecent shall be construed as suggestive of, or inciting to sexual immorality or unnatural vice or likely in any similar way to corrupt or deprave'. In response to concern from some members of the Oireachtas that this would lead to widespread banning of books, the censorship board was instructed that a book should be banned only if in its 'general tendency [it was] indecent or obscene'. This phrase 'in its general tendency indecent or obscene' was, however, deleted from an Amending Act in 1946; that, as Connolly later claimed at a Tuairim meeting in 1959, was otherwise an improvement because it introduced an appeals board.[2] The deletion of the phrase was one of the actions that Connolly believed led to the banning of so many works of literary merit. While the censorship board banned over 1,800 books between 1929 and 1946, this number increased to almost 8,000 books between 1946 and 1965.[3]

Seán O'Faolain and others writing in the periodical *The Bell* during the early 1940s had argued that the censorship board was overly zealous in its task. This criticism led to a debate in the Seanad in 1942 and later, the amending Act. During the debate, Sir John Keane claimed that in banning books such as *Land of Spices* by Kate O'Brien the board was not taking the whole of a book into consideration, as it was instructed to do by the Act of 1929. Keane was, however, very much in a minority in the Seanad, the vast majority of whose members supported the censorship board.

The increased number of books that were banned in the period following World War II was made more problematic by the fact that the system did not present authors with an opportunity to defend themselves before the censorship board. Clearly, not all of them wrote works that were of literary merit. Among these books, however, were novels by distinguished authors such as William Faulkner, Ernest Hemingway and Scott Fitzgerald.[4] Irish authors including Frank O'Connor and Kate and Edna O'Brien also had books banned. The controversy surrounding censorship centred on books by authors such as these who could claim to have written serious literary works. Increased criticism of the board, from, for example, a new organisation, the Irish Association of Civil Liberty, established in 1948, and in the *Irish Times* may have facilitated the appointment of what was effectively a new censorship board in 1956 and 1957. This change did not alter the machinery of censorship in any way. What was new was the attitude of those who decided which books were to be banned. Certainly, their actions resulted in less criticism from liberals or literati than in previous years.[5]

That is not to say that from the late 1950s the censorship board was free of controversy. The banning of books by authors such as those mentioned above reflected a concern with morality rather than the literary merit of a novel. Furthermore, if the appeals board confirmed a prohibition order, that book was banned in perpetuity. Authors such as Edna O'Brien not only were deprived of part of their income, but also, on occasion, encountered hostility because of the public perception of them as controversial writers. O'Brien's neighbours went so far as burning her book *Girl with green eyes*, in the grounds of her local church in 1962.[6] Though this is an extreme example, censorship thus alienated writers from the state and from the Catholic Church, which supported the system. Public opinion, insofar as it can be gauged, appears to have supported censorship as it existed in Ireland. While there were those including the Catholic hierarchy who enthusiastically defended censorship and others who criticised it, the majority of people acquiesced in the decisions that were taken. Furthermore, private censorship by library committees, organisations such as the Catholic Truth Society, customs officials or concerned citizens, who might highlight indecent literature to the censorship board, ensuring that it was not available in the local library or bookshop, seems to have been widespread.[7] This often resulted in the stigmatisation of authors who had books banned and made it difficult to argue against the law as it operated.

Tuairim and censorship

Tuairim and Peter Connolly sought to persuade the state of the need to reform the system of censorship. The first occasion on which Connolly, the Professor of English at St Patrick's College, Maynooth, spoke to Tuairim was in February 1959. This was the most significant meeting the society held in relation to censorship and was organised by the Dublin branch. Connolly examined the 'assumptions which underlie censorship' and focused on the author's intention and the general tendency of a novel rather than the traditional arguments over the extent to which the state should censor literature.[8] In his paper, subsequently published in *Christus Rex* in July 1959, Connolly pointed in a new direction in speaking 'as one with special interest in literature second only to a professional interest in morals'. He examined ecclesiastical and civil censorship and sought to 'synthesise...the perspective of each approach while maintaining the distinction between them'.[9] In a scholarly article, Connolly referred to Canon Law and responded to a statement by Pope Pius XII with a claim that 'You can't, in fact, make men good by Act of Parliament'. His argument was that the system of censorship in existence in Ireland was 'juvenile'. Because Connolly's concern was in relation to the individual, the creation of a 'fully rounded personality', he thought that the state, rather than setting standards, should attempt to provide the conditions for the 'moral and intellectual development' of its citizens.

Since censorship in Ireland inhibited that development, Connolly sought a 'more nuanced interpretation' of the term 'indecency' as defined in legislation.[10] He argued that the term 'indecent' could 'vary from one culture to the next, from country to country even in the Christian world, from one period to the next and simultaneously among the groups within any complex modern society'. For Connolly, this and other social values were continually changing, and the law should reflect as closely as possible these values while trying 'to balance the rival claims of various groups in society'. Such inclusive language was quite radical for the late 1950s. His views ran counter to the majority Catholic ethos, which held that the law should uphold Catholic morality. Unlike members of the Catholic hierarchy, Connolly did not feel that the availability of modern literature would involve a 'sacrifice of moral principle'. As a 'man of the Church', he combined a 'delight in the secular...with a fierce reverence for the sacred'.[11] Accordingly he was in a unique position to equip Irish Catholic culture better for any future confrontation with the secularist ideas already dominant in continental Europe. As Connolly said himself, 'The novels and the new ideas will seep through in any case but into a negative atmosphere in which the sense of intellectual adventure has gone stale and embittered.' He felt that the 'negative atmosphere' resulted from the effects of censorship in Ireland. For Connolly, if Catholicism was to survive in Ireland an 'intellectual Catholic elite' was required. It was perhaps not coincidental that Connolly was speaking to Tuairim when he made that remark. Open to individuals from all and no religions, the organisation shared Connolly's vision for a more open society where existing orthodoxies would be questioned and new ideas discussed freely. This was reflected in Tuairim's continued attempts to influence public opinion and legislation in a more liberal direction.

The 'cross-fertilisation of ideas' taking place between the secular, as represented in Tuairim, and the church, as reflected in Connolly's persona,[12] was particularly well reflected in a meeting organised by the Limerick branch (see Figure 9 for one of the Limerick branch's cultural activities). This event took place in April 1966. It drew a large audience and made quite an impact. In the most dramatic event that Tuairim organised on this and perhaps

9 Gemma Fallon seemed to enjoy a cheese, wine and art evening organised by the Limerick branch at King John's Castle.

on any subject, Connolly and Tuairim's John Dillon shared the society's platform with the controversial author Edna O'Brien, who had had her four books banned.[13] The branch was unusual for Tuairim in the extent of its commitment to cultural issues, and its support for O'Brien contrasted with the view of many individuals, who would have been uneasy with the female characters in her novels since they challenged the 'patriarchal structure of a traditional family life'.[14] More were shocked by the graphic sexual content of her books. The *Irish Times* stated that at the Tuairim meeting one lady spoke of 'vulgarity and a gentleman stood up and agreed with her'.[15] Others were indignant as to how a professor in Maynooth could speak about these 'godless works'.[16] Indeed, many individuals would have found a priest sharing a public platform, never mind defending such an author, deeply objectionable. Given that she was, in certain quarters, reviled for being banned and rarely had an opportunity to speak in public, the meeting fulfilled a valuable purpose. Though many people in attendance appeared to be hostile towards O'Brien, others admired the author and her novels. For instance, one of the several priests in attendance commented that 'he had read two of her books within the last week and that they were marvellous'.[17] Furthermore, O'Brien stated that 'she was overwhelmed by the enthusiastic audience accorded her in Limerick'.[18] Certainly most of the people present appeared to be familiar with O'Brien's work; when asked if they had read at least one of the books, a large number of them raised their hands. This highlights the ineffectiveness of the censorship system in Ireland. The reality was that in the 1950s and 1960s a person who wished to read a book that had been banned was usually able to acquire it. As Connolly put it in his article, there were many 'loopholes' and banned novels could 'be obtained by hook or by crook'.

Connolly proceeded to deliver an assessment of O'Brien's work. He was, as ever, fair in his approach. In his critique, he made use of the 'ideas and distinctions' that were in the article, 'The moralists and the obscene', which he had published in *The Irish Theological Quarterly* in 1965.[19] There he had contrasted what was 'legitimate treatment of erotic material' with what was 'pornography'.[20] Both that article and his critique of O'Brien's novels at Tuairim's meeting indicated that the 'quality' rather than the 'quantity' of the erotic material was the vital consideration for Connolly. He praised the 'high spirits…and…cheerful, natural ribaldry which expressed for him the spirit of the countryside' of the author's first two novels.[21] He was, however, more critical of the latter two novels and especially the last. Nevertheless, even here, Connolly, according to the *Irish Times*, criticised the 'sexual imagery…less for its quantity than for its quality and for the fact that it seemed to add very little to [her fourth] book'.

Many of the questions asked at Tuairim's meeting were concerned with the morality of O'Brien's novels rather than the quality of her literature. This suggests that Connolly's concern with the negative atmosphere which resulted from the operation of censorship in Ireland was well founded. At least some people present focused on a few passages in her novels rather than considering the totality of her work. In replying to one comment that the 'facts of life could be described without obscenity', she suggested, 'perhaps the word you really meant to use is frankness'.[22] Furthermore, she claimed that these criticisms said more about those who uttered them than they did about her, and in denying an 'allegation that she made money writing dirty books,' she maintained that 'writing is very arduous'.[23] O'Brien outlined the motivation behind her writing when she stated that 'only to give a fraction of someone's innermost thought is to abuse them and diminish them. What makes us love people is their imperfection as much as their perfection'.[24] She thought that every person was 'capable of a great depth and variation of thought, from the almost mythical to the obscene or impure'. O'Brien aimed to write the truth about people's emotions and passions. It was her perception of the truth of the lives of young women growing up in Ireland that made many individuals uncomfortable.

This is reflected in the questions that were directed at O'Brien. Some of them were so pointed that Connolly and Tuairim's John Dillon assisted her with them. When O'Brien was asked if she lived in England because Ireland was a 'Christian society', Connolly, according to the *Irish Times*, explained O'Brien's attitude as it had been conveyed to him over dinner:

> It was because she felt the time to write while living in Ireland was difficult because of the narrowness of the atmosphere, because of the pressures on the right hand in a country which was 'rather jittery' about its literature. It was a social not a religious pressure and other writers in other countries – Ibsen in Norway, for instance, had experienced it as well.

When asked whether 'hard-core pornography should be kept out of Ireland…O'Brien apologised and said that she had not seen any'. The *Irish Times* stated that Connolly was once again on his feet, 'noting that we should do our best to keep out this sort of stuff, but that the other job – that of cultivating discrimination in the literary field – was simply not being done well enough'.

Raising the consciousness of works of literary worth was one of Connolly's primary objectives. This explains his unease at the newspaper coverage of the meeting; it suggested that its significance lay in his defending a controversial writer rather than discussing the reasons for his defence. The coverage in the *Irish Times* was, for example, one of high praise for Tuairim and Connolly. Its editorial stated that Tuairim had helped 'send a wave of laughter around Ireland' and that Connolly 'has put everyone in the country in his debt'. The significance of the meeting for this and other newspapers was in the fact that a member of the Catholic Church had provided a critique of an author whose books were banned. This, they argued, was new and radical. Advertising the meeting, the *Limerick Leader* claimed that an evaluation of O'Brien's novels by 'a distinguished and liberal critic from the national seminary is an exciting departure'; the paper predicted 'an exciting confrontation'.[25] The reality, however, was that there were other priests in Maynooth such as Tuairim's Enda McDonagh and Fr. Denis Meehan, Professor of Divinity and Classics at Maynooth, who were also in contact with the society and who, like McDonagh and Connolly, sought a more intellectual Catholicism in Ireland. Nevertheless, Connolly's approach to censorship was, indeed, innovative; there was a significant contrast between him and, for example, Archbishop McQuaid, who was shocked at the content of O'Brien's novels. Even Connolly noted that the Tuairim meeting was an unusual event: he said that it was very rare for anyone in Ireland to consider or listen to an Irish writer before that person was 'dead or embittered'.[26] The newspapers thus had a point when they claimed that Tuairim's meeting marked a dramatic contrast with the silence with which prominent individuals in Irish society had traditionally treated Irish writers.

Connolly's objection to this type of coverage can be seen in a comment he made in an article in *Hibernia* in February 1964. He claimed that the '*Irish Times* still slants a lecture on censorship in the old way while passing over the fresh nuances introduced into the debate'. This was perhaps even more true of some of the correspondence to that newspaper: one letter described O'Brien's novels as 'malodorous' and another asked in relation to Connolly, 'What worth is moral teaching when the obscene is acclaimed?'[27] Connolly and O'Brien were thus to the forefront of the latest battle against censorship. It was nothing new for O'Brien to experience hostility from members of the public. As on past occasions, it did not deter her from giving her opinions forthrightly. While this time she did not directly object to censorship, she did argue that individuals could have different opinions about what was 'obscene', as with the word 'ugly'; O'Brien claimed that she could 'find soot in the chimney very beautiful; somebody else could find it ugly'.[28] Since books were banned for being 'obscene or indecent', this was a crucial point. Connolly was also distinguishing between what was and what was not 'obscene'. The implication for the censorship system was clear. In Connolly's view the definitions of the terms used in the censorship legislation were unsatisfactory, while O'Brien felt that that would always be the case.

The meeting served another valuable purpose in that at least in some quarters, O'Brien, as a writer, had not always been treated with the respect that she deserved. The *Limerick Leader* noted that 'Many take an agnostic view of Edna O'Brien's literary worth and allow her only woman's magazine class'.[29] That was partly because of the content of her novels. In supporting O'Brien and giving her an opportunity to present her views on writing and to respond to an assessment of her work by a well-known literary critic, Tuairim was hoping that the public would begin to see her as a serious writer. The fact that the literary critic was also a priest gave added weight to this attempt. It met, however, with mixed success. She was and continued to be a very popular writer but only recently have her achievements been properly recognised.[30]

Alongside this was the controversy, implied by some of the questions, over whether O'Brien could be seen as a Catholic writer. In this regard, the radical nature of Connolly's approach was reflected in his paper at Tuairim's meeting and in a review he wrote of *The lonely girl* in *Hibernia* in July 1962. Connolly revealed the extent to which Ireland had fallen behind 'contemporary standards of literature [and] contemporary taste', noting that while O'Brien's latest novel was banned in Ireland, its author was 'hailed in the *Catholic Herald* as "one of our best young Catholic writers"'.[31] Connolly's approach was more sophisticated in that he did not see any 'reason why O'Brien should be a "Catholic writer" if her bent is not in that direction'.[32] His view was that it was not; referring to the heroine, he explained that 'Kathleen's innocence [was] not amoral but premoral – what Frank O'Connor had differentiated from original sin by calling it original innocence'.[33] This certainly was very different from the usual approach taken in Ireland and quite revolutionary for one in Connolly's position. Connolly's view was that O'Brien's novels represented something 'new in Irish fiction'. He underlined his support for the author by stating that he would be more interested in her future career than in that of any other writer. This in turn was the major factor in his becoming embroiled in one of the 'censorship wars' which he had always perceived as futile.

Connolly's attitude towards past divisions between conservatives and liberals was indicated by his response to an article about him and another priest, Fr. John Kelly, SJ, by Peter Lennon, a journalist in *The Guardian*. Lennon's article 'Turbulent priests' placed Connolly and Kelly against Archbishop McQuaid, the Catholic Church and the UCD President, Michael Tierney, in a series in which he argued Ireland suffered from a 'Climate of Repression'.[34] In response, Connolly explained his aims in his reviews of films and books. His intention was to 'bypass the kind of anti-censorship wars which his own [Lennon's] tend to revive, in which he tries to enlist us all and which in my opinion are wholly outmoded'.[35] He continued that these 'censorship wars', which were 'valiantly' conducted by Seán O'Faolain and others in *The Bell* in the 1940s, 'pushed "liberal" litterateurs and conservative Irish readers farther and farther apart'. Connolly's approach was new in that he wrote:

> positive appreciations of contemporary films and books which would simply ignore polemics about our censorship. It would demonstrate to Irish readers that in the face of modern novels or films of whatever kind it was not necessary to bury one's head nor on the other hand sacrifice one jot of moral principle.

His paper at Tuairim's meeting and review in *Hibernia* were examples of his methods.

At a meeting of Tuairim's Dublin branch in February 1965, Connolly elaborated on the contrast between his approach and the controversies in the past. He viewed former arguments as counter-productive in that they 'tended to move in cycles with, first, a narrowing of censorship, then a journalistic outcry, public interest and finally a broadening of censorship principles until they again narrowed'.[36] Connolly believed that Lennon undermined the cause he claimed to support. While Lennon was justified in some his arguments as to the quality of intellectual life, many individuals saw his articles as 'tendentious'.[37] For instance, the poet John Jordan claimed that they contained 'intemperate language [which] will only mobilise sympathy for those he criticises' and were full of 'rumour and surmise'.[38] With the exception of the London branch, which was more forthright than Tuairim in Ireland, the society similarly thought that a moderate approach was more likely to influence policy formulation. Rational arguments and reasonable views would, it was believed, be more difficult for the Catholic hierarchy and others to oppose. This was reflected in the society's support for Connolly. Though the latter's wish to avoid becoming involved in a heated debate on censorship was partly due to his belief as to their futility, Connolly also needed to protect the platform – his position in Maynooth – from which he developed his ideas. This was an important factor in his reaction to Lennon's criticism of the institution of which he was a member.

Connolly also reiterated the importance of the writer, which was evident when he discussed the author's intention during the first Tuairim meeting. His support for writers was reflected in his call to the press and to literary periodicals to review extensively books that had been banned. Connolly thought that the views of the writer should be central to any system of censorship and claimed that the 'voice of the practising writer' should be added to the censorship board.[39] As James Murphy put it in *No bland facility*, Connolly was simultaneously 'irenic [and] subversive of the narrow ideas which formed the basis of Ireland's consensus on censorship'. Connolly 'hoped for a gradual growth of a climate of Catholic opinion which would make a juvenile standard of censorship – though not all censorship – untenable'.[40] While not against censorship in principle, he articulated the need for a change in how the system operated in Ireland.

Tuairim, the Church and the State

Despite the emergence of increasingly critical views, the Catholic hierarchy remained committed to censorship throughout this period. This was reflected in the views of Bishop Cornelius Lucey of Cork and Archbishop John Charles McQuaid. A few days after Tuairim's 1965 meeting, the Dublin Archbishop maintained that 'our good ordinary people demand from the civil authority that we shall be protected from the public activities of those who neither accept nor practice the natural and the Christian moral law'.[41] This statement was typical of McQuaid and his view that legislation, such as censorship, should reinforce Catholic morality. It reflected a paternalistic attitude that was dominant in the Irish Catholic Church before Vatican II and served as a reminder that powerful forces continued to resist reforms throughout this period. However, the reality was that significant changes had occurred in the church and in Irish society. Nevertheless, similarly to McQuaid, Lucey, in 1962 and again in 1966, argued for a strict form of censorship. Lucey actually went further than McQuaid and called for the judicial system to replace the censorship board, which would have marked a return to the methods used in Ireland before the 1929 Censorship of Publications Act. Lucey's proposal was, surprisingly, the same as that put forward at a Tuairim meeting. Sharing the branch's platform in 1965 with Peter Connolly and Fergus Lenihan, the film critic of the *Irish Times*, Jim Fitzgerald, a stage and television producer, claimed that the judicial system would be more lenient. Whereas Fitzgerald probably shared Connolly's view that a writer should be given an opportunity to defend herself or himself against a charge that his or her work was 'obscene', Lucey was anxious that those who wrote or published such work would be punished.

A government memorandum of 1967, which examined Lucey's views, suggested that the bishop probably thought that Irish juries would conservatively interpret what was indecent or obscene. The Minister for Justice, Brian Lenihan, did not share this view. Lenihan's opinion was that juries, particularly in Dublin, would be much more liberal than Lucey had suggested. Since he believed that Lucey and others would demand a system which was 'at least as effective' as that it replaced, they would not be satisfied with the legal process, which he claimed would result in further controversy as to its effectiveness in keeping out 'evil literature'.[42] That in turn would lead to a reaction from 'intellectuals and liberals'. The minister was 'firmly convinced that in all circumstances the censorship system, reasonably operated (as in his opinion, it largely is by the present board) is the best system, for the present at any rate, and sees no advantage in its abolition'.

Lenihan was, however, actually considering liberalising the censorship laws in relation to books. A more 'liberal-minded' film censorship appeals board was already in place.[43] Failing to realise that this innovation had already been introduced, Fergus Lenihan, at Tuairim's meeting in 1965, had called for 'new legislation…to compel the censor to grade all films'; this would end the practice of banning all films that were not suitable for children.[44] Reporting on the Limerick branch's meeting in April 1966, the *Irish Times* expressed the hope that the Minister for Justice would also change the laws in relation to books. The main anomaly that Lenihan intended to address was that once a work was banned, it was banned in perpetuity. In April 1967, he introduced a bill which, as a result of the consequent debate in the Oireachtas, reduced to twelve years the period for which a book was banned. It did not, however, provide for a writer to be part of the censorship board. Lenihan did not believe that a representative of any group had an automatic right to be a member thereof. His view diverged from that of the Fine Gael members Garret FitzGerald and Michael O'Higgins, who also called for the terms used in the legislation to be clarified. In the Seanad, FitzGerald, who was on the liberal wing of the party, argued that the phrase 'general tendency indecent or obscene', deleted in 1946, should be re-introduced, prior to stating that he was 'indebted to Connolly's article for much of what he had said'.[45] More surprisingly, O'Higgins, who was generally identified with the conservative wing of the party, was the first TD during this debate to call for a book to be banned for a shorter period than the twenty years that had been proposed originally by the minister. The influence of what he called Peter Connolly's 'very informative and authoritative article' was explicit in the proposals that he and FitzGerald put forward.[46]

Brian Lenihan thought that definitions were not, however, nearly as important as a sensible attitude from the censorship board. The present board, he emphasised in the Dáil, contained members with 'commonsense views'. More striking were the differences that the Minister had with

Connolly over the extent to which a writer's intention should be a factor in considering whether a book should be banned or not. According to Tuairim's Donal Barrington, he and Lenihan had discussed Connolly's views.[47] Lenihan believed, however, that the censorship board was representing the reading public; as such, it should assess the impact a book would make on these people rather than examining the author's objective when writing a book. In this, he seems to have been influenced by the view of the chairperson of the censorship board, Judge William Conroy, who claimed that to give 'an author…or publisher…in effect a public hearing…would [make] the legislation quite unworkable'.[48] Lenihan defended the present board and admitted that the changes he was making did not affect the 'basic principle' of censorship.

Unlike the minister, the Fine Gael members Garret FitzGerald and Michael O'Higgins called for the terms used in the legislation to be clarified. Though all three men wished to see censorship removed from being an area of controversy in Irish life, the minister did not believe that Connolly's proposals would do that. His focus was on changing the law in a limited manner. The simple provision in the legislation, that of limiting the time period for which a book was banned, released 'over 5,000 titles'.[49] This undoubtedly contributed to the further liberalisation of Irish society. While Lenihan did not introduce the changes proposed by Connolly, the minister was aware of his writings. Furthermore, Lenihan was close to Tuairim members, including Barrington, and attended and spoke at a number of the society's meetings. On one occasion in 1966, speaking to Tuairim's Limerick branch, Lenihan described the society's contributions to reform as 'invaluable' and stressed the importance of the law's being 'in line with informed and responsible opinion'.[50] While he did not specifically mention any area in which he found Tuairim's contribution particularly helpful, the society, through the meetings it held, facilitated the emergence of a public opinion that was conducive to reform.

In influencing the public in this matter, Tuairim played a valuable role in providing a platform for individuals, especially Connolly, to develop their ideas. While Connolly's speeches and writings did not directly influence Lenihan, their role in facilitating the creation of a climate of opinion where the minister could reform the censorship laws is illustrated by the comments made by FitzGerald and O'Higgins. From the distinct wings of Fine Gael, each credited Connolly with influencing his views. This underlines the extent to which the system was seen as being in conflict with the newly tolerant climate. During the debates in the Oireachtas, they, along with other TDs and senators, called for the reduction of the period for which books were to be banned. Indeed, Lenihan did not go as far as many of them had hoped. Given the opposition from the Catholic hierarchy to any change to the censorship laws, Lenihan's was, nevertheless, still a courageous step. The impact of Connolly's article in *Christus Rex* in changing attitudes is underlined by descriptions thereof in both contemporary and historical accounts of that period. By way of illustration, Connolly remarked in 1964 that 'For the one Parish Priest who told that you were undermining the simple faith of the people a score of priests and as many lay-people showed that they were reassured in theirs'.[51]

Conclusion

The reform of the censorship laws in 1967 successfully ended Connolly's struggle to influence debate on this matter. Tuairim, which facilitated him in developing his ideas, played a subsidiary yet important role in influencing attitudes to censorship. Moving the public towards an appreciation of the literary merits of novels was a longer-term process, as many people remained ambivalent towards authors such as Edna O'Brien. The progressive nature of Tuairim in this regard was reflected in Connolly's statement that 'Irish newspapers do not invite priests to review controversial films or books'.[52] Tuairim's willingness to invite both a priest and an author to speak on the latter's banned books underlines the society's determination to tackle controversial issues and its ability to attract well-known individuals. The debate on censorship also indicates a willingness on the part of certain politicians to engage with Tuairim. This suggests a contrast between the politicians who had been active since independence and the new generation that emerged in the 1950s and 1960s. The arguments of the minister, Brian Lenihan indicate that they did not, however, always agree with the ideas put forward at Tuairim's meetings. But in relation to censorship, Connolly's ideas perhaps more than anyone else's influenced public opinion and facilitated the subsequent change in the censorship laws. These ideas were quite radical for Ireland in the late 1950s. Furthermore, the exchange of views between clergy and laity at Tuairim's meetings was unusual for Ireland at this time. In facilitating such developments, Tuairim made an important contribution to the discussion of new ideas and the creation of an open society.

Notes

1 Michael Adams, *Censorship: the Irish experience* (Tuscaloosa: University of Alabama Press, 1968), p. 54. Mary Kenny, *Goodbye to Catholic Ireland: a social, personal and cultural history from the fall of Parnell to the realm of Mary Robinson* (London: Sinclair-Stevenson, 1997), pp. xvi, xviii–xix, 141–61. See also Brian Fallon, *An age of innocence, 1930–1960* (Dublin: Gill and Macmillan, 1998), p. 206; Márie McGonagle, 'Ireland', in Derek Jones (ed.), *Censorship: a world*

encyclopaedia, vol. ii (London: Fitzroy Dearborn, 2001), p. 1215; Senia Pašeta, 'Censorship and its critics in the Irish Free State, 1922–1932', *Past & Present*, 181 (November 2003), 193–218; Whyte, *Church and state*, pp. 37–49, 93–5, 315–17, 343–6. See also Kevin Rockett, *Irish film censorship: a cultural journey from silent cinema to internet pornography* (Dublin: Four Courts, 2004).

2 Peter Connolly, 'Censorship', *Christus Rex*, 13 (June 1959), 164–6.
3 NAI, DT, S18301, Censorship of Publications Act, 1967, 'Memorandum for the Government: Censorship of Publications Act', September 1966. See also Adams, *Censorship*, p. 118.
4 Connolly, 'Censorship', p. 166.
5 Adams, *Censorship*, pp. 120, 146–55, 250–3.
6 Julia Carlson, 'Interview with Edna O'Brien: the personal experience of censorship', in Julia Carlson (ed.), *Banned in Ireland: censorship and the Irish writer* (Athens: University of Georgia Press, 1990), p. 72.
7 See Carlson, 'Introduction', in Carlson (ed.), *Banned in Ireland*, pp. 9–18; Adams, *Censorship*, p. 146; Ferriter, *Occasions*, pp. 308, 385, 388; Kenny, *Goodbye to Catholic Ireland*, pp. 141, 148–9, 155, 159–60.
8 Connolly, 'Censorship', p. 151. Many of the quotations that follow are from this article.
9 James H. Murphy, 'Introduction', in James H. Murphy (ed.), *No bland facility: selected writings on literature, religion and censorship* (Gerrard's Cross: Colin Smythe Limited, 1991), p. 7.
10 Fuller, *Irish Catholicism*, pp. 63–4.
11 Patrick Hannon, 'Heart in pilgrimage', in Murphy (ed.), *No bland facility*, pp. 44, 49.
12 Fuller, *Irish Catholicism*, p. 62.
13 *Irish Times*, 23 April 1966. See also *Limerick Leader*, 16 April 1966. The novels in question were *The country girls* (1960), *Girl with green eyes* – originally *The lonely girl* (1962), *Girls in their married bliss* (1964) and *August is a wicked month* (1965). See also Finn, 'Priests, politics and poetry'.
14 George O'Brien, 'Contemporary prose in English: 1940–2000', in Margaret Kelleher and Philip O'Leary (eds), *The Cambridge history of Irish literature*, vol. ii, *1890–1900* (Cambridge: Cambridge University Press, 2006), pp. 427, 429.
15 *Irish Times*, 23 April 1966.
16 Interview with John Dillon, Dublin, 13 June 2005.
17 *Irish Times*, 23 April 1966.
18 *Evening Herald*, 23 April 1966.
19 Fuller, *Irish Catholicism*, p. 136. See also Murphy, 'Introduction', p. 11. See Peter Connolly, 'The moralists and the obscene', *Irish Theological Quarterly*, 32 (1965), 116–28.
20 Fuller, *Irish Catholicism*, p. 136.
21 *Irish Times*, 23 April 1966.
22 *Evening Herald*, 23 April 1966.
23 Ibid; *Irish Times*, 23 April 1966.
24 *Irish Times*, 23 April 1966. See also Cliodhna Ní Anluain, *Reading the future:*

       Irish writers in conversation with Mike Murphy (Dublin: Lilliput Press, 2000), p. 208. See also Carlson, 'Interview with Edna O'Brien', p. 71.
25 *Limerick Leader*, 16, 22 April 1966.
26 *Irish Times*, 23 April 1966. See also Cooney, *McQuaid*, p. 348.
27 *Irish Times*, 27, 28 April, 3 May 1966. There were other letters, such as one on 2 May 1966, that supported Connolly and O'Brien.
28 *Evening Herald*, 23 April 1966.
29 *Limerick Leader*, 22 April 1966.
30 For example, Carlson, 'Interview with Edna O'Brien', p. 69; *Irish Times*, 16 September 2006; Kathryn Laing, Sinéad Mooney and Maureen O'Connor (eds), *Edna O'Brien: new critical perspectives* (Dublin: Carysfort Press, 2006); Lisa Colletta and Maureen O'Connor (eds), *Wild colonial girl: essays on Edna O'Brien* (Madison: University of Wisconsin Press, 2006).
31 Connolly, 'Censorship', pp. 169–70; *Hibernia*, July 1962.
32 *Hibernia*, July 1962.
33 *Irish Times*, 23 April 1966.
34 *The Guardian*, 8, 9, 10, 11 January 1964. In 1967, Lennon made the controversial documentary film *The Rocky Road to Dublin*, which characterised the atmosphere in Ireland during the 1960s as repressive and stultifying.
35 *Hibernia*, February 1964.
36 *Irish Times*, 12 February 1965.
37 Adams, *Censorship*, pp. 157–8, Fuller, *Irish Catholicism*, p. 253; Murphy, 'Introduction', p. 3. However, see Kenny, *Goodbye to Catholic Ireland*, p. 256. See also Finn, 'The influence of *Tuairim*', pp. 356–9.
38 *Hibernia*, February 1964.
39 *Irish Times*, 12 February 1965. Connolly also recommended that the 'role of the Censorship Board…be complemented by education'.
40 *Hibernia*, February 1964; Murphy, 'Introduction', p. 5.
41 *Irish Times*, 18 February 1965.
42 NAI, DT, S18301, Censorship, 'Memorandum to the government: Censorship of Publications Act', 1 March 1967, p. 8. See also *Irish Times*, 7 May 1962, 16 May 1966.
43 Whyte, *Church and state*, pp. 343–4.
44 *Irish Times*, 12 February 1965.
45 Seanad Éireann Debates, vol. 63, col. 322, 'Censorship of publications Bill, 1967', 7 June 1967.
46 Dáil Éireann Debates, vol. 63, col. 694, Censorship, 10 May 1967.
47 Ferriter, *Occasions*, p. 388.
48 Interview with Barrington, 19 May 2005.
49 Adams, *Censorship*, p. 199.
50 NAI, DJ, 2005/14/167, Ireland and the English Common Law, 'Address by minister to Limerick branch of Tuairim', 14 January 1965.
51 *Hibernia*, February 1964. See also Fuller, *Irish Catholicism*, p. 62; Adams, *Censorship*, p. 157.
52 *Hibernia*, July 1964.

Conclusion

Tuairim influenced the key policy decisions which shaped modern Ireland. Investment in education, reforms to censorship and the system of childcare as well as moves towards a more conciliatory policy in relation to Northern Ireland were all policies on which Tuairim's members voiced influential arguments. In relation to debates on these and other matters, the society's views were often the precursor to subsequent developments. Tuairim made its most significant impact on the discourse surrounding Northern Ireland, where its ideas, most particularly its advocation of the principle of consent, foreshadowed the Good Friday Agreement. In facilitating changes in this area, Tuairim could be said to have been far-sighted. The society also initiated and contributed to discussion on topical issues such as electoral reform and more broadly facilitated the development of an increasingly independent-minded citizenry within Ireland.

The significance of Tuairim was that it influenced thinking in policy-making circles and encouraged the transition towards a more liberal climate. Its influence was partly due to its presence in key networks – political, legal and educational – concerned with national policy and its administration.

Another critical factor in the extent to which Tuairim impacted on government thinking was timing. The society was at its most active during the late 1950s and early 1960s, a period when new policies – the basis of the present policies in relation to Northern Ireland, the economy and education – emerged. On the other hand, the society's timing was unfortunate in relation to the university question. When Tuairim's pamphlet was published in 1960, the government was effectively already committed to UCD's move to Belfield. Furthermore, Tuairim was short-sighted in its judgement as to the appropriate numbers in a third-level institution. It seems that the significance it attached to the university question blinded it as to the implications of such a limit to student numbers for Ireland's future.

Tuairim's members themselves claimed that its independence of the

Catholic Church and political parties enabled the society to confront sensitive issues such as education. This independence marked it apart from other organisations. The drive to establish a secular society was particularly innovative in an Irish context during the 1950s. This, combined with the range of issues that Tuairim considered, proved attractive to many people and was particularly welcome during the 1950s when there were relatively few outlets for the younger generation.

An additional importance of Tuairim lies not in its existence but in its legacy, that is, its contribution to the market for ideas as well as the roles that many of its members went on to play in Irish life. Garret FitzGerald, Barry Desmond and Michael Woods became well known and influential politicians. Donal Barrington, Ronan Keane, Miriam Hederman O'Brien are among those to have made equally important contributions to the country's legal system and the infrastructure of ideas. This latter point was central to Tuairim's mission. The diffusion of new ideas and the extent to which Tuairim helped to create a space to debate made it easier for those who came after Tuairim to have their voices heard. Tuairim went as far as to welcome, even foster, alternative points of view. The society did not, however, specify which policy was to be implemented. Its hospitality towards a variety of opinions reflected the society's commitment towards opening up debate. It could also be said that Tuairim acted contrary to its own interests. It not only encouraged its members to become involved in other organisations but actively sought to put forward viewpoints to which the majority of the members of the society were opposed.

More generally, during the 1960s, the ideas market became more congested. It was ironic that at this very time, Tuairim's increasing respectability meant that it was not as attractive as it had been to those who were demanding change. At the same time, the need for new policies had become less acute. The absence of Peter Tyrell's account from Tuairim's pamphlet on industrial schools also indicates that Tuairim was not entirely independent of the conventions of its era. Even allowing for the logic of its age limit, the society could not adapt to the changed circumstances of the 1970s. The new generation which emerged during the 1970s were unconvinced of the need for an organisation that examined a wide variety of issues. Tuairim's ineffectiveness in relation to television, henceforth the dominant medium, underlined its demise.

It was a further irony that Tuairim's relative unattractiveness to the younger generation was related to the sense that during the 1960s the society was not as radical as previously had been the case. It had gone from arguing for a more complete understanding of Northern Ireland and recognition of the need for planning the Irish economy to reform of the Oireachtas. While this could be seen as a progression in the range of issues dealt with by the society, Tuairim was remarkably consistent in what it argued. In relation to Northern Ireland, for example, it appealed for moderation throughout its existence. Tuairim had similar values during the 1970s to those it had in the 1950s. As liberal values became increasingly prevalent in society, Tuairim, however, found that its level of activity decreased through the loss of its most dynamic members.

The coverage that Tuairim received in the media reflected the increasing liberalisation of the 1960s. The transformation taking place was most evident with *Hibernia* and the *Irish Times*. The extent to which the latter increasingly reflected liberal values was echoed in the coverage it gave to Tuairim. In an even more comprehensive manner, *Hibernia* was transformed from a Catholic periodical in the 1950s to an influential and irreverent magazine by the end of the 1960s. While Tuairim's members made a significant contribution in the early stages of *Hibernia*'s transition, most but not all of them were critical of the hard-line stance it took in respect of Northern Ireland during the late 1960s and early 1970s.

On a more general level, the complex nature of debates during these decades was evident in Tuairim and the reaction that the society and its ideas provoked. While the opposition of the Catholic hierarchy to Tuairim's views was hardly surprising, the fact that many priests spoke at the organisation's meetings and that some were members of the society highlights the fact that the Catholic Church included diverse views in this period. Similarly, members of the same political party and even of the same family (as in the case of John A. Costello and his son Declan), reacted in different ways to Tuairim. Rather than being simply battles between different generations, between conservatives and liberals, between church and state, or between a conservative establishment and groups such as Tuairim, the opposing sides often consisted of individuals whose positions had evolved and who found themselves in perhaps surprising alliances. Discussion and divisions existed at different times within and between Tuairim, the government, opposition parties, civil servants, the church and a range of influential individuals. In regard to university education, for example, a reform-minded Minister for Education such as Patrick Hillery viewed Tuairim with hostility whereas Seán MacEntee, who has been generally seen as a conservative figure, praised the society. A juxtaposition of Hillery's opposition to Tuairim with MacEntee's support illustrates the deepening complexity of the debates during these years. Members of the government reacted in different ways to Tuairim and the views it put forward on the electoral system and the Oireachtas on the one hand and, on the other, on Northern Ireland and economic policy; this is a further indication of the diversity of positions held by different individuals. While Tuairim's position as a body which included a wide variety of viewpoints made it an unreliable ally in relation to such conflicts, this allowed the organisation to develop a place of its own in Irish society.

The reason why certain politicians including Hillery regarded Tuairim with such hostility remains unclear. To what extent was it due to anti-intellectualism in Irish life and in its politics? In a general sense, politicians such as Hillery, Seán Lemass and John A. Costello and many civil servants could not be said to be anti-intellectual in that they were interested in ideas. That much is reflected in the influence that Tuairim had in a range of policy areas. As Tom Garvin has suggested in *Judging Lemass*, it could, nevertheless, be argued that they were anti-intellectual in the impatience they displayed towards academic research or what they perceived to be impractical ideas. Rather than anti-intellectualism the evidence suggests that Tuairim was regarded with suspicion because of the resistance of parts of the political and religious establishments to the society's liberalising agenda and the independent thinking that it promoted. Hillery's view of Tuairim and that of John A. Costello reflected their reaction to what they perceived to be the society's challenge to the moral parameters formed by church and state. In a less forthright but perhaps an even more determined manner, Lemass also defended the way in which the political system operated. While this could equally be said to have represented anti-intellectualism in that his determination to retain control of the policy process meant that intellectuals were excluded, other individuals were similarly ignored. Lemass, Hillery and Costello each disagreed with some of the ideas that Tuairim put forward. Hillery and Costello may have disliked everything the society stood for but, like Lemass, they were motivated by a resistance to what they perceived as unwarranted external interference. The reality is that when they did not perceive their immediate interests to be directly threatened, they could be and were open to being influenced by the ideas put forward by Tuairim and others. Moreover, aside from the initial response of the Minister for Justice, Gerald Boland, to Tuairim's establishment, no member of the government felt it necessary to use the state's power to undermine the society. Tuairim was allowed to exist and was able to operate in an unfettered manner.

Tuairim's methods were the main reason why the society could articulate a vision for a better Ireland and influence those in positions of authority. Its moderate approach was effective in reaching through to important individuals. In this context, the Department of Education's attitude during the 1960s suggests that a distinction needs to be made between the more tolerant climate evident later in that decade and that at the start of the 1960s, when the orthodoxy in place since independence had yet to be broken down. Even here, Hillery's reaction underlines the effectiveness of the society's methods. Rather than ignore Tuairim as Eamon de Valera chose to do during the debate on the electoral system, Hillery felt compelled to respond. The understanding within Tuairim seems to have been that it was more difficult to oppose arguments that were put in moderate terms than those in sensationalist terms. The tone and the language used were usually conciliatory. While Tuairim's methods and style were designed to seek solutions rather than to provoke, the society in Ireland as well as in London could be forthright and pointed in what it said. The London branch's more direct approach was due to the fact that it was located outside Ireland and thus part of a different milieu. That branch highlighted the organisationally diffuse nature of the Irish in London but also the significant contribution that was made by parts of the diaspora to the modernisation of Ireland.

Much work remains to be done on the role of intellectuals and ideas in Ireland. This book has considered intellectual engagement with Irish political discourse. It has concurred with the view of Joe Lee and Donal Barrington that the main problem was with the market for ideas. Tuairim was one response to deficiencies in their supply, while its existence facilitated improvements in demand thereof. Though progressive developments occurred in the intellectual market during the 1950s and 1960s, criticisms continue to be made as to the quality of public discussion and the extent to which the state has promoted the acquisition of knowledge.

As to the scholarship on intellectuals in other societies, Tuairim shared certain perceived characteristics and dilemmas with such individuals. These included an interest in a range of ideas, a reputation for valuable contributions to debate, a tendency to be regarded with suspicion and the need to be independent. The question that then arises is whether intellectuals were able to remain truly autonomous or served a particular class or the state. Scholars such as Stefan Collini in *Absent minds* have challenged the idea prevalent in the past that an intellectual needs to be independent. Sociological literature has tended to place these individuals in class terms, but more recently the setting and countries in which intellectuals exist have been examined. Perhaps unusually for intellectuals in this period, Tuairim did not perceive itself to be a part of any particular class or feel the need to act as one. While its members were primarily middle-class, the individuals in Tuairim were altruistic in their intentions and actions. Each member decided whether a matter was to be pursued. In response to accusations of partiality, Tuairim insisted that it was independent, but by the late 1960s it was more critical of Fianna Fáil than the opposition political parties, while it was more sympathetic to nationalists in relation to Northern Ireland. Reliant on volunteers, the society was able to retain an independence of the political and religious establishment, but in addressing itself to the public it could not be truly independent. The reality was that Tuairim was to a certain extent constrained in the views it put forward. It did not, for example, advocate the legalisation of divorce or abortion. Possessing only the power to influence, Tuairim was in any case too diverse in its membership to attempt to alter Irish society or its politics fundamentally. Tuairim focused on what was achievable in the short to medium term. That is not to gainsay that Tuairim lacked ambition: its wish for a more open society was reflected in its methods. This, in itself, could be said to have had revolutionary implications for the Ireland of the 1950s and 1960s.

Tuairim and its members did not fit comfortably into the definitions of intellectuals which have traditionally been used. There was a sense that an intellectual had to be either affiliated to the church or to the state or be independent. He (or occasionally she) was a member of the literary community, or perhaps a scholar or represented a particular section of society. That was not the case with Tuairim. The society was unusual in that it provided a forum for men and women from different backgrounds to debate the pressing issues facing Irish society. While its inclusivity was somewhat diminished by its age limit, it had always been the intention of Tuairim's founding members that having proposed solutions to problems in Irish society they would seek to have their ideas implemented from within the establishment.

In terms of Irish historiography, Tuairim's existence and activities support the case made by Dermot Keogh and Diarmaid Ferriter, who have argued that the 1950s witnessed the emergence of an inquisitive culture that challenged the conservative consensus in place since independence. Historians have also pointed to continuing problems in the 1960s. In relation to one such issue, that of children in institutional care, this book has underlined the need to examine the evidence available to a contemporary audience and to attempt to understand their actions. Elsewhere, specifically with regard to Northern Ireland, Tuairim has been described as revisionist. Unconnected to this, the revisionist controversy in Irish history ran parallel to Tuairim's existence. As a term, 'revisionism' arguably does much to explain the society and its modus operandi. Tuairim questioned national myths in a whole range of areas. The term also intimates the academic basis of Tuairim and the society's determination to be aloof from the nationalist narrative of Ireland.

Other issues raised by Tuairim include questions about the quality of civil society in Ireland. In independent Ireland, there had always been lay writers, such as Seán O'Faoláin and other contributors to *The Bell*, who advocated an independence of mind among the country's citizens. They tended, however, to be minority voices that did not significantly alter the dominant political culture. The increased questioning of traditional attitudes in the 1950s was facilitated by the resolution of the controversy over the extent of independence gained by the Irish state. This combined with the emergence of an educated middle class, born since the establishment of the state, helped sustain the new culture of enquiry. Tuairim was a leading part of this culture. In this way, Tuairim undoubtedly strengthened civil society and hence, democracy in Ireland. The nature of civil society and how it changed during this period, however, needs further research. In this regard, a comparative study of Ireland and other Western countries would be revealing. It would help to shed further light on which institutional factors facilitated and inhibited the influence of intellectuals in Ireland and why intellectuals and the infrastructure for ideas seemed underdeveloped in comparison to other societies. Such an approach would also illuminate the extent to which anti-intellectualism exists in Irish life. Moreover, further examination of the reasons why new policies emerged and old ideas endured would be welcome. Ideas, intellectuals and their role in persuading governmental institutions to adopt new policies constitute an area that has yet to be fully explored. The pressure for reform and resistance to change surrounding Tuairim highlight the connection between intellectual debate and policy formulation. This book has thus contributed to a more complete understanding of the process by which modern Ireland emerged: specifically it illuminates how the state's policy approach and the nature of public debate were transformed in this crucial period of Ireland's development.

Select bibliography

Primary sources

Government papers

National Archives of Ireland, Dublin
Department of Foreign Affairs
Department of Justice
Department of Taoiseach

Department of Education, Athlone

Department of Health, Dublin

Private papers

Dublin Diocesan Archive, Dublin
Archbishop John Charles McQuaid

History Department, Trinity College, Dublin
Tuairim's Dublin branch

National Library of Ireland, Dublin
Leslie Daiken
Owen Sheehy Skeffington

National University of Ireland, Galway
Pearse O'Malley

University College Cork, Special Collections
Neville Keery

University College Dublin, Archives Department
Ernest Blythe
Fianna Fáil
Fine Gael

Tuairim members (papers currently in the author's possession)
Donal Barrington
John Boland
Barry Desmond
Val Finnegan
Miriam Hederman O'Brien
Brian O'Connor
Michael O'Hanrahan
Maurice Manning
William Peacocke
Joy Rudd

Correspondence
Paddy Barry
Rebecca Black
Tom Bogue
Donal Counihan
Dermot Devine
John Dillon
Tony Fahy
Desmond Fennell
Garret FitzGerald
Martin Hudner
Margaret Hurley
Áine Hyland
Paul Jackson
Roy Johnston
Patrick Kelleher
Thomas Kilroy
Ann Lewis
Seán Lyster
Myles McSwiney
Kathleen O'Higgins
Seán Redmond
W. E. Vaughan
Jean Whyte

Interviews
Donal Barrington
Ronan Brocklesby
Paul Callan
Arthur Carter
Francis Xavier Carty
Harold Clarke
John Coolahan
Declan Costello

Anthony Coughlan
Frank D'Arcy
Barry Desmond
John Dillon
Jim Doolan
Bríd Foy
Maurice Gaffney
Brian Geary
Norman Gibson
Paddy Glynn
Michael Gorman
Miriam Hederman O'Brien
Michael D. Higgins
Margaret Hurley
Ronan Keane
Hubert Kearns
Neville Keery
Pat Kelleher
Seán Kilfeather
Patrick Kilroy
Dermot Kinlen
John Madigan
Muriel McCarthy
Enda McDonagh
Aubrey McElhatton
Dermot Montgomery
John A. Murphy
Cian O'Carroll
Diarmuid Ó Cearbhaill
Helen Ó Ciosáin
Brian O'Connor
Michael O'Hanrahan
Basil O'Meara
Franklin O'Sullivan
Gearóid Ó Tuathaigh
William Peacocke
Michael Collins Powell
Seán Quinn
Seán Redmond
Anne Reidy
Geordie Rudd
Mona Stanton
W. E. Vaughan
Declan and Anna White
Michael Woods

Printed Sources

Parliamentary and other official publications

Department of Education, *Report of the Council of Education: (1) The function of the primary school (2) The curriculum to be pursued in the primary school from the infant age up to 12 years of age* (Dublin: Stationery Office, 1954).
Department of Education, *Report of the Council of Education: the curriculum of the secondary school* (Dublin: Stationery Office, 1960).
Programme for economic expansion (Dublin: Stationery Office, 1958).
Report of the Commission on accommodation needs of the constituent colleges of the National University of Ireland (Dublin: Stationery Office, 1959).
Report of the Commission to Inquire into Child Abuse, 2009.
Reports I & II, Commission on Higher Education, 1960–67 (Dublin: The Stationery Office, 1967).
Whitaker, T. K., *Economic development* (Dublin: The Stationery Office, 1958).

Dáil Éireann Debates.
Seanad Éireann Debates.

Newspapers

Catholic Herald
Clonmel Nationalist & The Munster Tribune
Cork Examiner
Evening Herald
Evening Mail
Focus
Free Press
The Guardian
Hibernia
Irish Democrat
Irish Independent
Irish Press
Irish Times
Limerick Leader
Limerick Weekly Echo
Northern Standard
Standard
Sunday Independent
Sunday Press

Periodicals

Administration
Catholic Truth Quarterly

Christus Rex
The Furrow
Hibernia
Institute of Public Administration, *Yearbook and diary* (Dublin: The Institute of Public Administration, 1970–73)
Irish Political Studies
The Irish Theological Quarterly
Studies
Weekly Bulletin of the Department of External Affairs

Tuairim's pamphlets (in chronological order)

Barrington, Donal, *Uniting Ireland* (Dublin: Tuairim, 1958).
Gibson, Norman, *Partition today: a Northern viewpoint* (Dublin: Tuairim, 1959).
Tuairim research group, *P.R. – for or against?* (Dublin: Tuairim, 1959).
Clear, John K., *Outlines of an Irish fishing industry* (Dublin: Tuairim, 1959).
Lynch, Patrick and Carter, C. F., *Planning for economic development* (Dublin: Tuairim, 1959).
Tuairim, *University College Dublin and the future: with special reference to the proposal to transfer University College, Dublin to a new site: a memorandum from a research group of Tuairim Dublin branch on the report of the commission on accommodation needs of the constituent colleges of the National University of Ireland* (Dublin: Tuairim, 1960).
O'Connor, Brian J., *Ireland and the United Nations* (Tuairim: Dublin, 1961).
Tuairim Dublin branch in association with Irish section of the European Association of Teachers, *Educating towards a united Europe* (Dublin: Tuairim, 1962).
Tuairim London research group, *Irish education* (London: Tuairim, 1962).
Dowdall, Finbarr, *Irish attitudes and Europe* (Cork: Tuairim, 1962).
Vermeulen, Adrianus, Jackson, Paul, Gavin Duffy, Colum and Thornley, David, *The European challenge: its social, legal and political prospects*, (Dublin: Tuairim, 1963).
Thornley, David, *Ireland: the end of an era?* (Dublin: Tuairim, 1965).
Tuairim London branch study group, *Some of our children: a report on the residential care of the deprived child in Ireland* (London: Tuairim, 1966).
Coughlan, Anthony, *Aims of social policy: reform in Ireland's social security and health services* (Dublin: Tuairim, 1966).
Whyte, John, *Dáil deputies: their work, its difficulties, possible remedies* (Dublin: Tuairim, 1966).
Carty, Xavier, *Government and people: a creative dialogue: a report of the 1969/70 communications conference* (Dublin: Tuairim, 1970).

Tuairim's *An Occasional Bulletin* (in chronological order)

An Occasional Bulletin, 1 (London: Tuairim, 1960).
An Occasional Bulletin, 2 (London: Tuairim, 1960).
An Occasional Bulletin, 3 (London: Tuairim, 1961).
An Occasional Bulletin, 4 (London: Tuairim, 1961).

An Occasional Bulletin, 5 (London: Tuairim, 1961).
An Occasional Bulletin, 6 (London: Tuairim, 1962).
An Occasional Bulletin, 7 (London: Tuairim, 1963).
An Occasional Bulletin, 8 (London: Tuairim, 1963).
An Occasional Bulletin, 9 (London: Tuairim, 1964).

Other Tuairim publications

Tuairim, *Picture lending scheme: list of exhibits* (Dublin: Tuairim, 1962).
Tuairim, *List of exhibits* (Dublin: Tuairim, undated).
Tuairim, *The castle poets* (Limerick: Tuairim, 1966).

Other publications by Tuairim members or in part relating to Tuairim

Barrington, Donal, 'After Sunningdale', *Administration*, 24:2 (1976), 235–61.
——, *The church, the state and the constitution* (Dublin: Catholic Truth Society of Ireland, 1959).
——, 'Council of Ireland in the constitutional context', *Administration*, 20:4 (1972), 28–49.
Connolly, Peter, 'Censorship', *Christus Rex*, 13 (June 1959), 151–70.
D'Arcy, Frank, 'A movement on the fence', *Catholic Truth Quarterly*, 11:1 (1959), 27–31.
Desmond, Barry, *Finally and in conclusion: a political memoir* (Dublin: New Island, 2000).
FitzGerald, Garret, *All in a life: an autobiography* (Dublin: Gill and Macmillan, 1992).
——, 'Irish economy north and south', *Studies*, 45:180 (Winter 1956), 373–88.
——, *Just Garret: tales from the political front line* (Dublin: Liberties Press, 2010).
——, *Planning in Ireland: a PEP study* (Dublin: Institute of Public Administration, 1968).
——, 'P.R.: the great debate', *Studies*, 48:189 (Spring 1959), 1–20.
——, *Reflections on the Irish state* (Dublin: Irish Academic Press, 2003).
Hederman, Miriam, *The road to Europe: Irish attitudes, 1948–61* (Dublin: Institute of Public Administration, 1983).
Hederman O'Brien, Miriam (ed.), *The clash of ideas: essays in honour of Patrick Lynch* (Dublin: Gill and Macmillan, 1988).
Hughes, Owen, 'Rates equalization', *Administration*, 9:2 (1961), 110–19.
Johnston, Roy H. W., *Century of endeavour: a biographical & autobiographical view of the twentieth century in Ireland*, (Carlow: Tyndall Publications, in association with Lilliput Press Dublin, 2006).
——, *A Century of endeavour: a father and son overview of the 20th century*, e-version, private source (2005).
Latchford, G. L., 'Adult education – the future', *Christus Rex*, 22 (April 1968), 134–43.
McCarthy, Charles *The decade of upheaval: Irish trade unions in the nineteen sixties* (Dublin: Institute of Public Administration, 1973).
——, *The distasteful challenge* (Dublin: Institute of Public Administration, 1968).

McDonagh, Enda, 'The Christian life, xi: tolerance', *The Furrow*, 12:1 (1961), 49–55.
——, 'Ireland's divided disciplines', in Furrow Trust (ed.), *The challenge of Northern Ireland* (Maynooth: Furrow Trust, 1984), pp. 29–35.
——, *Violence and political change* (London: Cambridge Terrace, 1978).
McKeown, Michael, *The Greening of a Nationalist* (Dublin: Murlough Press, 1986).
Meghen, P. J., 'New ways of financing local government', *Administration*, 9:2 (1961), 106–9.
O'Connor, James, 'The juvenile offender', *Studies*, 52:205 (Spring 1963), 69–86.
O'Doherty, E. F., 'Bilingual school policy', *Studies*, 47:187 (Autumn 1958), 259–68.
Scott, James 'A letter from Ireland', *The Furrow*, 9:4 (1958), 300–01.
——, 'Thoughts of the conversion of Ireland', *The Furrow*, 4:11 (1953), 615–18.
Thornley, David, 'The development of the Irish labour movement', *Christus Rex*, 18 (January 1964), 7–21.
Thornley, Yseult (ed.), *Unquiet spirit: essays in memory of David Thornley* (Dublin: Liberties Press, 2008).
Winder, Frank, 'Comment on University merger', *Studies*, 56:222 (Summer 1967), 190–5.

Other contributions to contemporary debate

Barrington, T. J., 'Big government and local community', *Christus Rex*, 24 (July 1970), 198–206.
——, *From big government to local government: the road to decentralisation* (Dublin: Institute of Public Administration, 1975).
——, 'The next necessary thing', *Administration*, 7:2 (1959), 119–41.
Barritt, Denis P., and Carter, Charles, *The Northern Ireland problem: a study in group relations* (London: Oxford University Press, 1962).
Blythe, Ernest, *An appeal to leaders of nationalist opinion in the north: a memorandum written in 1957* (Dublin: Elo Publications, 1997).
Chubb, Basil, '"Going about persecuting civil servants": the role of the Irish parliamentary representative', *Political Studies*, 11:3 (1963), 272–86.
——, and Lynch, Patrick (eds), *Economic development and planning* (Dublin: Institute of Public Administration, 1969).
Coughlan, Anthony, C., *Desmond Greaves, 1913–1988: an obituary essay* (Dublin: Irish Labour History Society, 1990).
Fennell, Desmond, *The northern Catholic: an inquiry* (Dublin, Mount Salus Press, 1958).
Gallagher, Eric, *Inter-denominational trust* (Dublin: Irish Association for Cultural, Economic and Social Relations, 1973).
Gallagher, Frank, *The indivisible island: the history of the partition of Ireland* (London: Gollancz, 1957).
Gibson, Norman, *Economic and social implications of the political alternatives that may be open to Northern Ireland* (Coleraine: New University of Ireland, 1974).
Grace, Edmond, 'Foreword', *Administration*, 20:4 (1972), 3–4.
Houlihan, P., 'Uniting Ireland: notes and comments', *Christus Rex*, 13 (December 1958), 73–4.

Irish National Teachers' Organisation, *A plan for education* (Dublin: Irish National Teachers' Organisation, 1947).

Kennedy, David, 'Whither northern nationalism', *Christus Rex*, 13 (October 1959), 269–83.

Lynch, Patrick, 'Administrative theory and the civil service', *Administration*, 4:4 (1956–57), 97–116.

——, 'Comment on foregoing article: the Irish economy viewed from without by C. F. Carter', *Studies*, 46:182 (Summer 1957), 145–7.

——, 'The economist and public policy', *Studies*, 43:167 (Autumn 1953), 256–60.

MacHale, J. P., 'The university merger', *Studies*, 56:222 (Summer 1967), 69–96.

Marsh, Thomas, 'A booklet on church and state', *Christus Rex*, 14 (July 1960), 180–3.

McCracken, J. L., *Representative government in Ireland: a study of Dáil Éireann, 1919–48* (London: Oxford University Press, 1958).

McKevitt, Peter, 'Planning, notes and comments', *Christus Rex*, 13 (June 1959), 214–17.

O'Brien, Conor Cruise, *Memoir: my life and times* (Dublin: Poolbeg Press, 1998).

——, *States of Ireland* (London: Granada Publishing, 1979).

O'Brien, John A., *The vanishing Irish: the enigma of the modern world* (London: W. H. Allen, 1954).

O'Connor, Seán, *A troubled sky: reflections on the Irish educational scene, 1957–1968* (Dublin: St Patrick's College, 1986).

O'Malley, Donogh, 'Statement on university education in Dublin', *Studies*, 56:222 (Summer 1967), 113–21.

O'Meara, John, *Reform in education* (Dublin: Mount Salus Press, 1958).

Redmond, Seán, *Desmond Greaves and the origins of the civil rights movement in Northern Ireland* (London: Connolly Publications, 2000).

Sheehy, Michael, *Divided we stand: a study in partition* (London: Faber & Faber, 1955).

Sibbett, R. M., *The sunshine patriots: the 1798 rebellion in Antrim & Down* (Belfast: GOLI Publications, 1997).

Tierney, Michael (ed.), *Daniel O'Connell* (Dublin: Browne and Nolan, 1949).

Whelan, Diarmuid, 'Document study: Peter Tyrell's account of Letterfrack, war and exile, Sheehy Skeffington papers, National Library of Ireland', *Saothar*, 31 (2006), 111–18.

——, *Founded on fear: Letterfrack industrial school, war and exile* (Dublin: Irish Academic Press, 2006).

Secondary Sources

Adams, Michael, *Censorship: the Irish experience* (Tuscaloosa: University of Alabama Press, 1968).

Arnold, Mavis and Laskey, Heather, *Children of the Poor Clares* (Belfast: Appletree Press, 1985).

Bannon, Michael J. (ed.), *Planning: the Irish experience, 1920–1988* (Dublin: Wolfhound Press, 1989).

Barrington, Ruth, *Health, medicine and politics in Ireland 1900–1970* (Dublin: Institute of Public Administration, 2000).
Bowman, John, *De Valera and the Ulster question, 1917–1973* (Oxford: Oxford University Press, 1989).
Boyce, D. George, *Nineteenth-century Ireland: the search for stability* (Dublin: Gill and Macmillan, 2005).
Brown, Terence, *Ireland: A social and cultural history, 1922–2002* (London: Harper Perennial, 2004).
Carlson, Julia (ed.), *Banned in Ireland: censorship and the Irish writer* (Athens: University of Georgia Press, 1990).
Carty, Francis Xavier, *Hold firm: John Charles McQuaid and the second Vatican Council* (Dublin: Columba Press, 2007).
Chubb, Basil, *The government and politics of Ireland* (Harlow: Pearson, 1992).
Coakley, John and Gallagher, Michael (eds), *Politics in the Republic of Ireland* (London: Routledge, 2003).
Collini, Stefan, *Absent minds: intellectuals in Britain* (Oxford: Oxford University Press, 2007).
Cooney, John, *John Charles McQuaid: ruler of Catholic Ireland* (Dublin: O'Brien Press, 1999).
Cradden, Terry, 'Labour in Britain and the Northern Ireland Labour Party', in Peter Catterall and Seán McDougall (eds), *The Northern Ireland question in British politics* (Basingstoke: Macmillan Press, 1996).
——, *Trade unionism, socialism & partition: the partition movement in Northern Ireland, 1939–1953* (Belfast: December Publications, 1993).
Daly, Mary E., *The buffer state: the historical roots of the Department of the Environment* (Dublin: Institute of Public Administration, 1997).
——, *The first department: a history of the Department of Agriculture* (Dublin: Institute of Public Administration, 2002).
——, *The slow failure: population decline and independent Ireland, 1920–1973* (Madison: University of Wisconsin Press, 2006).
——, *The spirit of earnest inquiry: the Statistical and Social Inquiry Society of Ireland, 1847–1997* (Dublin: Statistical and Social Inquiry Society of Ireland, 1997).
De Buitléir, Donal and Ruane, Francis (eds), *Governance and policy in Ireland: essays in honour of Miriam Hederman O'Brien* (Dublin: Institute of Public Administration, 2003).
Drake, David, *Intellectuals and politics in post-war France* (Basingstoke: Palgrave, 2002).
Edwards, Aaron, *A history of the Northern Ireland Labour Party: democratic socialism and sectarianism* (Manchester: Manchester University Press, 2009).
Fallon, Brian, *An age of innocence: Irish culture, 1930–1960* (Dublin: Gill and Macmillan, 1998).
Fanning, Bryan, *The quest for modern Ireland: the battle for ideas, 1912–1986* (Dublin: Irish Academic Press, 2008).
Fanning, Ronan, *Independent Ireland* (Dublin: Helicon, 1983).
——, *Irish Department of Finance, 1922–1958* (Dublin: Institute of Public Administration, 1978).

Farren, Seán, *The politics of Irish education, 1920–65* (Belfast: Institute of Irish Studies, 1995).
Feeney, Tom, *Seán MacEntee: a political life* (Dublin: Irish Academic Press, 2009).
Ferriter, Diarmaid, *Occasions of sin: sex and society in modern Ireland* (London: Profile Books, 2009).
——, *The transformation of Ireland, 1900–2000* (London: Profile Books, 2004).
Finn, Tomás, 'Priests, politics and poetry: *Tuairim* in Limerick, 1954–1975', *History Studies*, 7 (Limerick: University of Limerick, 2006), 15–30.
Foster, R. F., *Luck and the Irish: a brief history of change, 1970–2000* (London: Penguin Books, 2008).
Fuller, Louise, *Irish Catholicism since 1950: the undoing of a culture* (Dublin: Gill and Macmillan, 2002).
Gallagher, Michael, *The Irish Labour Party in transition, 1957–82* (Dublin: Gill and Macmillan, 1982).
——, Laver, Michael and Mair, Peter, *Representative Government in modern Europe* (New York: McGraw-Hill, 2001).
Garvin, Tom, *Judging Lemass: the measure of the man* (Dublin: Royal Irish Academy, 2009).
——, *News from a new republic: Ireland in the 1950s* (Dublin: Gill and Macmillan, 2010).
——, *Preventing the future: why was Ireland so poor for so long?* (Dublin: Gill and Macmillan, 2004).
Girvin, Brian and Murphy, Gary (eds), *The Lemass era: politics and society in the Ireland of Seán Lemass* (Dublin: University College Dublin Press, 2005).
Goldring, Maurice, *Pleasant the scholar's life: Irish intellectuals and the construction of the nation state* (London: Serif, 1993).
Gray, Tony, *Mr. Smylie, Sir* (Dublin: Gill and Macmillan, 1991).
Hart, Jennifer, *Proportional representation: critics of the British electoral system, 1820–1945* (Oxford: Clarendon Press, 1992).
Hennessey, Thomas, *A history of Northern Ireland, 1920–1996* (Dublin: Gill and Macmillan, 1997).
Hill, J. R. (ed.), *A new history of Ireland*, vol. vii: *Ireland, 1921–84* (Oxford: Oxford University Press, 2003).
Horgan, John, *Broadcasting and public life: RTE news and current affairs, 1926–1997* (Dublin: Four Courts Press, 2004).
——, *Irish media: a critical history since 1922* (London: Routledge, 2001).
——, *Labour: the price of power* (Dublin: Gill and Macmillan, 1986).
——, *Noel Browne: passionate outsider* (Dublin: Gill and Macmillan, 2000).
——, *Seán Lemass: the enigmatic patriot* (Dublin: Gill and Macmillan, 1997).
Howard, Katy and MacCarthaigh, Muiris (eds), *Recycling the State: politics of adaptation in Ireland* (Dublin: Irish Academic Press, 2007).
Jennings, Jeremy and Kemp-Welch, Anthony (eds), *Intellectuals in politics: from the Dreyfus affair to Salman Rushdie* (London: Routledge, 1997).
Kelleher, Margaret and O'Leary, Philip (eds), *The Cambridge history of Irish literature*, vol. ii: *1890–1900* (Cambridge: Cambridge University Press, 2006).
Kelly, Michael (ed.), *French culture and society: the essentials* (London: Arnold, 2001).

Kennedy, Dennis, *The widening gulf: northern attitudes to the independent Irish state 1919–49* (Belfast: Blackstaff Press, 1988).

Kennedy, Michael, *Divisions and consensus: the politics of cross-border relations* (Dublin: Institute of Public Administration, 2000).

—— and Morrison Skelly, Joseph (eds), *Irish foreign policy, 1919–66: from independence to internationalism* (Dublin: Four Courts Press, 2000).

Keogh, Dermot, *Ireland and Europe, 1919–1989* (Cork: Hibernian University Press, 1990).

——, *Ireland and the Vatican: the politics and diplomacy of church–state relations, 1922–1960* (Cork: Cork University Press, 1995).

——, *Jack Lynch: a biography* (Dublin: Gill and Macmillan, 2008).

——, *Twentieth-century Ireland: nation and state* (Dublin: Gill and Macmillan, 1994).

——, O'Shea, Finbarr and Quinlan, Carmel (eds), *The lost decade: Ireland in the 1950's* (Cork: Mercier Press, 2004).

Lee, J. J., *Ireland, 1912–1985: politics and society* (Cambridge: Cambridge University Press, 1993).

Litton, Frank (ed.), *The constitution of Ireland, 1937–1987* (Dublin: Institute of Public Administration, 1988).

MacCarthaigh, Muiris, *Accountability in Irish parliamentary politics* (Dublin: Institute of Public Administration, 2005).

Maguire, Moira, *Precarious childhood in post-independence Ireland* (Manchester: Manchester University Press, 2009).

Maher, D. J., *The tortuous path: the course of Ireland's entry into the EEC, 1948–73* (Dublin: Institute of Public Administration, 1986).

Manning, Maurice, *James Dillon: a biography* (Dublin: Wolfhound Press, 1999).

Maye, Brian, *Fine Gael, 1923–1987: a general history with biographical sketches of leading members* (Dublin: Blackwater Press, 1983).

McCarthy, John F. (ed.), *Planning Ireland's future: the legacy of T. K. Whitaker* (Dublin: Glendale, 1990).

McCartney, Donal, *UCD: a national idea: the history of University College Dublin* (Dublin: Gill and Macmillan, 1999).

McDermott, Eithne, *Clann na Poblachta* (Cork: Cork University Press, 1998).

McGarry, John and O'Leary, Brendan, *Explaining Northern Ireland: broken images* (Oxford: Blackwell Publishers, 1996).

McIntosh, Gillian, *The force of culture: unionist identities in twentieth-century Ireland* (Cork: Cork University Press, 1999).

Meenan, James, *Centenary history of the Literary and Historical society of University College Dublin, 1855–1955* (Dublin: A. & A. Farmar, 2005).

Moloney, Ed, *A secret history of the IRA* (New York: W. W. Norton & Company, 2002).

Murphy, Gary, *In Search of the Promised Land: the politics of post-war Ireland* (Cork: Mercier Press, 2009).

Murphy, James H. (ed.), *No bland facility: selected writings on literature, religion and censorship* (Gerrard's Cross: Colin Smythe Limited, 1991).

Murphy, John A., *Ireland in the twentieth century* (Dublin: Gill and Macmillan, 1975).

O'Brien, Mark, *De Valera, Fianna Fáil and the Irish press* (Dublin: Irish Academic Press, 2001).
——, *The Irish Times: a history* (Dublin: Four Courts Press, 2008).
O'Dowd, Liam (ed.), *On Intellectuals and Intellectual life in Ireland: international, comparative and historical contexts* (Belfast: Institute of Irish Studies, 1996).
O'Halloran, Clare, *Partition and the limits of Irish nationalism: an ideology under stress* (Dublin: Gill and Macmillan, 1987).
Prince, Simon, *Northern Ireland's '68: civil rights, global trouble and the origins of the troubles* (Dublin: Irish Academic Press, 2007).
Puirséil, Niamh, *The Irish Labour Party, 1922–73* (Dublin: University College Dublin Press, 2007).
Rafter, Kevin, *The Clann: the story of Clann na Poblachta* (Cork: Mercier Press, 1996).
Raftery, Mary, and O'Sullivan, Eoin, *Suffer the little children: the inside story of Ireland's Industrial schools* (Dublin: New Island, 1999).
Savage, Robert J., *A loss of innocence?: Television and Irish society, 1960–1972* (Manchester: Manchester University Press, 2010).
Sheehy Skeffington, Andrée, *Skeff: the life of Owen Sheehy Skeffington, 1909–1970* (Dublin: Lilliput Press, 1981).
Shovlin, Frank, *The Irish literary periodical, 1932–1958* (Oxford: Clarendon Press, 2003).
Staunton, Enda, *The nationalists of Northern Ireland* (Dublin: Columba Press, 2001).
Walsh, John, *Patrick Hillery: the official biography* (Dublin: New Island, 2008).
——, *The politics of expansion: the transformation of educational policy in the Republic of Ireland, 1957–72* (Manchester: Manchester University Press, 2009).
Whitaker, T. K., *Protectionism or free trade – the final battle* (Dublin: Institute of Public Administration, 2006).
Whyte, John, *Church and state in modern Ireland, 1923–1979* (Dublin: Gill and Macmillan, 1980).
——, 'How much discrimination was there under the Unionist regime, 1921–1968?', in Tom Gallagher and James O'Connell (eds), *Contemporary Irish studies* (Manchester: Manchester University Press, 1983).
——, *Interpreting Northern Ireland* (Oxford: Clarendon Press, 1991).

Index

Page numbers in *italic* refer to illustrations

Administration 4, 22, 63, 65–6, 137

Barrington, Donal ix, xii, 1, 8, 15,
  18–19, 22, 26–7, 34, 67, 70, *75*,
  155, 221, 226, 229
  Catholic Church 20, 36
  Hibernia 35, 42, 60, 66
  Northern Ireland 103–7, 109–10,
    113–28, 130, 132–3, 137
  Tuairim and politics 16–17, 42, 50,
    74–5, 134, 136
  UCD see University College Dublin
    155, 159, 163–4, 171
Barrington, T. J. 66, 82, 86, 88
Belfast branch 19, 33, 123–4
Belfast Telegraph 106, 113, 119, 179,
  181
Blythe, Ernest 7, 71, 103–4, 111–15,
  122–3, 127
Boland, Gerald 17, 20, 169, 228
Boland, John 38, 132–3
Booth, Lionel 71–2, 75–6, 169
Brookeborough, Basil 103–4, 110, 116,
  118
Browne, Noel 65, 169–70

Carter, Charles 63–8
Catholic Church 1–4, 6, 10, 14–15, 19,
  21, 35, 39, 48, 60, 62, 66, 108,
  132, 150–4, 171–3

Ban on Trinity College 156,
  171–2
Censorship 212–13, 216, 218–19,
  226–7
Constitution of Ireland 20
Ecumenical developments 4, 19, 36–8,
  219
Education 174, 181, 184, 187
Catholic Truth Society 20, 22, 212
Childers, Erskine ix, x, 45, 62, 74, *75*,
  82, 84–5, 120–1, *167*
Christus Rex 4, 7, 22–3, 25, 65–6, 117,
  122, 153, 194, 212, 222
Chubb, Basil 71, 78–9, 81, 185
Civil Service 7, 9, 14, 17, 22, 25, 39–40,
  49, 61, 63–8, 75, 80, 82–4, 86,
  90, 153, 186, 195, 227–8
Connolly Association 8, 32, 35, 39,
  102, 125, 131–3, 136
  Irish Democrat 8, 35, 125–6, 132
Connolly, Peter, 24, 210–22
Constitution of Ireland 1, 15, 20, 68,
  130–1, 137, 168, 175, 191
Cork branch 8, 19–20, 28–31, 33–4,
  43, 45, 70–1, 89, 110, 128, *129*,
  183–4, 188, 196
Costello, Declan 40–1, 43, 74, *75*, *81*
Costello, John A. 40–4, 228
Cruise O'Brien, Conor ix, 16, 31, *32*,
  128–9, 135

Dáil Éireann xiv, 7, 39, 41, 43–4, 59–61, 65, 116, 119, 122, 131, 153, 159–60, 163, 185, 195, 211, 220–1, 226–7
   Oireachtas reform 9, 45–6, 59–60, 78–91
   P.R. 68–78
   University education 164–5, 167–71
Daly, Miriam 32–3, 131, 174–5, 181–2, 185–7
Davis, Thomas 26, 47, 106, 155
   Young Irelanders 47, 106, 154–5
Department of Education xi, 6, 8, 82–3, 85, 150, 152–4, 158, 163, 165–8, 172, 174–7, 179, 184–8, 190–5, 228
   Colley, George 17, 45, 174, 179, 184, 187–9
   Comprehensive schools 182, 185–7
   Hillery, Patrick *x*, 159, 165, 167–9, 171–2, 179, 182, 184–8, 227–8
   O'Connor, Seán 6, 186
   O'Malley, Donogh 45, 168, 173, 184, 187, 189, 195
Department of External Affairs 40
Feehan, Tadhg 40, 132
Department of Finance 17, 59, 61–3, 65, 67–8, 75, 82–3, 90, 107, 165
   Dolan, James 82–4
   Murray, Charlie 82–3
   Ó Cearbhaill, Diarmuid 17, 75, 83
Department of Health xi, 8, 153, 190–2, 193–5
   Clandillon, Fidelma 153, 190–1, 194–5
Desmond, Barry xii, 8, 16, 43, 77–8, 81, 87–8, 90, 186, 226
De Valera, Eamon 23, 36, 60, 69–71, 74–7, 104, 118–20, 157, 228
Devlin Report 63, 68, 86–7
Devlin, Paddy 125–6, 128
Doolan, Jim, *ix*, xii, 8, 17, 188
Dublin branch 8–9, 36, 39, 41, 46, 87, 107, 123–4, 126–7
   Censorship 24, 212–13, 218–222
   Development 14–20, 23–30, 34

   Political reform 78–91
   Primary and post-primary education 10, 150, 153, 173–80, 182–4, 188–9, 196, 225
   Proportional representation 68–78
   University education 6, 10, 24, 45, 119, 150, 154–173, 196–7, 225, 227

Economic Development 20, 61–4

Fennell, Desmond 103, 109, 123
Fianna Fáil 7, 16–17, 41, 43–6, 60–2, 68–71, 74–80, 82, 87–8, 91, 105, 116–17, 120–1, 130, 138, 158, 168, 170, 174, 179, 186–7, 195, 229
Fine Gael 16, 40–5, 60, 69–71, 74, 77–9, 81–2, 89–90, 111, 119, 121, 128–30, 154, 164–5, 168–70
FitzGerald, Garret ix, 1, 6, 16, 18, 22, 26, 43, 69–72, 78, 82–3, 86, 90, 104, 121, 124, 127–30, 137, 155–6, 172, 220–1, 226

Good Friday Agreement 10, 121, 137–8, 225
Gibson, Norman 103, 105, 107–13, 118, 132–3

Haughey, Charles *x*, 45–6, 82, *167*
Hederman O'Brien, Miriam xii, 1, 8, 16, 18–9, 26–8, 60, 226
Hibernia 7, 35–6, 42, 60, 65–6, 75, 77, 102, 111–12, 124, 127, 132–6, 164, 179–81, 183, 186–7, 193–4, 216–18, 227

Industrial schools 3, 6, 8, 10, 33, 150, 152–3, 189–97, 226
   Tyrell, Peter 192–3, 226
IRA 103–5, 115, 118, 127, 129–30, 132, 134–5
Irish Association 102, 108, 113, 117, 121, 124, 127–8, 136
Irish Examiner ix, 8 , 180

Irish Independent ix, x, 7, 26, 69, 164, 179, 194
Irish Press 7, 30, 69, 111–2, 117–8, 164, 179–80, 186, 195
Irish Times ix, x, 7, 21, 39–41, 65–6, 69, 73, 77, 81, 110–12, 151–19, 121, 133, 152, 155–6, 164, 179–80, 182, 185–6, 194, 212, 214–16, 219–20, 227

Johnston, Roy 32, 131–3

Keane, Ronan 16–7, 70–2, 159, 226
Keery, Neville 82, 85, 87–9
Kelly, John 111, 135
Kilroy, Patrick 15–18, 35
Kilroy, Thomas 174, 177–9

Labour party 1, 16, 18, 43, 46, 48, 69–71, 76–7, 79, 81–2, 89–91, 106, 128–30, 170, 186
Lenihan, Brian x, 45, 71, *167*, 210, 220–2
Liberal Party, Northern Ireland 106, 122–3, 126, 127
Limerick branch x, 19, 28–9, 33–4, 43, 78, 210, 213–14, 220–1
London branch 6, 8–10, 14, 19, 30–3, 38–40, 47–9, 110, 131–3, 150, 153, 173–97, 218, 229
Lynch, Jack 75–6, 85, 87, 91, 121, 157–8
Lynch, Patrick 43, 59, 63–8, 82, 84, 86, 172, 179, 188

MacAonghusa, Prionsias 73, 127, 135
MacEntee, Seán 45, 76, 157, 159, 165, 172, 227
McCarthy, Charles 82, 86, 174, 177–8
McDonagh, Enda 8, 18, 20, 38, 127–8, 131, 175, 182, 216
McHugh, Roger 156–7, 159, 164–5
McKeown, Michael 35, 124–5, 134–5

McQuaid, John Charles 6–7, 19–20, 25, 35–8, 49, 154–5, 163, 171, 184–5, 216, 218–19

NILP 106, 122–3, 125–6

O'Brien, Edna 210–12, 214–17, 222
O'Connell, Daniel 47, 154–5
O'Meara, John 151, 157, 178
O'Sullivan, Franklin 17, 46, 60, 85, 87, 128

Proportional representation (PR) 68–78, 80, 84

Queen's University Belfast 16, 32, 39, 63, 107, 119, 154

Rudd, Joy 8, 31, 132, 174–5, 182–3, 185, 188–9, 193
Ryan Report 6, 152–3, 194
Ryan, Richie 41, 43, 81

Scott, James 16, 20, 35, 124, 127, 134, 136
SDLP 111, 125, 128, 130–1
Seanad Éireann xiv, 17, 26, 65, 74, 87, 119–20, 211, 220–1
   University education 168, 170–1
Sheehy, Michael 103–4, 113, 115
Sheehy Skeffington, Owen 8, 119, 170, 193
Sinn Féin 39, 64, 127, 129, 135
Studies 4, 7, 22, 25, 63, 104, 151, 153, 194

Television 2, 30, 46, 78, 85, 88, 113, 127, 180, 219, 226
Thornley, David *ix*, 1, 7, 16–18, 22, 37, 39, 44, 48, 60–1, 69, 78–80, 85, 88–9, 110, 129, 185
Tierney, Michael 154–8, 163–4, 170–1, 218
Trinity College Dublin 1, 8, 10, 16–7, 38–9, 81, 110, 119, 150, 154–6, 158–60, 162–73, 179, 197

University College Cork 26, 29, 71, 154, 156–8, 160–1, 164, 170
University College Dublin 17–18, 22, 26, 37, 39, 63, 65, 111, 150–1, 184, 187, 194, 196–7, 225
  Move to Belfield 6, 10, 24, 154–73
  Relations with Trinity College Dublin 10, 119, 155–6, 158, 160, 162–73, 196–7
University College Galway 17, 26, 154, 156–8, 160–1, 166

Vocational Education 151, 176, 180–2, 186–90
  McCarthy, Charles 82, 86, 174, 177–8

Whitaker, T. K. 61–4, 67, 82, 84, 86, 107
Woods, Michael 16, 43, 82, 121, 137, 226
Whyte, John 17, 39, 60, 69, 78–81, 88, 113, 115, 127

EU authorised representative for GPSR:
Easy Access System Europe, Mustamäe tee 50,
10621 Tallinn, Estonia
gpsr.requests@easproject.com

www.ingramcontent.com/pod-product-compliance
Ingram Content Group UK Ltd.
Pitfield, Milton Keynes, MK11 3LW, UK
UKHW021848140426
5217IPUK00022B/1649